Also by Thomas L. Friedman

From Beirut to Jerusalem (1989)

The Lexus and the Olive Tree

THE
LEXUS
AND THE
OLIVE
TREE

❧

Thomas L. Friedman

❧

FARRAR   STRAUS   GIROUX

New York

Farrar, Straus and Giroux
19 Union Square West, New York 10003

Distributed in Canada by Douglas & McIntyre Ltd.
Printed in the United States of America
Designed by Jonathan D. Lippincott
First published in 1999 by Farrar, Straus and Giroux
Revised edition, 2000

Library of Congress Cataloging-in-Publication Data
Friedman, Thomas L.
    The Lexus and the olive tree / by Thomas L. Friedman.
        p.   cm.
    Includes bibliographical references and index.
    ISBN 0-374-18552-2 (alk. paper)
    1. International economic relations.   2. Free trade.
    3. Capitalism—Social aspects.   4. Technological innovations—
    Economic aspects.   5. Technological innovations—Social aspects.
    6. Intercultural communication.   7. United States—Foreign economic
    relations.   I. Title.
    HF1359.F74 1999
    337—dc21   99-10742

Grateful acknowledgment is made for permission to reprint an excerpt from the musical *Ragtime*.
Lyrics by Lynn Ahrens © Hillsdale Music, Inc. & Pen and Perseverance, Inc.

    Part of the chapter "The Groundswell" was first published in slightly different form in *The
Economist*. © 2000 The Economist Newspaper Group, Inc. Reprinted with permission. Further
reproduction prohibited.

For Ann

CONTENTS

Foreword

Welcome to the updated and expanded edition of *The Lexus and the Olive Tree*. Readers of the original version of the book will notice that several things have changed in this new version. But what has not changed is the core thesis of this book: that globalization is not simply a trend or a fad but is, rather, an international system. It is the system that has now replaced the old Cold War system, and, like that Cold War system, globalization has its own rules and logic that today directly or indirectly influence the politics, environment, geopolitics and economics of virtually every country in the world.

So what has changed? I have reorganized the early chapters to make my core thesis a little easier for the reader to identify and digest, and I have used the year since the book was originally published in April 1999 to gather more evidence and to update and expand the book with all the technological and market innovations that are enhancing globalization even further. I have also re-examined some of the more controversial sub-theses of this book. One is my Golden Arches Theory—that no two countries that both have McDonald's have ever fought a war against each other since they each got their McDonald's. I feel the underlying logic of that theory is stronger than ever, and I have responded to those who have challenged it in the wake of the Kosovo war. Another change is that the chapter originally entitled "Buy Taiwan, Hold Italy, Sell France" is now broken into two parts. The new chapter, called "Shapers, Adapters and Other New Ways of Thinking About Power," builds on a question I raised in the first edition: if economic power in the globalization system was first based on PCs per household in a country, and then on degree of Internet bandwidth per person in a country, what comes next? This chapter tries to answer that question by looking at evolving new ways of measuring economic power in the globalization era. Finally, I have tried to answer some of the most oft-asked questions I got from readers of the first edition: "Now that you have described this new system, how do I prepare my kids for it?" and "Is God in cyberspace?"—which is another way of saying, "Where do moral values fit in?"

The new world order is evolving so fast that sometimes I wish this were an electronic book that I could just update every day. My more realistic hope is that when the day comes years from now when this book can no longer reside on the Current Affairs shelf in bookstores, it will find a comfortable home in the History section—remembered among the books that caught the start, and helped to first define, the new system of globalization that is now upon us.

Thomas L. Friedman
Bethesda, Maryland
January 2000

Opening Scene:
The World Is Ten Years Old

It's aggravating—we have nothing to do with Russia or Asia. We're just a little domestic business trying to grow, but we're being prevented because of the way those governments run their countries.

—Douglas Hanson, CEO of Rocky Mountain Internet, Inc.,
speaking to The Wall Street Journal *after the 1998 market*
meltdown forced him to postpone a $175 million junk bond issue

On the morning of December 8, 1997, the government of Thailand announced that it was closing 56 of the country's 58 top finance houses. Almost overnight, these private banks had been bankrupted by the crash of the Thai currency, the baht. The finance houses had borrowed heavily in U.S. dollars and lent those dollars out to Thai businesses for the building of hotels, office blocks, luxury apartments and factories. The finance houses all thought they were safe because the Thai government was committed to keeping the Thai baht at a fixed rate against the dollar. But when the government failed to do so, in the wake of massive global speculation against the baht—triggered by a dawning awareness that the Thai economy was not as strong as previously believed—the Thai currency plummeted by 30 percent. This meant that businesses that had borrowed dollars had to come up with roughly one-third more Thai baht to pay back each $1 of loans. Many businesses couldn't pay the finance houses back, many finance houses couldn't repay their foreign lenders and the whole system went into gridlock, putting 20,000 white-collar employees out of work. The next day, I happened to be driving to an appointment in Bangkok down Asoke Street, Thailand's equivalent of Wall Street, where most of the bankrupt finance houses were located. As we slowly passed each one of these fallen firms, my cabdriver pointed them out, pronouncing at each one: "Dead! . . . dead! . . . dead! . . . dead! . . . dead!"

I did not know it at the time—no one did—but these Thai investment houses were the first dominoes in what would prove to be the first global financial crisis of the new era of globalization—the era that followed the Cold War. The Thai crisis triggered a general flight of capital out of virtually all the Southeast Asian emerging markets, driving down the value of currencies in South Korea, Malaysia and Indonesia. Both global and local investors started scrutinizing these economies more closely, found them wanting, and either moved their cash out to safer havens or demanded higher interest rates to compensate for the higher risk. It wasn't long before one of the most popular sweatshirts around Bangkok was emblazoned with the words "Former Rich."

Within a few months, the Southeast Asian recession began to have an effect on commodity prices around the world. Asia had been an important engine for worldwide economic growth—an engine that consumed huge amounts of raw materials. When that engine started to sputter, the prices of gold, copper, aluminum and, most important, crude oil all started to fall. This fall in worldwide commodity prices turned out to be the mechanism for transmitting the Southeast Asian crisis to Russia. Russia at the time was minding its own business, trying, with the help of the IMF, to climb out of its own self-made economic morass onto a stable growth track. The problem with Russia, though, was that too many of its factories couldn't make anything of value. In fact, much of what they made was considered "negative value added." That is, a tractor made by a Russian factory was so bad it was actually worth more as scrap metal, or just raw iron ore, than it was as a finished, Russian-made tractor. On top of it all, those Russian factories that were making products that could be sold abroad were paying few, if any, taxes to the government, so the Kremlin was chronically short of cash.

Without much of an economy to rely on for revenues, the Russian government had become heavily dependent on taxes from crude oil and other commodity exports to fund its operating budget. It had also become dependent on foreign borrowers, whose money Russia lured by offering ridiculous rates of interest on various Russian government-issued bonds.

As Russia's economy continued to slide in early 1998, the Russians had to raise the interest rate on their ruble bonds from 20 to 50 to 70 percent to keep attracting the foreigners. The hedge funds and foreign banks kept buying them, figuring that even if the Russian government couldn't pay them back, the IMF would step in, bail out Russia and the foreigners would get their money back. Some hedge funds and foreign banks not only continued to put their own money into Russia, but they went out and borrowed even more money, at 5 percent, and then bought Russian T-bills with it that paid 20 or 30 percent. As Grandma would say, "Such a deal!" But as Grandma would also say, "If it sounds too good to be true, it usually is!"

And it was. The Asian-triggered slump in oil prices made it harder and harder for the Russian government to pay the interest and principal on its T-bills. And with the IMF under pressure to make loans to rescue Thailand, Korea and Indonesia, it resisted any proposals for putting more cash into Russia—unless the Russians first fulfilled their promises to reform their economy, starting with getting their biggest businesses and banks to pay some taxes. On August 17, 1998, the Russian economic house of cards came tumbling down, dealing the markets a double whammy: Russia both devalued and unilaterally defaulted on its government bonds, without giving any warning to its creditors or arranging any workout agreement. The hedge funds, banks and investment banks that were invested in Russia began piling up massive losses, and those that had borrowed money to magnify their bets in the Kremlin casino were threatened with bankruptcy.

On the face of it, the collapse of the Russian economy should not have had much impact on the global system. Russia's economy was smaller than that of the Netherlands. But the system was now more global than ever, and just as crude oil prices were the transmission mechanism from Southeast Asia to Russia, the hedge funds—the huge unregulated pools of private capital that scour the globe for the best investments—were the transmission mechanism from Russia to all the other emerging markets in the world, particularly Brazil. The hedge funds and other trading firms, having racked up huge losses in Russia, some of which were magnified fifty times by using borrowed money, suddenly had to raise cash to pay back their bankers. They had to sell anything that was liquid. So they started selling assets in financially sound countries to compensate for their losses in bad ones. Brazil, for instance, which had been doing a lot of the right things in the eyes of the global markets and the IMF, suddenly saw all its stocks and bonds being sold by panicky investors. Brazil had to raise its interest rates as high as 40 percent to try to hold capital inside the country. Variations on this scenario were played out throughout the world's emerging markets, as investors fled for safety. They cashed in their Brazilian, Korean, Egyptian, Israeli and Mexican bonds and stocks, and put the money either under their mattresses or into the safest U.S. bonds they could find. So the declines in Brazil and the other emerging markets became the transmission mechanism that triggered a herdlike stampede into U.S. Treasury bonds. This, in turn, sharply drove up the value of U.S. T-bonds, drove down the interest that the U.S. government had to offer on them to attract investors and increased the spread between U.S. T-bonds and other corporate and emerging market bonds.

The steep drop in the yield on U.S. Treasury bonds was then the transmission mechanism which crippled more hedge funds and investment banks. Take for instance Long-Term Capital Management, based in Greenwich, Connecticut. LTCM was the Mother of All Hedge Funds. Because so many hedge funds were attracted to the marketplace in the late 1980s, the field became fiercely competitive. Everyone pounced on the same opportunities. In order to make money in such a fiercely competitive world, the hedge funds had to seek ever more exotic bets with ever larger pools of cash. To guide them in placing the right bets, LTCM drew on the work of two Nobel Prize–winning business economists, whose research argued that the basic volatility of stocks and bonds could be estimated from how they reacted in the past. Using computer models, and borrowing heavily from different banks, LTCM put $120 billion at risk betting on the direction that certain key bonds would take in the summer of 1998. It implicitly bet that the value of U.S. T-bonds would go down, and that the value of junk bonds and emerging market bonds would go up. LTCM's computer model, however, never anticipated something like the global contagion that would be set off in August by Russia's collapse, and, as a result, its bets turned out to be exactly wrong. When the whole investment world panicked at once and decided to rush into U.S. T-bonds, their value soared instead of fell, and the value of junk bonds and emerging market bonds collapsed instead of soared. LTCM was like a wishbone that got pulled apart from both ends. It had to be bailed out by its bankers to prevent it from engaging in a fire sale of all its stocks and bonds that could have triggered a worldwide market meltdown.

Now we get to my street. In early August 1998, I happened to invest in my friend's new Internet bank. The shares opened at $14.50 a share and soared to $27. I felt like a genius. But then Russia defaulted and set all these dominoes in motion, and my friend's stock went to $8. Why? Because his bank held a lot of home mortgages, and with the fall of interest rates in America, triggered by the rush to buy T-bills, the markets feared that a lot of people would suddenly pay off their home mortgages early. If a lot of people paid off their home mortgages early, my friend's bank might not have the income stream that it was counting on to pay depositors. The markets were actually wrong about my friend's bank, and its stock bounced back nicely. Indeed, by early 1999 I was feeling like a genius again, as the Amazon.com Internet craze set in and drove my friend's Internet bank stock sky high, as well as other technology shares. But, once again, it wasn't long before the rest of the world crashed the party. Only this time, instead of Russia breaking down the front door, it was Brazil's turn to upset U.S. markets and even dampen (temporarily) the Internet stock boom.

As I watched all this play out, all I could think of was that it took nine months for the events on Asoke Street to affect my street, and it took one week for events on the Brazilian Amazon (Amazon.country) to affect Amazon.com. USA *Today* aptly summed up the global marketplace at the end of 1998: "The trouble spread to one continent after another like a virus," the paper noted. "U.S. markets reacted instantaneously . . . People in barbershops actually talked about the Thai baht."

It wasn't long, though, before Amazon.com started to soar again, pulling up all the Internet stocks, which in turn helped pull up the whole U.S. stock market, which in turn created a wealth effect in America, which in turn encouraged Americans to spend beyond their savings, which in turn enabled Brazil, Thailand and other emerging markets to export their way out of their latest troubles by selling to America. Amazon.com, Amazon.country — we were all becoming one river.

If nothing else, the cycle from Asoke Street to my street, and from Amazon.country to Amazon.com and then back again to Amazon.country, served to educate all of us about the state of the world today. The slow, fixed, divided Cold War system that had dominated international affairs since 1945 had been firmly replaced by a new, very greased, interconnected system called globalization. If we didn't fully understand that in 1989, when the Berlin Wall came down, we sure understood it a decade later. Indeed, on October 11, 1998, at the height of the global economic crisis, Merrill Lynch ran full-page ads in major newspapers throughout America to drive this point home. The ads read:

The World Is 10 Years Old
It was born when the Wall fell in 1989. It's no surprise that the world's youngest economy — the global economy — is still finding

its bearings. The intricate checks and balances that stabilize economies are only incorporated with time. Many world markets are only recently freed, governed for the first time by the emotions of the people rather than the fists of the state. From where we sit, none of this diminishes the promise offered a decade ago by the demise of the walled-off world . . . The spread of free markets and democracy around the world is permitting more people everywhere to turn their aspirations into achievements. And technology, properly harnessed and liberally distributed, has the power to erase not just geographical borders but also human ones. It seems to us that, for a 10-year-old, the world continues to hold great promise. In the meantime, no one ever said growing up was easy.

Actually, the Merrill Lynch ad would have been a little more correct to say that *this* era of globalization is ten years old. Because from the mid-1800s to the late 1920s the world experienced a similar era of globalization. If you compared the volumes of trade and capital flows across borders, relative to GNPs, and the flow of labor across borders, relative to populations, the period of globalization preceding World War I was quite similar to the one we are living through today. Great Britain, which was then the dominant global power, was a huge investor in emerging markets, and fat cats in England, Europe and America were often buffeted by financial crises, triggered by something that happened in Argentine railroad bonds, Latvian government bonds or German government bonds. There were no currency controls, so no sooner was the transatlantic cable connected in 1866 than banking and financial crises in New York were quickly being transmitted to London or Paris. I was on a panel once with John Monks, the head of the British Trades Union Congress, the AFL-CIO of Britain, who remarked that the agenda for the TUC's first Congress in Manchester, England, in 1868, listed among the items that needed to be discussed: "The need to deal with competition from the Asian colonies" and "The need to match the educational and training standards of the United States and Germany." In those days, people also migrated more than we remember, and, other than in wartime, countries did not require passports for travel before 1914. All those immigrants who flooded America's shores came without visas. When you put all of these factors together, along with the inventions of the steamship, telegraph, railroad and eventually telephone, it is safe to say that this first era of globalization before World War I shrank the world from a size "large" to a size "medium."

This first era of globalization and global finance capitalism was broken apart by the successive hammer blows of World War I, the Russian Revolution and the Great Depression, which combined to fracture the world both physically and ideologically. The formally divided world that emerged after World War II was then frozen in place by the Cold War. The Cold War was also an international system. It lasted roughly from 1945 to 1989, when, with the fall of the Berlin Wall, it was replaced by another system: the new era of globalization we are now in. Call it "Globalization Round II." It turns out that the roughly seventy-five-year period from the start of World War I to the end of the Cold War was just a long time-out between one era of globalization and another.

While there are a lot of similarities in kind between the previous era of globalization and the one we are now in, what is new today is the degree and intensity with which the world is being tied together into a single globalized marketplace and village. What is also new is the sheer number of people and countries able to partake of today's globalized economy and information networks, and to be affected by them. The pre-1914 era of globalization may have been intense, but many developing countries in that era were left out of it. The pre-1914 era may have been large in scale relative to its time, but it was minuscule in absolute terms compared to today. Daily foreign exchange trading in 1900 was measured in the millions of dollars. In 1992, it was $820 billion a day, according to the New York Federal Reserve, and by April 1998 it was up to $1.5 trillion a day, and still rising. Around 1900, private capital flows from developed countries to developing ones could be measured in the hundreds of millions of dollars and relatively few countries were involved. By 2000, it was being measured in the hundreds of billions of dollars, with dozens of countries involved. This new era of globalization, compared to the one before World War I, is turbocharged.

But today's era of globalization is not only different in degree; in some very important ways it is also different in kind—both technologically and politically. Technologically speaking, it is different in that the previous era of globalization was built around falling transportation costs. Thanks to the invention of the railroad, the steamship and the automobile, people could get to a lot more places faster and cheaper and they could trade with a lot more places faster and cheaper. But as The Economist has noted, today's era of globalization is built around falling telecommunications costs—thanks to microchips, satellites, fiber optics and the Internet. These new information technologies are able to weave the world together even tighter. These technologies mean that developing countries don't just have to trade their raw materials to the West and get finished products in return; they mean that developing countries can become big-time producers as well. These technologies also allow companies to locate different parts of their production, research and marketing in different countries, but still tie them together through computers and teleconferencing as though they were in one place. Also, thanks to the combination of computers and cheap telecommunications, people can now offer and trade services globally—from medical advice to software writing to data processing—services that could never really be traded before. And why not? A three-minute call (in 1996 dollars) between New York and London cost $300 in 1930. Today it is almost free through the Internet.

These technologies are making it possible not only for traditional nation-states and corporations to reach farther, faster, cheaper and deeper around the world than ever before, but also for individuals to do so. I was reminded of this point close to home, when in the summer of 1998 my then seventy-nine-year-old mother, Margaret Friedman, who lives in Minneapolis, called me sounding very upset. "What's wrong, Mom?" I asked. "Well," she said, "I've been playing bridge on the Internet with three Frenchmen and they keep speaking French to each other and I can't understand them." When I chuckled at the thought of my card-shark mom playing bridge with three Frenchmen on the Net, she took a little umbrage. "Don't laugh," she said, "I was playing bridge with someone in Siberia the other day."

To all those who say that this era of globalization is no different from the previous one, I would simply ask: Was your great-grandmother playing bridge with Frenchmen on the Internet in 1900? I don't think so.

But, as I said, this new era of globalization is also different politically from that of the 1900s. That earlier era was dominated by British power, the British pound and the British navy. Today's era is dominated by American power, American culture, the American dollar and the American navy. American power after World War II deliberately set out to forge an open international trading system to stimulate employment and counterbalance Soviet communism. It was America that drove the creation of the International Monetary Fund, the General Agreement on Tariffs and Trade (GATT) and a host of other institutions for opening markets and fostering trade around the world. And it was the American fleet that kept the sea lanes open for these open markets to easily connect. So when the Information Revolution flowered in the late 1980s—and made it possible for so many more people to act globally, communicate globally, travel globally and sell globally—it flowered into a global power structure that encouraged and enhanced all these trends and made it very costly for any country that tried to buck them.

In short, there are some things about this new era of globalization that we've seen before (but which are much more intense now), some things that we've never seen before and some things that are so new we don't even understand them yet. For all these reasons, I would sum up the differences between the two eras of globalization this way: If the first era of globalization shrank the world from a size "large" to a size "medium," this era of globalization is shrinking the world from a size "medium" to a size "small."

This book is an effort to explain how this new era of globalization became the dominant international system at the end of the twentieth century—replacing the Cold War system—and to examine how it now shapes virtually everyone's domestic politics, commerce, environment and international relations. In that sense, it is meant as a contribution to the body of literature that has been attempting to define the post–Cold War world. Among the most widely read of this genre are Paul M. Kennedy's *The Rise and Fall of the Great Powers: Economic Change and Military Conflict from 1500 to 2000*, Francis Fukuyama's *The End of History and the Last Man*, the various essays and books of Robert D. Kaplan, and Samuel P. Huntington's *The Clash of Civilizations and the Remaking of World Order*.

While all of these works contained important truths, I think none of them really captured the post–Cold War world in any holistic way. Kaplan's reporting was vivid and honest, but he took the grimmest corners of the globe and overgeneralized from them to the fate of the rest of the world. Huntington saw cultural conflicts around the world and wildly expanded that into an enduring, sharply defined clash of civilizations, even proclaiming that the next world war, if there is one, "will be a war between civilizations." I believe both Kaplan and Huntington vastly underestimated how the power of states, the lure of global markets, the diffusion of technology, the rise of networks and the spread of global norms could trump their black-and-white (mostly black) projections.

Both Kennedy and Huntington tried to divine the future too much from the past and the past alone. Kennedy traced (quite brilliantly) the decline of the Spanish, French and British empires, but he concluded by suggesting that the American empire would be the next to fall because of its own imperial overreaching. His implicit message was that the end of the Cold War not only meant the end of the Soviet Union but would also herald the decline of the United States. I believe Kennedy did not appreciate enough that the relative decline of the United States in the 1980s, when he was writing, was part of America's preparing itself for and adjusting to the new globalization system—a process that much of the rest of the world is going through only now. Kennedy did not anticipate that under the pressure of globalization America would slash its defense budget, shrink its government and shift more and more powers to the free market in ways that would prolong its status as a Great Power, not diminish it.

Huntington's view was that, with the Cold War over, we won't have the Soviets to kick around anymore, so we will naturally go back to kicking the Hindus and Muslims around and them kicking us. He implicitly ruled out the rise of some new international system that could shape events differently. For Huntington, only tribalism could follow the Cold War, not anything new.

Fukuyama's pathbreaking book contained the most accurate insight about what was new—the triumph of liberalism and free-market capitalism as the most effective way to organize a society—but his title (*The End of History*) implied a finality to this triumph (much more than the book itself does) that does not jibe with the world as I find it.

In a way, each of these works became prominent because they tried to capture in a single catchy thought "The One Big Thing," the central moving part, the essential motor, that would drive international affairs in the post–Cold War world—either the clash of civilizations, chaos, the decline of empires or the triumph of liberalism.

My argument is different. I believe that if you want to understand the post–Cold War world you have to start by understanding that a new international system has succeeded it—globalization. That is "The One Big Thing" people should focus on. Globalization is not the only thing influencing events in the world today, but to the extent that there is a North Star and a worldwide shaping force, it is this system. What is new is the system; what is old is power politics, chaos, clashing civilizations and liberalism. And what is the drama of the post–Cold War world is the interaction between this new system and all these old passions and aspirations. It is a complex drama, with the final act still not written.

That is why under the globalization system you will find both clashes of civilization and the homogenization of civilizations, both environmental disasters and amazing environmental rescues, both the triumph of liberal, free-market capitalism and a backlash against it, both the durability of nation-states and the rise of enormously powerful nonstate actors. What I have tried to write is a guidebook for how to follow that drama and how to think about managing it.

Just one last word before we start. The publisher and editor of the first edition of this book, Jonathan Galassi, called me one day and said, "I was telling some friends of mine that you're writing a book about globalization and they said, 'Oh, Friedman, he loves globalization.' What would you say to that?" I answered Jonathan that I feel about globalization a lot like I feel about the dawn. Generally speaking, I think it's a good thing that the sun comes up every morning. It does more good than harm, especially if you wear sunscreen and sunglasses. But even if I didn't much care for the dawn there isn't much I could do about it. I didn't start globalization, I can't stop it—except at a huge cost to human development—and I'm not going to waste time trying. I am a journalist, not a salesman for globalization. As you will see from the book, I am keenly aware of globalization's downsides. The question in my mind is what to do about them. I believe the best way for us to deal with the brutalities of globalization is by first understanding the logic of the system and its moving parts, and them figuring out how this system can benefit the most people while inflicting the least amount of pain. That is the spirit that motivated this book.

The first part of the book explains how to look at today's globalization system and how the system works. The second part explains how nation-states, communities, individuals and the environment interact with this system. The third part explains the backlash against globalization. And the fourth explains the unique role the United States plays, and needs to keep playing, in stabilizing this new system.

(I)

Seeing the System

The New System

What was it that Forrest Gump's mama liked to say? Life is like a box of chocolates: you never know what you're going to get inside. For me, an inveterate traveler and foreign correspondent, life is like room service—you never know what you're going to find outside your door.

Take for instance the evening of December 31, 1994, when I began my assignment as the foreign affairs columnist for *The New York Times*. I started the column by writing from Tokyo, and when I arrived at the Okura Hotel after a long transpacific flight, I called room service with one simple request: "Could you please send me up four oranges." I am addicted to citrus and I needed a fix. It seemed to me a simple enough order when I telephoned it in, and the person on the other end seemed to understand. About twenty minutes later there was a knock at my door. A room service waiter was standing there in his perfectly creased uniform. In front of him was a cart covered by a starched white tablecloth. On the tablecloth were four tall glasses of fresh-squeezed orange juice, each glass set regally in a small silver bowl of ice.

"No, no," I said to the waiter, "I want oranges, oranges—not orange juice." I then pretended to bite into something like an orange.

"Ahhhh," the waiter said, nodding his head. "O-ranges, o-ranges."

I retreated into my room and went back to work. Twenty minutes later there was another knock at my door. Same waiter. Same linen-covered room service trolley. But this time, on it were four plates and on each plate was an orange that had been peeled and diced into perfect little sections that were fanned out on a plate like sushi, as only the Japanese can do.

"No, no," I said, shaking my head again. "I want the whole orange." I made a ball shape with my hands. "I want to keep them in my room and eat them for snacks. I can't eat four oranges all cut up like that. I can't store them in my mini-bar. I want the whole orange."

Again, I did my best exaggerated imitation of someone eating an orange.

"Ahhhh," the waiter said, nodding his head. "O-range, o-range. You want whole o-range."

Another twenty minutes went by. Again there was a knock on my door. Same waiter. Same trolley, only this time he had four bright oranges, each one on its own dinner plate, with a fork, knife and linen napkin next to it. That was progress.

"That's right," I said, signing the bill. "That's just what I wanted."

As he left the room, I looked down at the room service bill. The four oranges were $22. How am I going to explain that to my publisher?

But my citrus adventures were not over. Two weeks later I was in Hanoi, having dinner by myself in the dining room of the Metropole Hotel. It was the tangerine season in Vietnam, and vendors were selling pyramids of the most delicious, bright orange tangerines on every street corner. Each morning I had a few tangerines for breakfast. When the waiter came to get my dessert order I told him all I wanted was a tangerine.

He went away and came back a few minutes later.

"Sorry," he said, "no tangerines."

"But how can that be?" I asked in exasperation. "You have a table full of them at breakfast every morning! Surely there must be a tangerine somewhere back in the kitchen?"

"Sorry." He shook his head. "Maybe you like watermelon?"

"O.K.," I said, "bring me some watermelon."

Five minutes later the waiter returned with a plate bearing three peeled tangerines on it.

"I found the tangerines," he said. "No watermelon."

Had I known then what I know now I would have taken it all as a harbinger. For I too would find a lot of things on my plate and outside my door that I wasn't planning to find as I traveled the globe for the *Times*.

Being the foreign affairs columnist for *The New York Times* is actually the best job in the world. I mean, someone has to have the best job, right? Well, I've got it. The reason it is such a great job is that I get to be a tourist with an attitude. I get to go anywhere, anytime, and have attitudes about what I see and hear. But the question for me as I embarked on this odyssey was: Which attitudes? What would be the lens, the perspective, the organizing system—the superstory—through which I would look at the world, make sense of events, prioritize them, opine upon them and help readers understand them?

In some ways my predecessors had it a little easier. They each had a very obvious superstory and international system in place when they were writing. I am the fifth foreign affairs columnist in the history of the *Times*. "Foreign Affairs" is actually the paper's oldest column. It was begun in 1937 by a remarkable woman, Anne O'Hare McCormick, and was originally called "In Europe," because in those days, "in Europe" was foreign affairs for most Americans, and it seemed perfectly natural that the paper's one overseas columnist would be located on the European continent. Mrs. McCormick's 1954 obituary in the *Times* said she got her start in foreign reporting "as the wife of Mr. McCormick, a Dayton engineer whom she accompanied on frequent buying trips to Europe." (*New York Times* obits have become considerably more politically correct since then.) The international system which she covered was the disintegration of balance-of-power Versailles Europe and the beginnings of World War II.

As America emerged from World War II, standing astride the world as the preeminent superpower, with global responsibilities and engaged in a global power struggle with the Soviet Union, the title of the column changed in 1954 to "Foreign Affairs." Suddenly the whole world was America's playing field and the whole world mattered, because every corner was being contested with the Soviet Union. The Cold War international system, with its competition for influence and supremacy between the capitalist West and the communist East, between Washington, Moscow and Beijing, became the superstory within which the next three foreign affairs columnists organized their opinions.

By the time I started the column at the beginning of 1995, though, the Cold War was over. The Berlin Wall had crumbled and the Soviet Union was history. I had the good fortune to witness, in the Kremlin, one of the last gasps of the Soviet Union. The day was December 16, 1991. Secretary of State James A. Baker III was visiting Moscow, just as Boris Yeltsin was easing Mikhail Gorbachev out of power. Whenever Baker had met Gorbachev previously, they had held their talks in the Kremlin's gold-gilded St. Catherine Hall. There was always a very orchestrated entry scene for the press. Mr. Baker and his entourage would wait behind two huge wooden double doors on one end of the long Kremlin hall, with

Gorbachev and his team behind the doors on the other end. And then, by some signal, the doors would simultaneously open and each man would stride out and they would shake hands in front of the cameras in the middle of the room. Well, on this day Baker arrived for his meeting at the appointed hour, the doors swung open and Boris Yeltsin walked out, instead of Gorbachev. Guess who's coming to dinner! "Welcome to Russian soil and this Russian building," Yeltsin said to Baker. Baker did meet Gorbachev later in the day, but it was clear that power had shifted. We State Department reporters who were there to chronicle the event ended up spending that whole day in the Kremlin. It snowed heavily while we were inside, and when we finally walked out after sunset we found the Kremlin grounds covered in a white snow blanket. As we trudged to the Kremlin's Spassky Gate, our shoes crunching fresh tracks in the snow, I noticed that the red Soviet hammer and sickle was still flying atop the Kremlin flagpole, illuminated by a spotlight as it had been for some seventy years. I said to myself, "That is probably the last time I'll ever see that flag flying there." In a few weeks it was indeed gone, and with it went the Cold War system and superstory.

But what wasn't clear to me as I embarked upon my column assignment a few years later was what had replaced the Cold War system as the dominant organizing framework for international affairs. So I actually began my column as a tourist without an attitude — just an open mind. For several years, I, like everyone else, just referred to "the post–Cold War world." We knew some new system was aborning that constituted a different framework for international relations, but we couldn't define what it was, so we defined it by what it wasn't. It wasn't the Cold War. So we called it the post–Cold War world.

The more I traveled, though, the more it became apparent to me that we were not just in some messy, incoherent, indefinable post–Cold War world. Rather, we were in a new international system. This new system had its own unique logic, rules, pressures and incentives and it deserved its own name: "globalization." Globalization is not just some economic fad, and it is not just a passing trend. It is an international system — the dominant international system that replaced the Cold War system after the fall of the Berlin Wall. We need to understand it as such. If there can be a statute of limitations on crimes, then surely there must be a statute of limitations on foreign policy clichés. With that in mind, the "post–Cold War world" should be declared over. We are now in the new international system of globalization.

. . .

W hen I say that globalization has replaced the Cold War as the
     defining international system, what exactly do I mean?

I mean that, as an international system, the Cold War had its own
structure of power: the balance between the United States and the
U.S.S.R. The Cold War had its own rules: in foreign affairs, neither superpower would encroach on the other's sphere of influence; in economics, less developed countries would focus on nurturing their own national
industries, developing countries on export-led growth, communist countries on autarky and Western economies on regulated trade. The Cold
War had its own dominant ideas: the clash between communism and
capitalism, as well as detente, nonalignment and perestroika. The Cold
War had its own demographic trends: the movement of people from east
to west was largely frozen by the Iron Curtain, but the movement from
south to north was a more steady flow. The Cold War had its own perspective on the globe: the world was a space divided into the communist
camp, the Western camp, and the neutral camp, and everyone's country
was in one of them. The Cold War had its own defining technologies: nuclear weapons and the second Industrial Revolution were dominant, but
for many people in developing countries the hammer and sickle were still
relevant tools. The Cold War had its own defining measurement: the
throw weight of nuclear missiles. And lastly, the Cold War had its own
defining anxiety: nuclear annihilation. When taken all together the elements of this Cold War system influenced the domestic politics, commerce and foreign relations of virtually every country in the world. The
Cold War system didn't shape everything, but it shaped many things.

Today's era of globalization is a similar international system, with
its own unique attributes, which contrast sharply with those of the Cold
War. To begin with the Cold War system was characterized by one overarching feature—division. The world was a divided-up, chopped-up place
and both your threats and opportunities in the Cold War system tended to
grow out of who you were divided from. Appropriately, this Cold War system was symbolized by a single word: the *wall*—the Berlin Wall. One of
my favorite descriptions of that world was provided by Jack Nicholson in
the movie *A Few Good Men*. Nicholson plays a Marine colonel who is the
commander of the U.S. base in Cuba, at Guantánamo Bay. In the cli-
mactic scene of the movie, Nicholson is pressed by Tom Cruise to explain how a certain weak soldier under Nicholson's command, Santiago,

was beaten to death by his own fellow Marines: "You want answers?" shouts Nicholson. "You want answers?" I want the truth, retorts Cruise. "You can't handle the truth," says Nicholson. "Son, we live in a world that has walls and those walls have to be guarded by men with guns. Who's gonna do it? You? You, Lieutenant Weinberg? I have a greater responsibility than you can possibly fathom. You weep for Santiago and you curse the Marines. You have that luxury. You have the luxury of not knowing what I know—that Santiago's death, while tragic, probably saved lives. And my existence, while grotesque and incomprehensible to you, saves lives. You don't want the truth because deep down in places you don't talk about at parties, you want me on that wall. You need me on that wall."

The globalization system is a bit different. It also has one overarching feature—integration. The world has become an increasingly interwoven place, and today, whether you are a company or a country, your threats and opportunities increasingly derive from who you are connected to. This globalization system is also characterized by a single word: the Web. So in the broadest sense we have gone from a system built around division and walls to a system increasingly built around integration and webs. In the Cold War we reached for the "hotline," which was a symbol that we were all divided but at least two people were in charge—the United States and the Soviet Union—and in the globalization system we reach for the Internet, which is a symbol that we are all increasingly connected and nobody is quite in charge.

This leads to many other differences between the globalization system and the Cold War system. The globalization system, unlike the Cold War system, is not frozen, but a dynamic ongoing process. That's why I define globalization this way: it is the inexorable integration of markets, nation-states and technologies to a degree never witnessed before—in a way that is enabling individuals, corporations and nation-states to reach around the world farther, faster, deeper and cheaper than ever before, and in a way that is enabling the world to reach into individuals, corporations and nation-states farther, faster, deeper, cheaper than ever before. This process of globalization is also producing a powerful backlash from those brutalized or left behind by this new system.

The driving idea behind globalization is free-market capitalism—the more you let market forces rule and the more you open your economy to free trade and competition, the more efficient and flourishing your economy will be. Globalization means the spread of free-market capitalism to

virtually every country in the world. Therefore, globalization also has its
own set of economic rules—rules that revolve around opening, deregu-   1.
lating and privatizing your economy, in order to make it more competitive and attractive to foreign investment. In 1975, at the height of the
Cold War, only 8 percent of countries worldwide had liberal, free-market
capital regimes, and foreign direct investment at the time totaled only
$23 billion, according to the World Bank. By 1997, the number of coun-
tries with liberal economic regimes constituted 28 percent, and foreign
investment totaled $644 billion.

Unlike the Cold War system, globalization has its own dominant culture, which is why it tends to be homogenizing to a certain degree. In previous eras this sort of cultural homogenization happened on a regional
scale—the Romanization of Western Europe and the Mediterranean
world, the Islamification of Central Asia, North Africa, Europe and the
Middle East by the Arabs and later the Ottomans, or the Russification of
Eastern and Central Europe and parts of Eurasia under the Soviets. Culturally speaking, globalization has tended to involve the spread (for better
and for worse) of Americanization—from Big Macs to iMacs to Mickey
Mouse.

Globalization has its own defining technologies: computerization,   3.
miniaturization, digitization, satellite communications, fiber optics and
the Internet, which reinforce its defining perspective of integration. Once
a country makes the leap into the system of globalization, its elites begin
to internalize this perspective of integration, and always try to locate themselves in a global context. I was visiting Amman, Jordan, in the summer of
1998 and having coffee at the Inter-Continental Hotel with my friend
Rami Khouri, the leading political columnist in Jordan. We sat down and
I asked him what was new. The first thing he said to me was: "Jordan was
just added to CNN's worldwide weather highlights." What Rami was saying was that it is important for Jordan to know that those institutions
which think globally believe it is now worth knowing what the weather is
like in Amman. It makes Jordanians feel more important and holds out
the hope that they will be enriched by having more tourists or global investors visiting. The day after seeing Rami I happened to go to Israel and
meet with Jacob Frenkel, governor of Israel's Central Bank and a University of Chicago–trained economist. Frenkel remarked that he too was
going through a perspective change: "Before, when we talked about
macroeconomics, we started by looking at the local markets, local financial systems and the interrelationship between them, and then, as an af-

terthought, we looked at the international economy. There was a feeling that what we do is primarily our own business and then there are some outlets where we will sell abroad. Now we reverse the perspective. Let's not ask what markets we should export to, after having decided what to produce; rather let's first study the global framework within which we operate and then decide what to produce. It changes your whole perspective."

While the defining measurement of the Cold War was weight—particularly the throw weight of missiles—the defining measurement of the globalization system is speed—speed of commerce, travel, communication and innovation. The Cold War was about Einstein's mass-energy equation, $e = mc^2$. Globalization tends to revolve around Moore's Law, which states that the computing power of silicon chips will double every eighteen to twenty-four months, while the price will halve. In the Cold War, the most frequently asked question was: "Whose side are you on?" In globalization, the most frequently asked question is: "To what extent are you connected to everyone?" In the Cold War, the second most frequently asked question was: "How big is your missile?" In globalization, the second most frequently asked question is: "How fast is your modem?" The defining document of the Cold War system was "The Treaty." The defining document of globalization is "The Deal." The Cold War system even had its own style. In 1961, according to *Foreign Policy* magazine, Cuban President Fidel Castro, wearing his usual olive drab military uniform, made his famous declaration "I shall be a Marxist-Leninist for the rest of my life." In January 1999, Castro put on a business suit for a conference on globalization in Havana, to which financier George Soros and free-market economist Milton Friedman were both invited.

If the defining economists of the Cold War system were Karl Marx and John Maynard Keynes, who each in his own way wanted to tame capitalism, the defining economists of the globalization system are Joseph Schumpeter and Intel chairman Andy Grove, who prefer to unleash capitalism. Schumpeter, a former Austrian Minister of Finance and Harvard Business School professor, expressed the view in his classic work *Capitalism, Socialism and Democracy* that the essence of capitalism is the process of "creative destruction"—the perpetual cycle of destroying the old and less efficient product or service and replacing it with new, more efficient ones. Andy Grove took Schumpeter's insight that "only the paranoid survive" for the title of his book on life in Silicon Valley, and made it in many ways the business model of globalization capitalism. Grove

helped to popularize the view that dramatic, industry-transforming innovations are taking place today faster and faster. Thanks to these technological breakthroughs, the speed by which your latest invention can be
made obsolete or turned into a commodity is now lightning quick. Therefore, only the paranoid, only those who are constantly looking over their
shoulders to see who is creating something new that will destroy them
and then staying just one step ahead of them, will survive. Those countries that are most willing to let capitalism quickly destroy inefficient
companies, so that money can be freed up and directed to more innovative ones, will thrive in the era of globalization. Those which rely on their
governments to protect them from such creative destruction will fall behind in this era.

James Surowiecki, the business columnist for *Slate* magazine, review-
ing Grove's book, neatly summarized what Schumpeter and Grove have
in common, which is the essence of globalization economics. It is the notion that: "Innovation replaces tradition. The present—or perhaps the future—replaces the past. Nothing matters so much as what will come next,
and what will come next can only arrive if what is here now gets over-
turned. While this makes the system a terrific place for innovation, it
makes it a difficult place to live, since most people prefer some measure
of security about the future to a life lived in almost constant uncertainty . . . We are not forced to re-create our relationships with those closest to us on a regular basis. And yet that's precisely what Schumpeter, and
Grove after him, suggest is necessary to prosper [today]."

Indeed, if the Cold War were a sport, it would be sumo wrestling, says
Johns Hopkins University foreign affairs professor Michael Mandelbaum.
"It would be two big fat guys in a ring, with all sorts of posturing and rituals and stomping of feet, but actually very little contact, until the end of
the match, when there is a brief moment of shoving and the loser gets
pushed out of the ring, but nobody gets killed."

By contrast, if globalization were a sport, it would be the 100-meter
dash, over and over and over. And no matter how many times you
win, you have to race again the next day. And if you lose by just one-
hundredth of a second it can be as if you lost by an hour. (Just ask French
multinationals. In 1999, French labor laws were changed, requiring—*requiring*—every employer to implement a four-hour reduction in the legal
workweek, from 39 hours to 35 hours, with no cut in pay. Many French
firms were fighting the move because of the impact it would have on their
productivity in a global market. Henri Thierry, human resources director

for Thomson–CSF Communications, a high-tech firm in the suburbs of Paris, told *The Washington Post*: "We are in a worldwide competition. If we lose one point of productivity, we lose orders. If we're obliged to go to 35 hours it would be like requiring French athletes to run the 100 meters wearing flippers. They wouldn't have much of a chance winning a medal.")

To paraphrase German political theorist Carl Schmitt, the Cold War was a world of "friends" and "enemies." The globalization world, by contrast, tends to turn all friends and enemies into "competitors."

If the defining anxiety of the Cold War was fear of annihilation from an enemy you knew all too well in a world struggle that was fixed and stable, the defining anxiety in globalization is fear of rapid change from an enemy you can't see, touch or feel—a sense that your job, community or workplace can be changed at any moment by anonymous economic and technological forces that are anything but stable. The defining defense system of the Cold War was radar—to expose the threats coming from the other side of the wall. The defining defense system of the globalization era is the X-ray machine—to expose the threats coming from within.

Globalization also has its own demographic pattern—a rapid acceleration of the movement of people from rural areas and agricultural lifestyles to urban areas and urban lifestyles more intimately linked with global fashion, food, markets and entertainment trends.

Last, and most important, globalization has its own defining structure of power, which is much more complex than the Cold War structure. The Cold War system was built exclusively around nation-states. You acted on the world in that system through your state. The Cold War was primarily a drama of states confronting states, balancing states and aligning with states. And, as a system, the Cold War was balanced at the center by two superstates: the United States and the Soviet Union.

The globalization system, by contrast, is built around three balances, which overlap and affect one another. The first is the traditional balance between nation-states. In the globalization system, the United States is now the sole and dominant superpower and all other nations are subordinate to it to one degree or another. The balance of power between the United States and the other states, though, still matters for the stability of this system. And it can still explain a lot of the news you read on the front page of the papers, whether it is the containment of Iraq in the Middle East or the expansion of NATO against Russia in Central Europe.

The second balance in the globalization system is between nation-states and global markets. These global markets are made up of millions of investors moving money around the world with the click of a mouse. I call them "the Electronic Herd," and this herd gathers in key global financial centers, such as Wall Street, Hong Kong, London and Frankfurt, which I call "the Supermarkets." The attitudes and actions of the Electronic Herd and the Supermarkets can have a huge impact on nation-states today, even to the point of triggering the downfall of governments. Who ousted Suharto in Indonesia in 1998? It wasn't another state, it was the Supermarkets, by withdrawing their support for, and confidence in, the Indonesian economy. You will not understand the front page of newspapers today unless you bring the Supermarkets into your analysis. Because the United States can destroy you by dropping bombs and the Supermarkets can destroy you by downgrading your bonds. In other words, the United States is the dominant player in maintaining the globalization gameboard, but it is not alone in influencing the moves on that gameboard. This globalization gameboard today is a lot like a Ouija board—sometimes pieces are moved around by the obvious hand of the superpower, and sometimes they are moved around by hidden hands of the Supermarkets.

The third balance that you have to pay attention to in the globalization system—the one that is really the newest of all—is the balance between individuals and nation-states. Because globalization has brought down many of the walls that limited the movement and reach of people, and because it has simultaneously wired the world into networks, it gives more power to individuals to influence both markets and nation-states than at any time in history. Individuals can increasingly act on the world stage directly—unmediated by a state. So you have today not only a superpower, not only Supermarkets, but, as will be demonstrated later in the book, you now have Super-empowered individuals. Some of these Super-empowered individuals are quite angry, some of them quite wonderful—but all of them are now able to act directly on the world stage.

Without the knowledge of the U.S. government, Long-Term Capital Management—a few guys with a hedge fund in Greenwich, Connecticut—amassed more financial bets around the world than all the foreign reserves of China. Osama bin Laden, a Saudi millionaire with his own global network, declared war on the United States in the late 1990s, and the U.S. Air Force retaliated with a cruise missile attack on him (where he resided in Afghanistan) as though he were another nation-state. Think about that. The United States fired seventy-five cruise missiles, at $1 million apiece, at a person! That was a superpower against a Super-empowered angry man. Jody Williams won the Nobel Peace Prize in 1997 for her contribution to the international ban on landmines. She achieved that ban not only without much government help, but in the face of opposition from all the major powers. And what did she say was her secret weapon for organizing 1,000 different human rights and arms control groups on six continents? "E-mail."

Nation-states, and the American superpower in particular, are still hugely important today, but so too now are Supermarkets and Super-empowered individuals. You will never understand the globalization system, or the front page of the morning paper, unless you see it as a complex interaction between all three of these actors: states bumping up against states, states bumping up against Supermarkets, and Supermarkets and states bumping up against Super-empowered individuals.

Unfortunately, for reasons I will explain later, the system of globalization has come upon us far faster than our ability to retrain ourselves to see and comprehend it. Think about just this one fact: Most people had never even heard of the Internet in 1990, and very few people had an E-mail address then. That was just ten years ago! But today the Internet, cell phones and E-mail have become essential tools that many people, and not only in developed countries, cannot imagine living without. It was no different, I am sure, at the start of the Cold War, with the first appearance of nuclear arsenals and deterrence theories. It took a long time for leaders and analysts of that era to fully grasp the real nature and dimensions of the Cold War system. They emerged from World War II thinking that this great war had produced a certain kind of world, but they soon discovered it had laid the foundations for a world very different from the one they anticipated. Much of what came to be seen as great Cold War architecture and strategizing were responses on the fly to changing events and evolving threats. Bit by bit, these Cold War strategists built the institutions, the perceptions and the reflexes that came to be known as the Cold War system.

It will be no different with the globalization system, except that it may take us even longer to get our minds around it, because it requires so much retraining just to see this new system and because it is built not just around superpowers but also around Supermarkets and Super-empowered individuals. I would say that in 2000 we understand as much about how today's system of globalization is going to work as we understood about how the Cold War system was going to work in 1946—the year Winston Churchill gave his speech warning that an "Iron Curtain" was coming down, cutting off the Soviet zone of influence from Western Europe. We barely understood how the Cold War system was going to play out thirty years after Churchill's speech! That was when Routledge published a collection of essays by some of the top Sovietologists, entitled *Soviet Economy Towards the Year 2000*. It was a good seller when it came out. It never occurred at that time to any of the authors that there wouldn't be a Soviet economy in the year 2000.

If you want to appreciate how few people understand exactly how this system works, think about one amusing fact. The two key economists who were advising Long-Term Capital Management, Robert C. Merton and Myron S. Scholes, shared the Nobel Prize for economics in 1997, roughly one year before LTCM so misunderstood the nature of risk in today's highly integrated global marketplace that it racked up the biggest losses in hedge fund history. And what did LTCM's two economists win their Nobel Prize for? For their studies on how complex financial instruments, known as derivatives, can be used by global investors to offset risk! In 1997 they won the Nobel Prize for managing risk. In 1998 they won the booby prize for creating risk. Same guys, same market—new world.

Information Arbitrage

At the wonderful science museum in Barcelona, I saw an exhibit that beautifully illustrated "chaos." A nonlinear version of a pendulum was set up so that the visitor could hold the bob and start out in a chosen position and with a chosen velocity. One could then watch the subsequent motion, which was also recorded with a pen on a sheet of paper. The visitor was then invited to seize the bob again and try to imitate exactly the previous initial position and velocity. No matter how carefully that was done, the subsequent motion was quite different from what it was the first time . . . I asked the museum director what the two men were doing who were standing in a corner watching us. He replied, "Oh, those are two Dutchmen waiting to take away the 'chaos.' " Apparently, the exhibit was about to be dismantled and taken to Amsterdam. But I have wondered ever since whether the services of those two Dutchmen would not be in great demand across the globe, by organizations that wanted their chaos taken away.

—*Murray Gell-Mann, author of* The Quark and the Jaguar

Like everyone else trying to adjust to this new globalization system and bring it into focus, I had to retrain myself and develop new lenses to see it. In order to explain how, let me start with a confession that I have wanted to unburden myself of for a long, long time. Are you ready? Here it is: I used to make up the weather reports from Beirut.

Well, actually, I didn't make them up. That would be wrong. I "estimated" them. It was 1979 and I was working as a cub reporter in Beirut for United Press International. I often had to work the late-night shift, and one of the responsibilities of the late person was to file the weather report from Beirut, which would be included in UPI's worldwide weather roundup that went out to newspapers each day, with the highs and lows. The only problem was that there was no weatherman in Beirut, or at least none I was aware of. The country was in the midst of a civil war. Who cared what the temperature was? People were just glad to be alive. The

only temperature you cared about in Beirut in those days was your own—
98.6 degrees. So I estimated what the temperature was, often by ad hoc
polling. Gathering the weather report basically involved my shouting
down the hall or across the room: "Hey, Ahmed, how does it feel out
there today?"

And Ahmed or Sonia or Daoud would shout back, "Ya'ani, it feels
hot."

"About ninety degrees?" I would ask. "Sure, Mr. Thomas, whatever
you say," the answer would come back. "Something like that." So I would
write, "High 90 degrees." Then I would ask later, "Kinda cool out there
now?" "Sure, Mr. Thomas," the answer would come back. "About
seventy-two degrees, would you say?" "Sure, Mr. Thomas, whatever you
say," the answer would come back. And so I would write, "Low 72 degrees." And thus was the weather report filed from Beirut.

Years later I would recall those moments when I found myself working in the Business Day section of *The New York Times*. I was occasionally assigned to write the daily dollar or stock market stories and had to
call around to brokers after the markets closed to find out where the dollar finished against other major currencies, or to ascertain why the Dow
Jones Industrial Average moved up or down. I was always amazed that
whichever way the markets moved, whether the dollar fell or rose, some
analyst always had a pithy one-liner explaining why $1.2 trillion in trans-
actions on six different continents across twenty-four different time zones
resulted in the dollar falling or rising against the Japanese yen by half a
penny. And we all believed this explanation. But somewhere in the back
of my mind I used to wonder whether these commentators weren't just
pulling my leg. Somewhere in the back of my mind I used to wonder
whether this wasn't just the Wall Street version of the weather report from
Beirut, with someone shouting down the hall at the offices of Merrill
Lynch or PaineWebber the equivalent of "Hey, Ahmed, why did the dollar go down today?" And whatever the stock boy or the secretary or the
first broker to walk by his desk happened to answer ended up in the next
day's newspaper as the global explanation for the behavior of thousands of
different traders around the world.

In 1994 I was the *New York Times* international trade and finance correspondent, covering the United States–Japan trade talks. One afternoon,
I was sitting at my desk, scrolling through the news wires on my computer, when I noticed two items move on Reuters, one right after the
other:

Dollar Ends Higher on Optimism over Trade Talks
NEW YORK (Reuters)—The dollar finished higher against most lead-
ing currencies Friday as optimism grew that Washington and
Tokyo would reach a trade agreement.

Blue Chip Stocks End Lower on Uncertainty over Trade Talks
NEW YORK (Reuters)—Blue chip stocks closed lower Friday amid
uncertainty over U.S.-Japan trade talks ahead of a midnight deadline for possible sanctions.

"Hey, Ahmed, what do you think of the U.S.-Japan talks?"

What I was doing back in those days filing the weather report from
Beirut, and what Reuters was doing with its stock and currency stories, was trying to order the chaos—without much success in either of our
cases. I knew when I began my foreign affairs column in 1995 that I would
not survive very long if all I was doing to order the chaos was the political
equivalent of just guessing the temperature in Beirut. So what to do? How
to understand and explain this incredibly complex system of globalization?

The short answer is that I learned you need to do two things at once—
look at the world through a multilens perspective and, at the same time,
convey that complexity to readers through simple stories, not grand theories. I use two techniques: I "do information arbitrage" in order to understand the world, and I "tell stories" in order to explain it.

What is information arbitrage? Arbitrage is a market term. Technically
speaking, it refers to the simultaneous buying and selling of the same securities, commodities or foreign exchange in different markets to profit
from unequal prices and unequal information. The successful arbitrageur is a trader who knows that pork bellies are selling for $1 per pound
in Chicago and for $1.50 in New York and so he buys them in Chicago
and sells them in New York. One can do arbitrage in markets. One can
do it in literature. It was said of the great Spanish writer José Ortega y
Gasset that he "bought information cheap in London and sold it expensive in Madrid." That is, he frequented all the great salons of London and
then translated the insights he gained there into Spanish for Spanish
readers back home. But whether you are selling pork bellies or insights,
the key to being a successful arbitrageur is having a wide net of infor-
mants and information and then knowing how to synthesize it in a way
that will produce a profit.

Today, more than ever, the traditional boundaries between politics, culture, technology, finance, national security and ecology are disappearing. You often cannot explain one without referring to the others, and you cannot explain the whole without reference to them all. Therefore, to be an effective foreign affairs analyst or reporter, you have to learn how to arbitrage information from these disparate perspectives and then weave it all together to produce a picture of the world that you would never have if you looked at it from only one perspective. That is the essence of information arbitrage. In a world where we are all so much more interconnected, the ability to read the connections, and to connect the dots, is the real value added provided by a journalist. If you don't see the connections, you won't see the world.

I wish I could say I understood all this when I began my career, but I didn't. I came to this approach entirely by accident, as successive changes in my career kept forcing me to add one more lens on top of another, just to survive. Here's what happened:

I began my journalistic life as the most narrow of reporters. For the first decade of my career I covered the "Mother of All Tribal Wars"—the Arab-Israeli conflict, first from Beirut and then from Jerusalem. In those days, journalism for me was basically a two-dimensional business. It was about politics and culture, because in the Middle East your culture pretty much defined your politics. Or, to put it another way, the world for me was all about watching people clinging to their own roots and uprooting their neighbors' olive trees.

Then in 1988 I left Jerusalem, after a decade in the Middle East, and came to Washington, where I became the *New York Times* diplomatic correspondent. The first story I was assigned to cover was Secretary of State–designate James A. Baker III's confirmation hearing before the Senate. I am embarrassed to say that since both my B.A. and M.A. were in Arabic and Middle Eastern Studies, and since I had spent almost my entire journalistic career up to that point covering the Middle East, I really did not know very much about any other parts of the world, and I certainly did not know anything about most of the issues the senators were quizzing Mr. Baker about, such as the START treaty, the Contras, Angola, the CFE (Conventional Forces in Europe) arms control negotiations and NATO. My head was swimming as I came out of the hearing. I had no idea what the lead was. I didn't even know what half the acronyms stood for. I couldn't keep straight whether the Contras were our guys or their guys, and I thought CFE was a typo and was actually "cafe" without the "a." As I took a taxi back to the *Times* bureau, all I could see in my head was a banner headline in *The Washington Post* the next morning about something Baker had said that I would not even have mentioned in my story. Only thanks to help from the *Times*'s Pentagon reporter, Michael Gordon, did I manage to pull a story together that day. But I knew then and there that two dimensions weren't going to cut it anymore. Fortunately, thanks to four years of covering diplomacy, including some 500,000 miles on the road with Baker, I managed to add a new dimension to politics and culture—the national security, balance-of-power dimension. This comprises the whole nexus of issues revolving around arms control, superpower competition, Cold War alliance management and power geopolitics. Thus my old two-dimensional view of the world was transformed. I remember once flying with Baker to Israel, and his plane got diverted briefly over the Tel Aviv airport and was sent on a big, wide arc over the West Bank before coming in for its landing. I found myself looking out the window of the Secretary of State's airplane, down at the West Bank, and thinking, "You know, in raw power terms, this place really isn't very important anymore. Interesting, yes. But geopolitically important, no."

Following my tour at the State Department, and then a mercifully brief stint as a White House correspondent (none dare call that journalism), I added another lens in 1994 when the *Times* asked me to start a new beat that would cover the intersection between foreign policy and international finance. It was becoming apparent that with the end of the Cold War and the collapse of the Soviet Union, finance and trade were taking on a bigger role in shaping international relations. Having a beat that was at the intersection of economics and national security policy-making was something of an experiment for me and the *Times*. I was technically assigned to be the Treasury-trade correspondent, but given my background covering the State Department and the White House, I was asked to integrate it all. We described the beat variously as "Commercial Diplomacy" or "Foreign Affairs and Finance." What I discovered when I stood at that intersection were two things. First was that with the end of the Cold War system, this intersection was going to produce a huge amount of news. The other thing I discovered was that nobody else was there. Instead, there were a lot of trade reporters who didn't cover diplomacy. There were a lot of finance reporters who didn't cover national security affairs. There were a lot of diplomatic reporters who didn't cover finance. And there were White House reporters who didn't cover trade, finance or foreign affairs, but only what the President said or did.

For me, adding the financial markets dimension to politics, culture and national security was like putting on a new pair of glasses and suddenly looking at the world in 4-D. I saw news stories that I would never have recognized as news stories before. I saw causal chains of events that I never could have identified before. I saw invisible hands and handcuffs impeding leaders and nations from doing things that I never imagined before.

Alas, four dimensions were not enough. Once I was assigned to be the foreign affairs columnist, I gradually realized that what was driving the rise and power of markets, what was reshaping how nations and individuals interacted with one another, and what was really at the heart of globalization, was the recent advances in technology—from the Internet to satellite telecommunications. I realized that I could not explain to myself, let alone to readers, the forces that were shaping global politics unless I better understood these technologies that were empowering people, companies and governments in all sorts of new ways. Who controls the guns in a society is always critical. But who controls the phones and how they work also matters. How many troops and nukes your country possesses is always critical. But how much bandwidth you have for your Internet also matters. So I had to add yet another dimension—technology—and become a 5-D reporter. It meant adding Silicon Valley to the list of world capitals—Moscow, Beijing, London, Jerusalem—that I felt I had to visit once a year just to stay abreast of what was going on.

Finally, the more I observed the system of globalization at work, the more obvious it was that it had unleashed forest-crushing forces of development and Disney-round-the-clock homogenization, which, if left unchecked, had the potential to destroy the environment and uproot cultures at a pace never before seen in human history. I gradually realized that if I didn't bring this environmental perspective into my analysis, I would be leaving out one of the major forces that could limit development and trigger a backlash against globalization. So I added the sixth dimension to my arbitrage—educating myself in environmentalism—and began including environmental side trips to my travels to understand how ecosystems were being affected by globalization and how their degradation was affecting globalization.

Now that I am up to six D's, I don't know what's next. But if and when a new dimension becomes apparent, I will add it. Because I am a "globalist." That is the school of thought to which I belong. That means I am not a realist, who thinks everything in foreign affairs can be explained by the quest for power and geopolitical advantage—and markets don't really matter. I am not an environmentalist, who looks at the fate of the world only through the prism of the environment and what must be done to save it—and development doesn't matter. I am not a technologist—one of those Silicon Valley techno-nerds who believe that history began with the invention of the microprocessor and that the Internet will determine the future of international relations—and geopolitics doesn't matter. I am not an essentialist who believes that people's behavior can be explained by some essential cultural or DNA trait—and technology doesn't matter. And I am not an economist who believes that you can explain the world with reference only to markets—and power politics and culture don't matter.

I believe that this new system of globalization—in which walls between countries, markets and disciplines are increasingly being blown away—constitutes a fundamentally new state of affairs. And the only way to see it, understand it and explain it is by arbitraging all six dimensions laid out above— assigning different weights to different perspectives at different times in different situations, but always understanding that it is the interaction of all of them together that is really the defining feature of international relations today. And therefore being a globalist is the only way to systematically connect the dots, see the system of globalization and thereby order the chaos.

If I am wrong about this world, that will be apparent soon enough. But if I am not wrong, there are a lot of people who are going to have to go back to school. I believe it is particularly important for both journalists, who are charged with explaining the world, and strategists, who are responsible for shaping it, to think like globalists. There is increasingly a seamless web between all of these different worlds and institutions, and reporters and strategists need to be as seamless as that web. Unfortunately, in both journalism and academe, there is a deeply ingrained tendency to think in terms of highly segmented, narrow areas of expertise, which ignores the fact that the real world is not divided up into such neat little beats and that the boundaries between domestic, international, political and technological affairs are all collapsing.

Let me offer just one example. For years, the Clinton Administration kept threatening to impose trade sanctions on Japan unless it eliminated certain official and hidden tariffs on a variety of goods. But every time the savvy U.S. Trade Representative Mickey Kantor would seem to have won the argument inside the Administration for taking action, and the President was about to lower the boom on Japan, at the last minute Clinton would back off. Here is what I imagine was going on inside the Oval Office at the time:

Kantor would walk into the Oval Office, pull up a chair next to the President and say, "Mr. President, those damn Japanese are stonewalling, they are sticking it to us again. They are not allowing our exports in. It's time we really lowered the boom. Sanctions, Mr. President. Big-time sanctions. This is the time for them. This is the place for them, and, by the way, Mr. President, the unions will love us for it."

"Mickey, you are dead right," the President would say. "Go for it." But just as Kantor was about to leave to lower the boom on Tokyo, Treasury Secretary Robert Rubin would come in the side door of the Oval Office.

"Ah, Mr. President," Rubin would say, "you realize that if we impose trade sanctions on Japan the dollar is going to nosedive and the Japanese could start selling all the U.S. Treasury bills they hold, and domestic U.S. interest rates will rise."

The President would then motion to Kantor, who was halfway out the door. "Yo, Mickey, Mickey, Mickey. Come back here for a second. We've got to think this over."

A few days later, Kantor would be back. He would make the same arguments. This time the President would be really convinced. He would tell Kantor: "I am not going to take it from those Japanese anymore, Mickey. Sanctions. Lower the boom."

Just as Kantor would be about to leave to lower the boom on Tokyo, Defense Secretary William Perry would come in the side door of the Oval Office.

"Ah, Mr. President," Perry would say, "you realize that if we impose trade sanctions on Japan, the Japanese will not renegotiate our base agreement at Okinawa, or pay for that North Korean nuclear reactor we're counting on."

The President would then frantically motion to Kantor, who was trying to get out the door. "Yo, Mickey, Mickey, Mickey. Come back here for a second. We've got to think this over."

This is an imaginary scene, but I would bet a lot of money it bears a close resemblance to what was actually going on, and the reporter who will capture it properly for readers will not be the trade reporter, Treasury reporter or Pentagon reporter, but the one who is moving back and forth, arbitraging all three beats at the same time.

The Yale international relations historians Paul Kennedy and John Lewis Gaddis see one of their jobs as training the next generation of American strategists. To their great credit, they decided they had to find a way to broaden their curriculum in order to produce a new generation of strategists who could think as globalists and not just particularists. In an essay they jointly authored, Gaddis and Kennedy argued that while it is important that we have particularists in every subject—having a pool of people with deep knowledge of different spheres is always important—it is also important that the particularists alone not be the ones making and analyzing foreign policy.

"These people," the two Yale historians wrote, "are perfectly competent at taking in parts of the picture, but they have difficulty seeing the entire thing. They pigeonhole priorities, pursuing them separately and simultaneously, with little thought to how each might undercut the other. They proceed confidently enough from tree to tree, but seem astonished to find themselves lost in the forest. The great strategists of the past kept forests as well as the trees in view. They were generalists, and they operated from an ecological perspective. They understood that the world is a web, in which adjustments made here are bound to have effects over there—that everything is interconnected. Where, though, might one find generalists today? . . . The dominant trend within universities and the think tanks is toward ever-narrower specialization: a higher premium is placed on functioning deeply within a single field than broadly across several. And yet without some awareness of the whole—without some sense of how means converge to accomplish or to frustrate ends—there can be no strategy. And without strategy, there is only drift."

Some people are starting to catch on. That's why in the late 1990s the super-secret National Security Agency (NSA), which eavesdrops all over the globe, vacuuming up huge amounts of intelligence, decided it had to shift its internal way of handling information from the Cold War motto of "need to know," meaning you only got to see information if you had a need to know it, to "need to share," meaning we'll never understand the big picture unless we all share our little ones.

Maybe that explains why I gradually found that some (but by no means all) of my best intellectual sources these days were neither professors of international relations nor State Department diplomats, but rather the only real thriving school of globalists in the world today—hedge fund managers. I found myself drawn more and more to smart hedge fund managers—as opposed to diplomats or professors—because the best of them tended to be extremely well informed about global affairs and had a natural ability and willingness to arbitrage and interpolate information from all six dimensions before drawing their conclusions. One of the best of this group is Robert Johnson, who used to be a partner of George

Soros. Johnson and I often remarked, after one of our conversations analyzing the world, that we were both basically doing the same thing—the only difference was that at the end of the day he was making a bet on a stock or bond and I was writing an opinion about some aspect of international relations. But we both had to go through the same arbitrage process to get there.

While six-dimensional information arbitrage is the best way to see the system of globalization, it is too complex a system to be explained by grand theories alone. The best way to explain it is often through simple stories. I mentioned that one afternoon to Robert Hormats, the vice-chairman of Goldman Sachs International, and he observed: "To understand and then to explain globalization it is useful to think of yourself as an intellectual nomad. In the world of the nomad, there is no carefully defined turf. That's why the nomads were the ones who developed the monotheistic religions of Judaism and Islam. If you were sedentary you could develop all sorts of mythologies about this rock or that tree, and think that God was in that rock or that tree, alone. But the nomads always saw more of the world. They knew that God was not in that rock. He was everywhere. And the nomads, sitting around their campfires or walking from oasis to oasis, then conveyed that complex truth through simple stories."

In the old days a reporter, columnist or statesman could get away with thinking of his "market" as City Hall, or the Statehouse, or the White House, or the Pentagon, or the Treasury Department, or the State Department. But the relevant market today is the planet Earth and the global integration of technology, finance, trade and information in a way that is influencing wages, interest rates, living standards, culture, job opportunities, wars and weather patterns all over the world. It is not that the system of globalization explains everything happening in the world today. It is simply that to the extent that one system is influencing more people in more ways at the same time, it is globalization.

Murray Gell-Mann, the Nobel laureate, former professor of theoretical physics at Caltech and one of the founders of the Santa Fe Institute, once argued in a series of lectures that what I call information arbitrage is not much different from the approach taken by scientists trying to make sense of complex systems. He is right. And there is no more complex political system today than globalization, and understanding it requires the journalist and strategist to be equally complex.

"Here on earth, once it was formed, systems of increasing complexity have arisen as a consequence of the physical evolution of the planet, biological evolution and human cultural evolution," said Gell-Mann. "The process has gone so far that we human beings are now confronted with immensely complex ecological, political, economic and social problems. When we attempt to tackle such difficult problems, we naturally tend to break them up into more manageable pieces. That is a useful practice, but it has serious limitations. When dealing with any non-linear system, especially a complex one, you can't just think in terms of parts or aspects and just add things up and say that the behavior of this and the behavior of that, added together, makes the whole thing. With a complex non-linear system you have to break it up into pieces and then study each aspect, and then study the very strong interaction between them all. Only this way can you describe the whole system."

That to me is the essence of what I consider the globalist school in international relations. But to have a globalist school, we need more students, professors, diplomats, journalists, spies and social scientists trained as globalists.

"We need a corpus of people who consider that it is important to take a serious and professional crude look at the whole system," says Gell-Mann. "It has to be a crude look, because you will never master every part or every interconnection. You would think most journalists would do this. But they don't. Unfortunately, in a great many places in our society, including academia and most bureaucracies, prestige accrues principally to those who study carefully some [narrow] aspect of a problem, a trade, a technology, or a culture, while discussion of the big picture is relegated to cocktail party conversation. That is crazy. We have to learn not only to have specialists but also people whose specialty is to spot the strong interactions and the entanglements of the different dimensions, and then take a crude look at the whole. What we once considered the cocktail party stuff—that's a crucial part of the real story."

So, on to my cocktail party.

The Lexus and the Olive Tree

Jerusalem, December 29, 1998: Shimon Biton places his cellular phone up to the Western Wall so a relative in France can say a prayer at the holy site *(Photograph by Menahem Kahana, Agence France-Presse)*

Once you recognize that globalization is the international system that has replaced the Cold War system, is this all you need to know to explain world affairs today? Not quite. Globalization is what is new. And if the world were made of just microchips and markets, you could probably rely on globalization to explain almost everything. But, alas, the world is made of microchips and markets and men and women, with all their peculiar habits, traditions, longings and unpredictable aspirations. So world affairs today can only be explained as the interaction between what is as new as an Internet Web site and what is as old as a gnarled olive tree on the banks of the river Jordan. I first started thinking about this while riding on a train in Japan in May 1992, eating a sushi box dinner and traveling at 180 miles per hour.

I was in Tokyo on a reporting assignment and had arranged to visit the Lexus luxury car factory outside Toyota City, south of Tokyo. It was one of the most memorable tours I've ever taken. At that time, the factory was producing 300 Lexus sedans each day, made by 66 human beings and 310 robots. From what I could tell, the human beings were there mostly for quality control. Only a few of them were actually screwing in bolts or soldering parts together. The robots were doing all the work. There were even robotic trucks that hauled materials around the floor and could sense whenever humans were in their path and would "beep, beep" at them to move. I was fascinated watching the robot that applied the rubber seal that held in place the front windshield of each Lexus. The robot arm would neatly paint the hot molten rubber in a perfect rectangle around the window. But what I liked most was that when it finished its application there was always a tiny drop of rubber left hanging from the tip of the robot's finger—like the drop of toothpaste that might be left at the top of the tube after you've squeezed some onto your toothbrush. At the Lexus factory, though, this robot arm would swing around in a wide loop until the tip met a tiny, almost invisible metal wire that would perfectly slice off that last small drop of hot black rubber—leaving nothing left over. I kept staring at this process, thinking to myself how much planning, design and technology it must have taken to get that robot arm to do its job and then swing around each time, at the precise angle, so that this little thumbnail-size wire could snip off the last drop of hot rubber for the robot to start clean on the next window. I was impressed.

After touring the factory, I went back to Toyota City and boarded the bullet train for the ride back to Tokyo. The bullet train is aptly named, for it has both the look and feel of a speeding bullet. As I nibbled away on one of those sushi dinner boxes you can buy in any Japanese train station, I was reading that day's *International Herald Tribune*, and a story caught my eye on the top right corner of page 3. It was about the daily State Department briefing. State Department spokeswoman Margaret D. Tutwiler had given a controversial interpretation of a 1948 United Nations resolution, relating to the right of return for Palestinian refugees to Israel. I don't remember all the details, but whatever her interpretation was, it had clearly agitated both the Arabs and the Israelis and sparked a furor in the Middle East, which this story was reporting.

So there I was speeding along at 180 miles an hour on the most modern train in the world, reading this story about the oldest corner of the world. And the thought occurred to me that these Japanese, whose Lexus factory I had just visited and whose train I was riding, were building the greatest luxury car in the world with robots. And over here, on the top of page 3 of the *Herald Tribune*, the people with whom I had lived for so many years in Beirut and Jerusalem, whom I knew so well, were still fighting over who owned which olive tree. It struck me then that the Lexus and the olive tree were actually pretty good symbols of this post–Cold War era: half the world seemed to be emerging from the Cold War intent on building a better Lexus, dedicated to modernizing, streamlining and privatizing their economies in order to thrive in the system of globalization. And half of the world—sometimes half the same country, sometimes half the same person—was still caught up in the fight over who owns which olive tree.

Olive trees are important. They represent everything that roots us, anchors us, identifies us and locates us in this world—whether it be belonging to a family, a community, a tribe, a nation, a religion or, most of all, a place called home. Olive trees are what give us the warmth of family, the joy of individuality, the intimacy of personal rituals, the depth of private relationships, as well as the confidence and security to reach out and encounter others. We fight so intensely at times over our olive trees because, at their best, they provide the feelings of self-esteem and belonging that are as essential for human survival as food in the belly. Indeed, one reason that the nation-state will never disappear, even if it does weaken, is because it is the ultimate olive tree—the ultimate expression of whom we belong to—linguistically, geographically and historically. You cannot be a complete person alone. You can be a rich person alone. You can be a smart person alone. But you cannot be a complete person alone. For that you must be part of, and rooted in, an olive grove.

This truth was once beautifully conveyed by Rabbi Harold S. Kushner in his interpretation of a scene from Gabriel García Márquez's classic novel *One Hundred Years of Solitude:*

> Márquez tells of a village where people were afflicted with a strange plague of forgetfulness, a kind of contagious amnesia. Starting with the oldest inhabitants and working its way through the population, the plague causes people to forget the names of even the most common everyday objects. One young man, still unaffected, tries to limit the damage by putting labels on everything. "This is a table," "This is a window," "This is a cow; it has to be milked every morning." And at the entrance to the town, on the

main road, he puts up two large signs. One reads "The name of our village is Macondo," and the larger one reads "God exists." The message I get from that story is that we can, and probably will, forget most of what we have learned in life—the math, the history, the chemical formulas, the address and phone number of the first house we lived in when we got married—and all that forgetting will do us no harm. But if we forget whom we belong to, and if we forget that there is a God, something profoundly human in us will be lost.

But while olive trees are essential to our very being, an attachment to one's olive trees, when taken to excess, can lead us into forging identities, bonds and communities based on the exclusion of others. And when these obsessions really run amok, as with the Nazis in Germany, or the murderous Aum Shinrikyo cult in Japan or the Serbs in Yugoslavia, they lead to the extermination of others.

Conflicts between Serbs and Muslims, Jews and Palestinians, Armenians and Azeris over who owns which olive tree are so venomous precisely because they are about who will be at home and anchored in a local world and who will not be. Their underlying logic is: I must control this olive tree, because if the other controls it, not only will I be economically and politically under his thumb, but my whole sense of home will be lost. I'll never be able to take my shoes off and relax. Few things are more enraging to people than to have their identity or their sense of home stripped away. They will die for it, kill for it, sing for it, write poetry for it and novelize about it. Because without a sense of home and belonging, life becomes barren and rootless. And life as a tumbleweed is no life at all.

So then what does the Lexus represent? It represents an equally fundamental, age-old human drive—the drive for sustenance, improvement, prosperity and modernization—as it is played out in today's globalization system. The Lexus represents all the burgeoning global markets, financial institutions and computer technologies with which we pursue higher living standards today.

Of course, for millions of people in developing countries, the quest for material improvement still involves walking to a well, subsisting on a dollar a day, plowing a field barefoot behind an ox or gathering wood and carrying it on their heads for five miles. These people still upload for a living, not download. But for millions of others in developed countries, this quest for material betterment and modernization is increasingly conducted in Nike shoes, shopping in integrated markets and using the new network technologies. The point is that while different people have different access to the new markets and technologies that characterize the globalization system, and derive highly unequal benefits from them, this doesn't change the fact that these markets and technologies are the defining economic tools of the day and everyone is either directly or indirectly affected by them.

The Lexus versus the olive tree, though, is just a modern version of a very old story—indeed one of the oldest stories in recorded history—the story of why Cain slew Abel. The Hebrew Bible says in Genesis: "Cain said to his brother Abel; And when they were in the field, Cain rose up against his brother Abel and killed him. Then the Lord said to Cain, 'Where is your brother Abel?' And he said, 'I do not know. Am I my brother's keeper?' And the Lord said, 'What have you done? The voice of your brother's blood is crying to me from the ground.' "

If you read this paragraph closely you notice that the Hebrew Bible never tells us what Cain actually said to Abel. The sentence reads that "Cain said to his brother Abel," and then it just stops. We are not privy to the conversation. What happened in the conversation between them that got Cain so angry that he would actually kill his brother Abel? My theology teacher, Rabbi Tzvi Marx, taught me that the rabbinic sages in Genesis Rabbah, one of the fundamental rabbinic commentaries on the Bible, give three basic explanations of what was said. One is that the two brothers were arguing about a woman—Eve. After all, there was only one woman on earth at the time, their mother, and they were arguing over which brother would get to marry her. They were arguing over sexual fulfillment and procreation. Another interpretation posits that Cain and Abel had basically divided up the world between them. Cain had all the real estate—or as the Bible says, "Cain became a tiller of the soil"—and Abel had all the movables and livestock—"Abel became a keeper of sheep." And according to this interpretation, Cain told Abel to get his sheep off Cain's property and this triggered a fight over territory that eventually ended with Cain slaying Abel in the heat of the argument. They were fighting over economic development and material fulfillment. The third interpretation is that the two brothers had already neatly divided everything in the world between them, except one critical thing that was still up for grabs: Where would the Temple be built that would reflect their particular religious and cultural identity? Each wanted to control that Temple and have it reflect his identity. Each wanted that Temple in his olive grove. They were fighting over the issue of identity, and which of them would be the keeper of their family's source of legitimacy. So, the rabbis noted, all the basic elements of human motivation are potentially there in one story: the need for sexual intimacy, the need for sustenance and the need for a sense of identity and community. I will leave matters of sex for somebody else. This book is about the other two.

That's why I like to say that information arbitrage provides the lenses we need to look into today's world, but lenses alone are not enough. We also need to know what we are looking at and for. And what we are look-ing at and for is how the age-old quests for material betterment and for individual and communal identity—which go all the way back to Genesis—play themselves out in today's dominant international system of globalization. This is the drama of the Lexus and the olive tree.

In the Cold War system, the most likely threat to your olive tree was from another olive tree. It was from your neighbor coming over, vio-lently digging up your olive tree and planting his in its place. That threat has not been eliminated today, but, for the moment, it has been dimin-ished in many parts of the world. The biggest threat today to your olive tree is likely to come from the Lexus—from all the anonymous, transna-tional, homogenizing, standardizing market forces and technologies that make up today's globalizing economic system. There are some things about this system that can make the Lexus so overpowering it can overrun and overwhelm every olive tree in sight—breaking down communities, steamrolling environments and crowding out traditions—and this can produce a real olive tree backlash. But there are other things about this system that empower even the smallest, weakest political community to actually use the new technologies and markets to preserve their olive trees, their culture and identity. Traveling the world in recent years, again and again I have come on this simultaneous wrestling match, tug-of-war, balancing act between the Lexus and the olive tree.

The Lexus and olive tree wrestling with each other in the new system of globalization was reflected in Norway's 1994 referendum about whether or not to join the European Union. That should have been a slam dunk for Norwegians. After all, Norway is in Europe. It is a rich, de-veloped country and it has a significant amount of intra-European trade.

Joining the EU made all the economic sense in the world for Norway in a world of increasing globalization. But the referendum failed, because too many Norwegians felt joining the EU would mean uprooting too much of their own Norwegian identity and way of life, which, thanks to Norwegian North Sea oil (sold into a global economy), the Norwegians could still afford to preserve—without EU membership. Many Norwegians looked at the EU and said to themselves, "Now let me get this straight. I am supposed to take my Norwegian identity and deposit it into a Euro-Cuisinart, where it will be turned into Euromush by Eurobureaucrats paid in Eurodollars at the Euro-Parliament in the Eurocapital covered by Eurojournalists? Hey, no, thanks. I'd rather be Sten from Norway. I'd rather cling to my own unique olive tree identity and be a little less efficient economically."

The olive tree backlashing against the Lexus is the August 1999 story from France, by *The Washington Post*'s Anne Swardson, about Philippe Folliot, the mayor of the southwestern French village of St. Pierre-de-Trivisy—population 610. Folliot and the St. Pierre-de-Trivisy town council slapped a 100 percent tax on bottles of Coca-Cola sold at the town's campground, in retaliation for a tariff that the United States had slapped on Roquefort cheese, which is produced only in the southwestern French region around St. Pierre-de-Trivisy. As he applied some Roquefort to a piece of crusty bread, Folliot told Swardson, "Roquefort is made from the milk of only one breed of sheep, it is made in only one place in France, and it is made in only one special way. It is the opposite of globalization. Coca-Cola you can buy anywhere in the world and it is exactly the same. [Coke] is a symbol of the American multinational that wants to uniformize taste all over the planet. That's what we are against."

The Lexus and the olive tree in a healthy balance was the story related to me by Glenn Prickett, a senior vice president at the environmental group Conservation International, about when he visited the Kayapo Indian village of Aukre, which is located in a remote corner of the Brazilian Amazon rain forest reached only by small-engine plane. "Touching down on the grass landing strip we were met by the entire village in traditional dress—and undress—and painted faces, with a smattering of American baseball caps bearing random logos," recalled Prickett. "I was there with Conservation International to inspect the progress of a biological research station we were running upriver with the Kayapo. The Kayapo have defended a large chunk of intact Amazon for centuries through sheer force. Now they are learning to protect it through alliances with international scientists, conservationists and socially conscious businesspeople. Their village has a little main street with a Conservation International store and a branch of the Body Shop, the ecoconscious soap makers. So after a two-day stay at the biological research station, we came back to the village to do a final bit of business. We had arranged for an open-air market of Kayapo culture, artifacts, baskets, war clubs, spears and bows and arrows to be set up. Then our group proceeded to buy all of it for very steep prices in U.S. dollars. We then went and sat in the men's hut in the center of this Kayapo village, which could have come out of prehistory. While sitting in this hut with the leading men of the village, I noticed that they were all watching a single TV, connected to a large satellite dish. The men were flipping the channels back and forth between a Brazilian soccer match and a business channel that carried the running price of gold on world markets. The Kayapo men wanted to be sure that they were charging the small miners, whom they let dig on the edges of their rain-forest property, the going international rate for whatever gold they found. They then used these profits earned on the world gold market to protect their own unique lifestyle in the middle of the Amazon rain forest."

The Lexus struggling with the olive tree was a scene I witnessed at NATO headquarters in Brussels. I was sitting on a couch in the lobby, waiting for an appointment. Nearby was a Russian journalist, speaking Russian into her cell phone. But what struck me most was the fact that she was walking in circles next to the Coke machine, underneath a television tuned to CNN that was broadcasting the surprise entry of Russian troops into Pristina, Kosovo—ahead of NATO forces. A Russian journalist, circling the Coke machine, under the CNN screen, speaking Russian into a cell phone, in NATO headquarters, while Kosovo burned—my mind couldn't contain all the contradictions.

The Lexus being exploited by the olive tree was the report in *The Economist* of August 14, 1999, entitled "Cyberthugs." It stated that "The National Criminal Intelligence Service blamed the increasingly sophisticated nature of football hooligans for the organized violence last weekend between fans of Millwall and Cardiff City. Rival bands of thugs are apparently prepared to cooperate by fixing venues for fights via the Internet. Information is exchanged in closed or open Websites. Some even report the violence as it happens: 'It's kicking off right now as I speak,' wrote Paul Dodd, a particularly dopey hooligan known to cyber nerds and police alike. The police now say they surf for such Websites, hoping to discover other planned attacks."

West Side Story meets the World Wide Web.

The olive tree exploiting the Lexus is also the story that came to light in the summer of 1999 about Adolf Hitler's racist manifesto *Mein Kampf,* which is banned in Germany by the German government. You cannot sell it in any German bookstore, or publish it in Germany. But Germans found that they could order the book over the Internet from Amazon.com and it would come in the mail in a way that the German government was powerless to stop. Indeed, so many Germans ordered *Mein Kampf* from Amazon.com that in the summer of 1999 Hitler made Amazon.com's top-ten best-seller list for Germany. Amazon.com at first refused to stop shipping *Mein Kampf* to Germany, insisting that the English translation was not covered by censorship, and that it was not going to get in the business of deciding what its customers were allowed to read. However, after this was publicized, Amazon.com was so bombarded with angry E-mails from all over the world that it stopped selling Hitler's works.

The olive tree trumping the Lexus, and the Lexus then coming right back to trump the olive tree, was the nuclear-testing saga that unfolded in India in the late 1990s. In the spring of 1998 India's newly elected nationalist Bharatiya Janata Party (BJP) decided to defy the world and resume testing its nuclear weapons. Asserting India's right to test had been a key plank in the BJP's election campaign. Shortly after the tests I visited India, where I talked to rich and poor, government and nongovernment types, villagers and city slickers. I kept waiting to meet the Indian who would say to me, "You know, these nuclear tests were really stupid. We didn't get any additional security out of them and they've really cost us with sanctions." I am sure that sentiment was there—but I couldn't find anyone to express it. Even those Indian politicians who denounced the nuclear tests as a cheap, jingoistic maneuver by India's new Hindu nationalist government would tell you that these tests were the only way for India to get what it wants most from the United States and China: R-E-S-P-E-C-T. I finally realized the depth of this sentiment when I went to see a saffron-robed Indian human rights campaigner, Swami Agnivesh. As the two of us sat cross-legged on the floor of his living room in his simple Delhi home, I thought, "Surely he will disavow this test." But no sooner did we start talking than he declared to me: "We are India, the second-largest country in the world! You can't just take us for granted. India doesn't feel threatened by Pakistan, but in the whole international game India is being marginalized by the China-U.S. axis." The next day I went out to Dasna, a village north of New Delhi, where I randomly

stopped shopkeepers to talk. Dasna is one of the poorest places I have
ever seen. Nobody seemed to have shoes. Everyone seemed to be skin
and bones. There were more water buffalo and bicycles than cars on the
road. The air was heavy with the smell of cow dung used for energy. But
they loved their government's nuclear sound-and-light show. "We are
nine hundred million people. We will not die from these sanctions," pro-
nounced Pramod Batra, the forty-two-year-old village doctor in Dasna.
"This nuclear test was about self-respect, and self-respect is more important than roads, electricity and water. Anyway, what did we do? We exploded our bomb. It was like shooting a gun off into the air. We didn't
hurt anybody."

But while India's olive tree impulse seemed to have prevailed over its
needs for a Lexus, when this happens in today's globalization system
there is always a hidden long-term price. While in New Delhi, I stayed at
the Oberoi Hotel, where I swam laps in the pool at the end of each day to
recover from the sweltering 100-degree heat. My first day there, while I
was doing my breaststrokes, there was an Indian woman also swimming
laps in the lane next to me. During a rest stop we started talking and she
told me she ran the India office of Salomon Brothers–Smith Barney, the
major American investment bank. I told her I was a columnist who had
come over to write about the fallout from the Indian nuclear tests.

"Have you heard who's in town?" she asked me as we each trod water.
"No," I said, shaking my head. "Who's in town?"

"Moody's," she said. Moody's Investors Service is the international
credit-rating agency which rates economies, with grades of A, B and C, so
that global investors know who is pursuing sound economics and who is
not, and if your economy gets a lower rating it means you will have to pay
higher interest rates for international loans. "Moody's has sent a team
over to re-rate the Indian economy," she said.

"Have you heard anything about what they decided?"

No, I hadn't, I replied.

"You might want to check," she said, and swam away.

I did check. It turned out that the Moody's team had moved around
New Delhi almost as quietly and secretly as India's nuclear scientists had
prepared their bomb. I couldn't find out anything about their decisions,
but the night I left India, I was listening to the evening news when the
fourth item caught my ear. It said that in reaction to the Indian government's new bloated, directionless budget, and in the wake of the Indian
nuclear tests and the U.S. sanctions imposed on India for blowing off
some nukes, Moody's had downgraded India's economy from "invest-

ment grade," which meant it was safe for global investors, to "speculative grade," which meant it was risky. The Standard & Poor's rating agency also changed its outlook on the Indian economy from "stable" to "negative." This meant that any Indian company trying to borrow money from international markets would have to pay higher interest. And because India has a low savings rate, those foreign funds are crucial for a country that needs $500 billion in new infrastructure over the next decade in order to be competitive.

So yes, the olive tree had had its day in India. But when it pushes out like that in the system of globalization, there is always a price to pay. You can't escape the system. Sooner or later the Lexus always catches up with you. A year and a half after India's nuclear test, I picked up *The Wall Street Journal* (Oct. 7, 1999) to read the following headline: "India's BJP Is Shifting Priority to the Economy." The story noted that the BJP came to power some two years earlier "calling for India to assert its nuclear capability—a pledge it fulfilled two months later with a series of weapons tests that sparked global sanctions and stalled investment." Upon its reelection, though, Prime Minister Atal Bihari Vajpayee wasn't even waiting for the votes to be counted before signaling his new priority: economic reform. "The priority is to build a national consensus on the acceptance of global capital, market norms and whatever goes with it. You have to go out and compete for investments," Vajpayee told the *Indian Express* newspaper.

An example of the Lexus and olive tree forces in balance was the Gulf Air flight I took from Bahrain to London, on which the television monitor on my Business Class seat included a channel which, using a global positioning satellite (GPS) linked into the airplane's antenna, showed passengers exactly where the plane was in relation to the Muslim holy city of Mecca at all times. The screen displayed a diagram of the aircraft with a white dot that moved around the diagram as the plane changed directions. This enabled Muslim passengers, who are enjoined to pray five times a day facing toward Mecca, to always know which way to face inside the plane when they unrolled their prayer rugs. During the flight, I saw several passengers near me wedge into the galley to perform their prayer rituals, and thanks to the GPS system, they knew just which way to aim.

The Lexus ignoring the olive tree in the era of globalization was a computer part that a friend of mine sent me. On the back was written: "This part was made in Malaysia, Singapore, the Philippines, China, Mexico, Germany, the U.S., Thailand, Canada and Japan. It was made in so many different places that we cannot specify a country of origin."

The Lexus trumping the olive tree in the era of globalization was the small item that appeared in the August 11, 1997, edition of *Sports Illustrated*. It said: "The 38-year-old Welsh soccer club Llansantffraid has changed its name to 'Total Network Solutions' in exchange for $400,000 from a cellular phone company."

The Lexus and olive tree working together in the era of globalization was on display in a rather unusual *Washington Times* story of September 21, 1997, which reported that Russian counterintelligence officers were complaining about having to pay twice as much to recruit a CIA spy as a double agent than the other way around. An official of Russia's Federal Security Service (the successor to the KGB), speaking on condition of anonymity, told the Itar-Tass news agency that a Russian spy could be bought for a mere $1 million, while CIA operatives held out for $2 million to work for the other side.

At roughly the same time that this report appeared, Israel's *Yediot Aharonot* newspaper published what seemed to me to be the first-ever totally free-market intelligence scoop. *Yediot* editors went to Moscow and bought some Russian spy satellite photographs of new Scud missile bases in Syria. Then *Yediot* hired a private U.S. expert on satellite photos to analyze the pictures. Then *Yediot* published the whole package as a scoop about Syria's new missile threat, without ever having once quoted a government official. Who needs Deep Throat when you have deep pockets?

Finally, my favorite "Lexus trumps olive tree in the era of globalization" story is about Abu Jihad's son. I was attending the Middle East Economic Summit in Amman, Jordan, in 1995, and was having lunch by myself on the balcony of the Amman Marriott. Out of the blue, a young Arab man approached my table and asked, "Are you Tom Friedman?" I said yes.

"Mr. Friedman," the young man continued politely, "you knew my father."

"Who was your father?" I asked.

"My father was Abu Jihad."

Abu Jihad, whose real name was Khalil al-Wazir, was one of the Palestinians who, with Yasser Arafat, founded el-Fatah and later took over the Palestine Liberation Organization. Abu Jihad, meaning "father of struggle," was his nom de guerre, and he was the overall commander of Palestinian military operations in Lebanon and the West Bank in the days when I was the *New York Times* correspondent in Beirut. I got to know him in Beirut. Palestinians considered him a military hero; Israelis considered him one of the most dangerous Palestinian terrorists. An Israeli hit team assassinated Abu Jihad in his living room in Tunis on April 16, 1988, pumping a hundred bullets into his body.

"Yes, I knew your father very well—I once visited your home in Damascus," I told the young man. "What do you do?"

He handed me his business card. It read: "Jihad al-Wazir, Managing Director, World Trade Center, Gaza, Palestine."

I read that card and thought to myself, "That's amazing. From Jesse James to Michael Milken in one generation."

The challenge in this era of globalization—for countries and individuals—is to find a healthy balance between preserving a sense of identity, home and community and doing what it takes to survive within the globalization system. Any society that wants to thrive economically today must constantly be trying to build a better Lexus and driving it out into the world. But no one should have any illusions that merely participating in this global economy will make a society healthy. If that participation comes at the price of a country's identity, if individuals feel their olive tree roots crushed, or washed out, by this global system, those olive tree roots will rebel. They will rise up and strangle the process. Therefore the survival of globalization as a system will depend, in part, on how well all of us strike this balance. A country without healthy olive trees will never feel rooted or secure enough to open up fully to the world and reach out into it. But a country that is only olive trees, that is only roots, and has no Lexus, will never go, or grow, very far. Keeping the two in balance is a constant struggle.

Maybe that's why of the many stories you will read in this book my favorite comes from my old college friend Victor Friedman, who teaches business management at the Ruppin Institute in Israel. I telephoned him one day to say hello and he told me he was glad that I called because he no longer had my phone numbers. When I asked why, he explained that he no longer had his handheld computer, in which he kept everything— his friends' addresses, E-mail addresses, phone numbers and his schedule for the next two years. He then told me what happened to it.

"We had a [desktop] computer at home that broke down. I took it to be repaired at a computer shop in Hadera [a town in central Israel]. A couple weeks later the shop called and said my PC was repaired. So I tossed my palm computer into my leather briefcase and drove over to Hadera to pick up my repaired PC. I left the shop carrying the big PC computer and my briefcase, which had my palm computer inside. When I got to the car, I put my briefcase down on the sidewalk, opened the trunk of my car and very carefully placed my repaired PC in the trunk to make sure that it was secure. Then I got in the car and drove off, leaving my briefcase on the sidewalk. Well, as soon as I got to my office and looked for my brief-case I realized what had happened—and what was going to happen next—and I immediately called the Hadera police to tell them 'Don't blow up my briefcase.' [It is standard Israeli police practice to blow apart any package, briefcase or suspicious object left on a sidewalk, because this is how many Palestinian bombs against Israeli civilians have been set off. Israelis are so well trained to protect against this that if you leave a package for a minute, the police will already have been called.] I knew no one would steal the briefcase. In Israel, a thief wouldn't touch such an ob-ject left on the sidewalk. But I was too late. The police dispatcher told me that the bomb squad was already on the scene and had 'dealt with it.' When I got to the police station they handed me back my beautiful leather briefcase with a nice neat bullet hole right through the middle. The only thing it hurt was my handheld computer. My Genius OP9300 took a direct hit. My whole life was in that thing and I had never made a backup. I told the police I felt terrible for causing such a problem, and they said, 'Don't feel bad, it happens to everyone.' For weeks I walked around campus with my briefcase with the bullet hole in it to remind my-self to stop and think more often. Most of my management students are in the Israeli Army and as soon as they saw the briefcase and that bullet hole they would immediately crack up laughing, because they knew just what had happened."

After Victor finished telling me this story, he said, "By the way, send me your E-mail address. I need to start a new address book."

$$\left(\begin{array}{c}4\end{array}\right)$$

... And the Walls Came
Tumbling Down

In the summer of 1998, Guilherme Frering, chairman of the board of the giant Brazilian mining company Caemi Minerção e Metalurgia, described for me the incredible changes in Brazil's economy over the previous decade. In passing he made the following remark: "You realize, the Berlin Wall fell here too. It wasn't just a local event in Europe. It was a global event. It fell on Brazil. The big changes to the Brazilian economy happened at exactly the same time that the Berlin Wall fell."

To illustrate his point, he cited this story: In November 1988, militant steelworkers went on strike at the government-controlled National Steel Company (CSN) mill in Volta Redonda, which is located northwest of Rio de Janeiro and is the largest steel plant in South America. Some 2,500 angry Brazilian steelworkers took over the factory and demanded retroactive pay raises and reduced work hours, from eight hours to six hours a day. Clashes between the workers and local police eventually escalated to a point where the Brazilian Army had to be called in. Three steelworkers were killed and thirty-six wounded in the battle for control of the mill. The Brazilian Army accused the workers of a "veritable urban guerrilla warfare operation," in which they used stones, Molotov cocktails, iron bars and firearms to defend their state-provided jobs and benefits. During Brazil's twenty-one-year military dictatorship, which only ended in 1985, Brazil's ruling generals had always been very sensitive about control of the huge steel mill, going so far as to declare Volta Redonda a "town of national security" and having its mayors appointed by the government. After explaining all this to me, Frering added this kicker: "Roughly four years after that bloody strike, after the Berlin Wall had fallen, those very same CSN steelworkers were demanding—demanding—that the mill be privatized, because they understood that this was the only way it could remain competitive and keep most of them employed. Today CSN is fully privatized and has been participating, as a major shareholder, in the privatization of other state-owned factories in Brazil."

Frering's remarks were like a lightbulb turning on in my head: Of course he was right! The Berlin Wall didn't just fall in Berlin. It fell East and West, and North and South, and it hit both countries and companies, and hit them all at roughly the same time. We focused on the Berlin Wall's fall in the East because that was so dramatic, and so palpable: a cement wall crumbling on the evening news. But in fact, similar, less palpable walls fell all over the world. And it is the fall of all those walls all over the world that made this era of globalization and integration possible. So this raises a very important question: What blew down the walls? Or as my kids might ask, "Daddy, where did globalization come from?"

I would begin my answer like this: The Cold War world was like a broad plain, crisscrossed and divided by fences, walls, ditches and dead ends. It was impossible to go very far, or very fast, in that world without running into a Berlin Wall or an Iron Curtain or a Warsaw Pact or somebody's protective tariff or capital controls. And behind these fences and walls, countries could preserve their own unique forms of life, politics, economics and culture. They could be in the First World, the Second World or the Third World. They could have widely differing economic systems—a centrally planned communist economy, a welfare-state economy, a socialist economy or a free-market economy. And they could maintain widely different political systems—anything from democracy to dictatorship to enlightened authoritarianism to monarchy to totalitarianism. And differences could remain sharp, black and white even, because there were walls aplenty to protect them, and they were not easily penetrated.

What blew away all these walls were three fundamental changes—changes in how we communicate, how we invest and how we learn about the world. These changes were born and incubated during the Cold War and achieved a critical mass by the late 1980s, when they finally came together into a whirlwind strong enough to blow down all the walls of the Cold War system and enable the world to come together as a single, integrated, open plain. Today, that plain grows wider, faster and more open every day, as more walls get blown down and more countries get absorbed. And that's why today there is no more First World, Second World or Third World. There's now just the Fast World—the world of the wide-open plain—and the Slow World—the world of those who either fall by the wayside or choose to live away from the plain in some artificially walled-off valley of their own, because they find the Fast World to be too fast, too scary, too homogenizing or too demanding. Here's how it happened.

The Democratization of Technology

Deputy U.S. Treasury Secretary Larry Summers likes to tell the story that in 1988 he was working on Michael Dukakis's presidential campaign and was sent one day to Chicago to give a talk on behalf of Dukakis. While in Chicago, he was assigned a car by the Dukakis campaign staff that had—are you sitting down?—a phone in it.

"I thought it was sufficiently neat to have a cell phone in my car in 1988," Summers recalled, "that I used it to call my wife to tell her I was in a car with a phone."

Nine years later, in 1997, Summers, on Treasury business, was visiting Ivory Coast, in West Africa. As part of his official visit he had to inaugurate an American-funded health project in a village upriver from the capital, Abidjan. The village, which was opening its first potable water well, could be reached only by dugout canoe. Summers, the big cheese from America, was made an honorary African chief by the villagers and decked out in African robes. But what he remembered most vividly was that on his way back from the village, as he stepped into the dugout canoe to go back downriver, an Ivory Coast official handed him a cell phone and said, "Washington has a question for you." In nine years Summers went from thinking it was neat to have a phone in his car in Chicago to expecting to have a phone in his dugout canoe in Abidjan.

Summers's phone adventures were made possible thanks to the first and most important change that was nurtured during the Cold War—the change in how we communicate with one another. I call this change "the democratization of technology," and it is what is enabling more and more people, with more and more home computers, modems, cellular phones, cable systems and Internet connections, to reach farther and farther, into more and more countries, faster and faster, deeper and deeper, cheaper and cheaper than ever before in history.

There is a bank in the Washington, D.C., area, Valley Spring, which offers all sorts of Internet and telephone banking services for its customers. The bank's advertising jingle neatly sums up the democratization of technology. It says: "Let us put a bank in your home." Thanks to the democratization of technology, we can all now have a bank in our homes, an office in our homes, a newspaper in our homes, a bookstore in our homes, a brokerage firm in our homes, a factory in our homes, an investment firm in our homes, a school in our homes . . .

The democratization of technology is the result of several innovations that came together in the 1980s involving computerization, telecommunications, miniaturization, compression technology and digitization. For instance, advances in microchip technology have resulted in computing power doubling roughly every eighteen months over the past thirty years, while advances in compression technology mean that the amount of data that can be stored on a square inch of disk surface has increased by 60 percent every year since 1991. Meanwhile, the cost of that storage capacity has fallen from five dollars a megabyte to five cents, making computing power stronger and more accessible every day. And innovations in telecommunications have steadily brought down the cost of a phone call and data transfers, while constantly increasing the speed, distance and amounts of information that can be transmitted on a phone line, cable or radio signal.

Not only can you call *to* anywhere cheaply, you can call *from* anywhere cheaply, including from your laptop, your mountaintop, your airplane seat or the top of Mount Everest. This is possible because innovations in miniaturization have steadily reduced the size and weight of computers, phones and pagers. Now they can be taken to more and more far-flung places and afforded by people with less and less income. The July 1998 issue of *Golf* magazine reported that many golf courses are starting to install the Spyder-9000 computer system in their golf carts, "which allows cart riders to keep score electronically, measure yardages digitally, view videotaped hole previews, view video golf tips, order lunch, check stock prices, and watch TV commercials." The only thing it doesn't do is putt for you.

All these innovations have reinforced, and been reinforced by, the revolution in digitization. Digitization is the wizardry by which we turn voices, sounds, movies, television signals, music, colors, pictures, words, documents, numbers, computing language and any other form of data you can think of into computer bits and then transfer them by telephone lines, satellites and fiber-optic cables around the world. Computer bits are the basic molecules of computing and are nothing more than different combinations of 1's and 0's. Digitization involves reducing any sound, picture, number or letters into a different code of 1's and 0's, and then transmitting them through telecommunications to another point where those 1's and 0's are decoded for the receiver and reconstituted into something very close to the original. Nicholas Negroponte, author of *Being Digital*, has a vivid way of describing digitization: "It is as if we suddenly have been able to make freeze-dried cappuccino which is so good that by adding water it comes back to us as rich and aromatic as any freshly brewed in an Italian cafe." And as Negroponte also points out, we can now freeze-dry more things, by turning them "from atoms to bits," from sights and sounds to 1's and 0's, and then send them more places more cheaply than ever before.

Think of the process like this: The microchip and the computer are like a furnace that can convert all sorts of things made of atoms into bits. Satellites, phone lines and fiber-optic cable are like the pipes that run out of this furnace to the rest of the world. And as these pipes become more sophisticated—as they increase in "bandwidth," which is the measure of how many 1's and 0's your digital pipe can transfer in one second—we can use them to carry more and more of the atoms that our furnace has forged into bits.

This process of digitization is so central to understanding this era of globalization, and what makes it unique, that it is worth stopping for a minute here and giving a real-life example of how it works. Consider a simple phone call. You pick up your phone in New York and dial a friend in Bangkok. When you speak into the mouthpiece of your phone, the pressure of the air from your breath hits a diaphragm in the phone's handset. The diaphragm then moves back and forth with the sound of your voice. That diaphragm is connected to a magnet, which is located next to a coil of electrical wire. As the diaphragm moves the magnet, the magnetic field creates a current in the wire. The magnetic field fluctuates as your voice fluctuates and therefore the current in the wire fluctuates as your voice fluctuates. So now we have the sound coming out of your mouth being converted into a fluctuating electric signal that goes up and down like a wave as the pitch of your voice changes. You've seen this if you have ever watched a voice being tracked on an oscilloscope.

How do we turn that into bits that can be transmitted? Basically, what you do is imagine that these electrical waves are going up and down on a grid. You slice up each wave into tiny segments and measure the height of each slice and then give it a number, expressed in 0's and 1's. So, for instance, a height of 10 might be expressed as 11110000 and 11 expressed as 11111000 and so on. Each 1 and 0 is translated into an electrical impulse, which, when strung together, is known as a square wave. Unlike an analog voice wave, which goes up and down like the waves of an ocean and is more susceptible to minor distortions and variations in the transmission process, a square wave simply goes up for 1's and down for 0's. It is much easier for the device receiving such a signal to read exactly what it is. All it has to ask is: Is it up or down—as opposed to trying to read a wave. This is why digital copies are always so much sharper and why anything that is sent as a string of 1's and 0's from your mouth or fax or computer in New York will automatically come out as the same 1's and 0's on the other end.

But let's say you're a long talker. And you are deep in conversation with your friend from Bangkok. So there are a lot of electronic impulses of 1's and 0's that need to be transmitted. Thanks to the miracle of technology, these 1's and 0's can be compressed. (Basically, you have the computer say 8×1 and 8×0, instead of 11111111 and 00000000.) Now we have your voice compressed down into a nice little package of bits. It's time to move them. We can do this in several ways. The simplest is by emitting a fluctuating current, where, in crude terms, it is one volt for 1's and two volts for 0's. Or we can move them over a fiber-optic cable, which works by emitting impulses of light. You flash a light on for 1's and off for 0's. (A compact disc is simply a flat platter of plastic coated with a layer of aluminum. They dig little holes in the platter for the 1's and leave it flat for the 0's. All your CD player does is shine a little laser light on each track of the platter, read the 1's and 0's, and turn them back into the same beautiful sounds they started out as.) Or we can use radio waves, with a high sound for 1's and a low sound for 0's. Whatever way we choose, chances are it will come out as a perfect copy every time. In the case of your phone call to Bangkok, your voice might have gotten converted to fiber-optic light impulses, and then when those impulses reached Bangkok and your friend's telephone receiver, they were turned back into sound waves by having a tiny device that translates each 1 and 0 into a certain amount of voltage that hits the electric coil in the phone. When that coil gets hit, it creates a magnetic field that drives the magnet back and forth, which moves the diaphragm in the phone earpiece, which pushes the air, which turns back into your voice. Presto! Negroponte's perfect cappuccino every time.

So when I say that the innovations in computerization, miniaturization, telecommunication and digitization have democratized technology, what I mean is that they have made it possible for hundreds of millions of people around the world to get connected and exchange information, news, knowledge, money, family photos, financial trades, music or television shows in ways, and to a degree, never witnessed before. In the old days, if you were living in New York and your child was living in Australia and had a new baby boy, he used to have go out, get a camera, buy some Kodak film, take the baby pictures, have them developed, put them in an envelope and send them by mail. If you were lucky you got to see your first grandchild's cute face ten days later. Not anymore. Now your kid can take those baby pictures with a digital camera, record them digitally on a 3.5-inch floppy disk, edit them digitally on his computer and then transmit them digitally to you over the Internet—all before the baby is ten hours old.

Former NBC News president Lawrence Grossman neatly sums up this democratization of technology: "Printing," he says, "made us all readers. Xeroxing made us all publishers. Television made us all viewers. Digitization makes us all broadcasters."

Grossman's observation highlights another factor that makes this era of globalization different in both degree and kind from previous eras. Put simply, this democratization of technology "globalizes production." Today, we can all be producers. Today's globalization isn't just about developing countries shipping raw materials to developed ones, letting them produce the finished goods and then shipping them back. No, today, thanks to the democratization of technology, all sorts of countries have the opportunity to assemble the technologies, raw materials and funding to be producers, or subcontractors, of highly complex finished products or services, and this becomes another subtle factor knitting the world more tightly together. I will discuss this in detail later. Suffice it to say for now, though, that this democratization of technology is how Thailand, in fifteen years, went from being primarily a low-wage rice-producing country to being the world's second-largest producer of pickup trucks, rivaling Detroit, and the fourth-largest maker of motorcycles.

And this democratization of technology doesn't just apply to cars and scooters. As Teera Phutrakal, a mutual fund manager in Bangkok, remarked to me once: "At our mutual fund we didn't have to reinvent the wheel, we just had to import it. Some of the technology we bought we got at one-tenth of what [our parent firm] Bankers Trust paid for it. Take, for instance, this automated voice response system where investors call in, press 1 to find out the asset value of the funds, press 2 to get bid offers, press 3 to sell. If you want to buy or redeem [your mutual fund shares] you can do it all by telebanking now, and all of these bells and whistles come in much cheaper for us. We just waited for them to be developed outside. This is the real beauty of globalization. We are a local house with local knowledge, but now we have global technology and reach."

What this democratization of technology means is that the potential for wealth creation becomes geographically dispersed, giving all kinds of previously disconnected people the chance to access and apply knowledge. In Kuala Lumpur, I met a Hong Kong Chinese woman who told me she once called the local Hong Kong number for Dell Computer's technical assistance and a customer-service specialist speaking perfect Cantonese, the Hong Kong dialect, answered. My Hong Kong friend remarked to the Dell specialist how heavily it was raining in the central district of Hong Kong that day and she asked whether it was raining as heavily at the Dell office. The Dell specialist responded that it wasn't raining where she was at all, because she was thousands of miles away in Penang, Malaysia. That specialist was a Malaysian Chinese who was now able to get a good service job with Dell, while living in a relative backwater like Penang. The democratization of technology made that possible. India is rapidly becoming the back office for the world. *The Economist* reported on September 18, 1999, that Indian phone operators, based in India, are now working for GE Capital. On any given day they might be calling from India to someone in Texas about why their credit card payments are late. I can't say I was particularly happy to learn, though, that these Indian operators "assume Western names and reportedly pick up the twang of the region they cover." Swissair moved its entire accounting division, including computers, from high-wage Switzerland to low-wage India to take advantage of lower labor costs for secretaries, programmers and accountants. Thanks to digitization and networking, these jobs can be done anywhere that you have a high concentration of English-speaking high school and college graduates. This could be a huge boon for India, Pakistan, the Philippines, South Africa and English-speaking communities all over the developing world. British Airways World Network Services, based in Mumbai, India, keeps track of the airline's frequent-flier miles. Selectronic, a telecomputing firm in Delhi, plucks doctors' dictation from a toll-free number in the United States, transcribes the recordings and sends the results back as text to an American HMO. The *Far Eastern Economic Review* (Sept. 2, 1999) reported that America Online now has six hundred Filipino customer-service reps in Manila who answer 10,000 to 12,000 technical and billing enquiries a day, mostly from the United States, which amounts to about 80 percent of AOL's customer E-mail. The AOL subsidiary in the Philippines paid its college-educated workers in 1999 about $5.50 a day, the *Review* reported, which is 35 percent more than the legal minimum wage, but roughly what an unskilled American worker would make in an hour. That is a meager wage, but it is a first step to bringing a whole new generation of educated Filipinos into the Fast World, and you can bet the smartest ones will soon go off and start their own little tech companies, maybe POL, next to their AOL office. This rapidly expanding market for services and telecomputing could be the foundation of Asia's next boom. But to participate, countries such as Thailand, which got into the globalization game by offering cheap manufacturing, will now have to upgrade the education and skills level of its people in order to compete for the best telecomputing jobs and services.

I was once musing with Geoff Baehr, chief of network designs for Sun Microsystems, about where all this democratization of technology and the means of production might lead. The more Baehr and I thought about all this, the more devilish our thoughts became. "Now that we can provide all these previously nontradable services through networks, like the Internet, why not outsource your government too?" asked Baehr. Think about it—you could outsource your commando operations and border guard jobs to the Russians. You could have the Indians keep your country's books and the Swiss run your customs service. You could have the Germans run your central bank. You could have Italians design all your shoes. You could have the British run your high schools. The Japanese could run your elementary schools and your trains . . .

The Democratization of Finance

The democratization of technology certainly helped foster the second major change driving globalization, and that is the change in how we invest. I call this "the democratization of finance." For much of the post–Cold War era, most large-scale domestic and international lending or underwriting was done by big commercial banks, investment banks and insurance companies. These white-shoe institutions always preferred lending to companies with proven track records and "investment-grade" ratings. This made bank lending very undemocratic. The old-line banks had a very limited notion of who was creditworthy, and if you were an upstart, trying to get access to cash often depended on whether you had an "in" at the bank or insurance company. These traditional institutions also tended to be run by slow-moving executives and decision-making committees, who were risk-averse and not particularly swift at responding to changes in the marketplace.

The democratization of finance actually began in the late 1960s with the emergence of the "commercial paper" market. These were bonds that corporations issued directly to the public in order to raise capital. The creation of this corporate bond market introduced some pluralism into the world of finance and took away the monopoly of the banks. This was followed in the 1970s by the "securitization" of home mortgages. Investment banks started approaching banks and home mortgage companies, buying up their whole portfolio of mortgages, and then chopping them up into $1,000 bonds that you and I and my Aunt Bev could buy. We got a chance to earn a little more interest on a pretty secure investment, and the interest and principal on the bonds was paid out from the monthly cash flow from people paying off their home mortgages. Securitization opened the doors for all kinds of companies and investors who never had access to cash before to raise money.

It was in the 1980s, though, that this democratization of finance really exploded, and the man who truly pushed out the last barriers was the brilliant, mercurial but ultimately corrupt junk bond king, Michael Milken. Milken, a graduate of the Wharton School of Business and Finance at the University of Pennsylvania, got his start with the Drexel brokerage firm in Philadelphia in 1970. At the time, none of the big banks or investment houses cared to have much to do with selling low-rated "junk bonds," which in those days were primarily blue-chip companies that had fallen from grace or start-ups with little capital and no track record. Milken thought the major banks were stupid. He did his own calculations, studied some of the little-noticed academic research on the subject of junk bonds and concluded the following: Companies that were not considered investment grade were being asked to pay interest rates 3 to 10 percentage points higher than the norm—if they could get any loans at all.

But in fact these companies went bankrupt only slightly more often than the top-rated blue-chip companies, whose bonds offered much lower rates of return. Therefore, these so-called junk bonds actually offered a chance to make a lot more money, without a lot more risk. And if you put a lot of different junk bonds together into a single fund, even if a few of them defaulted, the total fund would still pay an average return three or four percentage points higher than the blue chips, with virtually no extra risk. As *Business Week* put it in March 1995: Milken, armed with this insight, "set about the arduous task of convincing a skeptical world that he'd discovered the investment equivalent of the free lunch."

Since traditional banks and investment houses were skeptical, and continued to shun this business, Milken quickly moved from trading those junk bonds that already existed, from fallen grade-A companies, to underwriting a whole new market full of only junk players—risky companies, fallen companies, new companies, entrepreneurs and start-ups who could not get credit from the traditional banks, even financial pirates who wanted to take over other companies but couldn't raise the cash to do it through conventional bank channels. Because of his contacts, Milken could also sell the junk bonds he issued to mutual funds, private investors and pension funds, who realized that he was right about their providing higher returns for not much higher risks. This gave you, me and my Aunt Bev a chance to buy a slice of these deals that had previously been off-limits to the little guy.

Many of these deals had convulsive impacts on the companies and workers involved. Nevertheless, it didn't take long for Milken's insight to be copied far and wide. Soon there was a flourishing junk bond—or "high-yield"—industry, offering the public a share of all sorts of firms and deals.

A similar democratization of finance was happening internationally as well. For decades, big banks lent large amounts of money to foreign governments, states and corporations and then carried these loans on their books at par value. That meant that if your bank lent a country or company $10 million, it showed up on its books as a $10 million loan to be repaid in full, whether or not this country or company had assets worth $10 million on that particular day. Because these loans were made primarily by banks and carried on their books, when a country like Mexico got into financial trouble, as it did in 1982, by borrowing abroad to finance populist consumption at home, banks bore the brunt of the problem. Mexico's President could fly to New York City, call together the twenty leading banks holding Mexico's foreign debt, and say to them essentially: "Gentlemen, we're broke. And you know what they say: If a man owes you a thousand dollars that's his problem. If a man owes you ten million dollars that's your problem. Well, we're your problem. We can't pay our debts. So you are going to have to cut us some slack, renegotiate our loans and extend us fresh credit." The bankers would nod their heads and work out some deal, involving loan extensions (usually at even higher interest rates). What choice did they have? Mexico was *their* problem, and the U.S. bankers did not want to have to go back to their shareholders and say that this Mexican loan that they were carrying on their books as a $10 million asset was actually worth nothing. Better to just carry the Mexicans along. And because twenty banks managed most of the debt, they could get together and settle the whole thing in a single boardroom.

John Page, who was then an economist working in the Latin American Department of the World Bank, explained to me exactly how it worked. Page, who speaks Spanish, was down in Mexico in 1982 meeting with José Angel Gurria, who was then the Director General of Public Credit in Mexico's Ministry of Finance. Gurria was legendary for his ability to get foreign bankers—from big bankers in New York to little bankers in West Texas—to extend loans to the Mexican government.

"I was in Gurria's office one day, and we were speaking Spanish and the phone rang," Page recalled. "It was the president of a small Texas bank whom Gurria had persuaded to take on some Mexican debt, and this guy was worried about reports that the Mexican economy was in trouble. Gurria switched from talking to me in Spanish to talking to this American banker in perfect colloquial English. He said: 'Hey, Joe, good to hear from you . . . No, no, don't worry. Things are fine down here. Your money's perfectly safe. How's the family? . . . Great. How's that daughter of yours? Is she still in school? . . . Good talking to you. Call anytime. Stay in touch.' And then, without missing a beat, he hung up the phone and went right back to talking to me in Spanish. In thirty seconds he had solved his problem with a key investor."

But then a funny thing happened on the way to globalization. This international debt market got securitized, just like Milken's companies and friends. What this meant was that when Latin America got into another debt crisis in the late 1980s, then–Treasury Secretary Nicholas Brady tried a Milkenesque solution. In 1989, the Latin American debts of the major commercial banks were converted into U.S. government–backed bonds, and those bonds were then either held by the banks as assets or sold to the general public, to mutual funds and to pension funds, with higher than normal rates of interest. Suddenly you and I and my Aunt

Bev could buy a piece of Mexico's debt, Brazil's debt or Argentina's debt—either directly or through our pension and mutual funds. And those bonds traded every day, with their value going up and down according to each country's economic performance. They didn't just sit on a bank's books at par value. Said Joel Korn, who headed Bank of America Brazil at the time: "What Brady did was really a revolution. Before him, the U.S. Treasury Department was simply pressing the U.S. banks and the IMF to keep throwing good money after bad at these Latin American countries. What Brady did was put together a market-based solution. Banks were given U.S. government guarantees to extend new loans to Latin America, on condition that the countries made economic reforms. After extending these loans, the banks, instead of just carrying them on their books, chopped these loans up into U.S. government–backed bonds that were sold to the public. That brought thousands of new players into the game. Instead of a country just dealing with a committee of twenty major commercial banks, it suddenly found itself dealing with thousands of individual investors and mutual funds. This expanded the market, and it made it more liquid, but it also put a whole new kind of pressure on the countries. People were buying and selling their bonds every day, depending on how well they performed. This meant they were being graded on their performance every day. And a lot of the people doing the buying and grading were foreigners over whom Brazil, Mexico or Argentina had no control." These bondholders were not like the banks, who, because they were already so exposed to these countries, felt they had to keep lending more money to protect their earlier loans. If a country didn't perform, the public bondholders would just sell that country's bonds, say goodbye and put their money into the bonds of a country that did perform.

So when Mexico got in trouble again for excessive spending in 1995, all sorts of big and little guys started selling their Mexican bonds, driving down their value, and Gurria could not just call up twenty bankers and ask them to roll over the debt and cut him some slack. Mexico's debt had been democratized into too many hands. So this time Mexico had to call up the U.S. Treasury and ask for help, and Uncle Sam would only give Mexico the money on very strict terms and Mexico had to put up its oil reserves as collateral. The only way the U.S. government was going to bail out Mexico was on the condition that it ran its economy as well as New Mexico. Soon, lots of emerging economies started selling bonds the Brady way, often denominated in dollars. Today there are sixteen countries issuing Brady bonds worth roughly $150 billion. There is nothing new about governments issuing bonds to foreign holders. That has been around for many years. What is new is the degree to which these bonds are now widely dispersed to individuals, pension funds and mutual funds. In the early part of this century it was mostly the wealthy who took part in international bond deals. Now the retirement fund of Orange County, the school janitor, not to mention you and me and my Aunt Bev, can all play.

This is because the democratization of lending coincided, in America, with the democratization of investing, thanks primarily to pension reform and the creation of personal 401(k) pension accounts. America is moving from a country in which companies guaranteed an employee's pension through a defined "set of benefits" to a country in which many companies now just guarantee a defined "contribution," and the individual manages his or her own money and shifts it around, according to where he or she can get the best return. And with people now living longer, and wondering whether social security will be there when they want to retire, they are not only turning to these mutual funds and pension funds in an aggressive manner but also managing them very aggressively for higher returns. Your parents probably had very little idea where or how their pension funds were invested. Now many workers are offered a menu of funds, with different kinds of returns and risks, and they move their money around like chips on a roulette table, rewarding the successful mutual funds and punishing the less successful.

The online brokerage firm E*Trade ran a brilliant commercial that illustrated this point. The commercial opens with a man sitting in his convertible, his golf clubs poking out of the backseat. He is parked on the side of the road because a cop has just pulled him over. The cop walks up alongside his car and the following conversation ensues:

Cop: "Evening."
Convertible guy: "I know. I know. License and registration."
Cop: "Ohh, Kirk Brewer. I've been wanting to talk to you."
Convertible guy: "Me?"
Cop: "Well, you're the fund manager for my Large Cap [mutual] fund."
Convertible guy (kind of proud): "Oh, yeah."
Cop: "So I noticed you made the top ten [best performing mutual funds]."
Convertible guy: "Yeah."

Cop: "But not the top five."
Cop turns and looks at the golf clubs in the backseat.
Convertible guy is looking a little nervous: "Uh . . . Well . . ."
Cop: "Let's put the clubs away and get back to the office."
Then comes a voiceover that says: "Make your fund manager work harder. It's time for the E*Trade Mutual Fund Center."
Finally, the camera pans back to the cop, who is last seen removing the golf clubs from the convertible guy's car and taking them away. The message is clear: even the motorcycle cop knows where his pension is and moves it around among the best performers.

This democratization of investing was also enhanced internationally when the system of fixed exchange rates and strict controls on international flows of capital, which was set up after World War II at Bretton Woods, came apart in the early 1970s. We forget now, but between the end of World War II and 1970, it was very difficult for a Japanese, Mexican or European investor to buy stocks or bonds in America, and it was very difficult for an American to do so in their countries. But when the system of fixed exchange rates and capital controls came unstuck, developed countries gradually democratized their capital markets, opening them to any foreign traders who wanted to play, and then the developing countries followed suit.

Soon all sorts of products were available: Mexican bonds, Lebanese bonds, Turkish bonds, Russian bonds, German bonds, French bonds. You could take your choice, and people did. The more individual investors could move their money in and out of these highly competitive global mutual funds, the more these fund managers would move their money between companies and countries, constantly demanding higher, more sustained returns. Each fund wanted to beat out the other funds to attract more money. Thanks to this democratization of finance, we have gone from a world in which a few bankers held the sovereign debts of a lot of countries, to a world in which a lot of bankers held the sovereign debts of a lot of countries, and finally to a world today in which many individuals, through pension funds and mutual funds, hold the sovereign debts of many countries.

It is important to note that a lot of the junk bond money was also used to trigger a boom in company takeovers in America. Here again, the little guy, who could never participate in such potentially lucrative deals, could suddenly do so indirectly through his pension fund and mutual fund. This process of takeovers, though, put company managers under greater scrutiny, particularly if they underperformed. The process also helped to drive the streamlining of the American economy in the 1980s and prepare America for the era of globalization better and sooner than any other major country in the world. Many companies saw their efficiency improve as a result, although some had the life squeezed right out of them.

One of the main reasons Japan has so many lagging domestic companies is that for years finance there was not at all democratized. Japan's big banks dominated finance, so unknown upstarts had a much harder time raising cash, capital for hostile takeovers was not easily available, and banks pumped capital into companies that were affiliated with them, without regard to risk or competitiveness. Takeovers were also frowned upon for cultural reasons and because so many bank boards and corporate boards were in bed with each other. Moreover, Japanese workers had little choice in or control over their pensions. They could not just shuffle their money around, so the pressure on local Japanese companies, mutual funds and pension funds to perform to ever higher global standards was diminished. That is why Japan had a more genteel economy, but one that was much less efficient at Schumpeter's creative destruction. It's also why capital in Japan eventually became so misallocated that a huge bubble emerged at the end of the 1980s and thousands of inefficient domestic firms were allowed to linger on life support.

But that started to change by the year 2000, as Japan opened up its financial service sector and American companies started pouring in, such as GE Capital. The foreign competitors forced Japanese banks to become more serious lenders and this, in turn, forced Japanese companies to become more efficient producers. This has led to a more rational use of capital in Japan and to more accessible capital for start-ups and new players. Money is no longer reserved for the good-old-boy networks. The GE Capital–owned finance company Lake started operating "automated loan kiosks" all over Japan in the late 1990s. You just walked up, showed your license or some other form of identification so that an instant credit check could be run on you, signed an automated loan contract and got your loan within the hour. How's that for democratized finance?

The Democratization of Information

John Burns was the *New York Times* bureau chief in New Delhi in the late 1990s. I happened to visit him in the summer of 1998 when the World Cup soccer matches were being played and Burns was trying to follow the games on TV. One morning Burns told me the following tale: "We have four satellite dishes on the roof of our house [in New Delhi], which are costing the *Times* thousands of dollars a year. It's like we're running an uplink station here. Anyway, I got fed up because despite all these satellite dishes I couldn't even get the Indian channel that televises the World Cup. It has something to do with weather interference and the satellites needing to be adjusted and the man who is supposed to do it turns up intermittently. So I am complaining about all this over breakfast and our cook, Abdul Toheed, who is seventy-one years old and the former shoeshine boy of the last British commander in India, says to me, 'I don't know what you're upset about. I get all the channels on my TV. You are wasting your time and money with your satellites. Come back to my quarters.' He and his wife live in a little compound in the back of our house. So I go back there, and his wife is listening to the BBC. I said to him, 'What's she doing? She doesn't speak English.' And he says to me, 'She's learning.' Then he hands me the television remote, and with increasing astonishment I start at Channel 1 and go all the way to Channel 27. He had television stations from China, Pakistan, Australia, Italy, France—all these channels to choose from, and it was only costing him 150 rupees a month [$3.75]. With all my satellite dishes, I only had fourteen channels. He had just gotten some friend of his who has his own pirate cable system to run a cable along the telephone wires and into his house behind my house. It was all unofficial and illegal, but he now lives in the wired world and his wife is learning English. Meanwhile, I'm still struggling to get Indian television."

Burns's story illustrates the third change that made globalization possible—the change in how we look at the world. I call this change "the democratization of information." Thanks to satellite dishes, the Internet and television we can now see through, hear through and look through almost every conceivable wall.

This breakthrough began with the globalization of television. Throughout much of the Cold War era, television and radio broadcasting was a restricted business, because the spectrums and technologies available for transmission were limited. Governments either directly ran most television broadcasting or highly regulated it. This began to break down first in the United States with the advent of cable television, which could carry many more channels than could be broadcast over the air. Then, in the 1980s, other versions of multichannel television began to spread around the world—thanks largely to the falling cost of putting satellites into orbit. There is some irony in this: The Cold War drove both the Soviet Union and America to be constantly trying to put smaller and smaller, stronger and stronger and cheaper and cheaper satellites into space in order to spy on each other. That same technology, though, paved the way for transmitting television signals cheaply, which, in turn, helped to break down the walls of communism that much faster.

At first, only big cable systems could afford to build the antennas to pull down those satellite signals, but thanks to the democratization of technology, and particularly miniaturization, soon millions of people around the world could pull down those signals on a pizza-sized satellite receiver dish mounted on their balconies. Suddenly the restrictions on broadcasting were gone and a huge new audience was created. Once digital television gets fully up and running, broadcasters will be able to offer not just five or fifty stations but five hundred channels.

In addition, information is increasingly being democratized thanks to advances in compression technology, such as the digital video disk. DVDs are CDs, five inches wide, that can hold a full-length feature film, with surround-sound quality, in multiple languages, that you are able to play on a laptop or palm-held video player. I remember visiting the Persian Gulf back in the late 1970s and customs agents used to rifle through people's luggage to make sure they were not bringing in any salacious or politically explosive videotapes. I would like to see them try to find a DVD in my suitcase. There was an explosion of DVD players all over China in the late 1990s—with every Hollywood movie being pirated and distributed to millions of Chinese homes. And increasingly they won't have to wait for Hollywood. Inexpensive digital movie cameras and digital projectors, which operate without film, will make everyone a potential movie mogul. And not only will you be able to shoot your own digital movie at low cost, but with the Internet, you will be able to distribute it yourself all around the world at low cost.

As important as television and satellite dishes have been to democratizing information, the spread of the Internet topped them all. The Internet is the pinnacle of the democratization of information: no one owns the Internet, it is totally decentralized, no one can turn it off, it can potentially reach into every home in the world and many of its key advances were done by collaboration among individuals—many who have never met each other—who worked together over the network, contributing their ideas for free. As central as the Internet is in our lives today, few people actually appreciate how it evolved. It's a fascinating story. The Internet was actually born as part of the U.S. reaction to the October 4, 1957, launch into space of the Sputnik satellite on board a Soviet rocket. Weighing only 184 pounds and roughly the size of a basketball, Sputnik not only set in motion the space age, it actually set in motion the cyberspace age.

At an October 9, 1957, news conference, President Dwight D. Eisenhower was asked by legendary reporter Merriman Smith the following: "Russia has launched an earth satellite. They also claim to have had a successful firing of an intercontinental ballistic missile, none of which this country has done. I ask you, sir, what are we going to do about it?" What Ike decided to do about it was to launch a crash program to catch up with the Soviet Union. As part of that effort, he concluded that the U.S. government needed a single manager for all space and strategic missile research. Eisenhower eventually won approval from Congress to set up something called the Advanced Research Projects Agency, or ARPA. The space and missile research programs were eventually broken off and turned into NASA, and ARPA was left as the Pentagon's arm for promoting computer science research and information processing. Information processing was at the time a relatively new field. And, as Stephen Segaller, author of *Nerds 2.0.1: A Brief History of the Internet*—the best book on this subject—points out, it was the Information Processing Techniques Office, an obscure division of ARPA, that would build the original Internet prototype and lay the foundations for what is now the age of networks.

Its original concoction was first unveiled in 1969 and was called ARPAnet—a crude private computer network linking the U.S. Defense Department with key university researchers and government labs. Funded by the Pentagon, ARPAnet was designed to enable a handful of researchers to exchange ideas and data, and to save money by sharing costly computer time and equipment, through a network system. With computing power scarce at the time, it was important that someone at a lab at UCLA be able to run a program on a machine in Cambridge, Massachusetts, and that researchers in both places be able to swap data.

"Thirty years ago, on Oct. 29, 1969, the inaugural message was sent over the first thin reed of what was to become the Internet," wrote *The New York Times* on October 12, 1999. "It was nothing so portentous as 'What hath God wrought,' the words christening the telegraph in 1844. It was just the simple word 'login.' There were only two nodes on what was then known as ARPANET . . . As the story has become enshrined in the folklore, a UCLA student named Charley Kline tapped out the letters 'L' and 'O,' which were dutifully echoed back by a computer at the Stanford Research Institute, a center about 300 miles northwest in what was not yet Silicon Valley."

It wasn't until 1972, though, that the Internet pioneers discovered E-mail. Time-sharing computers in those days had a mail-drop system inside them, where different people could have their own mailbox and leave messages for other people on that same computer. One day, according to Segaller, Ray Tomlinson, who worked for the computer research firm Bolt, Beranek and Newman, wrote a simple file-transfer program to open a connection, send a file from one computer's mailbox system to another and then confirm that the file had been transferred. Tomlinson later told Segaller, "Once we had the ability to transfer a file from one machine to another, it became fairly clear that one thing you could do was just write the file across the network and send mail to somebody else. I also happened to be working on one piece of software to be used to compose and send E-mail, called 'send message.' And it seemed like an interesting hack to tie those two together to use the file-transfer program to send the mail to the other machine. So that's what I did . . . and it worked." Others heard about it, other networks adopted it and, presto, E-mail was born!

It was also Tomlinson, writes Segaller, who invented the use of the @ sign in E-mail to identify the E-mail user with his or her institution. When the researchers involved in the early Internet discovered the virtues of E-mail, its usage began to explode, as did the whole network, with more and more packets of data switching between universities, the federal government, companies and research firms all the time. Other networks, smaller than ARPAnet, also began to mushroom, but as Segaller notes, "they weren't able to inter-network. Each of them had their own 'protocols' that defined how one network would organize communication among its nodes." This started to become a problem. You couldn't send packets of data from one university network to another. This problem eventually gave birth to the Internet, which was essentially created when researchers Vint Cerf and Bob Kahn created a cross-network protocol, a sort of universal, one-size-fits-all computer lingo that allowed a packet of data to leave one network, travel and then enter the gateway of another network. Segaller explains that the solution was referred to in 1973 by its designers as "the inter-networking of networks"—or, for short, the Internet.

The whole thing didn't get popularized, though, until 1990, when an English software engineer based in Geneva, Tim Berners-Lee, created a vehicle for making it easy and virtually cost-free to locate information all over this network of networks. This became known as the World Wide Web. According to Segaller, at the time Berners-Lee embarked on the Web project, there were about 800 different computer networks attached to the Internet, with about 160,000 computers attached to them, all with files and databases containing information that one might want to access. Technically, all these computers and databases were connected, but sorting through them all and plucking out what you wanted wasn't easy, because there was no centralized database, address book or information manager. Berners-Lee's great innovation, as *The New York Times* once put it, "was to design the software standards for addressing, linking and transferring multimedia documents over the Internet." His key inventions were the uniform resource locator (URL)—a system of codes identifying every Web site and page of information, no matter where the computer servers that actually supported it were located; the hypertext transfer protocol (HTTP)—which provided an easy highway between every Web site and every user's computer; and finally, the hypertext mark-up language (HTML), which set the basic standards for how a Web site should be organized and appear when called up on a computer screen. Together, the URL, HTTP and HTML formed a system of hyperlinks—those underlined words, colored words and graphic icons you see on a computer screen, which, when you click on them, instantly transport you to a related Web page, even if it resides on a wholly different computer server in a wholly different country. That's why they called it a World Wide Web, because you could follow any strand out, around the world and back. In the old days, this book might have had an Internet file devoted to it, with all sorts of biographical and other information, but to get at it you would have had to negotiate a maze of different networks and codes, and even when you found it, it might not have been written in a program compatible with your computer, so you couldn't view it. Now, all you have to do is type in "www.lexusandtheolivetree.com" or click on a picture of my book on Amazon.com, and the World Wide Web will transport you right to the site.

But for the Internet to really take off and become a mass tool for research, commerce and communication, it needed three more inventions—the Web browser, the search engine and high-grade encryption technology so that people would not hesitate to type their credit card numbers onto a Web site in order to do business. The browser was a piece of software that really helped to turn the Internet into a form of television. That is, it allowed everyone to display what was on their Web address, so when you typed in a www address, or clicked on a hyperlink, a whole screen full of words or multimedia graphics would appear before your eyes. This browser—combined with a search engine that could find key words and places—meant that even a small child could navigate through the millions of Web sites and pieces of information on the Internet and find what he or she was looking for and then display it. Berners-Lee created a crude browser to make the World Wide Web work, but the pioneer commercial browser, called Mosaic, was put together by technologist Marc Andreessen in 1993. It was superseded a year later by a much more sophisticated product called Netscape Navigator. Netscape made browsing the Web simple, through colorful, interactive graphics that could find anything anywhere in cyberspace and display it on any computer.

The rise of Netscape coincided with the U.S. Congress's decision to approve Internet commerce and with the steep drop in the prices of both home computers and telephone calls. When mixed together they produced an explosion of Internet usage and a democratization of information that has been revolutionary. Kevin Maney summarized well the Internet's democratizing impact when he wrote in USA Today (Aug. 9, 1999): "As a world-changing invention, the Net echoes many of the characteristics of the printing press. It brings a dramatic drop in the cost of creating, sending and storing information while vastly increasing its availability. It breaks information monopolies. Think of all the medical information on the Web, which, until recently, only doctors could access. Think of what you can find about cars and prices, cracking the information that had been guarded by car dealers . . . Millions of people now post their own Web pages, detailing the minutia of their lives."

The result is that never before in the history of the world have so many people been able to learn about so many other people's lives, products and ideas. The next stage, the one that will characterize the early twenty-first century, is when everyone will have access to high-speed Internet communications right in their home or office or on their handheld notepad or beeper. Broadband access means that there will be enough bandwidth so that your Internet connection will be always on, just like your television can be, and the speed with which information will be retrieved, and the richness of the information that will be able to come up on your screen, will be many, many times greater than what it is today. Such high-speed, broadband connections will allow you to take part in a teleconference meeting via your laptop from anywhere on the road, without any problem. It will allow you to simply and easily download movies, music and videos. And it will make shopping via E-commerce a much more textured 3-D experience. There is a wonderful commercial that was run in 1999 by the Internet company Qwest. It showed a businessman, tired and dusty, checking into a motel in the middle of nowhere. He asks the bored-looking desk clerk whether they have room service and other amenities. She says yes. Then he asks her whether entertainment is available on his room television, and the clerk answers in a what-do-you-think-you-idiot monotone: "All rooms have every movie ever made in every language, any time, day or night."

That is what high-speed, broadband Internet access will make possible in every dusty, end-of-the-world motel.

Put all of this democratization of information together and what it means is that the days when governments could isolate their people from understanding what life was like beyond their borders or even beyond their village are over. Life outside can't be trashed and made to look worse than it is. And life inside can't be propagandized and made to look better than it is. Thanks to the democratization of information, we all increasingly know how each other lives — no matter how isolated you think a country might be. The minute you think you have devised a new, higher, thicker wall to hide behind, you discover that technology has found a way to lower it. And the minute you think you have drawn a new line in the sand to protect you, technology finds a way to erase it. Raul Valdes Vivo, the rector of the Cuban Communist Party's Nico Lopez school for advanced studies outside Havana, put it so well in an interview with National Geographic (June 1999). He was asked about the difficulties Castro's Cuba faced in maintaining socialist principles, even as it was increasingly being forced to adopt capitalist means to survive. "Cuba is no longer an island," he mused. "There are no islands anymore. There is only one world."

There is a story that in the 1980s the Soviets once ran a picture in

Pravda illustrating breadlines in America. Upon closer examination it turned out that the picture was of a group of people in Manhattan waiting in line for Zabar's bakery and delicatessen to open on a Saturday morning. Don't try that trick today—even in China. Not with the Internet around. What makes the Internet so dangerous for police states is that they can't afford not to have it, because they will fall behind economically if they do. But if they have it, it means they simply can't control information the way they once did. And what's really scary about the Internet for regimes such as China's is that it's interactive, it's alive. It's not just a radio, where you listen passively. It's not just a television, where you watch like a couch potato. On the Internet people are giving and taking, chatting and outreaching, uploading ideologies and downloading ideologies, buying and selling—and doing it all in a way that is virtually impossible to control.

On December 4, 1998, China put on trial a computer entrepreneur, being hailed as the first "cyberdissident," who gave E-mail addresses in China to a Chinese-language Internet magazine supporting democracy. The No. 1 Intermediate People's Court in Shanghai conducted a closed trial for the entrepreneur, Lin Hai, on charges of subversion for having given the addresses of 30,000 Chinese computer users to *VIP Reference,* a journal that Chinese dissidents publish in the United States. The Chinese-born editor of *VIP Reference* told the *Los Angeles Times* (Jan. 4, 1999): "We are destined to destroy the Chinese system of censorship over the Internet. We believe that the Chinese people, like any other people in the world, deserve the rights of knowledge and free expression." The title of this Internet magazine, which is E-mailed to 250,000 mainland Chinese, is a gibe at China's leaders. The top officials of the Communist Party in China have a daily news summary, prepared for their eyes only, made up of real news. It is called "Reference News." As the *L.A. Times* noted, the editors of *VIP Reference* say their Internet magazine is meant to bring real news to China's real VIPs—"ordinary people." The same thing is happening in finance. An Internet company formed in Chicago in 1998, called China Online, uses stringers inside China to gather market and other news. They file the information to Chicago via the Internet, and China Online then beams it back into China, again via the Internet. Among the things that China Online offers as a daily service is the black-market rate of the Chinese currency against the dollar in China's major cities. Its reporters go out into the market every day, check the rate with underground dealers, and then file it to Chicago.

This is very useful data for anyone doing business in China, particularly for Chinese. It is something the Chinese government would never provide to its own people, let alone to the world, but Beijing is now powerless to stop it.

In South Teheran, the poorest neighborhood of the Iranian capital, some families can afford a television and some can't. When I visited Teheran in 1997, I found that some of those in South Teheran who had televisions were setting up a few chairs and selling tickets when the most popular American television show came on each week (courtesy of a satellite). The most popular show was *Baywatch*, a Southern California fantasy, in which all the women wear only bikinis and are 36-24-36. The Iranian government banned satellite dishes, so my Iranian friends just hid them under the laundry lines or under their "satellite bushes," the plants they use to cover them up on their balconies.

Thanks to the information revolution and the falling costs of communicating by phone, fax, the Internet, radio, television and information appliances no wall in the world is secure anymore. And when we all increasingly know how each other lives, it creates a whole new dynamic to world politics. When it comes to atrocities happening in some dark corner of the world, leaders today no longer have the option not to know, only not to act. And when it comes to some opportunities being enjoyed in some bright corner of the world, leaders no longer have the option to deny them to their people, only not to deliver them. That's why the more we learn how each other lives, the more leaders all have to promise the same things. And when they can't deliver, they have a problem. And it's only going to become more acute. In a few years, every citizen of the world will be able to comparison shop between his own country and his own government and the one next door.

"Today, no country can ever truly cut itself off from the global media or from external sources of information; trends that start in one corner of the world are rapidly replicated thousands of miles away," notes Francis Fukuyama, author of *The End of History and the Last Man*. "A country trying to opt out of the global economy by cutting itself off from external trade and capital flows will still have to deal with the fact that the expectations of its population are shaped by their awareness of living standards and cultural products emerging from the outside world."

Sure, the president of a developing country can come to his people today and say, "Folks, we're going to stop moving into this globalization system. We are going to temporarily erect new tariff walls and impose controls again on foreign money flowing in and out. We will have less pain, less volatility in our economy, but also slower growth, because we won't be able to tap savings from the rest of the world. So, if you're not in the middle class yet, you may have to wait a bit." But when he does that someone in a village outside the capital is eventually going to protest, "But, Mr. President, I've been watching *Baywatch* for five years. You mean, no *Baywatch* for me? No Disney World? No bikinis?" Governments that want to avoid globalization not only have to prove that their alternative can still produce rising standards of living but—and this is critically important—they also have to do it in an environment in which we all increasingly know how everyone else lives.

Political scientists note that in the Cold War system, in the world of walls, leaders tended to invite their citizens to compare themselves to their fathers. They would say: "Are you doing better than your father? Yes? O.K., then shut up." But now people don't compare themselves to their fathers. They have so much more information. Now they compare themselves to their neighbors—everywhere. Because they can track them all over the world on television, over satellites, on DVDs and through the Internet. Now they even look into the living rooms of their worst enemies, who used to reside behind the thickest walls of all, and measure themselves against them.

My friend Laura Blumenfeld, a feature writer for *The Washington Post*, who has been traveling in the Middle East while researching a book on revenge, visited Syria with her mother in the spring of 1998. She told me the following story: "My mom and I hired a guide while we were in Damascus to take us around. His name was Walid. We got to know each other after a while, and we told him we had come from Israel. We eventually got into some very frank conversations. He told us that he liked to sit in his office at night, where he had a satellite dish, and watch Israel TV. As he described the scene, I pictured this man in this dark office, his eyes wide with fascination, watching this TV screen with people he hated but wanted to be like and was jealous of. He said, though, that of all the things that he watched on Israel TV, the thing that really bothered him was the yogurt commercials—the fact that the yogurt in Israel came in all these different fruit-colored containers— pink and orange, like in America—while in Syria they were just black or white. He even, dejectedly, pointed out to us the Syrian yogurt containers on the street one day. He also said to us, 'Our cornflakes wilt right after you put them in the milk, but I can see [from the television commercials on Israel TV] that Israel's cornflakes are crunchy and don't wilt.' Forget the Golan Heights, what really bothered him were the yogurt containers and Israel's cornflakes. One day he said to us, 'It's not fair that we are a hundred years behind the Israelis and they just got here.' "

This democratization of information is also transforming financial markets. Not only can investors now buy and sell stocks and bonds from all over the world, not only can they now do that buying and selling from their home computers, but Internet brokerage sites are now giving them—for free—the information and analytical tools to make those trades, without ever having to call a broker. The more people do that, the more they will demand more information and analyses about different economies and companies, and the more easily they will move their money around, punishing the bad performers and rewarding the good ones.

Charles Schwab, the discount brokers, began running an ad in late 1998 featuring a housewife boasting about her online trading and how she can get all the information she needs now from the Schwab Web site. The woman, named Holly, says in the ad: "A few years ago I was invited to join a women's investing group called Grow Now. We actually do a lot of work with the numbers. Then we discuss, vote and trade. And literally, everything I need is in the Schwab.com Analyst Center. Industry reports, information on management, earnings estimates, which give you some idea of how to evaluate stocks."

Soon everyone will have a virtual seat on the New York Stock Exchange. Indeed, the Schwab and E*Trade sites, and others like them, really bring together in one place the democratizations of technology, finance and information in the financial field. Another E*Trade ad remains to this day one of my favorite documents summarizing what happened when the three democratizations converged in the late 1990s, when all the walls came tumbling down. The two-page ad carried a banner headline that read: "AN INVESTOR'S DREAM. A BROKER'S NIGHTMARE. Introducing the new E*Trade. The Web's one-stop financial center. With 10X more research. More tools. More power. You can invest in stocks, options and over 4,000 mutual funds. Set up and track your portfolio. Place trades around the clock—online or by phone—for as low as $14.95. Free investing help and education, like mutual fund screening tools. Free real-time quotes, because old information is bad information. Also get breaking news. Charts. Analysis from leading sources. [And] unsurpassed security, using the leading Internet encryption technology . . . NOW OPEN FREE TO THE PUBLIC, 24 HOURS. CHECK IT OUT. GO NOW. GO FAST. SOMEDAY, WE'LL ALL INVEST THIS WAY."

My favorite line, though, was how E*Trade's television ads concluded: "E*Trade. Now the power is in your hands."

5

Microchip Immune Deficiency

SOONER OR LATER, ALL TYRANNIES CRUMBLE
Those That Keep Putting Their Customers
On Hold Tend to Crumble Sooner.

> —*ad in* The Washington Post *announcing* Star Power, *a new phone,
> cable and Internet service provider competing with Bell Atlantic*

You can never feel like you've won
You can never break even
You can never get out of the game

> —*motto for doing business on the Internet*

E or be eaten

> —*motto for adapting your company to the Internet*

N ow, some people will say, "Well, these changes in how people communicate, invest and see the world that made globalization possible are all well and good for developed societies, but what about the rest of the world? How can you talk about globalization being global when the vast majority of humanity still lives in villages without telephones, and has never touched a computer or sent an E-mail message?"

It is true that globalization today is not global, in the sense that we are still a long, long way away from a world in which everyone is online (although some 300,000 new users join the Internet each week). But globalization is global in the sense that almost everyone now is feeling—directly or indirectly—the pressures, constraints and opportunities to adapt to the democratizations of technology, finance and information that are at the heart of the globalization system. As Chen Yuan, the deputy governor of the Central Bank of China, once remarked to me: "Every country has a part that is underdeveloped. Even in the United States you can drive south from Washington to Virginia and still find some mountainous areas with remote villages. But you cannot say that this area is not in the process of globalization. China is the same."

Indeed it is. If there is a place that should have been beyond the frontiers of globalization, it is the village of Gujialingzi, a tiny hamlet in northeastern China, north of North Korea. I went there in the winter of 1998 with a team of international monitors to observe village elections in rural China. But I actually had an ulterior motive for going. I wanted to see what globalization looked like from beyond the frontier—from outside the system, as it were—and I discovered something fundamental on this trip: I couldn't get there. I couldn't get beyond the frontier. I couldn't get outside the system, which now extended deep into even the villages of northeastern China. When our monitoring team arrived in Gujialingzi, we found virtually all the voting-age adults gathered in the schoolyard. They were assembled to hear the two candidates for village chief deliver their campaign speeches. This place was dirt poor; in fact, the schoolrooms had dirt floors. The Chinese province within which it is located, Jilin, is in the heart of the former industrial belt of China, which is fast becoming a rust belt, because the state-owned industries there are not globally competitive and increasingly the Beijing government can't afford to subsidize these factories, or the social benefits they normally provide. Maybe that was why when the two candidates for village chief rose and delivered their campaign speeches in Gujialingzi they sounded as if they were running for mayor of an old steel-mill town in central Ohio.

The first to speak was the incumbent chief, Li Hongling. Here is an excerpt from his remarks: "Villagers, how are you? Let me remind you I am forty-seven years old, a member of the Communist Party with a junior high school education. I want to do something good for the village. As you know, I helped this village recover from the Cultural Revolution. Everywhere you can see my sweat. I visit everyone's home. I get ideas from you. I have never used the village's money to host a banquet. I have tried to handle everything legally. I promise to improve our elementary school and raise our incomes. If elected I vow that I will get our vegetables to the township more quickly. I will also improve the spirit of the village. We need more trees, and also fiber-optic cable so everyone can have a telephone. Under the leadership of the Party branch, I will correct all my shortcomings. This is my contract with you."

After polite applause, his challenger, Liu Fu, took the podium. He went right for the gender vote: "First let me say that tomorrow is Women's

Day and I want to express my congratulations to all the women. I am fifty-one years old, with a junior high education. I own my own bean curd business. I love this village. I love you all. Your poverty is my shame. Under the guidance of the Party I will turn a new chapter here. I promise to reduce gambling and pornography in the village and create more channels for making money. I won't be arrogant. I will reduce the village budget to save your money. I won't take any bribes, and even if my superior comes from the city, I won't take him for a banquet. We have too many official banquets. I have not been to a banquet or drunk one drop of alcohol in ten years. I will guard the money of the masses. No cadres from the village will be allowed to travel to the township on village money. I will bring technology here. I promise to give everyone the technology for making bean curd. I will drill more wells. The Cultural Revolution wasted ten years of our lives. We have to think now of better ideas for how to prosper. I will be very nonideological. As Deng Xiaoping said: 'Black cat, white cat. It doesn't matter. All that matters is that it catches mice.' I will improve our school. Knowledge is important. If you are ignorant you cannot build a socialist economy. And I will take care of all the bachelors here who do not have the income to find a wife. I will make you rich! Let's march together."

While the villagers voted and waited for the results to be announced, I did some exit polling, asking villagers at random which speech they liked most. The village butcher in a blue Mao cap stepped forward from a crowd and freely unburdened himself of his views: "When [the challenger] said he had never been to a restaurant, I believe him. There should be no more banquets for superiors who come to town. We end up paying for that."

Another villager then chimed in: "They are making government smaller in Beijing. They must do that here too . . . And he's right, we have to have a fiber-optic cable in here. We have no phones."

How do you know about fiber optics? I asked the villager.

"I don't know." He shrugged. "I just heard about it."

I got a similar response at a neighboring village, Heng Dao, where we also went to listen to campaign speeches. The incumbent, Jiang Ying, told his villagers: "I have tried to be very pragmatic in leading the village on the road to wealth. Our annual income is now 2,300 yuan per year. The budget is much smaller and during my tenure we've gotten many cadres off the village payroll. If elected, we need to introduce more science and technology into agriculture, get more enterprises here and speed up procedures for generating wealth . . . [because] the whole world is turning into one big market for merchandise."

I asked him where he got such ideas. The village has only one phone. He answered: "I read newspapers. I listen to radio . . . We have a window-frame factory here. Right now we only sell locally, but we were told that if we improve the quality, we can sell abroad, make more money."

So globalization isn't global, eh?

Don't believe it for a second. Tip O'Neill was wrong. All politics isn't local—not anymore. All politics is now global. Not every country may feel itself part of the globalization system, but every country is directly or indirectly being shaped and affected by this system. And that is why it is not a historical accident that East Germany, the Soviet Union, Asian capitalism, Brazilian state-owned industries, Chinese communism, General Motors and IBM all either collapsed or were forced to radically restructure at roughly the same time. They all got hit with the same basic disease that brought down the Berlin Wall and all the other walls that defined the Cold War. They all got hit with a disease I call Microchip Immune Deficiency Syndrome, or MIDS. Microchip Immune Deficiency Syndrome is the defining political disease of the globalization era. It can strike any company or country, large or small, East or West, North or South. If I were writing the entry in a medical dictionary for Microchip Immune Deficiency Syndrome, it would read as follows:

"MIDS: A disease that can afflict any bloated, overweight, sclerotic system in the post–Cold War era. MIDS is usually contracted by countries and companies that fail to inoculate themselves against changes brought about by the microchip, and the democratizations of technology, finance and information—which created a much faster, more open and more complex marketplace, with a whole new set of efficiencies. The symptoms of MIDS appear when a country or company exhibits a consistent inability to increase productivity, wages, living standards, knowledge use and competitiveness, and becomes too slow to respond to the challenges of the Fast World. Countries and companies with MIDS tend to be those run on Cold War corporate models—where one or a few people at the top hold all the information and make all the decisions, and all the people in the middle and the bottom simply carry out those decisions, using only the information they need to know to do their jobs. The only known cure for countries and companies with MIDS is 'the fourth democratization.' This is the democratization of decision-making and information flows, and the deconcentration of power, in ways that allow more people in a country or company to share knowledge, experiment and innovate faster. This enables them to keep up with a marketplace in which consumers are constantly demanding cheaper products and services tailored specifically for them. MIDS can be fatal to those companies and countries that do not get appropriate treatment in time. (See entries for *Soviet Union, East Germany* and *Pan Am.*)"

At some level there is nothing new about the basic concept of MIDS. Market economies have thrived over centuries by brutally killing off those firms that are less efficient, less able to adapt to new technologies and less able to remain in touch with the changing demands of consumers and to meet those demands with the minimum use of labor and capital. But what the democratizations of technology, finance and information did was put this process into hyperspeed in the 1980s, requiring companies and countries to move much faster in order to avoid contracting MIDS. Think of it as a three-stage evolution:

It began in the era before microprocessors and microchips made possible the personal computer and before the personal computer made possible the democratizations of technology, finance and information. This was an era that began with the end of World War I and lasted until the late 1970s. It was a time when both governments and corporations could be more lumbering and less efficient, because everyone was operating in a more protected game. As Alan Greenspan once described this restrictive Cold War system in a speech: "Adjustments were slower. International trade comprised a far smaller share of domestic economies. Tariff walls [restricted] competition, and capital controls often constrained cross-border currency flows. In retrospect, [this] economic environment appeared less competitive, more tranquil and certainly less threatening to those with only moderate or lesser skills. Indeed, before computer technology automated many repetitive tasks, the unskilled were able to contribute significant value-added and earn a respectable wage relative to the skilled. In this less demanding world, governments were able to construct social safety nets and engage in policies intended to redistribute income."

To be sure, added Greenspan, average standards of living were less than they could have been in this walled-up Cold War system, and the choice of products in the market was far less sensitive to changing consumer tastes than in today's microchip-based environment. The huge barriers to entry from one business to another guaranteed that change evolved much more leisurely, and it took much longer for a country or company to get into trouble. Even though both labor and product costs in those days were higher and less flexible than they needed to be, a significant portion of every society today looks back on this slower, less competitive Stone Age with a warm glow of nostalgia.

The most egregious example of this more controlled economic environment was the centrally planned, centrally controlled, top-down-directed economy of the Soviet Union. The purpose of the Soviet economy was not to meet the demands of consumers, but to reinforce the control of the central government. So all information flowed up and all orders flowed down. At a Soviet company that made bed frames the managers were paid by the central government not according to how many bed frames they sold, but on the basis of how much steel they consumed. The number of bed frames sold is a measure of consumer satisfaction. The amount of steel produced and used is a measure of state power. In the Cold War, the Soviet Union was only interested in the latter. And as long as the Cold War lasted, and the pace of change and information flows were controlled, the Soviets could get away with such an absurd system.

I will never forget a trip I took with Secretary of State Baker in 1992 to visit Chelyabinsk-70, the Soviet nuclear-bomb-designing complex located east of the Urals—a place so secret it was never registered on official Soviet maps. This was Russia's Los Alamos, home to its top nuclear scientists. What I remember most, though, was that we stayed overnight in nearby Sverdlovsk, at the October Hotel, and when I got in the elevator I noticed that the buttons read: 1, 3, 4, 5, 6, 7, 8, 9, 2. Someone forgot the second-floor button and then just tacked it on later. When you pressed the 2 button you went to the second floor—even though it was in the 10 spot. This was a hotel in the Soviet Union's most sophisticated military industrial complex! Only in a divided, chopped up, slowed-down, regulated Cold War system could the Russians get away with an elevator with the floor buttons out of sequence.

IBM in the 1970s and 1980s was a lot like Gosplan, the Soviet central planning system, with the top telling the bottom what the right products should be and what the customers should want. I once asked John Chambers, president of Cisco Systems, what it was like working for IBM in its Gosplan days. Chambers said that when he was at IBM in the early 1980s, it supposedly had an "open door" policy, whereby any employee could raise any question with any executive at any level and if he didn't like the answer he got he could go to the next higher level. "I tried that once," recalled Chambers, "and one of my friends in the company took me aside and said to me, 'You got away with it this time, but don't do it again.' At one point I told one of my superiors that the product line they were pushing would not be accepted by our customers and we would have to use up an enormous amount of resources to move it, but he didn't want to hear it. He said to me, 'I have my bonus riding on that, so go out and sell a lot of them.' "

IBM was safe as long as the barriers to entry into something as complex as the computer business were so high that the big, slow firms could be protected from mistakes, even failure, for a long time. And countries such as the Soviet Union were safe as long as the barriers to information were so high—and the awareness by its own people of competing lifestyles was so low—that the big, slow Kremlin could be protected from its mistakes, even failures, for a long time.

. . . And then came the 1980s.

The second stage in the evolution of MIDS as a disease came about with the destruction of this slow-moving world. At both the corporate and government levels, the democratizations of technology, finance and information started to converge in the late 1980s and created amazing new efficiencies and economies of scale in the marketplace, as well as a whole new place to do business, called cyberspace. This transformation became known as the Information Revolution. It will be seen in time as one of those great leaps forward in technology that occur every one hundred years, such as the discovery of electricity, which triggered a fundamental break from the previous era.

There are many ways to sum up what the Information Revolution and the three democratizations did to the marketplace. But for me it comes down to two simple concepts: First, it greatly lowered the barriers to entry into almost every business, by radically lowering the costs for new entrants. And, by doing so, it radically increased competition and the speed by which a product moved from being an innovation to being a commodity. Second, by lowering the barriers around companies, the Information Revolution also brought them closer to their customers, giving consumers much greater power to communicate their choices and to move quickly from companies that won't deliver them to companies that will.

Let's look at this in detail. The three democratizations lowered the barriers to entry because with a single personal computer, credit card, phone line, modem, color printer, Internet link, Web site and Federal Express delivery account, anyone could sit in the basement and start his or her own publishing house, retail outlet, catalogue business, global design or consulting firm, newspaper, advertising agency, distribution business, brokerage firm, gambling casino, video store, bank, bookstore, auto sales market or clothing showroom. And it could be done overnight at very low cost, and the company could become a global competitor by the next morning. You could be living on a block with three bookstores—Barnes & Noble, Crown Books and Borders—and practically overnight you could be giving them all a run for their money by creating "Borderless Books" in cyberspace by the name of Amazon.com. Amazon.com was created out of the democratization of technology (home computers for all), the democratization of finance (credit cards for all) and the democratization of information (the Internet for all) to become not just a neighborhood bookstore tailored to the specific buying habits of a community, but a twenty-four-hour-a-day bookstore, where you can shop anytime and the whole store is dedicated just to you.

When this sort of thing starts to happen across the American economy and across the world, it means that any product or service can be transformed, much more quickly, from being an innovation—that only one or two players can produce and that has a high-value-added component and fat profit margins—to being a commodity. A commodity is any product, service or process that can be provided by any number of firms, and the only distinguishing feature among these firms is who can do it cheapest. Having your product or service turned into a commodity is no fun, because it means your profit margins will become razor thin, you will have dozens of competitors and all you can do is make that product or service cheaper and sell more of it than the next guy, every day, or die.

In the walled-up Cold War system this process of going from innovation to commoditization happened at 10 miles per hour, because the barriers to entry into businesses were generally much higher and the barriers countries could erect around their economies were also much higher. In the globalization world, with the barriers now lowered or removed, this process is happening at 110 miles per hour. And as we evolve to an economy that will be increasingly defined by the Internet, the move from innovation to commoditization is going to reach Net speed, which is as fast as the speed of light. It isn't for nothing that Webheads like to say that competition on the Internet is like "Darwinism on steroids."

This is because the Internet offers the closest thing to a perfectly competitive market in the world today, explained Edward Yardeni, chief economist for Deutsche Bank. In the model of perfect competition, he noted, "there are no barriers to entry, no protection from failure for unprofitable firms, and everyone (consumers and producers) has easy and free access to all information. These just happen to be the three main characteristics of Internet commerce . . . The Internet lowers the cost of comparison shopping to zero. Increasingly, the consumer can easily and quickly find the lowest price for any good or service. In the cybereconomy, the low-cost producer will offer the lowest price and provide this information at no cost to any and all potential customers anywhere on the planet." In the low-tech economy, notes Yardeni, the cost of searching for the lowest price was relatively high. You had to climb over all sorts of walls and travel all sorts of distances to get the best deal, and this gave a built-in advantage to local or well-established companies and stores. Now manufacturers, service providers and retailers anywhere in the world can bid for business anywhere in the world, and consumers can seek out the lowest price anywhere in the world. In the past, companies made money by depending on the consumer's lack of information and lack of the technology to track it down. The Internet changes that forever. Any business that thinks it can survive by maintaining an information imbalance between buyers and sellers is fooling itself.

That's why it is going to be wonderful to be a consumer in the age of the Internet and it's going to be hell on wheels to be a seller or manufacturer. To some extent, every successful product business is going to have to become a service business. That is, every product business needs to learn to use technology to cut its costs, streamline its operations and speed up its innovation cycle so that it can play to that other feature of the Information Revolution—the ability of consumers to demand products tailored to their own personal needs. Human beings are collections of skin and bones, not digits, and therefore they will always crave, and pay a little more for, the human touch and the service or product tailored just for them. Therefore, every company now needs to use the Internet not just to improve its own business operations as an end in itself, but so that it will have more time, energy and money to tailor more products to more customers, because it is the tailored product and the personal touch that can never be commoditized. Therefore, the tailored product and human touch will always be able to earn a premium return.

Look at the brokerage business. You may think that being a stockbroker is a high-value-added service, which should pay a handsome salary. But when fifty online Internet brokerage sites suddenly appear in cyberspace and enable all your clients to buy and sell stocks for a fraction of what Merrill Lynch charges, and also give them market analyses online for free, your stockbroker's basic trading job has just been turned into a commodity. If you want to survive as a broker you are going to have to learn to use technology to understand the individual needs and demands of your customers better, learn to sell them a wider array of products than just stocks and bonds and, finally, get smarter as a broker so that you can offer them real value-added service in the form of advice and judgment. Merrill Lynch will have to charge less and less for stock transactions, now that the barriers to entry into its business have collapsed with online brokerage. But it can survive if it can provide high-touch, personal advice for navigating the global marketplace. *That* people will always pay for.

When the barriers to entry to your business start to fall this dramatically, you simply never know where your next competitor might come from. Because when the walls fall we are all increasingly in one another's business. Let me give a real-life example of this new world: One day I was flipping through a newsmagazine and I saw an ad for a new Sony digital camera system. So the first thing I said to myself was: "Wait a minute, did that ad say *Sony*? Sony was never in the camera and film business. I thought they made stereos, Walkmans and CDs." Well, yes, they do. But what is a CD? It is just a round piece of plastic coded with digits that are read by a light beam and turned into music. When you look at it that way, Sony is in the digits business, and with its digital know-how Sony can be in any business that can be converted into digits. Which brings me back to the ad for Sony's digital Mavica camera. The ad contained three pictures: The first was of the camera, which takes snapshots like your old Instamatic, only it records them digitally. Above the camera, the ad copy read: "This is your camera." Next to the camera was a 3.5-inch Sony floppy diskette. Above this diskette was written the words: "This is your film." And next to the diskette was a computer with a picture of a baby on the screen. Above the computer were the words: "This is your post office."

Now think about this ad and what it was saying. It was saying that someone back at Sony headquarters woke up one morning and said to himself, "Hey, what are we? We're just a big factory for digitizing stuff. It happens that all these years we've been digitizing music. But, hey, what the heck, if we can digitize anything, why don't we digitize your baby pictures too? Why don't we be Sony *and* Kodak? Because with our digital camera you can take digital pictures, store them on a diskette, edit them on a computer and then just print them out on your own printer." Then someone down in Sony's shipping and receiving office said, "Hey, while we're digitizing these baby pictures, we could also be E-mailing them around the world. Because once they are digitized our customers can edit them on their computers and then send them on modems to the grand-parents on different continents. So we can be Sony. We can be Kodak. And we can be Federal Express—all at the same time."

After seeing that ad, I said to myself: "I wonder how the folks at Kodak feel about this?" But then I was listening to the radio and heard an ad for Kodak, promoting all its new online computerized photo technology. Kodak seemed to be talking as though it had turned itself into a personal computer company which also developed film. That made me wonder how the folks at Compaq and Dell felt about Kodak talking like a com-puter company. But then I saw some ads for Compaq and Dell, and they were both boasting that they weren't just selling computers anymore—those are a commodity. They were now selling "business solutions" through computers, for whatever problem your company or country needed to solve. They each were presenting themselves as business con-sulting firms who happen to sell computers. Indeed, Compaq's ads often didn't even show pictures of their computers, they just said: "Compaq—better answers." Well, that made me wonder about a friend of mine who worked for PricewaterhouseCoopers. I had seen advertisements for his firm—an accounting-consulting giant—which said the firm was now pro-viding business solutions and better answers, not just preparing tax re-turns. So I asked my friend if he was worried about competition from Compaq and Dell in the business-consulting world. My friend told me that his firm wasn't afraid of the PC companies, but they were worried about the fact that Goldman Sachs, the investment bank, was now offer-ing tax-saving solutions, in the form of newly tailored tax derivatives. PricewaterhouseCoopers now has to worry that investment bankers are going to move into its tax-consulting business. My friend suggested I read something on the subject, so I figured I'd go over to Borders Books and try to find some literature, but my wife said she never goes to the bookstore anymore, because we have Amazon.com—"borderless books"—right in our basement now. So I went downstairs and clicked up Amazon.com and found that not only was it a bookstore, but it was also selling CDs. So I said to myself, "Hey, wasn't that Sony's business?"

This led me to wonder what all of this would mean for the marketing of this book you're reading. So I went up to New York and addressed the sales force of Farrar, Straus and Giroux, the publishers of the first edition, and I was seated next to Mark Gates, one of the company's top sales reps. We started talking about the book business and Gates was clearly upset. Why? He told me: "I just went into Brooks Brothers to look for a suit. So I go into the suit department and I see on one of the tables a stack of Michael Jordan's latest book, *For the Love of the Game.* It's on sale in the Brooks Brothers men's department, displayed on a pile of suits! So I go over to the salesman and say to him: 'You're not a bookstore. How would you like it if I told my bookstores they should start selling suits?' He laughed. He was a little embarrassed, but then he says to me: 'Have you looked at your electricity bill lately? Consolidated Edison has a special on for the Christmas holidays. They are offering the Jordan book at forty percent off and you can just charge it to your electric bill and they will mail it to you!' I really got depressed. I am forty-six years old. I don't plan to retire for nineteen years. But I'm asking myself now whether I will have any accounts in nineteen years. In my heart of hearts, I don't think so. All the lines are getting blurred now."

The New York Times ran a headline around this time which really stuck in my mind. It was about how AT&T was branching out into all sorts of new businesses, and the headline read: "AT&T: Ma Everything." Everyone today seems to be becoming either a niche, boutique player or Ma Everything. Everyone now is in everyone else's business.

No wonder then that the first to get hit with Microchip Immune Deficiency Syndrome in this era were the most top-heavy, overweight, slow systems like the Soviet Union and IBM, who, in a world without walls, completely lost touch with its customers and simply couldn't keep up with the speed of change in the marketplace at large. Next to catch the virus were the next closest things to Soviet central planning—the heavily state-controlled economies of Latin America, the most bloated welfare systems of Canada and Western Europe and the most overly centralized, slow-moving corporations of North America. By the late 1990s, the MIDS virus had spread to Asia and struck the top-heavy, state-directed economies of Indonesia, Malaysia, Thailand, China and even South Korea and Japan.

"I always felt that it was surely no accident that communism, planning ministries and corporate conglomerates all ran into great difficulties in the same era," Deputy Treasury Secretary Larry Summers once remarked to me, "because with the PC and the microchip it became much more efficient to empower individuals who could get more information and make more decisions themselves rather than having a single person at the top trying to direct everything."

The Buck Starts Here

The latest stage in this MIDS evolution is the one we are now in. It is the era of globalization in which governments and companies are either restructuring themselves in order to take advantage of the three democratizations, or failing to do so and finally succumbing to MIDS. It is in this stage that we see the fourth democratization—that of decision-making and the deconcentration of power and information—being used as the main technique to ward off or recover from MIDS.

To understand what I mean by the democratization of decision-making and the deconcentration of power and information, think again of the most extreme case, the former Soviet Union. Because the Soviet system was built for the sole purpose of control, it centralized all the main functions of leadership. It centralized decision-making—all decisions were made at the top and the top told you what to think, what to make, what to aspire to and what to like. It centralized information—all information flowed to the top and only the top few people had a complete picture of what was going on. And it centralized strategy—all strategic decisions about where the country was headed were made at the top.

What the democratization of decision-making and deconcentration of power does is to take a centrally controlled system like this, loosen it up and redefine the center so that decision-making and information flow both top-down and bottom-up. Each successful company or country will reorganize its center a little bit differently, depending on its marketplace, geography, population and level of development. Dell Computer now centralizes all of its billing, inventory management and distribution of computers for its European operations by having them flow through a single call center in Ireland. It is centralizing certain functions not for the purpose of control but to take advantage of new cost-saving efficiencies. At the same time, Dell has decentralized a lot of other decision-making to its individual sales and service centers in each European country, because each of these centers is closer to its customers, can tailor its services to their particular needs and tastes and can quickly adapt to any changes.

In today's hyperspeed, enormously complex globalization system, most of the information needed to answer most of the problems now rests in the hands of people on the outer edges of organizations, not at the center. And if your country or company has not democratized decision-making and deconcentrated power to enable these people to use and share their knowledge, it is going to be at a real disadvantage. As Warren Bennis, in his book *Organizing Genius,* puts it: "None of us is as smart as all of us."

One way to summarize this shift is to think of the sign that used to sit on the desk of every American leader or executive. It said: "The Buck Stops Here." That was a plausible motto during the Cold War since all information flowed to the top so that all decisions could flow down from the top, and the marketplace was slow enough to wait for one person. But today the best CEOs will be those who understand that their job is to chart the broad corporate strategies, to establish the broad corporate culture, to get the balls rolling on the right paths and then let those closest to the customers and to the rapidly changing marketplace manage those balls on their own.

Therefore the sign on the desk of the successful CEO in the era of globalization will not be "The Buck Stops Here." It will be "The Buck Starts Here." I, the boss, set the broad strategies, I keep everyone connected on the same path, I get the balls rolling, but you, the employees, gather the information, share it and make as many of the decisions as you can, quickly and close to the market.

Robert Shapiro, the chairman of Monsanto, is a classic example of a chief executive who revamped the center of his company so the buck could start, not stop there. "In the old days an event would happen somewhere out in the world," he explained to me, not far from the open cubicle he works in, which is the same size as his secretary's. "Some low-level person in your company would observe it, and of course it was mostly low-level people who were out there actually observing things. The observation that this low-level person would make would have something to do with what was going on with your customers or your competitors. This piece of information that this low-level person would generate on the periphery would then get passed up the hierarchical ladder—provided that the people at each step recognized its significance and were not threatened by it and therefore didn't try to kill it. But let's suppose it eventually made its way up to someone near the top who had the power to decide. Chances are that in today's globalization system by the time it got there this piece of information would no longer be timely. It would probably be distorted and, worse, the person who was supposed to make the decision about it would probably do so on the basis of his or her archaic experiences when he or she was down at the bottom of the ladder fifteen years ago. 'Ah yes,' he would say, 'I was confronted with a problem like that once in the era before the Flood.' Now, that was all O.K. when everyone was operating on the same general basis and there was no particular disadvantage from being a little slower, a little less at the cutting edge, a little farther from the customer. But that world is gone.

"So what we are doing at Monsanto is trying to redefine the center," Shapiro continued. "We are not just decentralizing everything and letting everyone go off and do their own thing. We are not saying that headquarters doesn't matter. But we are redefining what the center means in ways that are more inclusive, in ways that allow us to move faster and be more responsive to changes in the marketplace. In the past, I could justify [my leadership] by the fact that I had the broadest scope of information and therefore I had a perspective that no one else in the company had, so I was adding value to the process by making decisions by myself. But now, with E-mail, intranets and the Internet, everyone on the front lines has much of the information I have, and often more. Even if I wanted to, I could not deny them the information. So any hierarchy that bases itself on denying information to its citizens or employees is not going to work. Now it has to be much more of a team effort. I suspect I listen better to more people all the time now, because I know that they have much more information and therefore have a better basis for their point of view now—better than they used to have and better than I used to have. I can get in immediate contact now with that person at the bottom rung who is having the idea or the experience with the customer that normally would have to work its way up the ladder . . . As leader of the company, I have to make sure that my managers have the training in the culture, values and strategy of the company so that when they are gathering information they have an appropriate context to assess it and know whether it confirms or contradicts the path that we are on. But to do that they have to know the path that we are on and they have to have information about it all the time. My job is to make sure that happens."

My father-in-law, Matthew Bucksbaum, is the chairman of a large shopping-center development company, General Growth Properties, and he decided to test out this idea. His company is headquartered in Chicago but controls 130 shopping centers in cities around the United States, and each center has an individual manager, who lives in that city

and operates that center. Once a year they bring all their managers together for a convention. So at the 1999 meeting, Matthew wore a button
that said "The Buck Starts Here," and he gave each of his 130 shopping-
center managers a button that said "The Buck Stops Here."

This was Matthew's way of trying to inoculate his company against
MIDS, so that the Berlin Wall wouldn't fall on him. Every company has
to do this its own way. I have been collecting stories of different strategies
for avoiding getting hit with the Berlin Wall. I offer here three very different examples—one from a Minnesota farmer, one from a Baltimore
small businessman and one from an Internet doctor in cyberspace.

G ary Wagner, age forty-four, and his two brothers own a 4,200-acre
farm in the heart of Minnesota's Red River Valley, outside Crooks-
ton, on the border with North Dakota. As the 1990s rolled around, Gary
could see what was happening to the farm business: either you got big
and were able to take advantage of economies of scale and played in the
global farmers' market, or you got swallowed up by someone else who
could. Wagner and his brothers didn't want to get swallowed, so they
began to look for an edge. Maybe because Wagner's father died when he
was twenty-four and left him in charge of the farm, he was a little more
open to new ideas, like on the day in 1993 when the agro-research firm
AgLeader approached him with a wacky new technology. It was a
microchip-based sensor that could be attached to his wheat combine. As
Wagner would drive the combine to harvest his wheat, the sensor would
measure the exact stream of wheat coming in off every square foot of his
field. At the same time, Wagner's tractor would be connected by trans-
mitter to a global positioning satellite (GPS) in outer space that could
track his precise position in his field at all times. When he combined the
data from the sensor that was tracking the harvest and the data from the
satellite that was tracking his combine's movement, Wagner suddenly
found out exactly how much wheat was being harvested from every acre
of his field.

It took a little while to get the whole system coordinated. "The software programmer would sit on the back of the combine with me," said
Wagner, "and he would be writing the program on his laptop as we went
along, then go back to his hotel and make some adjustments and then
come out on the tractor and test it again." But once they got the system
working, the information it produced was well worth the effort.

"What I found out was something of a surprise," said Wagner. "It was a common belief that yield did not vary very much from one area of your field to another. You looked out at your field and it all looked very uniform to the eye. But once we generated a precise yield map from this program, we discovered that there was a major difference in yield between some acres and others, as much as 150 dollars an acre, which can be the difference between a profit and a loss on that acre. Once I had that information it was worth its weight in gold to me, because we have a choice every season of different varieties of crops to plant. By using these sorts of computerized yield monitors we can tell exactly which varieties of crops grow best in which soils under our management."

Previously, Wagner had to live under the central planning system of the agribusiness. Information flowed down to him from the top. He took the crop varieties recommended by the companies selling the seeds. But all the companies did was determine which average varieties would do best on an average farm like his in an average region like his. Their varieties were never tailored to every acre of his farm. Once he was armed with his own deeper information about his farm, Wagner was able to deconcentrate and "democratize" his fields. He was able to shift decision-making and information down to each acre and, in effect, let each acre tell him the precise crop variety, water level and fertilizer that it preferred in order to produce the highest yields, given its specific soil, moisture and slope of land. He could also program (centralize) all that information into his fertilizer applicator, and then tie that applicator in with the satellite. Once he had that system together, he could drive down his sugar-beet field and the satellite would know which acre he was on, the software program would know just how much fertilizer that specific acre liked and the fertilizer applicator would automatically dispense the exact amount of nitrates—more in some places, less in others—demanded by that specific acre. It saved on fertilizer, which was good for the environment, and maximized his yields, which was good for his pocketbook.

"Instead of having to work with information from a centralized pool that was based on averages for the region for the average farmer, we were able to tailor everything to ourselves," said Wagner. "The tuition was high. It was a big investment for us. But now it is paying off. Let's be honest, we are competing against our neighbors and we need an edge. Everyone has the same tractors, the same combines, the same basic land, the same water, so the only thing that can distinguish you from your competitor now is who has more knowledge."

Armed with more knowledge, Wagner can now delegate more things to his workers so he can concentrate on the key strategy, which is making his farm bigger so it will be the one that eats others and is not eaten itself.

For instance, he says, "We hire soil samplers to input some of the basic information we need in our database. In the past, they would just come and take a random set of samples around your field and tell you what you have. Now it is reversed. Because I know more about my fields, I can tell the soil samplers exactly where to take the samples and they use the GPS satellite to navigate to exactly those spots. So if I am looking for uniform areas in my fields to grow the exact same variety of crops, I can tell them just where to test. It means I can delegate more, and I get as good information as I would have gotten if I had done it myself. That allows me to concentrate on getting bigger. But the only way to get bigger and still be profitable is to get smarter. If I can show my bankers these kinds of improvements, they will be more willing to lend me the money I need to grow."

Wagner is still a pioneer in what is known as "precision farming." Most of his neighbors are still dubious. "I think if my dad were alive, he would have been interested, but he never would have approved us going down this track so fast," he says. "But because it's just my brothers and me in charge, and there is no big boss above us, we are a little more open to new ideas. The precision-farming community is still pretty small, though, so we keep in touch with each other via the Internet. We now have a precision farmers' chat room where we all share problems and solutions."

What was true for a farmer in Minnesota was also true for Jerry Portnoy's thirty-five-person company, Valley Lighting, Inc., of Baltimore.

"We are basically commercial lighting distributors," Portnoy explained to me in 1999. "We supply material to electrical contractors and developers for large commercial projects, both on a competitive bid and a negotiated basis. We bid, design and budget—do whatever is needed—to get our developers and contractors the best bang for their lighting buck. We only succeed when we add value to our customers' businesses. Now, you might say, how does a lighting company add value? We do it by providing you the lowest-cost lighting solution and service for whatever your requirements are."

In the early 1990s, though, right after a wall happened to fall in Berlin, Portnoy noticed his own marketplace suddenly changing.

"It was like somebody just pulled down a window shade, and an era was over," he said. "Our customers changed in their attitudes, becoming much more demanding; guys who used to give us commitments on jobs in an instant wouldn't give commitments; guys who used to negotiate with us alone suddenly started demanding bids from everybody and anybody. My salespeople started coming to me saying, 'We can't get orders, things have gotten much more competitive, and when we do get orders, we can't make a profit.' I started to feel that our company was at risk, but we really didn't understand what was happening. As you would say, the Berlin Wall was falling on us and we didn't know it."

In response to this situation, Portnoy and his partner decided to do a little tinkering. They set aside a pool of cash—$100,000—that would enable their salespeople to close deals for half of their normal profit margin. So, for instance, if a salesperson closed a deal for less than the company's traditional profit margin, he could take the difference out of this $100,000 pool.

"What I was trying to do," said Portnoy, "was really see how much faster and more efficient we could become, and to understand what in the world was going on out in the marketplace. By taking on these contracts I would be able to see if we could buy the raw materials, operate them efficiently and continue to service our clients—all at lower costs— and still make a profit. Well, a funny thing happened. My key producers were able to gross as many dollars as before, without having to dip into the 100,000-dollar pool. It was an ego thing for them. Nobody wanted to be the one who had to dip into the pool. They had to work much harder to stay where they were, but many of them were able to do it, at least for a while. But, I have to say, there was still a lot of frustration for my people at the way they were being treated by their customers. Coming out of the late 1980s, we all thought we were hotshots, and suddenly, boom, people were treating us like we were just some regular commodity-supply house. We continued to add value, but our customers wouldn't even acknowledge it. They said, 'Yeah, you give good service, but so what?' They were losing money, so all they could think about was going to the person with the lowest number. The whole construction industry was getting commoditized, so nobody had any cushions anymore. By the mid-1990s our salespeople were coming to me more often saying that they were going to have to allow some old relationships to erode. They were all complaining that they couldn't put good bids together like they used to, partly because to make the same amount of money they had to bid so many more jobs just to get one, so they had less time to study each component of a job and to understand exactly where the dollars and opportunities were. And remember, the secret to bidding is information and knowledge. The more you understand about a job and its different components, the more you can bid it right and come in with a low number that still allows you to make the necessary profit margins to survive."

By 1994, Valley Lighting was still not losing money, but it was making a lot less. MIDS was starting to set in. It was clear that the democratizations of finance, technology and information had fundamentally changed Portnoy's business environment and commoditized a lot of things that had not been commodities in the past.

"So I started to look around at my business, and I realized that what we were missing most was information," says Portnoy. "We didn't have enough information and knowledge to survive in this marketplace. Our promise to our customers had always been that by letting us handle their lighting demands we would always add more value to their project than we charged for our services. If you had budgetary constraints, we could find a way to give you ninety percent of the lighting look and feel you wanted at seventy percent of the cost, as opposed to our competitors, who would only give you seventy percent of the feel you wanted for seventy percent of the cost. I knew I had to get us back to that sort of value-added strategy in this new environment."

So Portnoy really got radical. He hired a software consultant and spent $20,000 to see if there was some software program on the market that could make his company smarter and faster, so that it could continue to provide its value-added service in this new market and avoid becoming a commodity.

"After a year or so of searching we just couldn't find a software package that fit more than fifty percent of our needs. So we decided to write our own software package," Portnoy explained. "I don't know anything about writing software. But two of my key lighting people were self-taught techies who, just as a hobby, loved this sort of software stuff. I hired a professional programmer, and he worked with my people and together they designed a system that could be applied to exactly the way we think our business should be run. I don't know how they did it. My job was simply to approve the budgetary dollars. But it was a big commitment for me. It ended up costing 350,000 dollars. But it saved our business. They developed a software program that allowed each of our salespeople and estimators to understand more about each component of a job and then to draw up bids and quotations so much more efficiently and quickly by just filling in a set of blanks that we knew were the critical variables. Even more important, the whole system operates as a continuum, so the original quotations automatically convert into purchase orders and the purchase orders automatically convert into delivery information and billing invoices and maintenance management. And all that information can be displayed on one screen, so that people are not having to stop and perform each stage separately. The same information, entered once, now gets used over and over and over. When we started, we operated with only stand-alone computers. But now we are a PC-based network, so the whole thing is integrated throughout our company. In the first six months of 1998 our sales and profits rose by thirty-three percent, with the same number of people. When you increase your business by one-third with the same people, it means that if you add more people you can really increase your business. And in this winner-take-all environment, you have to get bigger, smarter, faster than your competition, or get out of the way. I don't know if it's sustainable, but I know that it has given me an opportunity for survival into the next phase—until somebody becomes more efficient."

How has it changed your job as CEO? I asked Portnoy.

"To be honest, I know less of what is going on, on the ground, now, but it doesn't bother me. I have delegated my people to make more decisions with more information. My salespeople are not on commission. They work as a team, so they can be interactive and not compete with each other. They know if the company makes money, they will make money. It really encourages them to share information. They all have more information now and because of that they have more power. They can decide on their own what jobs they have a better chance of closing, which ones will yield the greatest gross profits and which ones will be easiest to service. And what's most important, with the new software, they now have time to think. And that is incredibly important, instead of just banging away all day on calculators. They can run the business now instead of the business running them. It's like they are all individual profit centers now—they each have their own business—and my job is to keep them together and give them the support they need, and the tools they need, to do what they do best."

The buck starts here.

Finally, the newest strategy for surviving the fall of the Berlin Wall— the one you will hear about most in coming years—can be summed

up by a 1999 ad for Computer Sciences Corporation. The headline on
the ad asked: "How long can you wait for e-business?" And the copy reads
as follows: "Inside every business, there's a huge e-business opportunity
ticking away. The power to move faster. The power to reach farther. The
power to claim a prime spot in the new e-economy. But wait too long and
your options expire."

In the 1980s the Internet was a novelty. By the 1990s it was a useful
technology. By the time the new millennium rolled around it was an indispensable tool for doing business. Which is why by the year 2000 Wall
Street was asking every company the same question: What is your IQ?
What is your Internet Quotient? To what degree have you understood
that the Internet is not a toy, is not just a useful appendage to your operations, but an indispensable tool for how you deal with customers, suppliers and other companies? After all, thanks to the Internet, noted Alan
Greenspan, companies can now have instantaneous information about
changing tastes in the marketplace, the status of inventories among suppliers and the location of every product in the production chain. This, in
turn, can enable them to remove large swaths of inventory, redundant
capital equipment and layers of workers, while arming them with detailed data to fine-tune products to the most specific customer needs and
desires. As more and more companies realized this, a whole new career
was born. I call it Internet doctoring. Internet doctors are companies like
Computer Sciences Corporation. They are the 911 that the CEO calls
when he wakes up one morning and says, "Oh my God. This Internet
thing is real! What is it going to do to my business and how do I survive?"

Alan S. Cohen is one of the first Internet doctors. He is to Internet
medicine what Hippocrates was to human medicine. He heads the management team that does Internet doctoring for telecommunications companies at Cisco Systems, a firm that not only builds the Internet but built
itself around the Internet. When a company dials "911-Get-Me-E-
Ready," Alan Cohen is the guy Cisco sends out to do a diagnosis and pre-
scribe some remedies. He operates on the theory that while there is a
huge market in selling technology, there is a monster market in teaching
a company how to use it to more efficiently relate to customers, suppliers
and itself.

"The first motivator for the CEO of a company to call for an E-doctor
is fear—fear that his fundamental business model is going to be threatened by E-commerce," explained Cohen. "So I'm an Internet doctor. A
doctor advises you on a couple of levels. Bad doctors treat only symptoms.

Good doctors treat root causes. Sometimes a company will come to us and say, 'I am not feeling well. I want to sell more on the Internet. Help me use the Internet to sell more.' The first thing I might say is: 'Well, the reason you aren't feeling well, and the reason you aren't selling more on the Net, is not just because you have no Internet retailing strategy. Forget about E-commerce for a minute. Your whole workforce is inefficient and your relationship with your suppliers is inefficient. You need to use the Internet to address that. Then we can talk about E-commerce.'

"Most of these executives who come to us looking for answers never saw the Internet or information technology as part of their core business functions," added Cohen. "Companies have tended to be broken into two basic parts—the guys who build and sell stuff, and everybody else. The Internet and information technologies were traditionally handled by the everybody-else department. It was kept separate from the guys who build and sell. In a lot of companies, the title CIO—Chief Information Officer—actually stood for 'Career Is Over.' Information technology was just viewed as a cost, and costs were something to be kept down. At Cisco, we start by taking a very different approach and we encourage others to start the same way. So when that executive calls our 911 number, what we try to do is give him some basic integrated rules to think about. I would list them as follows:

"Rule number one: To be successful in E-business you have to be an E-business. You don't just attach the Internet to a wall somewhere. You have to absorb it into everything you do. Start by getting rid of all the paper. No more paper. Sorry. You want to talk to me you can't do it on paper, you have to do it via E-mail and the Internet. Cisco now sells the vast majority of its equipment over the Net. Customers place their orders directly over Cisco's Web site, which cuts down on mistakes that inevitably arise when someone is taking down someone else's order on paper and then logging it into the system. Most orders that come into Cisco are never touched by human hands, but rather sail into its Web site and out of its factories. All those people who used to be involved in taking down orders and punching them into the system can focus instead on servicing customers and learning about their new needs. Cisco's suppliers can also see these orders, so they can ship the right number of replenishment parts to Cisco's factories, eliminating the need to hold lots of inventory. Cisco also put as much of its customer support as possible on its own Web site. That way customers can find their own answers to simple questions and Cisco's most sophisticated engineers can focus more on complex installation problems and servicing. Time is something that is being wasted if it is being spent on anything other than servicing, and delighting, a customer in a very tailored way.

"Cisco also has all its employee expenses and benefits online, so that employees don't need to spend more than a minute filing expenses and accessing benefits. They get reimbursed for expenses within two days by submitting them through the company's intranet system. We just bought a small start-up company for Cisco. We sent a team out to visit the company. Then we sent a memo around via E-mail to all the key executives about why we wanted to buy it. We sent the company's profile around by E-mail. We discussed it all over E-mail, and made the final decision in one face-to-face executive meeting. We got to this strategy, in part, because we started to grow so fast that we couldn't hire people fast enough. So we moved one business function at a time away from people into networks, where customers and suppliers, managers and new employees, sales people and manufacturing engineers could all access information and each other directly. And then we turned off the paper."

Cisco is so internally wired together—management, manufacturing, accounting and sales—that it doesn't have to wait for the end of the quarter any longer to close its books to find out where it stands, and to see which departments are making money and which are over budget. The company is so internally wired it can close its books in one hour—anytime it wants.

Rule number two, said Cohen, is: Make your CEO your Internet evangelist. Make him or her responsible for your E-commerce success. People don't listen to anyone but the boss. If the boss is not committed to really bringing the Internet into a business, then don't bother. Jack Welch at General Electric told each of his managers that they had to have an Internet strategy in place by a certain deadline. It came down as a mandate from the top, driven by fear of what the Internet might do to their business. Company cultures only really change from the top down. "As an Internet doctor, you have to identify the executive change agent who sees his career success tied up with E-development," said Cohen. "If the attitude of the boss is 'Get this stuff off my plate so I can just keep my country club membership,' that's not the guy you want to be with. You want the guy who is eager to create a new revenue stream and change the whole company.

"Rule number three is: Give everyone access to everything all the time. You need to have a freedom of information act for corporate data, so that your employees, suppliers and customers can serve themselves. When people can serve themselves, they will serve themselves. When the customer places his own order and can track it downstream, all sorts of efficiency and speed gets built into the system. There's a lot better chance that an order will be written up right if the customer writes it in himself. Our average customer logs on to our Web site for orders every other day, and they can immediately and directly gratify some information need. What's more, we have customers not just asking us stuff, but telling us stuff online about our products, so we can learn from it and so, too, can other Cisco customers.

"Rule number four is: Train and motivate your customers and employees to always go to the Web. When a customer calls our call center the operator there will tell him, 'Did you know you can see everything you are looking for, or answer that question, right online, without having to wait for an operator?' We have our own online university to train new employees and customers and to upgrade the skills of existing employees. Prospective employees can also come there to find out about Cisco, and see if they want to work here." The more classroom days that are converted to electronic courses delivered over the Internet, and the more customers serve themselves through the Cisco Web site rather than having a telephone operator take their call, the more people Cisco can serve at a lower cost.

Indeed, says Cohen, "We have changed the bonus system inside Cisco, so that for a manager to get a bonus he or she has to demonstrate each year that they are doing more things with fewer people—and the only way to do that is by leveraging the Internet. Today, about eighty percent of questions from Cisco customers and suppliers get answered on line. So we now do more business than ever with fewer technical support staff. Moreover, every vendor who does business with Cisco does it over the Internet. You want to be our HMO, sell us paper plates or toilet paper or computers, you have to have your catalogue logged into our online procurement system so we can order from it with one click and compare prices with one click. We don't carry any catalogues around here. Remember, there's no more paper. Throw it all away. You can't communicate with me on paper."

Once a business adopts a real Internet strategy, Cohen's group has developed a series of tests to see how it is doing. He calls them the "E-business cholesterol test." They try to measure a company's general Net-readiness. "A year later we are looking for measurable changes," says

Cohen. "For instance, how well has efficiency per employee improved? Are you getting more from the same gang? We figure we have saved 1.5 billion dollars in costs between 1996 and 1999 by routing all our business through the Internet. How well has customer satisfaction improved? Have customers noticed that they are now relating to you more through the Internet, and are they enjoying that? Has your market share improved? Are you able to lower your inventory carrying costs, because you are communicating more often and more transparently with both your customers and suppliers? Has the Internet enabled your customers to order things much more easily from me, and, as a result, is that customer not only more satisfied but someone who is ordering more things—things that he never even knew we sold before? Do I have more productivity per salesman? Lastly, are my people happier and are we worth more as a company—has the market recognized the efficiency gains we have made from our ability to execute an Internet strategy?"

In other words, has the market recognized that your company has developed a strategy for surviving the fall of the Berlin Wall?

In its own crude way, trying to survive the fall of the wall was what the Chinese government was trying to do by encouraging village elections, even if half of them were bogus. They were trying to push the buck, and decision-making, down to the local level, because Beijing concluded that the only way it could deal with the economic problems of the countryside was by allowing villagers to hold their own elections for chief and make more of their own decisions. China's authoritarian leaders hoped that these elections would produce better local leaders who would understand the needs and circumstances in the countryside better, be able to hustle more and, ideally, build up the local economies on their own. It was their way of deconcentrating power and decision-making—not in the political sphere, but in the economic sphere.

Holding such local elections will not be sufficient to keep the Chinese economy growing at the rate it needs to grow. It will require a lot more deconcentration of power. But I am sure that it was a necessary beginning, and the Chinese villagers I met were just as sure.

By the way, I never did tell you who won the election for chief in the village of Gujialingzi. We sat around there for hours while they tallied the votes on the blackboard of a schoolroom. I will never forget the scene of all those Chinese villagers, crammed into the doorway and pressed up against the windows, watching as each vote was recorded with a white chalk mark. Despite his appeal to the women's vote, Liu Fu, the challenger, was beaten by the incumbent. Several of us chatted with Liu afterward. He said he was sorry to lose, but he'd seen worse. A lot worse. During the Cultural Revolution he'd been banished and now, twenty years later, he was running for village chief (in an election monitored by a team from the United States).

Asked if he had ever lost hope during the Cultural Revolution, he answered with a Chinese proverb: "No hand can block out the sun."

6

The Golden Straitjacket

We're still very much in a straitjacket for the next year or two. The new government will have to be quite careful.

—*Umar Juoro, economic adviser to former Indonesian Prime Minister B. J. Habibie, describing to* The New York Times *how little room to maneuver the Indonesian government has on the economic front, because if it does anything rash it will get hammered by the IMF and the global markets,* October 23, 1999

While I was on that trip monitoring elections in Chinese villages and my interpreter and I were wandering through the village of Heng Dao, we dropped in on a farmer-turned-mechanic who had geese and pigs in the front yard, but a stereo and color television inside his brick hut. My interpreter, a Chinese student who was studying in America, noticed something I never would have—that there didn't seem to be any loudspeaker around. During Mao's day the Communist Party installed loudspeakers in the "brigades," as small villages were known, and used them to blare out propaganda and other messages exhorting the workers. We asked our host what happened to it.

"We took it down last year," the villager said of the loudspeaker. "No one wanted to listen to it anymore. We have stereo and TV now." What the villager didn't say was that he didn't need to hear the message from Beijing and the Communist Party anymore, because he knew what it was and it wasn't the teachings of Chairman Mao. The only message coming from them was much simpler: "You're on your own. Get a job. Send money."

A few months earlier I had been in Thailand, watching Thailand's crony capitalist economy going into a tailspin. I had arranged to interview Sirivat Voravetvuthikun, a Thai real estate developer who had gone bankrupt in the Thai economic crash. He and his wife had become the poster children for the Thai crash, because they had decided to go into the sandwich-selling business to make ends meet. This once-wealthy couple rented out some vacant space in downtown Bangkok, set up a sandwich-making operation with many of their former employees and started delivering fresh ham-and-cheese around the streets of Bangkok. Sirivat arrived at our interview carrying a yellow picnic box strapped around his neck like a sandwich vendor at an American baseball game. What I remembered most about our conversation, though, was the absence of bitterness in his voice, and the much more pungent air of resignation. His message was that Thailand had messed up. People knew it. They would now have to tighten their belts and get with the program and there wasn't much else to say. Wasn't he mad? I asked. Didn't he want to burn down some government building in anger at being wiped out?

No, Sirivat explained to me: "Communism fails, socialism fails, so now there is only capitalism. We don't want to go back to the jungle, we all want a better standard of living, so you have to make capitalism work, because you don't have a choice. We have to improve ourselves and follow the world rules . . . Only the competitive survive. It will probably require a national unity government, because the burden is so big."

A few months after this I attended a lecture in Washington by Anatoly Chubais, the architect of Russia's failed economic reforms and privatization. Chubais had come to Washington to make a last-ditch appeal to the IMF for more aid to Russia, but at the time the still-communist-dominated Russian Duma, or parliament, was resisting the IMF's conditions. The Duma was also regularly denouncing Chubais as a traitor and foreign agent for submitting to IMF demands that Russia radically reform its economy along real free-market lines. I asked Chubais how he answered his critics, and he told me: " 'O.K.,' I tell them, 'Chubais is a spy for the CIA and IMF. But what is your substitute? Do you have [any alternative] workable ideas?' " Chubais said he never gets any coherent answer, because the communists have no alternative.

I was in Brazil a few months later, where I interviewed Fabio Feldmann, the former environmental secretary of São Paulo and a federal deputy in the Brazilian parliament, who was campaigning for reelection in São Paulo. His office was a beehive of campaign workers, awash in posters and other campaign paraphernalia. Feldmann is a liberal, and I asked him about the nature of the political debate in Brazil today. He responded: "The [ideological] left in Brazil have lost their flag. The challenge of the federal government is jobs and employment. You have to generate *and* distribute income. And what is the program of the left? They don't have proposals to generate income, only to distribute it."

What are these stories telling us? Once the three democratizations came together in the late 1980s and blew away all the walls, they also blew away all the major ideological alternatives to free-market capitalism. People can talk about alternatives to the free market and global integration, they can demand alternatives, they can insist on a "Third Way," but for now none is apparent. This is very different from the first era of globalization. During the nineteenth and early twentieth centuries, when the Industrial Revolution and global finance capitalism roared through Europe and America, many people were shocked by their Darwinian brutality and "dark Satanic mills." They destroyed old orders and hierarchies, produced huge income gaps and put everyone under pressure, but they also produced sharply rising standards of living for those who could make a go of it. This experience triggered a great deal of debate and revolutionary theorizing, as people tried to find ways to cushion workers from the cruelest aspects of free-market capitalism in that day. As Karl Marx and Friedrich Engels described this era in *The Communist Manifesto*: "Constant revolutionizing of production, uninterrupted disturbance of all social conditions, everlasting uncertainty and agitation distinguish the bourgeois epoch from all earlier ones. All fixed, fast-frozen relations, with their train of ancient and venerable prejudices and opinions, are swept away, all new-formed ones become antiquated before they can ossify. All that is solid melts into air, all that is holy is profaned, and man is at last compelled to face with sober senses, his real conditions of life, and his relations with his kind."

Eventually, people came along who declared that they could take these destabilizing, brutalizing swings out of the free market, and create a world that would never be dependent on unfettered bourgeois capitalists. They would have the government centrally plan and fund everything, and distribute to each worker according to his needs and expect from each worker a contribution according to his abilities. The names of these revolutionary thinkers were Engels, Marx, Lenin and Mussolini, among others. The centrally planned, nondemocratic alternatives they offered — communism, socialism and fascism — helped to abort the first era of globalization as they were tested out on the world stage from 1917 to 1989.

There is only one thing to say about those alternatives: *They didn't work*. And the people who rendered that judgment were the people who lived under them. So with the collapse of communism in Europe, in the

Soviet Union and in China—and all the walls that protected these systems—those people who are unhappy with the Darwinian brutality of
free-market capitalism don't have any ready ideological alternative now.
When it comes to the question of which system today is the most effective
at generating rising standards of living, the historical debate is over. The
answer is free-market capitalism. Other systems may be able to distribute
and divide income more efficiently and equitably, but none can generate
income to distribute as efficiently as free-market capitalism. And more
and more people now know that. So, ideologically speaking, there is no
more mint chocolate chip, there is no more strawberry swirl and there is
no more lemon-lime. Today there is only free-market vanilla and North
Korea. There can be different brands of free-market vanilla and you can
adjust your society to it by going faster or slower. But, in the end, if you
want higher standards of living in a world without walls, the free market is
the only ideological alternative left. One road. Different speeds. But one
road.

When your country recognizes this fact, when it recognizes the rules
of the free market in today's global economy, and decides to abide
by them, it puts on what I call the Golden Straitjacket. The Golden
Straitjacket is the defining political-economic garment of this globalization era. The Cold War had the Mao suit, the Nehru jacket, the Russian
fur. Globalization has only the Golden Straitjacket. If your country has
not been fitted for one, it will be soon.

The Golden Straitjacket first began to be stitched together and popularized in 1979 by British Prime Minister Margaret Thatcher—who, as
the original seamstress of the Golden Straitjacket, will go down in history
as one of the great revolutionaries of the second half of the twentieth century. That Thatcherite coat was soon reinforced by Ronald Reagan in the
United States in the 1980s, giving the straitjacket, and its rules, some real
critical mass. It became a global fashion with the end of the Cold War,
once the three democratizations blew away all the alternative fashions
and all the walls that protected them. The Thatcherite-Reaganite revolutions came about because popular majorities in these two major Western
economies concluded that the old government-directed economic approaches simply were not providing sufficient levels of growth. Thatcher
and Reagan combined to strip huge chunks of economic decision-
making power from the state, from the advocates of the Great Society and

from traditional Keynesian economics, and hand them over to the free market.

To fit into the Golden Straitjacket a country must either adopt, or be seen as moving toward, the following golden rules: making the private sector the primary engine of its economic growth, maintaining a low rate of inflation and price stability, shrinking the size of its state bureaucracy, maintaining as close to a balanced budget as possible, if not a surplus, eliminating and lowering tariffs on imported goods, removing restrictions on foreign investment, getting rid of quotas and domestic monopolies, increasing exports, privatizing state-owned industries and utilities, deregulating capital markets, making its currency convertible, opening its industries and stock and bond markets to direct foreign ownership and investment, deregulating its economy to promote as much domestic competition as possible, eliminating government corruption, subsidies and kickbacks as much as possible, opening its banking and telecommunications systems to private ownership and competition, and allowing its citizens to choose from an array of competing pension options and foreign-run pension and mutual funds. When you stitch all of these pieces together you have the Golden Straitjacket.

Unfortunately, this Golden Straitjacket is pretty much "one size fits all." So it pinches certain groups, squeezes others and keeps a society under pressure to constantly streamline its economic institutions and upgrade its performance. It leaves people behind quicker than ever if they shuck it off, and it helps them catch up quicker than ever if they wear it right. It is not always pretty or gentle or comfortable. But it's here and it's the only model on the rack this historical season.

As your country puts on the Golden Straitjacket, two things tend to happen: your economy grows and your politics shrinks. That is, on the economic front the Golden Straitjacket usually fosters more growth and higher average incomes—through more trade, foreign investment, privatization and more efficient use of resources under the pressure of global competition. But on the political front, the Golden Straitjacket narrows the political and economic policy choices of those in power to relatively tight parameters. That is why it is increasingly difficult these days to find any real differences between ruling and opposition parties in those countries that have put on the Golden Straitjacket. Once your country puts it on, its political choices get reduced to Pepsi or Coke—to slight nuances of taste, slight nuances of policy, slight alterations in design to account for local traditions, some loosening here or there, but never any major deviation from the core golden rules. Governments—be they led by Democrats or Republicans, Conservatives or Labourites, Gaullists or Socialists, Christian Democrats or Social Democrats—that deviate too far from the core rules will see their investors stampede away, interest rates rise and stock market valuations fall. The only way to get more room to maneuver in the Golden Straitjacket is by enlarging it, and the only way to enlarge it is by keeping it on tight. That's its one virtue: the tighter you wear it, the more gold it produces and the more padding you can then put into it for your society.

No wonder so much of the political debate in developed countries today has been reduced to arguments over minor tailoring changes in the Golden Straitjacket, not radical alterations. When it came to economics, how much of a difference was there really between Bill Clinton and Bob Dole in the 1996 American presidential election? On broad economic issues, very little. Clinton essentially said, "We're in this Golden Straitjacket, but I have a way we can put a little more padding in the elbows and enlarge the middle a bit." And Dole said in effect, "No, no, you can't loosen the middle at all. Keep it on tight and we'll put a little less padding in the elbows." But they were really discussing the buttonholes on a jacket neither of them intended to alter very much—and they were hardly alone. In the 1997 British election campaign Tony Blair vowed in essence that if he won, "We'll keep the Golden Straitjacket on as tight as the Tories, but we'll add some padding to the shoulders and the chest," while his opponent, Conservative John Major, seemed to retort, "Don't you dare touch a thread on that jacket. Margaret Thatcher designed it to be snug and by God that's the way it should stay." No wonder Paddy Ashdown, the leader of Britain's Liberal Party, looked at Tony Blair and John Major during the 1997 British election, listened to their respective platforms and then declared that there was not a whit of difference between them. Ashdown sneered that Blair and Major were engaged in "synchronized swimming."

With the fall of the Cold War walls, and the rise of the Golden Straitjacket, I see a lot of synchronized swimming when I travel the world these days. Before the 1998 German elections, in which Social Democrat Gerhard Schroeder defeated Christian Democrat Helmut Kohl, the Associated Press quoted Karl-Josef Meiers of the German Society for Foreign Affairs as saying of the two German candidates: "You can forget the labels right and left. They're all sitting in the same boat." Korea's Lee Hong Koo learned firsthand about life in the Golden Straitjacket when he served as his country's Prime Minister in the mid-1990s. "In the old days we used to say, 'History dictated this or that,' " Lee remarked to me one day. "Now we say that 'market forces' dictate this and you have to live within [those forces]. It took us time to understand what had happened. We didn't realize that the victory of the Cold War was a victory for market forces above politics. The big decisions today are whether you have a democracy or not and whether you have an open economy or not. Those are the big choices. But once you've made those big choices, politics becomes just political engineering to implement decisions in the narrow space allowed you within this system." Lee was raised in Korea's long-dominant Grand National Party. But after Korea's economic meltdown in 1997–98, when the country found it had to put on the Golden Straitjacket much more snugly if it was to continue to thrive and attract foreign investment, the Korean public spurned the veteran, old-style Korean politicians and elected longtime liberal human rights advocate Kim Dae Jung as President, from the opposition National Congress for New Politics. But Kim asked Lee to go to Washington to be his ambassador anyway. As Lee told me: "It would have been unthinkable in the past that someone like myself, who was a presidential candidate from my party and former Prime Minister and party chairman, would go to Washington as an ambassador from another party, like President Kim's. But now, with what Korea has to do to get out of this economic crisis, the differences between me and Mr. Kim are insignificant. We don't have a lot of choices." How do you say "same boat" or "synchronized swimming" in Korean?

Manmohan Singh was India's Finance Minister when his country decided in 1991 to abandon decades of statist, quasi-socialist economics and don the Golden Straitjacket. Sitting in his office in the Indian Parliament in the summer of 1998, he spoke to me of the loss of control he felt once India embarked on this route.

"We learned that there were advantages to having access to international capital markets, [but] the government's ability to deliver and control shrank the more it opened to the world. If you are operating in a globalized economy, perceptions of other participants matter much more—whether they are right or wrong. Then you have to take those perceptions and make them an important input into your decision-making . . . We have a world where our fates are linked, but [India's specific] concerns and aspirations don't get taken into account. It brings a lot more anxiety. If you are operating an exchange-rate policy, or monetary policy, your policies become an adjunct of what Alan Greenspan does. It reduces your degree of freedom, even in fiscal policies. In a world in which capital is internationally mobile, you cannot adopt rates of taxation that are far from the rates that prevail in other countries and when labor is mobile you also can't be out of line with others' wages. It has reduced the amount of maneuverability . . . I have a friend from a neighboring country who also became a finance minister. The day he got his job I called to congratulate him. He said, 'Don't congratulate me. I am only half a minister. The other half is in Washington.' "

Not every country puts on the Golden Straitjacket all the way—some just go partway or a little at a time (India, Egypt). Some put it on and take it off (Malaysia, Russia). Some try to tailor it to their specific culture and wear a few of the buttons unfastened (Germany, Japan and France). Some think they can resist its pinch altogether because they have a natural resource such as oil (Iran, Saudi Arabia). And some are so poor and isolated, with a government able to force people to accept being poor, that they can get away with dressing their people not in a Golden Straitjacket, but in a plain old straitjacket (North Korea, Cuba, Sudan, Afghanistan). But over time, this Golden Straitjacket is becoming harder and harder for countries to avoid.

Often, when I make this point to non-Americans, I get some version of the following reaction: "Don't tell us we have to put on a straitjacket and plug into the global markets. We have our own culture, our own values, and we will do it our own way at our own pace. Your thesis is way too deterministic. Why can't we all just get together and agree on a different, less restrictive model?"

To which I answer the following: "I am not saying that you have to put on the straitjacket. And if your culture and social traditions are opposed to the values embodied in that jacket, I certainly sympathize with that. But I am saying this: Today's global market system, the Fast World and the Golden Straitjacket were produced by large historical forces that have fundamentally reshaped how we communicate, how we invest and how we see the world. If you want to resist these changes, that is your business. And it should be your business. But if you think that you can resist these changes without paying an increasingly steep price, without building an increasingly high wall and without falling behind increasingly fast, then you are deluding yourself."

Here's why: The democratizations of finance, technology and information didn't just blow away all the walls protecting alternative systems—from Mao's little red book to *The Communist Manifesto* to the welfare states of Western Europe to the crony capitalism of Southeast Asia. These three democratizations also gave birth to a new power source in the world—what I call the Electronic Herd.

The Electronic Herd is made up of all the faceless stock, bond and currency traders sitting behind computer screens all over the globe, moving their money around from mutual funds to pension funds to emerging market funds, or trading on the Internet from their basements. And it also consists of the big multinational corporations who now spread their factories around the world, constantly shifting them to the most efficient, low-cost producers. This herd has grown exponentially thanks to the democratizations of finance, technology and information—so much so that today it is beginning to replace governments as the primary source of capital for both companies and countries to grow. Indeed, as countries increasingly have to run balanced budgets to fit into the Golden Straitjacket, their economies become ever more dependent on the Electronic Herd for growth capital. So to thrive in today's globalization system a country not only has to put on the Golden Straitjacket, it has to join this Electronic Herd. The Electronic Herd loves the Golden Straitjacket, because it embodies all the liberal, free-market rules the herd wants to see in a country. Those countries that put on the Golden Straitjacket and keep it on are rewarded by the herd with investment capital. Those that don't put it on are disciplined by the herd—either by the herd avoiding or withdrawing its money from that country.

Moody's Investors Service, Duff & Phelps Credit Rating Co. and Standard & Poor's are the bloodhounds for the Electronic Herd. These credit-rating agencies prowl the world, constantly sniffing over countries. They are supposed to bark loudly when they see a country slipping out of the Golden Straitjacket (although sometimes Moody's and S&P also lose the scent or get caught up in euphorias, as in Southeast Asia, and don't bark until it's too late).

This interaction among the Electronic Herd, nation-states and the Golden Straitjacket is at the center of today's globalization system. I first realized this in February 1995, on the eve of President Clinton's first visit to Canada. I was covering the White House at the time, and in preparation for the President's trip I was keeping an eye out for articles in the *Financial Times* and other papers to see what the Canadians might be talking about in advance of their first visit from the "Man from Hope." I was intrigued to find that they weren't talking about the U.S. President at all. Instead, they were talking about the visit that had just been made to

Canada by the "Man from Moody's." Canada's Parliament at the time was debating the country's budget. A team from Moody's had just come to Ottawa and read the riot act to the Canadian Finance Ministry and legislators. The Moody's team told them that if they did not get their deficit-to-GDP ratio more in line with international norms and expectations, Moody's would downgrade their triple-A credit rating, and therefore Canada and every Canadian company would have to pay higher interest rates to borrow abroad. To underscore that point Canada's Finance Ministry issued a statement declaring: "The sheer magnitude of Canada's foreign debt in relation to the size of the economy means that Canada has become excessively vulnerable to the volatile sentiments of global financial markets. We have suffered a tangible loss of economic sovereignty." For those Canadians who might not have gotten the point, Finance Minister Paul Martin put it more bluntly: "We are in hock up to our eyeballs." No, the Canadians were not the least bit interested in the Man from Hope. It was the Man from Moody's, and the Electronic Herd, who had their undivided attention.

Where did this herd come from and how did it become a force so formidable that it could intimidate and enrich nation-states every bit as much as a superpower could?

no one on the other end of the phone! I know that's hard to accept. It's like telling people there's no God. We all want to believe that someone is in charge and responsible. But the global marketplace today is an Electronic Herd of often anonymous stock, bond and currency traders and multinational investors, connected by screens and networks. And, Mahathir, don't you play dumb with me. We both know your Central Bank lost three billion dollars speculating on the British pound in the early 1990s—so don't give me that innocence crap. The Electronic Herd cuts no one any slack. It does not recognize anyone's unique circumstances. The herd knows only its own rules. But the rules of the herd are pretty consistent—they're the rules of the Golden Straitjacket. Now, the herd feeds in 180 countries, Mahathir, so it doesn't have time to look at you in detail all the time. It makes snap judgments about whether you are living by its rules, and it rewards most lavishly those countries that are transparent about what they are doing. The herd hates surprises. For years Malaysia seemed to be living by those rules, and it attracted massive amounts of direct investment and portfolio investment, which enabled you to raise your per capita income from 350 dollars to 5,000 dollars in a couple of decades. But when you started to break the rules by overborrowing and then overbuilding, well, the herd sold you out. Did you really need to build the two tallest office buildings in the world? Have you rented even half their office space? I hear not. So the herd stampeded you and left you as roadkill. The KLCI Index, your Dow Jones, fell forty-eight percent in 1997, and your currency hit a twenty-six-year low. But when that happens you don't ask the herd for mercy, you don't denounce the herd as a 'Jewish conspiracy,' you just get up, dust yourself off, put your Golden Straitjacket on a little tighter and get back with the flow of the herd. Sure, this is unfair. In some ways the herd lured you into this problem: It kept offering you all this cheap money and you took it and then overbuilt your dams, your factory capacity and your office towers. But that's what's really scary, Mahathir: *The herd is not infallible.* It makes mistakes too. It overreacts and it overshoots. But if your fundamentals are basically sound, the herd will eventually recognize this and come back. The herd is never stupid for too long. In the end, it always responds to good governance and good economic management. Hey, America had similar fluctuations when it was an emerging market, with our railroad busts and booms. You just have to manage them and build in as many shock absorbers as possible. I track the herd's movements all day on the Bloomberg screen next to my desk. Democracies vote about a government's policies once every two or four years. But the Electronic Herd votes every minute of every hour of every day. Anytime you want to know, the herd will tell you exactly how you look in a Golden Straitjacket and whether it fits well or not. I know you think that I'm the all-powerful U.S. Treasury Secretary. But, Mahathir, I live just like you—in terror of the Electronic Herd. Those idiots in the media keep putting me on the front page, as if I'm actually in charge, and I'm sitting here terrified that if our Congress refuses to grant the President authority to expand free trade, or busts the budget ceiling, the herd is going to turn against me and trample the dollar and the Dow. So let me tell you a little secret, Mahathir—and don't tell anyone else. I don't even keep a phone on my desk anymore, because I know better than anyone: *There's nobody to call.*"

Like it or not, my imaginary Treasury Secretary is basically talking the truth. Countries cannot thrive in today's world without plugging into the Electronic Herd, and they cannot survive unless they learn how to get the best out of this herd without being overwhelmed or shocked by its inevitable surges. The Electronic Herd is just like a high-voltage wire that comes into your house. In normal times it can warm you, light your home and provide many of your energy needs. But if you don't have the right electricity regulators and surge protectors, and there is a sudden power surge or drop, it can shock you, fry you to a crisp and leave you for dead.

The Electronic Herd today consists of two basic groups. One group I call the "short-horn cattle." This includes all those people involved in the buying and selling of stocks, bonds and currencies around the world, and who can and often do move their money around on a very short-term basis. The short-horn cattle are currency traders, major mutual and pension funds, hedge funds, insurance companies, bank trading rooms and individual investors. They include everyone from Merrill Lynch to Crédit Suisse to Fuji Bank to the Charles Schwab Web site, where anyone with a PC and a modem can trade online from his living room.

The other group I call the "long-horn cattle." These are the multinationals—the General Electrics, the General Motorses, the IBMs, the Intels, the Siemenses—which are increasingly involved in foreign direct investment, building factories around the world or striking international long-term production deals or alliances with overseas factories to make or assemble their products. I call them the long-horn cattle because they have to make longer-term commitments when they invest in a country. But even they now move in and out, like a herd, with surprising speed.

Though the Electronic Herd was born and nurtured in the Cold War era, its members could never gather the critical mass, speed or reach in that overly regulated, walled-up system. Most countries maintained capital controls (at least until the 1970s), so capital could not move across borders the way it can in today's globalization system. This made it much harder to get a global herd together. In the relatively closed economies of the pre-1970s Cold War system, a government's own monetary policy completely dominated the setting of its own interest rates and a government's own fiscal policy was far and away the dominant instrument for stimulating growth. Also during the Cold War, the U.S. and Soviet governments could easily justify the high taxes needed for fiscal policy by invoking the Cold War: "We need your tax dollars to fight the enemy, put a man on the moon first and build a new highway system so we can move our army around faster." At the same time, many developing countries could muddle through by milking one of the superpowers—namely, the United States, the Soviet Union or China—or international lending institutions to fund a dam, support an army or build a highway. And because the citizens of these developing countries were not nearly as aware as they are today of how everyone else in the world was living, they were ready to tolerate the lower living standards that come from having a relatively closed economy.

But with the gradual lifting of capital controls in the 1970s, the democratizations of finance, technology and information, the end of the Cold War system and the fall of walls everywhere, there suddenly emerged a vast global plain where investor herds from many different countries could roam freely. It was on this wide-open plain, later expanded into cyberspace, that the Electronic Herd could really graze, grow, multiply and eventually gather in powerful Supermarkets. By the late twentieth century the dominant fact of the global financial system was that the private sector—what I call the Electronic Herd and the Supermarkets—had become, as U.S. Treasury Secretary Larry Summers once put it, "the overwhelming source of capital for growth," replacing the public sector. This has been true both within countries and between the developed countries and developing countries. According to the U.S. Treasury, in the 1990s nearly $1.3 trillion in private capital has flowed to the emerging market economies, compared to roughly $170 billion in the 1980s and a relative pittance in the 1970s. There is no better indicator for the way in which the Supermarkets have replaced the superpowers as sources of capital for growth.

The Supermarkets are the megamarkets of Tokyo, Frankfurt, Sydney, Singapore, Shanghai, Hong Kong, Bombay, São Paulo, Paris, Zurich, Chicago, London and New York. They are where the biggest members of the Electronic Herd come together, exchange information, execute their trades and issue stocks and bonds for different companies for the herd to feed upon. According to University of Chicago globalization expert Saskia Sassen, by the end of 1997 twenty-five Supermarkets controlled 83 percent of the world's equities under institutional management and accounted for roughly half of global market capitalization—around $20.9 trillion (*Foreign Affairs*, Jan. 1999).

This Electronic Herd—and the Supermarkets where it gathers to feed and procreate—have become important international actors in the globalization system. While they cannot go to war or invade a country, like nation-states, they are able to shape the behavior of nation-states in many areas. And that is why I contend that while the Cold War system was a system based on a balance between states, the globalization system is based on a balance between states and other states, and between states and the Electronic Herd and Supermarkets. Ever since the invention of the transatlantic cable, in the pre–World War I era of globalization, some sort of Electronic Herd has been at work, but during the Cold War system it was never as important as it is today. What is new about today's herd is not so much a difference in kind as in degree. Because of globalization, today's Electronic Herd—both its short-horn cattle and its long-horn cattle—combines size, speed and diversity to a degree never seen before in history. A mouse has a tail and a Tyrannosaurus Rex has a tail. They are both called "tails," but when one swings it has a very different effect on the world around it than the other. The Electronic Herd in the first era of globalization was like the tail of a mouse. Today's Electronic Herd is like the tail of a Tyrannosaurus Rex, and when it swings it reshapes the world around it in some fundamental ways. This chapter explains how this herd has become such an irresistible source for economic growth today and, at the same time, such an intimidating force that it can even topple governments when it swings.

The Short-Horn Cattle

The first thing that strikes one today about the short-horn cattle is the incredible diversity of financial products they can now feed on. The cornucopia of stocks and bonds, commodities and futures contracts, options and derivatives being offered from scores of different countries and markets around the world means that you can make a bet on almost anything today.

Indeed, when I look at the feed bag now being offered the Electronic Herd, I am always reminded of that scene from *Guys and Dolls* in which Nathan Detroit wants to bet Sky Masterson on whether Mindy's sells more cheesecake than strudel. It goes like this: Nathan Detroit: "I would be interested to hear. Offhand, would you say that Mindy's sells more cheesecake or more strudel?"

Sky says that going on his own preference, he would guess that Mindy's sells more cheesecake than strudel. What follows is a spirited exchange about how much Sky would be willing to bet on cheesecake over strudel—with Nathan, who has already checked with the kitchen and knows that strudel sells better than cheesecake, trying to lure Sky into putting his money where his stomach is. Now, Sky Masterson is a man who loves to bet. Normally, he would bet on cheese spreads as quickly as a Salomon Brothers bond trader would bet on interest-rate spreads. But Sky smells a setup. Nathan is just too eager to make a thousand-dollar bet.

So rather than taking it, Sky offers him some wisdom instead. "Nathan, let me tell you a story," he says. "On the day when I left home to make my way in the world my daddy took me to one side. 'Son,' my daddy says to me, 'I am sorry I am not able to bankroll you to a very large stock. But not having the necessary lettuce to get you rolling, instead I am going to stake you to some very valuable advice. One of these days in your travels a guy is going to show you a brand-new deck of cards on which the seal is not yet broken. Then this guy is going to offer to bet you that he can make the Jack of Spades jump out of this deck and squirt cider in your ear. But, son, you do not accept this bet, because as sure as you stand there you are going to wind up with an ear full of cider.' Now, Nathan, I do not suggest that you have been clocking Mindy's cheesecake . . ."

Nathan: "Would I do such a thing?"

Sky: "However" (cupping his hand over Nathan's bow tie), "if you are really looking for some action, I will bet you the same thousand bucks that you cannot name the color tie you have on. Have we got a bet?"

Nathan: "No bet."

Then, looking down at his bow tie, Nathan exclaims: "Polka dots! In the whole world nobody but Nathan Detroit could blow a thousand bucks on polka dots!"

Well, if Nathan and Sky were around today there would probably be a bond they could buy that would be based on the sales of both cheesecake and strudel at Mindy's. And there would probably be some customized financial instrument they could buy in order to hedge their bets, whether they put their money on strudel or cheesecake or polka dots. Because of the democratization of finance, and the explosion of securitization, almost anything today can be turned into a bond. You can even issue bonds in yourself and your own unique talents, as the singer David Bowie did. He raised $55 million in Bowie bonds in 1997, backed by his projected royalties. *The New York Times* said it all in a headline, "You too can be rated AAA."

My friend Lesley Goldwasser, a leading bond trader on Wall Street, is an expert in turning yet-to-be-made movies into bonds. She explains how it works: "Suppose you are a home mortgage company in Minneapolis and you have a hundred home mortgages out in the local market. And those hundred home mortgages involve an outlay by the mortgage company of a hundred million dollars and they bring in one million dollars a month in interest and principal payments. That mortgage company can bundle all its home mortgages together and then issue them as bonds that you or I can buy for a thousand dollars each. The advantage for the mortgage company is that it can get its hundred million dollars back right away, without having to wait for all these people to pay off their mortgages over thirty years. The advantage for the bondholders is that they are paid off by the cash flow from the interest and principal payments that come in each month, and the interest rate will be a few points higher than a money market or savings account would pay. What's more, the bonds will be backed up by actual homes, and since there are usually several hundred in each bundle, even if a few default the odds are that most of the others will pay off their loans accordingly. Well, people figured that if you could bundle home mortgages, why not bundle Hollywood movies— even unmade Hollywood movies. Say you are a movie company and you don't have any credit rating. What my investment bank will do is bundle together ten of your movie ideas. They don't even have to be in the production stage yet, just in the pipeline. We will then do a statistical analysis of the probability of how ten such movies will perform, based on historical precedents: One will be a megahit, one will be a big hit, two will be minor hits, two will be flops and four will more or less break even. On the basis of that probability analysis we'll figure out how much money you will earn over a period of five years. Let's say we think the movies will cost five hundred million dollars to make and will together earn six hundred million. Then we will advance your movie company four hundred million at an interest rate equal to that on a three-year Treasury bond, plus another percentage point or two. Your movie company will have to come up with the other hundred million in production costs itself. Then we'll take that four hundred million we loaned your movie company and chop it up into bonds, selling for a thousand dollars apiece, that you and I can buy. The interest and principal on those bonds will be paid by the movie receipts as they start to come in. Presto, your movie company, which has no credit rating and only a small amount of capital, gets money to make its films that it would never be able to raise from a bank, and you, the investor, get to buy a piece of it and earn a little higher return than you normally would at the bank. That's how it works. As long as what you are doing, manufacturing or performing produces a cash flow that can be statistically predicted over a period of time, we can turn it into a bond."

And it doesn't matter whether it is the cheesecake sales at Mindy's, home mortgages, credit card receivables, bad debts, auto loans, commercial loans, remakes of *Titanic*, Brazilian corporate debt, Lebanese government T-bills, auto financing for General Motors or the income stream of rock star David Bowie. The more capital controls have fallen between countries, the more everyone is offering everything for sale as stocks, bonds or derivatives. This move toward securitizing everything has "fundamentally changed the character of the credit markets," says the veteran Wall Street economist Henry Kaufman. It's easy to see why. In the old days your parents' home mortgage, car loan, credit card debts, life insurance policies or even the loans taken out by the government of Brazil from your parents' bank were never traded on an open market. They were carried on the books of your parents' bank or insurance companies at their original face value, and they were usually held by those institutions as assets until they reached their date of maturity. But as the 1980s rolled around and all of these things got securitized, packaged together and then sold as bonds to you and me and my Aunt Bev, they could be traded, and their prices would fluctuate every day in the marketplace—depending on how these bonds seemed to be performing, depending on general economic conditions and depending on their rates of return compared to other assets. The net effect, says Kaufman, is that this securitization has opened up literally trillions of dollars' worth of assets—which either were never traded before or no one ever dreamed could be turned into bonds—"to the harsh glare of changing market circumstances." All of this together has added incredible diversity to the markets—giving the Electronic Herd so many more things to feed on than ever before—and has added an element of fluctuation to assets that were never previously traded.

The people who can tell you this best are some of the lead bulls in the Electronic Herd. They remember what it was like to graze in the old fenced-in days of the Cold War. Leon Cooperman, the former director of research for Goldman Sachs, and now a hedge-fund manager at his own firm, Omega Advisors, remarked to me in 1998: "During my whole career at Goldman Sachs—1967 to 1991—I never owned a foreign stock or a foreign emerging market. Now I have hundreds of millions of dollars in Russia, Brazil, Argentina and Chile, and I worry constantly about the dollar-yen rate. Every night before I go to bed I call in for the dollar-yen quote, and to find out what the Nikkei is doing and what the Hang Seng Index is doing. We have bets in all these markets. Right now Paul over there"—he points to one of his traders, who is looking down at a hand-held device that provides him real-time quotes for all key stock and bond indexes—"is long on the Canadian dollar. We have bets all over the place. I would not have worried about any of these twenty years ago. Now I have to worry about all of them."

Cooperman then pulls out a copy of that day's *Wall Street Journal* and starts reading the different bets he can make: "Let's see here . . . Eurodollars, U.S. Treasury bonds, S&P futures, British pounds, soybeans, heating oil, light sweet crude, Singapore bonds, Venezuela bonds, NASDAQ 100, Japan index, Dow index, mutual funds, utility bonds, high-yield bonds, corporate bonds, intermediate bonds . . ." As I get up to leave a minute later, he is still reading the list.

This diversity of investment instruments and opportunities has been a godsend for both developed and developing countries and companies. It has enabled some of them to grow at previously unimaginable speeds. As *The Economist* once observed: "Poor countries, with large investment needs, are no longer hamstrung by a lack of capital. Savers are not confined to their home market, but can [now] seek investment opportunities that offer the highest returns around the world" (Oct. 25, 1997). Today, every major U.S. mutual-fund family offers at least one exotic "emerging market" investing option.

When you have so many different products, with so much information always available at such high speeds, your ability to get an edge on the competition and seize on an opportunity before everyone else sees it gets smaller and smaller. So investors have to do all sorts of different things now to find that little edge that might steal a march on the rest of the market.

"When I joined Goldman Sachs in 1967," Cooperman recalled, "I was the head of research and I hired analysts. In those days, a typical analyst covered seventy-five companies and maybe six different industries. I was recently talking to one of the analysts I had hired back then and he told me he was terribly overworked now because he had to cover twelve companies. I just laughed. Only twelve companies? But you have to look into those twelve companies so much more deeply now in order to get some edge that it takes up all of his time. It is the same with economic data. [In the old days] when the government would issue the unemployment number all everyone looked at was the rate of unemployment. Then they started to look underneath that general number at the payroll figures—are total payrolls up or down?—because that might indicate something [you could bet on]. Then they started looking at the composition of payroll figures. Who is up and who is down and what does that tell you? The amount of work you have to do to gain an edge to make money now is just so much greater."

I know a hedge-fund trader who spends hours poring over weather reports. Weather reports! The idea, he explained to me, "is to look for unconventional trends and how they might affect economic data. For instance, the fact that we had no winter in 1998 may have given us a stronger-looking economy than really is the case, so I might find a way to use that knowledge to make a certain bet on what will happen with interest rates. Or take the fact that we had terrible mudslides on the West Coast in the exact week when economic data was collected by the government for some major statistics, like the consumer price index. Since this economic data only matters at the margin, a few mudslides at the right time in a major state, like California, can make a difference in the statistics. So I might say, 'Gee, the stock of Home Depot, which sells all kinds of home-repair products, would probably benefit from mudslides and tornadoes.' Or I might notice that there happened to be a huge snowstorm the week that the government put together the unemployment numbers. And that might lead me to conclude that there is really a blip in those numbers. Maybe everyone is expecting 250,000 new nonfarm jobs to be created, but because of the weather, the number actually came in at only 150,000 new jobs, which suggests that the economy might be slowing and is softer than people thought, but in reality it is not, because this weather anomaly is reflected in the numbers. But because the numbers came in that way you know that people might conclude the economy is slowing and interest rates might be coming down and that would be good for bonds. So you might go long on bonds in advance of the unemployment numbers—just based on the weather report—ride them up when the unemployment numbers come in lower than expected, but sell them out quickly afterward, before the next month's numbers come in, because they will show that the previous month's numbers were anomalous due to the weather. It's an opportunity to make a few bucks by just using the weather report. You could use the weather that way to speculate on oil futures, heating oil or interest rates, electricity futures, natural gas futures, consumer price index futures, corn, soybeans, gasoline, unleaded gasoline, Brent crude, gas oil, hogs, copper, gold, silver . . ."

So many markets, so much information, so little edge. So when all else fails, don't call your broker, call the weatherman.

In order to make money in such a market, the short-horn cattle need not only that tiny extra edge: they also need to make larger and larger bets on top of it. Imagine a billion dollars stacked on the head of a pin and you have the right idea. This is usually done by fund managers employing exotic trading products—swaps, futures, forwards, options, derivatives and indexations—and then leveraging them by borrowing even more money than their investors have given them in order to expand each of their bets. This has contributed to the huge increase in the volume of transactions sloshing around the world every day. As a fund manager, when you win big now, you can win very, very big, and when you lose now, you can also lose very, very big. That is one reason why in recent years we have seen whole brokerage houses (Barings bank being the most prominent) brought down by the bets of a single broker using leverage. It is also what exaggerates the swings of the Tyrannosaurus Rex's tail. A friend of mine at a major American investment bank told me one of the bank's clients was a hedge fund that had $200 million in original capital. Through the miracle of leveraging, though, this hedge fund acquired $900 million in Russian bonds and $5 billion worth of Sallie Mae bonds. (These are bonds made up of bundled American student loans.) When Russia crashed in August 1998, this hedge fund lost virtually all its capital in Russia. So what did it do? It suddenly sold a large position of American student-loan bonds to pay off its Russian losses, sending the student-loan bond market

into a temporary tailspin and destroying some of my friend's positions in
that market, which should have had nothing to do with Russia.

Not only is the herd's feed bag more diverse, but so too is the herd itself, particularly the short-horn cattle. As Kaufman notes: "The relative
weight of traditional commercial banks, savings and loans and insurance
companies has diminished. Instead, a new breed of institutional participants has come to the fore. These institutions are distinguished by their
emphasis on short-term investment performance, their heavy use of leverage and their ability to move in and out of markets, whether equities,
bonds, currencies or commodities, wherever they believe the returns will
be the highest." The most prominent of these new players are the so-
called hedge funds, which bring together large pools of cash from
wealthy individuals and institutions, then magnify that pool by borrowing
from the banks to make high-risk, high-reward bets on currencies, stocks
and bonds around the world. But what has happened in recent years,
notes Kaufman, is that many major banks, brokerage firms, investment
banks, insurance companies, corporate treasury departments of major
multinationals and even the trading rooms of major world central banks
have felt a need to establish their own hedge-fund-like trading operations.
It is not unusual for a major investment bank to be the broker for a hedge
fund's trades and also to be mimicking that hedge fund's trades with its
own private trading operations.

Naturally, the more the fences come down, the more people start
roaming into areas they know nothing about. Imagine it working like this:
The Thai Farmers' Savings & Loan Bank gets a call from the Bangkok office of First Global Investment Bank, headquartered in the Cayman Islands, and they say, "Hey, you guys should really be in Russian bonds.
They're paying twenty percent, and even if the ruble devalues a bit, you
can still make a fortune." Suddenly the Thai Farmers' Savings & Loan is
sitting with $20 million in Russian bonds on its books, and when those
bonds tank, a bank that was chartered to make loans to Thai rice farmers
goes under. The world was shocked and amazed by how many Korean
banks were holding Russian bonds when Russia started to collapse in
1998. When credit becomes easily available, what tends to happen is that
"the marginal moron," the person who would never get funded in a more
cautious or recessionary period, is able to get money from investors and
banks and make bets along with the more serious players. These marginal
morons can really exaggerate swings in the global market.

The combination of the Supermarkets and the Internet has made global investing fast and easy not simply for the big guys, but for Mom and Pop as well, who can now trade from their bedroom through an online broker. Competition between these online brokers is now so intense that they charge virtually nothing to execute a trade. Because global investing has become so much easier and more accessible, it can lull people into thinking that every market in the world operates the same as Wall Street. As Treasury Secretary Larry Summers likes to say: "It is like when you build better highways, people tend to drive faster. And actually more people end up dying in auto accidents on these new highways, because they make a mistake in estimating how fast they can drive, and they end up driving much faster than they should."

So First Global Investment Bank calls the Thai Farmers' Savings & Loan and says, "You really should be in Turkish bonds. You could make a killing right now." The Thai banker says, "Turkish bonds are paying twenty-five percent, eh? I didn't know Turkey had a bond market. Sure, I'll take a few million. If you say so." But here's the rub. When people hear "Turkish bond market," they think, "Oh, Wall Street has a bond market, Frankfurt has a bond market, Tokyo has a bond market and now Turkey has a bond market. Isn't that nice." But while the Turkish bond market may quack like a market, walk like a market and look like a market, it is nothing like the Wall Street bond market. And you discover this when your Turkish bonds go down and you want to sell them. That's when you find out that the Turkish market is so small that when just a few major players want to sell their bonds, there are no buyers, there is no liquidity on the downside and therefore no exit. As Kaufman notes, globalization of markets creates the illusion that all markets "are efficient, liquid and symmetrical" and that there is perfect information and transparency in each market. Far from it. Just think about this: The total value of all Microsoft stock in late 1999 was around $600 billion. At that time, this one U.S. stock was worth far more than all the stocks on all the emerging-market stock markets in all the rest of the world put together.

And everybody is playing. In 1980, 4.6 million American households owned shares in mutual funds. By the year 2000, more than half the U.S. population was invested in the stock market, either through equities they purchased themselves or through mutual funds or through their pension-retirement plans. I did a short interview one day in mid-1999 for CNBC. I was listening to the show with half an ear before I went on the air. Appearing on the show before me was this stock guru who was dispensing advice about different stocks to callers telephoning from around the country. At one point the announcer said that the next caller was "Adam from Michigan." He sounded like a little boy. So Ron Insanta of CNBC asked him how old he was. Adam said he was twelve years old! He asked the guru, "I recently bought CVS [pharmacy stock] and I wonder how much it could go up?" (I found this a revealing but rather disturbing phenomenon.) Mutual-fund assets in retirement plans, such as IRAs, grew from $412 billion in 1992 to $1.6 trillion in 1997. Of these mutual-fund assets, about 10 percent were invested in global stocks. For the first time in American history both Joe Six-pack and Billionaire Bob are watching CNBC to see how their shares in the market are faring. Indeed, a 1998 commercial by Charles Schwab, the discount brokerage firm, shows a middle-class couple, Marion and Rick, sitting on a couch talking about their summer vacation.

Marion: "When we were traveling cross-country and we stopped at a place, they had the Business Channel. We started watching and the market was going down and we said that there were these stocks that we wanted to buy and from the road we called up . . ."

Rick: "Called up Schwab because we didn't have a phone modem in our motor home, so we couldn't trade online. Where were we?"

Marion: "Utah."

Rick: "Utah?"

Marion: "We were in Utah."

Rick: "On a pay phone talking to Schwab."

Marion: "Trying to get . . ."

Rick: "Buying the stocks. And there was a feeling of exhilaration. Hey, we've done it . . . And then we get back in the motor home, traveled on our way."

Marion: "And those purchases have done well."

Rick and Marion, welcome to the Electronic Herd. I am glad they did well, but the fact is this proliferation of investment instruments has lulled a lot of Ricks and Marions into markets they have no business being in. I cannot prove this, but I would guess that never before in history have more people invested more money in more places that they cannot find on the map. As Leon Cooperman points out: "In the last five years the guy who would normally take his savings and buy Treasury bills, to make sure he never lost any of that income, has gone out and bought bonds instead. And the guy who would normally buy bonds, because he was ready to take a little more risk to get a little more return, has gone out and bought emerging-market bonds, from places like Russia or Brazil, and the guy who would normally buy emerging-market bonds is now out buying emerging-market stocks. What has to happen, and it will happen, is that some people who have moved up this risk ladder will lose a lot of their money and then they will move back."

Global integration has raced ahead of education. Thanks to globalization, we all definitely know "of" one another more than ever, but we still don't know that much "about" one another. What's scary is that the diversity of players in the Electronic Herd has so expanded that it's not just the dentist in New Jersey who doesn't know what's going on, it's even some guys running big emerging-market funds. My favorite quote in this regard was the unnamed hedge-fund manager who told Moisés Naím, editor of *Foreign Policy* magazine, after the 1995 Mexican debt crisis: "We went into Latin America not knowing anything about the place. Now we are leaving without knowing anything about it."

While we are on the subject of the diversity of the Electronic Herd, there is one other critically important thing we should always keep in mind about it—this herd is not simply an exogenous force. It is not just made up of stateless offshore money funds, Internet investors from abroad and distant Supermarkets. It is also made up of locals in every country that has opened itself to the herd. What gives the herd its power is not only the fact that when capital controls in a country are lifted foreigners can easily come in and buy and sell currency, stocks and bonds. *It is the fact that the locals can easily go out!* The biggest untold secret about the Electronic Herd is that most stampedes don't begin with a hedge fund on Wall Street or a big bank in Frankfurt. They begin with a local banker, local financier or local money manager moving his money out of a country by converting from his local currency into dollars or betting against (shorting) his own country's currency in the forward market. The 1998 IMF study "Hedge Funds and the Financial Market Dynamics" noted that careful analyses of the 1994–95 Mexican peso crisis all found that "domestic residents and not international investors" played the leading role in that crisis. In a world of globalized financial markets, the IMF concluded the following: Foreign investors managing internationally diversified portfolios may find it difficult to keep abreast of conditions in myriad countries. The smaller the emerging market, the less the incentive for large investors to do so. Consequently, domestic residents with a comparative advantage in accessing and processing the relevant information about that market may often be the first to take a position against a fixed currency. And the deregulation of domestic financial markets and international financial transactions, which long inhibited position-taking by domestic residents, makes it much easier now for them to do so. In other words, it was *local* Mexican financiers, local Indonesian speculators, local Thai bankers who began the stampedes against their own currencies, stocks and bonds—with the rest of the Electronic Herd following. And of course this makes sense, because the local folks are almost always going to be better informed through family, friends and business contacts about what's really happening inside their country and therefore they are going to be the first to move to where the grass is safer. And today they can do it very easily—without having to smuggle out money or get some friend to open a foreign bank account for them, as was the case in the old days of capital controls.

Richard Medley, who does political and economic risk analysis for many international banks and hedge funds, told me he started warning his clients about a possible downturn in Asian markets and currencies five months before it actually happened in 1997, not because he was such a genius but because he was listening to the local herds. "The first thing I look for," he explained, "is when local financial institutions are demanding loans in a foreign currency instead of their local currency. If a Thai bank won't lend to a Thai businessman in Thai baht, but insists instead on lending in dollars or yen, it means it knows that something is wrong with the Thai currency and it might not hold its value. You have to depend on this sort of anecdotal evidence, because in many countries the economic data lags. In highly personalized economies, like those in Asia, I always assume that the locals know more than I do."

The Chinese government has been reluctant to make its currency fully convertible, as its neighbors have done, not just because it's afraid that it could not control the investments that would come in from outside but because Beijing fears it wouldn't be able to control what its own people would transfer abroad. They have good reason: A huge black market already exists in China for speculating against the Chinese currency. An American financial wire service reporter in Shanghai told me of a conversation he had with a Chinese friend who was complaining about the "conspiracy" of Western bankers and hedge funds who sold out the currencies of Thailand, Malaysia, South Korea and Indonesia during the 1997–98 Asian economic crisis.

"Why are they doing this to us?" the Chinese businessman asked this
American reporter.

"Tell me," the American financial reporter answered, "have you sold
any [Chinese] yuan for dollars lately?"

"Yes, I have," the Chinese businessman conceded. "I'm a little worried about the situation."

Remember: When the Electronic Herd starts to stampede, the first
bull is always a local.

Not only is the Electronic Herd bigger and more diverse than ever before but it is also much, much faster and much, much more connected. Joseph Sassoon, a partner in Goldman Sachs's London office,
joined the Electronic Herd back in 1982. "In London in 1982, because
we were five or six hours ahead of New York, we usually didn't find out
what the Dow closed at in New York until we came in the next morning,"
he once told me. "A few people had Quotron machines, but that was it.
Goldman Sachs thought it was really smart back then, because some guy
in the New York office realized one day that he could pay a kid to come
into the office at three-thirty a.m. New York time. The kid would make a
photocopy of the two key *Wall Street Journal* columns, 'Heard on the
Street' and 'Abreast of the Market'—stock-tip columns that often moved
the market—and then he would relay the contents to London. It gave us
a four-hour head start on all the other London brokerage firms, so we
could go out and push stocks with our clients that were being touted in
New York before our competition ever knew about it, because they were
waiting until their New York offices opened before getting the *Journal*. It
took them a while to figure out what we were doing. This was just 1982,
but when I tell people around our office about it today, they look at me
like I'm telling them about Great-grandpa."

No wonder. Walk around a hedge-fund office in New York today and
you will see people carrying around palm-held market monitors wherever
they go, which track any market, any stock or bond, in real time, so they
can be connected even when they go to the bathroom, let alone go home.
The wheels today have been so thoroughly greased that huge amounts of
what economist David Hale calls "gypsy capital" can move around the
world to exploit buying and selling opportunities anywhere, with transaction costs that are virtually zero, transmission costs that are virtually zero
and speeds that are virtually instantaneous. The state of play can be

summed up by the punch line from an ad that Crédit Suisse/First Boston began running in 1998 for its service, called Prime Trade, that offers the fastest possible execution of any trade in any of the world's listed derivatives exchanges. The ad says: "Prime Trade: Any market, Any time, Anywhere."

The fact that so many more people now have the instantaneous connections and information to trade from anywhere all the time is another reason today's Electronic Herd is so much bigger and potentially more volatile. It was long assumed that the more information investors had, the more stable this would make markets. But, in fact, the opposite seems to be true. I have learned that firsthand. Many passenger planes in the United States today provide a GTE cell-phone service, with a phone plugged into the middle seat in each row. In 1999, GTE connected those cell phones to the Dow Jones Industrial Average, the American Stock Exchange and the NASDAQ. So you can now sit in your seat, if you happen to be flying during trading hours, and watch in real time what the U.S. markets are doing every minute. In fact, if you are in the middle seat, you almost can't avoid watching it. The little screen on the back of the phone that tracks the markets is right in front of you. I found myself on a flight to Colorado one day tracking a stock I owned. I used a device in the GTE phone that enables you to get a quote on any stock off Bloomberg by punching in the stock's initials, using the letter keys on the phone's dialing pad. On this three-hour flight from Washington to Denver, I checked my stock five times, and sold it from a pay phone in Denver airport as soon as I landed. I never would have had the information or the ability to track and sell that stock with such immediacy a decade ago.

But that isn't necessarily going to make markets more stable. Edward Chancellor, in his book on the history of financial speculation, *Devil Take the Hindmost*, explains why the conventional wisdom was so wrong, about the impact of more information on the stability of the Electronic Herd. Most commentators, he noted, "viewed advances in information technology as a boon. If markets were inherently efficient, they would become even more so when supplied with better information. They might even become rather dull, like a reliable motorcar. In fact, there is little historical evidence to suggest that improvements in communications create docile financial markets or better informed investment behavior. If anything, the opposite appears to be the case. In the past, the wider availability of financial information and improvements in communications have tended to attract impulsive new players to the speculative game: the first generation of daily newspapers stimulated the South Sea Bubble, the new 'money market' columns of the British newspapers contributed to the mining mania of 1825, railways facilitated railway speculations in the 1840s, just as the ticker tape assisted stock market gambling in the Gilded Age and radio programmes in the 1920s excited a later generation of speculators. More recently, the Internet has brought the stock market into the home, where it has thrived . . . This has led to the appearance of hordes of 'day traders,' amateur speculators who operate mostly from their homes, using their computers to access the cheap share-dealing services provided by on-line brokerages. By the summer of 1998, five million Americans had accounts with Internet discount brokerages and around a million of them were day traders. Average turnover on these on-line accounts was twelve times heavier than at conventional brokerages. Some traders reportedly carried out a thousand trades a day." Indeed, NASDAQ market-makers will tell you that it isn't the long-horn cattle in the Electronic Herd—the big mutual funds—who push Internet stocks up and down like a roller coaster. It's the little short-horn day-traders, impulsively buying 200 or 300 shares at a time on one whiff of news or another. Most of them don't even know the companies they are buying or selling, but are just trading symbols.

To be sure, if the herd comes your way, it can, in short order, rain billions and billions of dollars on your country's stock and bond markets, as well as directly into plants and factories. That is why more and more countries are interested in doing whatever it takes to plug into this herd. But when for political, economic or social reasons markets in one country become unstable or weak, the Electronic Herd can transform what might have been a brutal but limited market adjustment downward into something much more painful and exaggerated, and it can also transmit instability much more quickly between markets, and from bad markets to good markets.

As Alan Greenspan has noted in speeches, the very same financial globalization "which has induced such dramatic increases in private capital flows has also exhibited significantly improved capacities to transmit ill-advised investments." The Federal Reserve chairman adds that "one can scarcely imagine the size of losses ($1 billion) of a single trader employing modern techniques that contributed to the demise of Barings in 1995 being accomplished in the paper-trade environment of earlier decades. Clearly, our productivity to create losses has improved measurably in recent years." Or as Egypt's Minister of Economy, Yousef Boutros-

Ghali, likes to say: "In the old days you panicked in a room with a hundred bankers, now you panic everywhere. Panic has been democratized." There is only one saving grace with all this. What goes around faster comes around faster, but then it also goes around faster again. While problems can come faster, so too can solutions—*provided your country does the right things.* When everything is speeded up, the world has a shorter memory. Mexico stiffs creditors in 1995 and by 1998 it's a darling of international investors again, and no one remembers 1995. Korea nearly goes bankrupt in 1997 and by 2000 Wall Street is lining up again to buy Korean bonds.

The Long-Horn Cattle

While it is often the big short-horn cattle of the Electronic Herd, such as George Soros, who make the headlines these days, the long-horn cattle play an increasingly important role. The long-horn cattle are multinational companies who engage in what is known as "foreign direct investment"—meaning that they don't just invest in a developing country's stocks or bonds, but rather invest directly in its factories, utilities, energy plants and a whole host of other projects that take time to plan and build and can't be pulled out overnight. The long-horn cattle are companies such as Ford, Intel, Compaq, Enron and Toyota. Thanks to globalization they are investing more money abroad in more ways and in more countries than ever before.

Under the Cold War system, when countries often protected their local markets with tariff walls, multinational companies would make long-term multimillion-dollar investments in big-market countries primarily for the purpose of jumping over those walls. In other words, Toyota would get around the American quota on Japanese auto imports by building a factory in the United States that would make Toyotas to be sold almost exclusively in the U.S. market, and Ford would so the same in Japan. In order to survive in a world of walls, multinationals had to build factories in key markets so that they could become better *local* producers and sellers in that market.

Once the democratizations of technology, finance and information blew away many of the Cold War walls, however, the long-horn cattle in the Electronic Herd had a much greater, and somewhat different, incentive to build factories abroad. Increasingly, there was a single, open global marketplace, and cyberspace, where a multinational company could sell anything anywhere or make anything anywhere. This has sharpened competition and squeezed profit margins in many industries. As a result, every big multinational needs to try to sell globally, in order to make up in volume for shrinking profit margins, and it needs to try to produce globally—by slicing up its production chain and outsourcing each segment to the country that can do it the cheapest and most efficiently—in order to keep manufacturing costs down and remain competitive. This has led to more multinationals investing in more cost-lowering production facilities abroad, or making alliances with cheaper subcontractors abroad— not to survive in a world of walls, *but to survive in a world without walls.* In the era of globalization, multinationals increasingly need to expand overseas, not because it's the only way to be an effective local producer in these countries, but because it's now the only way to become an effective global producer.

USA *Today*'s Kevin Maney had a story in the April 24, 1997, edition that captured how IBM is now using all sorts of foreign partners and subsidiaries to become a better, smarter global producer in a world without walls. Maney reported the following: "A group of computer programmers at Tsinghua University in Beijing is writing software using Java technology. They work for IBM. At the end of each day, they send their work over the Internet to an IBM facility in Seattle. There, programmers build on it and use the Internet to zap it 5,222 miles to the Institute of Computer Science in Belarus and the Software House Group in Latvia. From there, the work is sent east to India's Tata Group, which passes the software back to Tsinghua by morning in Beijing, back to Seattle and so on in a great global relay that never ceases until the project is done. 'We call it Java Around the Clock,' says John Patrick, vice president of Internet Technology for IBM. 'It's like we've created a forty-eight-hour day through the Internet.' "

In the 1970s, the Canadian-owned shoe company Bata might have had a dozen shoe factories in key markets around the world, but each would have been targeting that local market, adapting to the local styles and demands and selling virtually 100 percent of its output in that market. Today, by contrast, Nike can design a shoe in Oregon and transmit by fax or E-mail its latest design adjustments overnight to its factories and subcontractors all over Asia who will start turning out a new track shoe for global consumption the next day.

While it is true that the Fords, Ciscos, Nikes and Toyotas—the long-horn cattle—don't move their capital around as fast as the short-horn cattle, they are shifting it from country to country faster than many people realize. A lot of the foreign investing that the long-horn cattle do these days is not building factories anymore. It is developing alliances with locally owned factories, which serve as affiliates, subcontractors and partners of the multinational firms, and these production relationships can be and are moved around from country to country, producer to producer, with increasing velocity in search of the best tax deals and most efficient and low-cost labor forces. Cisco has thirty-four factories around the world manufacturing its equipment, but only two of them are owned by Cisco. The others are alliance partners intimately tied into the Cisco design, inventory and marketing system through the Internet. Cisco calls them "virtual manufacturing" facilities. Thanks to the Web, by which they are tied together, they behave as though they are one wholly owned factory, but they are not, and production can be shifted instantaneously between them.

The long-horn cattle can and do play off every developing country against the others. Each of these countries is desperate for multinational investments, because it is the quickest way for them to make technological leaps. Nike first established its Asian production facilities in Japan, but when that got too expensive it hopped over to Korea and then went to Thailand, China, the Philippines, Indonesia and Vietnam.

"They are a necessary good," says Brazilian management consultant Joel Korn, speaking about multinational firms. "Latin America is still highly dependent on external capital, because domestic savings are simply not enough to sustain high economic growth. So we need direct foreign investment. [These long-horn cattle] also bring international standards and technologies and help us become attuned to the patterns of different markets, and they also bring foreign partnerships, which themselves bring technology transfers and new markets of their own. If you don't let [the long-horn cattle] in today, it's as if you're living alone on a different planet."

Although this sort of globalized production began in the Cold War system, it has vastly expanded in the era of globalization, as the long-horn cattle have been very busy procreating. According to the World Bank, the share of total world output by the local affiliated factories of multinational corporations has gone from 4.5 percent of world gross domestic product in 1970 to double that amount today. While these percentages may seem small, the dollars behind them are enormous, because we are talking about total world output. In 1987, foreign direct investment in developing countries accounted for 0.4 percent of their total GDP. Today it is over 2 percent and it is now spread out, not just to the ten big emerging markets, but all over the world. If you look at all U.S.-owned foreign affiliates—companies such as Ford Motor Mexico, for instance—and ask what percentage of their sales were exported in 1966 and what percentage were sold to the local markets, the answer would be 20 percent was exported in 1966 and 80 percent locally consumed. Today, 40 percent is exported and only 60 percent locally consumed. No wonder Craig Barrett, the chairman of Intel, told me he has a string of ambassadors and statesmen from all over the world calling on him every month in Silicon Valley, with one message: "Come hither with your factory."

George St. Laurent is chairman of Vitech, the Brazilian-based computer manufacturer that he founded in Bahia state in northeastern Brazil, and he is a typical long-horn member of the Electronic Herd. He knows that in his own way he has a lot of power today, and he explained to me one afternoon in Brazil that he does not hesitate to let the Brazilian authorities know exactly what he needs if he is going to keep his computer company there, with all the jobs and technology transfers that come with it. He said: "I have to have a stable currency to continue to attract foreign capital, so they have to have their budget in balance and inflation under control and the size of the government down. One of our primary goals is to bring investment capital here, and the capital won't come in if it is not sure at what value it is going to be when it wants to go out. [Moreover,] I have to be convinced that the politicians have the same sense of client-supplier relations as I do. If you are my customer, to get you to buy my computer notebook I will get on my hands and knees. The politicians here don't like to think like that, because they are not used to ever having to assume the role of the vendor. They are used to having everyone come sit at the foot of their throne, and they dole out goodies and power as they see fit."

Indeed, as St. Laurent suggests, the increasing power of this Electronic Herd is something many traditional leaders are just beginning to understand and adjust to. I first discovered this while visiting Mexico at the depths of the 1995 peso crash. My education began on the flight in. I was feverishly filling out the customs form they passed out on the plane, when line 3 stumped me. It said you had to find and circle your occupation and listed nine different choices. "Columnist" was not one of them, but there was "farmer," "driver of a vehicle," "livestock raiser" and then one that just leapt out at me. It said: "bondholder." That word told me everything about Mexico's predicament at the time. Mexico had become so dependent for its economic growth on foreign investors who would buy its government and commercial bonds that foreign "bondholders" had their own category on the customs form.

Unfortunately for Mexico, most of the people who were checking that box at that time were going out, along with their money, not coming in. When I went to interview a shell-shocked official of Mexico's central bank, he asked me about these global bondholders who were dumping Mexican paper. "Why were they so mad? Why the vengeance?" he asked. I didn't know how to tell him that hell hath no fury like an American mutual-fund holder with a cell phone who just saw his investment devalued. Then I went to see Enrique del Val Blanco, an official of Mexico's Human Services Ministry, and he sounded to me like a man living through *Invasion of the Body Snatchers.* He told me: "Everyone feels their life is determined by someone outside, and everyone wants to know who is this person? Who is this force? We thought that we were on the path to the First World and suddenly something went wrong. One minute the World Bank and IMF were saying Mexico was the best example. Now we are the worst example. What did we do? We are losing control. If we don't find another type of development, we are finished. We surrender."

That same day I went across town to the Los Pinos presidential palace to see President Ernesto Zedillo, who was still reeling from the peso collapse. I don't remember much of what he said, but I will never forget the scene. I and my colleagues from the *Times* were ushered into the palace by a guard and told to go upstairs and down some halls to the President's office. It seemed as if no one was around. We went through one set of doors, then another, and then another, until we came to a secretary's small desk and she pointed us to the President's cavernous office. We walked in, and there, sitting alone at a table in the corner, was President Zedillo, listening to Tchaikovsky's "1812 Overture" on the office stereo, and looking a lot like Napoleon after Waterloo.

In the last decade a whole generation of postcolonial leaders—Zedillo, Mahathir, Suharto, even Boris Yeltsin—have found out what it is like to get hammered by the Electronic Herd. It is not pretty. The herd proved to be unlike any of their familiar domestic enemies. They could not arrest it, censor it, ban it, bribe it and often could not even see it. Some, like Zedillo, just bowed to its dictates. Mahathir and Suharto, though, adopted a different tack. They called the herd names, alleged conspiracies, vowed to avenge its brutalities and, in Mahathir's case, eventually tried to shut it out with capital controls. Mahathir and Suharto grew up in a Cold War system that often inhibited either superpower from really speaking harshly or directly to Third World leaders, whose support was coveted in the Cold War game. But once the Cold War system ended, those restraints went out the window. And today, the lead bulls of the herd, they're not like the State Department, the UN or the Nonaligned Movement. They don't tell you that they feel your pain, or that they understand your grievance because of your colonial experience. They don't tell you that you are so unique, so important to stability in the region, that they won't lay a finger on you. They just have their way with you and move on. The Electronic Herd turns the whole world into a parliamentary system, in which every government lives under the fear of a no-confidence vote from the herd.

I was speaking to Malaysia's then–Deputy Prime Minister, Anwar Ibrahim, in Kuala Lumpur at the height of the 1997 Asian economic crisis, before he was ousted by Mahathir. Anwar told me that as Mahathir kept accusing the Jews, Soros and other conspirators of deliberately driving down the Malaysian currency, Anwar and some of his colleagues finally went to Mahathir with a chart and said to him something like the following: "Look, you said this about Soros on Monday, and the Malaysian ringgit fell to here. You said this about the Jews on Tuesday, and the ringgit fell to here. You said this about global investors on Wednesday, and the ringgit fell to here. SHUT UP!"

In Suharto's case, the Electronic Herd actually helped to trigger the uprising that ousted him from power in early 1998, by so undercutting the Indonesian currency and markets that the Indonesian public and army lost all confidence in Suharto's leadership.

Supachai Panitchpakidi, Deputy Prime Minister and Minister of Commerce of Thailand, today wears the battle scars of someone whose country tried to box with the herd and lost: "We made one mistake—linking our currency [the baht] to the dollar for six months too long without devaluing," he said of the 1997 crisis. "It should not have been a disaster, but because of the bandwagon effect [of the herd], everyone jumped on our currency. So instead of just going down fifteen or twenty percent, it went down fifty percent. Because the market is globalized [the herd] learned about our lack of reserves. The first time they attacked our currency was in February, and then in March, and then in April. And each time the Thai Central Bank defended the currency with reserves and each time our Central Bank came out and said, 'We won.' But they actually lost each time. Because the reserves were being run down. We thought the world didn't know about our reserve levels, but the markets knew—our own people didn't know—but the markets knew. My friends in Singapore and Hong Kong knew, and they were calculating each time we defended our currency how much reserves the Thai government had left to intervene with. When you ask our former Prime Minister he will tell you that none of this information was being presented to him. But the market had it figured out and they knew when there had been a turning point, when we couldn't defend the currency anymore. And that's when they really went after us."

Adjusting to the power of the Supermarkets and the Electronic Herd requires a whole different mind-set for leaders, particularly in emerging markets. In the past, members of the Electronic Herd competed to see who could make themselves most attractive to governments, both domestic and foreign. For it was governments that passed out most of the goodies. Now governments compete to see who can make themselves the most stable, inviting and attractive to the Herd. Because it is now the Electronic Herd that increasingly passes out the goodies. To put it in a phrase: All world leaders have to think like governors now. Governors in American states get to make some decisions, just like presidents and prime ministers. They even get to send out the National Guard sometimes. But their main job these days is enticing the Electronic Herd and Supermarkets to invest in their states, doing whatever it takes to keep them there and constantly living in dread that they will leave. That's why the world today is increasingly ruled by governors, no matter what their specific title happens to be. And that is why the preeminent political leader of the globalization era is the governor of all governors, the governor of the United States, William Jefferson Clinton.

Kings, dictators, emirs, sultans, traditional presidents and prime ministers—they're all being reduced to governors now. In the fall of 1997, I visited Qatar, the tiny Arab oil state off the east coast of Saudi Arabia, and was invited one afternoon to have lunch with the emir, Sheikh Hamad bin Khalifa al-Thani. He is a delightful man, and smart like a fox, but he is a man used to giving orders, not taking them. He was asking me about the economic crisis in Malaysia and Southeast Asia and I was telling him how the Electronic Herd and the Supermarkets were punishing Malaysia for Mahathir's excesses, including his building of the world's two tallest buildings. Sheikh Hamad listened, and then said something that sounded so much like a governor, not an emir. He said, "Well, I guess I better not build any tall buildings here. The markets might not like that."

The way in which leaders, individuals, investors and companies are all learning to adjust to this new system of globalization is really the hallmark of the late twentieth century. There is just one more thing I have to say about it, though: You ain't seen nothin' yet.

As I have tried to explain, the democratizations of technology, finance and information—which have changed how we communicate, how we invest and how we look at the world—gave birth to all the key elements in today's globalization system. They are what blew away the walls. They are what created the networks which enable each of us now to reach around the world and become Super-empowered individuals. They are what created the links and the space for the Electronic Herd and the Supermarkets to really emerge. They are what blew away all the old ideologies, other than free-market capitalism. They are what created the incredible new efficiencies that every business either has to adapt to or die. They are what lowered the barriers to entry into virtually every business. They are what is forcing people to change from thinking locally first and then globally, to thinking globally first and then locally.

It is because of the Internet that I say you ain't seen nothin' yet. The rise of the Internet, which came in the last stages of the democratizations of technology, finance and information, certainly contributed to this new era of globalization. But as the Internet proliferates, it is going to become the turbocharged engine that drives globalization forward. The Internet will ensure that how we communicate, how we invest and how we look at the world will be increasingly global. Because from the moment you log onto the Internet you can communicate with anyone globally practically for free, from the moment you log onto the Internet you can invest in any market globally practically for free and from the moment you start a business that has an Internet Web site, wherever you are in the world, you will have to think globally—in terms of both who your competitors might be and who your customers might be.

In early 1998 I went out to Silicon Valley to talk about some of this with John Chambers, the president of Cisco Systems, which makes the pipes and black boxes that connect the Internet around the world. He said to me at the time: "The Internet will change everything. The Industrial Revolution brought together people with machines in factories, and the Internet revolution will bring together people with knowledge and information in virtual companies. And it will have every bit as much impact on society as the Industrial Revolution. It will promote globalization at an incredible pace. But instead of happening over a hundred years, like the Industrial Revolution, it will happen over seven years."

As Chambers spoke, I wrote down what he had to say and even quoted it in a column, but it never really sank in with me. I took it to be the sort of typical exaggerated talk you hear from technologists. "Yeah, yeah, yeah," I thought, "the Internet is going to change everything. That's what they always say." But the more I wrote this book, the more I realized that what Chambers said not only was true, it was understated.

A few months after I visited Chambers, his office sent me a box of cups, pens and a shirt bearing Cisco's new advertising campaign logo, which you may have seen on TV. It's very simple. Cisco's TV ads consist of people, young and old, from all over the world looking straight into a camera and asking: "Are you ready?" Again, when I got the box of stuff with that logo on it in the spring of 1998, I looked at it and said to myself, "What's all this junk? What a strange ad campaign. I mean, 'Are you ready' for what?"

But as 1999 became the year of the Internet, the year when the Internet achieved a critical mass and really did begin to define both commerce and communication, I started to understand exactly what Cisco meant by "Are you ready?" The Internet is going to be like a huge vise that takes the globalization system that I have described in this section of the book—the Fast World, the Electronic Herd, the Supermarkets, the Golden Straitjacket—and keeps tightening and tightening that system around everyone, in ways that will only make the world smaller and smaller and faster and faster with each passing day.

Think about it: thanks to the Internet, we now have a common, global postal system, through which we can all send each other mail. We now have a common global shopping center, in which we can all buy and sell. We now have a common global library, where we can all go to do research, and we now have a common global university where we can all go to take classes. By 1999 more than half the adult U.S. population, 100 million people, were online. It is increasingly common in America to run into people who have bought not just a book online, but also a mortgage, a new computer and a car. And it's not just happening in America. Look at India. In the poor regions around Delhi, an Indian start-up cellular phone company, called the Usha Group, has Indian-style Avon ladies who go house-to-house in the poorest villages, carrying cellular phones to people who don't have phones in their homes. For a small fee, villagers can use the phones for a few minutes to make all their calls. Now Usha is installing public call centers in many of these villages—with cheap Internet access.

Treasury Secretary Larry Summers likes to tell this story: "Some time ago, I visited Mozambique—by some measures the world's poorest country—to discuss issues relating to debt relief. Seated at a lunch with the local business community, I inquired of the person next to me how business was. He responded, 'Pretty good, but I am worried about the future.' When I asked why, he explained that he was the monopoly Internet provider in Mozambique but feared that competition was coming and would erode his profits."

And he was right to worry. Adjusting to this next phase of Internet-driven globalization, with the world getting smaller and faster by the day, is going to be a huge challenge for all of us—individuals, countries and companies. The next two sections of the book—"Plugging into the System" and "The Backlash Against the System"—explain what I mean.

Are you ready?

II

Plugging into the System

DOScapital 6.0

MOSCOW (AP)—A Moscow art gallery owner was questioned by prosecutors today after a life-sized cake depicting Vladimir Lenin was devoured by guests and art critics at a recent exhibition. The Moscow *Times* reported Tuesday that Sergei Taraborov was questioned by prosecutors after 20 Communist members of parliament complained the cake violated laws against insulting national figures.

—*AP Moscow, September 8, 1998*

H ow much money are you carrying?"
The question was fired at me in a Jesse James tone of voice by an Albanian customs agent at Tirana Airport as I was trying to leave the country. As soon as the words were out of her mouth, I had the sinking feeling that I was about to be separated from my cash.

"I have 3,500 dollars," I said, patting my money belt.

"3,500 dollars," she repeated, her eyes lighting up. "He has 3,500 dollars," she said to her male colleague, who was standing next to her at the baggage X-ray machine.

"Where are you from?" he asked me, apparently trying to size up how vulnerable I was and to make sure I wasn't a diplomat. I told him I was a writer for *The New York Times*. "*The New York Times?*" the customs man repeated, as he gave me the once-over. "Let him go."

Who'd have thunk that *The New York Times* carried such clout in Tirana! I practically ran onto the plane. I had reason to be nervous. I had been to this play before—in another country where the rule of law was also not exactly king, Iran. Only there it didn't have such a happy ending. There it began the same way at Teheran International Airport, as I was trying to get through customs at 4 a.m. I was ordered by a customs agent to open my suitcase and to hand him my customs declaration form. On it was a line for how much cash you are carrying, and I filled in the exact amount, $3,300.00, which I still had on me. Since American credit cards aren't accepted in Iran, I had to bring a lot of cash. The thin, mustachioed Iranian customs agent perused the form and then said to me with a lean hungry look, "Mister, mister, you can only take 500 dollars out of the country."

"Oh no," I said, "what do I do?"

The Iranian customs agent leaned over and whispered in my ear, "For 300 dollars, I can take care of it." There was a long line of Iranians behind me watching this whole scene—all, no doubt, knowing exactly what was happening. I reached into my money belt and pulled out three crisp $100 bills and crumpled them up into a ball in my hand.

"Be careful," the customs agent hissed at me—as if somebody in the line behind us was actually going to report on what was happening. Then the two of us pretended to be rummaging through my open suitcase, and with a quick snatch of his hand he grabbed the $300 out of my fingers. It happened so fast—like a trout going for a fly—that you would have needed slow-motion instant replay to see it. Then, with his other hand, he handed me a new, blank customs form, which he asked me to fill out, declaring that I was taking only $500 out of the country. But even that wasn't the end. When I went upstairs to the boarding gate, I found that there was a body search after I went through the metal detector. I went into the cubicle behind the curtain and the Iranian soldier there asked me to open my money belt. I panicked, thinking to myself: "How am I going to explain the 3,000 dollars? What do I say: 'Hey, I already bribed your colleague downstairs to get this far, so get lost?' " Fortunately, he just looked at the money, rattled off something in Farsi and let me go.

Seasoned world travelers will know that my Iranian and Albanian adventures were hardly out of the ordinary. One encounters many manifestations these days of this phenomenon best described as "kleptocracy." Kleptocracy goes beyond the normal run-of-the-mill bribery and corruption that one can always find in developing countries, and to a lesser degree in developed ones as well. Kleptocracy is when many or all the key functions of the state system—from tax collection to customs to privatization to regulation—have become so infected by corruption that legal transactions become the exception rather than the norm. The norm, which becomes both tolerated and expected, is that officials at every level will use their powers to extort whatever money they can from citizens, investors or the state itself, and citizens and investors will assume that the only way to get decisions or service is by paying someone off.

States range from full-fledged kleptocracies—where the state is built around theft, such as Nigeria—to budding kleptocracies—where corrup-

tion is rampant, tolerated and expected but some legal and even democratic norms exist alongside it, such as India. The difference between full-
fledged kleptocracy and budding kleptocracy is best illustrated by the old
joke they like to tell around the World Bank about the Asian and African
Ministers of Infrastructure who exchange visits to one another's countries.
First the African visits the Asian minister in his country, and at the end of
the day the Asian takes the African to his home for dinner. The Asian
minister lives in an absolutely palatial residence. So the African minister
asks his Asian counterpart, "Wow, how can you afford such a home on
your salary?" The Asian minister takes the African over to a big bay window and points to a new bridge in the distance. "You see that bridge over
there?" the Asian minister asks the African. "Yes, I see it," the African says.
Then the Asian minister points a finger at himself and whispers: "Ten percent," signaling 10 percent of the cost of the bridge went into his pocket.
Well, a year later the Asian went to visit the African minister in his country, and found that he lived in an even more palatial home than his Asian
counterpart. "Wow, how can you afford such a home on your salary?" the
Asian asked the African. The African pulled his Asian counterpart over to
the big bay window in his living room and pointed out to the horizon.
"Do you see that bridge over there?" the African asked the Asian. "No,
there is no bridge there," answered the Asian. "That's right," the African
minister said, pointing to himself: "One hundred percent."

What are the tangible signs that you are in either a budding or a full-
fledged kleptocracy? Well, here are a few indicators that I've collected
over the years:

Kleptocracy is Moscow in 1995 (and 1996, 1997, 1998, 1999!), at a
time when street crime was widespread in the wake of the collapse of the
Soviet Union. As soon as I checked into the Penta Hotel in downtown
Moscow, I took my cash down to the front desk and told the clerk there
that I wanted to rent a hotel safe-deposit box. I wasn't going to take any
chances walking around Moscow with a pocket full of dollars.

"Sorry," said the desk clerk. "They're all being used. There's a waiting
list. Would you like me to put you down?"

I had to laugh. A waiting list for hotel safe-deposit boxes? It was like
the punch line to a bad joke: "How do you know when you're in a really
dangerous city? Answer: When all the hotel safe-deposit boxes have been
taken." No wonder an investor I met in Moscow who had just bought into
a Russian bank found that it had more security men than executives. He
told me of a Western restaurant chain that just dispatched a team of audi-

tors to find out why its Moscow franchise was doing so much business and making so little money. They found that almost every employee was involved in some form of larceny—from chefs stealing hamburgers to managers taking kickbacks.

Kleptocracy is the fact that in Albania tax cheating was so rampant that in 1997 the thirty-fifth-highest taxpaying company in the country was an Albanian-American pizza parlor, and auto theft was so rampant that American officials estimated that 80 percent of the cars on the road in Albania were stolen from somewhere else in Europe.

Kleptocracy is corruption in Russia, which goes so high into the Kremlin leadership that Russians joke about the man who drives into Moscow from the countryside and parks his new car right outside the Kremlin's Spassky Gate, in Red Square. A policeman comes along and tells the man: "Look, you can't park here. This is the gate that all our leaders use." The man answers: "Don't worry. I locked my car."

Kleptocracy is the story told to me by a friend who lived in Indonesia during the reign of the wildly corrupt Suharto family. He was a longtime reporter in Jakarta for a Singapore-based newspaper and had to regularly get his residency papers renewed. Corruption in Indonesia ran so deep, he explained to me, that officials would "actually give you a receipt for your bribes. Really. I get my immigration papers renewed each year. I pay the bribe and get a receipt. The accountants in my office want documentation and the official I pay off provides it." It's no wonder that under Suharto Indonesians had a saying: If your neighbor steals your goat, whatever you do don't take him to court, because by the time you get done paying off the police and the judges, you'll end up losing your cow as well.

Kleptocracy is when officials and regulators who are responsible for overseeing rules believe the rules don't apply to them. Nayan Chanda, editor of the *Far Eastern Economic Review*, once related to me an experience he had visiting China: "I was in Beijing and we were riding on the Second Ring Road with a Foreign Ministry translator, his official driver and our office assistant. As we were going down the highway, the Foreign Ministry driver suddenly made a U-turn and went straight up the highway entry ramp, honking furiously. The cars were coming down the entry ramp onto the highway and we were veering around them. I was stunned and terrified. I said to the translator, 'What is he doing!!!' He answered that the driver had noticed a large traffic jam up ahead and decided to go around it by exiting on the entry ramp. I closed my eyes, ducked down be-

hind the seat and prayed that I was going to get out of this alive. I came
out alive. But the thought occurred to me later: What about the foreign
businesses that are all going into China? The Chinese sign a deal with
them, get their technology and then change the rules and tell them to go
home. Will they get out alive?"

Not if the regulators in China are on the take. The head of the China
branch of one of the biggest Canadian banks told me in 1997 that the
bank transferred several thousand dollars once from its Hong Kong
branch to its Shanghai branch and it took eighteen days for the transfer to
clear. "We think we know what happened," the banker told me one day
over lunch in Shanghai. "Someone in the Central Bank took the money,
speculated with it on the Shanghai stock exchange for seventeen days and
then put it back on the eighteenth day, when the money showed up in
our account."

Kleptocracy is the billions of dollars that have been made in corrupt
privatization programs throughout Eastern Europe and Russia, where
tiny oligarchical elites, often in cahoots with local mafia and government officials, have managed to gain control of the formerly state-owned
factories and natural resources at below-market rates, making them overnight billionaires. Real estate prices from Paris to Tel Aviv to London
were all boosted by these Russian oligarchs and other rip-off artists who
spirited assets out of that country at a staggering rate. America, when it
was an emerging market, had its robber barons, just as Russia now has its
robber barons. But America's robber barons invested their money in
America's stock market and real estate, whereas now, thanks to globalization and the free movement of capital, Russia's robber barons also
invest their money in America's stock market and real estate, impover-
ishing their own country.

Sometimes, though, kleptocracy isn't just rich oligarchs ripping off
their country, but simply little people trying to survive in a country with
no social safety net. I was once changing planes in Jakarta Airport and
had to shuttle from the domestic terminal to the international one. I went
out to the sidewalks with my bags and waited in line behind a sign that
read: "Free Inter-Terminal Airport Shuttle." When the bus came, I
loaded my bags and was the only one on the bus. As I walked past the driver to get off at the next terminal, he stopped me. "Mister," he said, and
then pointed up to a crude sign he had scrawled above his seat in red
Magic Marker. The sign said the ride cost 4,900 rupiah (about $2 at the
time). I just shrugged and gave him the money.

Kleptocracy was going, in the summer of 1998, with John Burns, the *New York Times* bureau chief in New Delhi, to visit the Indian Parliament, where India's laws are promulgated. While we were waiting in the lobby to be cleared through, Burns noticed a book for sale in the Parliament bookstore: *Who's Who of the Indian Parliament*—with biographies and pictures of every Indian legislator. Burns decided he wanted to buy a copy. "Who do I go to, to buy a book?" Burns asked the clerk standing next to the book display. "Here, sir," the clerk said, "seven hundred rupees." The man then left to retrieve a copy. When he returned, Burns asked him for a receipt. "We close at noon," the man said, "this will have to be an 'out of office' sale"—meaning no receipt. He then handed John the book and pocketed the money for himself. I found this rather charming—having to bribe someone in the lobby of the Indian legislature for a book about Indian lawmakers.

I guess this explains why the *Times of India* reported on December 16, 1998, that an eighteen-month-long search in the corruption-riddled Indian state of Punjab had been called off. The search was for an official who could be given a 100,000-rupee ($2,380) award for providing "honest" government service, in a state where everything from electricity hookups to public school enrollments requires paying a bribe to someone. But no official could be found who was appropriate for the award. Instead of identifying a recipient for the award, the New Delhi newspaper said the search produced evidence that may be used to bring charges against 300 corrupt officials.

What does all this have to do with globalization? Let me try to answer by using some simple analogies from the world of computers. I like to compare countries to three parts of a computer. First, there is the actual machine, the "hardware." This is the basic shell around your economy. And throughout the Cold War system you had three kinds of hardware in the world—free-market hardware, communist hardware and hybrid hardware that combined features of both.

The second part is the "operating system" for your hardware. I compare this to the broad macroeconomic policies of any country. In the communist countries the basic economic operating system was central planning. There was no free market. The government decided how capital should be allocated. I call that communist economic operating system DOScapital 0.0.

In the hybrid states the operating systems were various combinations of socialism, free markets, state-directed economics and crony capitalism, in which government bureaucrats, businesses and banks were all tied in with one another. I call this DOScapital 1.0 to 4.0, depending on the degree of government involvement and the sophistication of the economy. Hungary, for instance, is DOScapital 1.0, China is DOScapital 1.0 in the hinterland and 4.0 in Shanghai, Thailand is DOScapital 3.0, Indonesia is DOScapital 3.0, and Korea is DOScapital 4.0.

Last come the big industrial capitalist systems. Some of these have operating systems that are based on free markets but still have significant welfare-state components. This group includes France, Germany and Japan, and I call their operating systems DOScapital 5.0. Others, though, such as the United States, Hong Kong, Taiwan and the United Kingdom, have liberalized their economies and have put on the full Golden Straitjacket. They have DOScapital 6.0.

In addition to the type of hardware enclosing an economy and its basic operating system, there is also the "software" it needs to get the most out of both. Software, for me, is all the things that fall broadly in the category of the rule of law. Software is a measure of the quality of a country's legal and regulatory systems, and the degree to which its officials, bureaucrats and citizens understand its laws, embrace them and know how to make them work. Good software includes banking laws, commercial laws, bankruptcy rules, contract laws, business codes of conduct, a genuinely independent central bank, property rights that encourage risk-taking, processes for judicial review, international accounting standards, commercial courts, regulatory oversight agencies backed up by an impartial judiciary, laws against conflicts of interest and insider trading by government officials, and officials and citizens ready to implement these rules in a reasonably consistent manner.

In the Cold War, the big struggle was over whose hardware would dominate the world. The Soviets and Americans didn't pay all that much attention to how well their hardware was actually working in any particular allied country. They just wanted to make sure that other countries were using their brand, with their stickers. Indeed, a country could get by for a long time with a terrible operating system inside, and corrupted software, because the Soviets and Americans were so anxious to have it on their team, they would just subsidize it or offer free repairs—as long as that country stuck with the superpower's brand. Both superpowers lived in fear of the "domino theory," which stated that if a certain key country would change hardware, all its neighbors would change too.

This struggle ended with the collapse of the Cold War system. Suddenly, the communist, socialist and even hybrid models were all discredited. Suddenly, we found ourselves at a remarkable moment in history: For the first time, virtually every country in the world had the same basic hardware—free-market capitalism. Once that happened, the whole game changed. Countries no longer had to decide which hardware to choose, just how to make the best of the only hardware that seemed to work—free-market capitalism.

But there is a saying in the world of computer technology: "The hardware always runs ahead of the software and the operating systems." That is, the engineers keep inventing faster and faster chips and only later do the operating systems and the more sophisticated software get developed to really take advantage of this new hardware and get the most out of it. This dictum also applies to the world of globalization. What the world has witnessed since the collapse of communism and socialism in Russia, Eastern Europe and the Third World is a large number of countries adopting the basic hardware of free markets, and even plugging their hardware into the high-voltage Electronic Herd, but often without the operating system, software and other institutions needed to effectively manage and rationally allocate the currents of capital and energy that can flow in and out once a country is connected to that herd.

This, we are discovering, is one of the central problems in the transition from the Cold War system to the globalization system: the problem of "premature globalization." I repeat: You cannot thrive today without plugging into the Electronic Herd and the Supermarkets, and you cannot survive today unless you have an operating system and software that will allow you to get the most out of them and protect you from their worst excesses when they stampede.

It was inevitable that as everyone moved to the same brand of hardware—free markets—there would be lags in how different countries developed their operating systems and the software to catch up. Hey, it's easy to buy a computer, especially when there is only one brand. Any moron can go out to Computer City and pick one up. And in the transition from the Cold War system to the globalization system many countries did just that, without ever thinking about whether they had the operating system and software to effectively operate that computer. These countries just said, "Hey, this looks easy. I'll just plug my dandy new hardware into this Electronic Herd right here . . ."

But it was actually much harder than it looked. It's easy to declare a free market in your country. What's difficult is to establish evenhanded enforcement of equitable laws and commercial codes, with courts that will protect people from unfettered capitalism. It's easy to open a stock market. Even Mongolia has a stock market today. But it's very difficult to build a Securities and Exchange Commission (SEC) that can control insider trading. It's easy to suddenly loosen the reins on the press and permit the free flow of economic information. But it's very difficult to establish and protect a truly independent free press that will expose corruption inside government and unmask flimflam companies that are cheating their shareholders.

This process of building software and operating systems is emerging as the weak link in the globalization chain. That is, we know now that globalization leads to more commerce, trade and economic development; more economic development leads to more prosperity for more people; and more prosperity tends to lead to more pluralism and political liberalization; and greater liberalization tends to lead to democratization. But for this chain reaction to get going your country needs to get its basic operating system and software in place, and taking this first step often clashes with a country's culture, history and imbedded institutions or the lack of them. Therefore, this first step turns out to be much more difficult than originally thought in the euphoria that followed the fall of the Berlin Wall.

Think about Poland and the Soviet Union. They emerged from the Cold War at roughly the same time. Both initially experienced economic downturns; Poland soon started growing, though, but Russia didn't. The reason was partly due to the fact that Poland, which had a history of capitalism before the communists took over, was able to put in place relatively quickly a lot of the basic software and operating systems needed to succeed in the globalization era. But Russia, with no history of capitalism or democracy, has had a much harder time, and paid the price. I always remember a joke that Secretary of State James A. Baker III told reporters traveling with him—a joke that Soviet President Mikhail Gorbachev told him. Gorbachev was trying to underscore to Baker how difficult it was for Russia to make the psychological transition to capitalism, after so many years of communism, and he did it with this yarn: A Russian peasant finds a lamp by the side of the road and rubs it. Out pops a genie. The genie tells the peasant he can have any wish.

The peasant tells the genie, "You know, I have only three cows, but my neighbor Igor has ten cows."

"So you want twenty cows?" the genie asks the peasant.

"No," says the peasant, "I want you to kill seven of Igor's cows."

In the Cold War system, the big divide in the world was between communist and capitalist economies, with a few hybrids in between. Now that virtually everyone has the same hardware, the big divide in the world is increasingly going to be between free-market democracies and free-market kleptocracies. Those countries that are able to develop the operating systems and software to go with free markets will move in the direction of free-market democracies. Those countries that are unable, or unwilling, to develop the software and operating systems will move in the direction of free-market kleptocracies, where the state basically gets taken over by robber barons and criminal elements, none of whom have an interest in the real rule of law.

Goodbye, communists versus capitalists. Hello, free-market democrats versus free-market kleptocrats.

Since most people are familiar with what the best free-market democracies look like, let me illustrate what the worst free-market kleptocracies look like. Then you can locate any country on the spectrum in between.

The purest form of free-market kleptocracy that I have ever seen was Albania in the 1990s. Albania had been one of the most isolated communist countries for fifty years, having adopted a Maoist, pro-China stance in the Cold War. Following the collapse of the Berlin Wall, the communist regime in Albania also collapsed in 1991. Rudimentary elections were held in Albania, and a quasi-democratic government was established in Tirana. Finally, the Albanians thought, we are getting what everyone else has: free-market hardware. Unfortunately, that's all they got. Albania was all hardware, with no software and no operating system.

While I was visiting Tirana in 1998, Fatos Lubonja, a forty-seven-year-old Albanian writer and editor of the Albanian literary journal *Endeavor*, described to me what it was like to live in the Albanian kleptocracy. "After communism," he said, "we had total equality here. We were all at zero. Few people had property or contacts. So a hierarchical system only emerged after that. Basically, people looked at politics as a business, because being a politician meant that you could open or close doors. You could give or not give stamps. The free market was considered free to do anything. So the boldest people started doing all sorts of things, and the criminals discovered that they needed politicians for some things and politicians discovered they needed money to stay in power. People had no experience. They were not educated [in government affairs]. They did not realize that without the software, Albania would be a jungle, and so people suffered, and many were kidnapped by gangsters or left the country. [Soon people realized that] Albania could not compete in the free market except with an illegal economy. So we created this criminal bourgeoisie. They don't pay taxes. They are not responsible for the social lives of the people or for infrastructure. They just take and take. If you can't compete on microchips you will compete on mafia. As for building a real free-market democracy, we are at zero point. The first five years were just the last mutation of communism. Instead of building a free-market economy that would reward initiative and risk, we created a criminal economy linked with the pyramid schemes. People put their money in these pyramids. And instead of investing they were just drinking coffee and waiting for money to come to them, which is what the pyramid owners promised. This reminded me of how we used to wait for aid from China, and live off that [in the Cold War]. Whatever it was, it was not real economics."

Indeed, what happened in Albania was that instead of a proper banking system, the government tolerated, and to some degree even nurtured, Ponzi schemes—one of the oldest forms of swindle. So well established were these Ponzi schemes in Albania that one of the most brazen of them even sponsored an Italian race-car team, as though it were MasterCard International. The organizer of a typical Ponzi scheme came to people and told them if they would deposit their savings in the "fund" they would earn 20, 30, even 50 percent on their money in six months. Because the Ponzi funds had few if any real investments to earn such high returns on, the way they paid out this high interest was by constantly luring in new investors to pay off old ones—while always skimming a little cash off for the fund managers. It all works fine until you run out of new investors.

"The Ponzi schemes began with efforts to raise cash to finance the purchase of gasoline that could be smuggled at very high prices into neighboring Montenegro and Serbia, which were under international sanctions during the Balkan war," Carlos Elbirt, head of the World Bank office in Tirana, explained to me. "But after the sanctions were lifted on Serbia, there was no real business activity behind the Ponzi schemes, so they just became a business of getting new money to finance old money. When the people running these things were really desperate for new cash, they offered fifty percent interest on your money. It was hard for me to convince even my own Albanian [World Bank] staff that these Ponzi schemes were doomed to fall. My staff would nod their heads at my graphs and then put more money into their Ponzi scheme. They were just too tempting, and everyone was doing it. It was like a fever. People sold their homes and put the money in Ponzi schemes and then in two or three months they bought back their old home and a new one. The IMF and the central bank warned the Albanian government, 'Money doesn't grow on trees,' but the government would not step in."

This was in part because the Albanian government did not have enough people who knew better and in part because many of its own officials were caught up in Ponzi fever. "If I went to an ambassador's residence on his country's national day, you would see an owner of the pyramid schemes there," said Elbirt. "They were totally accepted and legitimized, and that is what led a lot of common people to them."

Eventually, though, the Albanian pyramid savings funds collapsed in 1997, as these things always do, leading to a total breakdown of law and order, with furious Albanians ransacking their own state in an effort to get their money back. Elbirt and other foreign diplomats had to be evacuated for their safety. They drove in a British-organized convoy from Tirana to the port of Durrës. Once they got to Durrës, the helicopter that was supposed to lift them out couldn't land because there was so much shooting. So the convoy was moved to a different area of the port, which was controlled by the Italians. The diplomats had all been driven to Durrës in their official cars with their official drivers, and their drivers were all parked in the port, waiting to take the cars back to Tirana. But anarchy reigned, and a group of half-drunk Albanian thieves set upon the port and began stealing all the cars. Elbirt said the most striking moment came when a thief showed up, took out a "big, big gun," demanded the keys to the car of one of the evacuees and then sped away with it, all in less than a minute. Ten minutes later, though, the thief returned, and demanded all the official registration papers for the car he had just stolen. It was as though the thief had an inkling that just in case Albania ever got some software, he might need the ownership documents.

Said Elbirt: "He was very polite. Once the actual robbery was over, it seems he just wanted to make the transaction official."

The story of Albania in the 1990s is an extreme example that proves a simple point: Those people who worried or predicted that, because of globalization and the increasing irrelevance of borders, the nation-state would begin to wither away or diminish in importance are dead wrong. In fact, they speak utter nonsense. Because of globalization and the increasing openness of borders, the quality of your state matters more, not less. Let me repeat that a little louder: IN THE GLOBALIZATION SYSTEM YOUR STATE MATTERS MORE, NOT LESS. Because the quality of your state really means the quality of the software and operating system you have to deal with the Electronic Herd. The ability of an economy to withstand the inevitable ups and downs of the herd depends in large part on the quality of its legal system, financial system and economic management—all matters still under the control of governments and bureaucrats. Chile, Taiwan, Hong Kong and Singapore all survived the economic crises of the 1990s so much better than their neighbors because they had better-quality states running better-quality software and operating systems.

Thai Prime Minister Chuan Leekpai told me in early 1998, after his country got battered in the Asian economic crisis: "If you are going to be part of this global market you had better be able to defend yourself from this market . . . One of the lessons this crisis has taught us is that many of our structures and institutions were not ready for this new era. Now we have to adapt ourselves to meet international standards. The whole of society expects it. They are looking for better government and transparent government."

But while the state matters more now, not less, what has changed is what we mean by the state. In the Cold War, it was the *size* of the state that mattered. You needed a big state to fight the communists, maintain the walls around your country and sustain a generous welfare system to buy off your workers so they wouldn't go communist. In the era of globalization it is the *quality* of the state that matters. You need a smaller state, because you want the free market to allocate capital, not the slow, bloated government, but you need a better state, a smarter state and a faster state, with bureaucrats that can regulate a free market, without either choking it or letting it get out of control. The trick for governments today is to get the quality of their states up at the same time that they get the size of their states down. One of the most important and enduring competitive advantages that a country can have today is a lean, efficient, honest civil service.

That's why the big issue for many of the former communist and hybrid, state-dominated economies is whether, once they start to get the size of their government down (by liberalizing, deregulating and privatizing their state-owned industries) they can also get the quality of their government up. Because less government without better government is really dangerous. You need a balance. You want a state that is strong enough and involved enough to maintain a level and fair playing field, to ensure that the best innovators and entrepreneurs win, but not one that is so strong and so involved that it is either picking winners or protecting losers from winners or protecting losers from internal or external competition. If your market is all stoplights and no freeways, it breeds stagnation. And if your free market is all freeways and no stoplights, it breeds chaos. In the case of Russia and Albania premature globalization, after the collapse of communism, led to all freeways and no stoplights. Russia plugged into the Electronic Herd with virtually no operating system and no software. As a result, Russia had people taking advantage of the privileges of a free market—taking in foreign investments, issuing stocks and bonds, making international loans—without sufficient oversight or taxation to generate incomes to pay the bondholders back. And when the herd finally realized that Russia was nothing more than a piece of free-market hardware with no operating system or software inside, the herd surged and melted down the tangled mess of wires that made up the Russian economy.

In post-communist Poland, the economy sagged and then surged as reforms kicked in, because investors found there was a level playing field there, where the most productive companies won. "In Russia you didn't do well by doing better, or by operating in accordance with best practices," said Bill Lewis, who headed a McKinsey consulting firm's study of the Russian economy. "You did well by seeking favors, tax preferences and subsidies."

What happened in Southeast Asia was another form of premature globalization. Thailand, Malaysia, South Korea and Indonesia are different from Russia. They had rudimentary free-market hardware all along. And they even had early versions of the operating system—from DOScapital 3.0 to 4.0. These early versions of DOScapital—when combined with lots of savings, lots of government-backed credit, lots of natural resources and lots of people ready to labor very hard—worked well to get them from $500 per capita income to $5,000. Because, as we all know, when you first get a computer, any operating system will do, and it will always make you more productive than you were with a typewriter. But these early versions of DOScapital were relatively slow and rife with crony capitalism. In Indonesia, for instance, the management of state-owned banks was dominated by the Finance Ministry.

"When politicians, members of the President's family or Finance Ministry officials came calling, bankers felt compelled to extend loans even for projects they figured would be unprofitable, and when repayment of the loans became doubtful, they concealed the problems," wrote Shiraishi Takashi, a Kyoto University expert on Southeast Asian finance. "Private sector banks were also accumulating bad debts. Their function was to serve the business groups that had set them up, and when a member of the group ran into trouble, they would lend it additional funds brought in from foreign sources at high interest rates."

As the Electronic Herd shifted into high gear in the 1990s, and increased in power from a 286 chip to a Pentium II, it offered these Southeast Asian countries more and more money. Local banks, most of which were barely regulated, started excessively buying dollars, converting them into local currencies at a fixed rate, not hedging them in any way, and then lending that money out to their cronies for an increasing number of nonproductive investments—from one too many golf courses to the world's tallest office towers to egomaniacal expansions of South Korean conglomerates. The Southeast Asian nations needed to update their old DOScapital 3.0 to 4.0 and move closer to DOScapital 6.0. They needed more liberalized operating systems that would reduce the role of governments, let markets more freely allocate resources to their most productive uses, encourage more internal competition and weed out losers through effective bankruptcy laws. And they needed more sophisticated software that would improve the quality of governance, regulate a faster, more open economy, discipline company managers, open them up for shareholder scrutiny and be strong enough and flexible enough to handle any sudden large-scale withdrawal of foreign investment from the herd. Just throwing lots of capital and labor at an industry wasn't enough anymore to produce sustained, high growth.

Unfortunately, the Southeast Asians just stuck with DOScapital 3.0. Big mistake. DOScapital 3.0 was fine for getting from $500 to $5,000 per capita income, when the herd was moving at the speed of a 286 chip. But when they wanted to move from $5,000 per capita income to $15,000, and the herd moved from a 286 chip to a Pentium II, and they were still running DOScapital 3.0, their hardware naturally froze up. Have you ever seen what happens when you use an old, slow version of the DOS operating system and Windows software in a new Pentium II computer?

What happens is that you get messages on your screen, such as "You Have Performed an Illegal Function," "Out of Memory" and "Cannot Save Item." This, in short, is what happened to the Southeast Asians in 1997–98, only the messages that came up on their screens read: "You Have Performed a Series of Irrational Investments. Cannot Save Items. Delete Memory of All Inefficient Industries. Contact Service Provider and Download New Software and Operating System." And this is what they have been trying to do ever since.

What you found in all these Southeast Asian countries was that they replicated the outward configurations of the Western financial systems, but in many cases it was replication by rote. There was something missing inside—a key element of the DOS operating system. It was a basic feel and understanding of how real free markets, and a free-market-based society, work—that they are not run by the arbitrary judgments of individuals, but by the anonymous working out of every value judgment in the marketplace. The huge Korean conglomerates, the so-called chaebols, would never have been able to build up the huge debt-to-equity ratios they did without the intervention of government officials arbitrarily directing capital their way. All this borrowing enabled them to grow at astronomical rates for a time, but in the end, it caught up with them.

Former Korean Prime Minister Lee Hong Koo told me that it took his government several years to understand this: "I was Prime Minister in 1995 when Korea was admitted to the OECD and reached $10,000 a year per capita income," he said. "We thought we had really finally arrived. We thought that because we had graduated from high school with honors, we were going to be great college students. But the qualities needed at one stage were very different at the next. We didn't realize that our big state bureaucracy, which we were so proud of, was more a stumbling block than a positive force. We lived by the formula that manufacturing plus exports equals economic growth and success. We learned that was wrong from the crisis [of the late 1990s], but the tuition is too high. We learned that the communist loss was a loss against capitalism and if capitalism won that meant that capital was in control. There was this rapid globalization of capital in the 1990s, but we had not prepared our institutions to deal with the global capital markets. We didn't have the mechanisms to deal with them. We were defenseless. We treated our banks as if they were a national service organization, as if they were an extension of government. We thought you should not make money from money. We thought you should make money from making things. So the job of banks was to promote growth. So they were part of the government bureaucracy. We didn't understand that banks and capital flows were the heart of the new economy and either you reform them or else."

As Harvard University economist Dani Rodrik has demonstrated through his own research, it "is not whether you globalize that matters, it is how you globalize." Countries that have built up sophisticated, honest and credible financial and legal infrastructures—and this takes time—are much better positioned to fend off speculative attacks on their currencies, are much better able to withstand sudden outflows of capital by the herd, and are much faster at taking steps to minimize their impact. Yes, there are some exceptions. Even a country with a sound operating system and software can run into trouble—witness Sweden in 1992 or America and its savings and loan debacle. But Sweden and the United States also bounced back quickly because of the underlying quality of their operating systems and software. As Alan Greenspan has noted in speeches, those countries with advanced financial operating systems and software "generally have been able to discourage speculative attacks against a well-entrenched currency, because their financial systems are robust and are able to withstand large and rapid capital outflows [and to mobilize] the often vigorous policy responses required to stem such attacks."

For all these reasons there is now a growing awareness among leaders of developing countries that what they need in order to succeed in the globalization system is not just an emerging market but what former U.S. ambassador to Hungary Donald Blinken called "an emerging society." It does not pay to privatize your economy in a societal and governance vacuum. "Putting the market before the society," said Blinken, "is an invitation to trouble and disappointment."

Therefore, it is critically important that both investors and politicians begin to broaden their definition of what constitutes a healthy emerging market, by looking at what constitutes a healthy emerging society. In retrospect, the biggest mistake the world made with Russia, when it succeeded the Soviet Union, was casting Russia's transition into the global system as primarily a "financial problem," and leaving it for the IMF to sort out—as if the only problem was freeing up prices the right way and trusting the free market to take care of everything.

World Bank president James Wolfensohn has proposed that we revise our methodology for measuring countries from the current checklist, which is almost entirely confined to financial statistics—GDP, GNP, per capita income—to "a new form of accounting" that would measure a country's health as an emerging society and not just as an emerging market. Countries must be graded on the quality of their governing software, judicial system, procedures for settling disputes, social safety net, rule of law and economic operating systems.

These so-called "second-generation" reforms needed to produce an emerging society take a lot more patience and hard work. "In the old days," a World Bank official once said to me, "you came into a developing country and you went to the governor of the Central Bank and you had one simple piece of advice: 'stop printing so much money.' Then you went over to the Minister of Finance and said, 'stop running such a big budget deficit so your Central Bank can stop printing so much money.' In other words, all you had to do was talk to two people and give two simple messages. But now we know that a lot more is required." And in order to get these second-generation software reforms in place, which really transform a country from an emerging market to an emerging society, you need to involve many, many more actors and it requires a much, much wider political consensus.

It has been said of America that it is a system designed by geniuses so that it could be run by idiots. What developing countries need most from America today is not aid. Rather, it is an understanding of what is the real source of American prosperity: the combination of the right operating system—free markets—with the right software, political institutions and political consensus that can protect property and innovation, maintain a level playing field, ensure that the most productive players usually win, and provide some minimum safety nets to catch the losers.

While all sorts of would-be Western geo-architects are talking about designing a new global central bank and new global governing institutions to control the Electronic Herd, leaders of many developing countries are coming to realize that none of that will protect them unless they have better local government. The bank laws and the legislatures that pass them, the executives and regulators who enforce them, and the courts that adjudicate them are all local institutions, and the focus must be on improving those bodies—not waiting for some celestial solution of global government. While many Western thinkers don't get this, the countries that have actually gone through economic crises in the 1990s get it very well.

"There are some voices, some very loud voices, saying that perhaps integration has gone too far and too quickly—especially in financial markets," Mexico's President Ernesto Zedillo told me in the winter of 1997.

"Well, I happen to believe just the opposite. Globalization poses challenges, but it offers tremendous opportunities. The fact that finance capital can move instantaneously indeed poses a risk, but jumping from that to say that we need to control movements of capital is totally wrong." Yes, he added, we need a strong IMF to help in emergencies and to alert us to distortions in countries or individual banks. But at the end of the day, said President Zedillo, "all of these [global] financial flows end up in a local financial system, or as resources to be lent by local banks." So what matters, he added, is whether you have the local financial and political institutions to properly regulate the whole process.

In the Cold War countries did not care very much what sort of operating system or software their neighbors had, since they were not highly integrated. But today, in the globalization era, the ability of the herd to transmit instability from bad countries to good countries has vastly increased. The domino theory today belongs to the world of finance, not politics.

That's why one has to be a bit worried about the quick "recovery" the Asian economies made from the crisis of 1997–98. It wasn't because they had actually put in place all the reforms they needed to upgrade from DOScapital 1.0 to 6.0. In many cases it was because their currencies had become very cheap and they were the beneficiaries of strong U.S. demand for imports, particularly of electronics and computer parts made in Southeast Asia.

The Wall Street Journal (Oct. 28, 1999) profiled Indonesia's Rini Soewandi, who was appointed head of the Indonesia automaker Astra International after the company was nearly wiped out by Asia's late-1990s economic downturn. She really expressed the growing awareness among Asian entrepreneurs of the changes that they need to put in place to thrive, but also how difficult they are to put in place.

"I follow the American way of doing business, but in my soul I'm a Javanese," said the forty-one-year-old Ms. Soewandi. The article then went on to say the following: "Ms. Soewandi is making a tough leap, attempting to transform the business soul of Astra, one of Southeast Asia's oldest and largest companies, from a clubby conglomerate to one of the region's first American-style public corporations . . . The remaking of Astra signals the start of a new struggle for Southeast Asia as it looks beyond the crisis. With the worst behind them, many companies are waking up to the longer-term problem of surviving in a newly opened market. Most have avoided the issue, hoping that recovery will restore their fortunes. But Astra is meeting its troubles head-on and effecting a cultural makeover — moving from profligacy to transparency, from ego-driven conglomerate to market-driven niche player. 'It's a race against time,' Ms. Soewandi says. 'We're [trying] to do two huge things at once—survive the crisis and invent an entirely new business model that will carry us into the furture. It's very difficult for a company to do one, let alone both.' "

While the rest of the world clearly has a stake in how these Asian trading partners manage their internal economic affairs, the ability of the U.S. government, or any others, to actually help them build the necessary software is very limited. They have to come to the task on their own. The U.S. Secretary of State likes to shuttle in an airplane, but to build software you have to shuttle in a taxicab—from the local Ministry of Justice to the stock market to the Ministry of Trade to the corporate headquarters. This is the stuff of micropolitics and microdiplomacy, which is totally foreign to most of today's diplomats.

So how to get at it? It would be nice if every society were able to get all its software and operating systems in place before it ever plugs into the Electronic Herd. But that is not realistic. The process is going to be much more chaotic—two steps forward, one step back. We now know it will be a process of countries, such as Russia or Brazil or Thailand, plugging in a little, getting burned by the herd and the herd getting burned by them, both of them learning certain lessons, implementing reforms, bouncing back a little, getting slapped down again, and then beginning the whole process anew, hopefully each time in a wiser manner. This is going to be a long-drawn-out learning process—one that could take a generation in a country such as Russia—that will dominate domestic politics and international relations in the era of globalization.

In this dialectical process, the Supermarkets and the Electronic Herd could end up playing a more important role than the American superpower in driving political reform. It would be great if every democracy movement could be spurred by a hero like Andrei Sakharov. It would be wonderful if every country could be nudged toward the rule of law by reading James Madison. But in the era we are heading into, the main engine of change could well be Merrill Lynch. The next chapter explains why.

Globalution

Story #1: In the winter of 1998 I interviewed the Prime Minister of Thailand, Chuan Leekpai. Half joking, half serious, I began the interview by looking across the table at him and saying: "Mr. Prime Minister, I have a confession to make. I helped oust your predecessor— and I didn't even know his name. You see, I was sitting home in my basement watching the Thai baht sink (and watching your predecessor completely mismanage your economy). So I called my broker and told him to get me out of East Asian emerging markets. I could have sold you out myself, via the Internet, but I decided to get my broker's advice instead. It's one dollar, one vote, Mr. Prime Minister. How does it feel to have Tom Friedman as a constituent?"

The Prime Minister laughed, but he knew just what I meant: joining the global economy and plugging into the Electronic Herd is the equivalent of taking your country public. It is the equivalent of turning your country into a public company, only the shareholders are no longer just your own citizens. They are the members of the Electronic Herd, wherever they might be. And, as I noted earlier, they don't just vote once every four years. They vote every hour, every day through their mutual funds, their pension funds, their brokers and, more and more, from their own basements via the Internet.

Story #2: In the fall of 1997, I visited Moscow with a delegation of American business executives and academics. Our group included Donald Rice, the former chief operating officer of the American high-tech giant Teledyne, now head of a biotechnology firm. During the visit, Don mentioned to me one day that he had been discussing business opportunities with a Russian entrepreneur who was interested in partnering with an American company. Rice is a seasoned business executive, and before he went very far with the Russian businessman he asked him a simple question: "Have you paid your taxes?" The Russian entrepreneur said, well, not exactly. Sorry, Rice told him, if he had not paid his taxes there was no way they could be partners, because Rice's company was a public company and if one of its international subsidiaries wasn't paying its taxes this would show up in Rice's annual audit. So the Russian entrepreneur now has a choice. He can be a bad Russian citizen, continue not to pay his Russian taxes and compete alone, or he can become a better Russian citizen and possibly partner with a cutting-edge American firm. The more countries link up with the herd, the more they will face the choice of Don Rice's Russian entrepreneur—either run with the Electronic Herd and live by its rules or run alone and live by your own rules but accept the fact that you are going to have less access to capital, less access to technology and ultimately a lower standard of living for your people.

What these two stories vividly illustrate are the conflicting effects that globalization has on democratization. The Electronic Herd will, on balance, pressure countries to put in place better software and operating systems that constitute the building blocks of democracy. At the same time, though, the Electronic Herd and the Supermarkets are fast becoming two of the most intimidating, coercive, intrusive forces in the world today. They leave many people feeling that whatever democracy they have at home, whatever choices they think they are exercising in their local or national elections, whoever they think they elected to run their societies, are all just illusions—because it is actually larger, distant, faceless markets and herds that are dictating their political lives.

The paradox of globalization is that some days the herd rides into town like the Lone Ranger, guns blazing, demanding the rule of law, and the next day it stomps right out of town like King Kong, squashing everyone in its path. One day the herd is 1776 and the next day it's 1984. Let me show you how it can be both at once.

I call the process by which the herd helps to build the foundation stones of democracy "revolution from beyond," or "globalution." I first discovered globalution in Indonesia during a visit in 1997, in the waning months of the Suharto era. I was having dinner with Wimar Witoelar, a popular Jakarta talk-show host, who was describing for me the young generation of the Indonesian middle class. He remarked that what many of these educated twenty- and thirty-year-olds had in common was that they wanted to get rich, without having to be corrupt, and they wanted democracy, but they didn't want to go in the streets and fight for it. This generation of Indonesians understood that under Suharto there would never be a democratic revolution from above, but they were terrified of democratic revolution from below, because if the urban poor revolted it would be the year of living dangerously all over again. So their whole strategy was *revolution from beyond*, or globalution. Their whole strategy was to do everything they could, sometimes consciously, sometimes unconsciously, to integrate Indonesia into the global system. They hoped that by tying Indonesia into these global institutions and markets—whether it was to the World Trade Organization, Pizza Hut, APEC, ASEAN, Merrill Lynch, PricewaterhouseCoopers or human rights nongovernmental organizations (NGOs)—they might be able to import from beyond the standards and rules-based systems that they knew would never be initiated from above and could never be generated from below.

For instance, the Indonesian press couldn't directly rebuke the Suharto regime for its rampant nepotism, so instead it reported with great relish on how the United States and Japan were taking Indonesia before a WTO court to protest the fact that Indonesia's national car factory—then controlled by the President's son—was being protected by tariffs out of line with WTO standards. The strategy of Indonesia's globalutionaries was, in short, to Gulliverize the Suharto regime by globalizing Indonesian society. Indonesian military analyst Juwono Sudarsono described globalution to me as meaning that "the global market will force upon us business practices and disciplines that we cannot generate internally." Another Indonesian reformer expressed it more simply. He told me that he and his son got their revenge on Suharto once a week "by eating at McDonald's."

The traditional foreign policy establishment, particularly the far left and far right, underestimate the power of the Electronic Herd and globalization to contribute to democratization. As Johns Hopkins University foreign policy expert Michael Mandelbaum notes: "We still live with the image of the revolutions of 1776, 1789, 1917 and 1989, which leaves the impression that democracy can only be produced by people rising up and throwing out a corrupt government. It is either the Minutemen on Lexington Common or the throngs in Paris storming the Bastille, or Solidarity rising in Poland, or People Power rising in the Philippines. As such, our image of how democratization happens is never that some foreign businessman shows up and tells your government that he can't make enough money to employ that country's people unless that government institutes better legal safeguards, international accounting standards and transparency."

Just because the United States does not, every day, order China to democratize, and just because the Chinese people are not rising up, every day, demanding the right to write op-ed pieces in the Asian *Wall Street Journal*, doesn't mean that a process of democratization isn't being nurtured there. We keep looking at democratization as an event—like the fall of the Berlin Wall—but it's actually a process.

Of course, for this process of democratization to end up in successful liberal democracy, it needs to be pushed by more than just market forces, notes Larry Diamond, co-editor of the *Journal of Democracy*, and one of the most thoughtful scholars on worldwide democratization trends. The herd is necessary but not sufficient. "It is also important that the United States government speak out, forcefully and consistently, for democratization," he explained. "It is important that the European Union and the United Nations Development Program and the ever-widening network of nongovernmental organizations that monitor and promote human rights support democratization initiatives in emerging markets. It is important that the globalization of information is constantly informing more and more people about how others live. It is important that economic development within countries creates new middle classes around the world, with their natural demands for more participation in decision-making and political pluralism. It is not an accident that every country with a per capita income above $15,000 is a liberal democracy, except Singapore, which is a city-state and almost certainly will become a liberal democracy once there is a generational change. It is important that the end of the Cold War and the collapse of communism have discredited all models other than liberal democracy."

You need all these factors working together.

My simple point is that not only will the Electronic Herd and the Supermarkets take their place among these other forces that Diamond explains are critical for promoting democratization, but in this era of globalization the herd and the Supermarkets may well turn out to be the most important of these forces. This is because of the herd's ability to get deep inside the wiring of countries, in ways that governments and even human rights organizations cannot. The herd can impose pressures that few governments can resist. It has a self-interest in doing so and it generates in others the self-interest to comply.

To be sure, the herd is driven to get inside that wiring not because it values democracy per se. It doesn't. It values stability, predictability, transparency and the ability to transfer and protect its private property from arbitrary or criminal confiscation. But to secure these things, the herd needs developing countries to put in place better software, operating systems and governance—which are the building blocks of democracy. In today's world, you cannot get from Mao to Merrill Lynch without some Madison as well. Let's look in detail at how the herd is forcing in place some of these building blocks of democracy.

Transparency

The Wall Street Journal reported that when senior finance officials from the United States, Japan, China and eleven other Asian countries gathered for a meeting in Malaysia in November 1997, they found that the Malaysian Central Bank had put up an electronic scoreboard, the sort you usually find at an NBA basketball game, which displayed a running tally of Malaysia's currency reserves to reassure visitors about the soundness of the country's economy.

Not every country is going to go so far as to put up such a scoreboard in the arrival terminal of their airport—or maybe they will. In recent years, the Electronic Herd has learned, usually the hard way, to demand more transparency in financial reporting. Countries that plug into the herd have increasingly learned, also the hard way, that the more transparent they are about their financial data and transactions, the less likely the herd is to make a sudden stampede away from them.

Think of the Electronic Herd as being like a herd of wildebeests grazing over a wide area of Africa. When a wildebeest on the edge of the herd sees something move in the tall, thick brush next to where it's feeding, that wildebeest doesn't say to the wildebeest next to it, "Gosh, I wonder if that's a lion moving around there in the brush." No way. That wildebeest just starts a stampede, and these wildebeests don't stampede for a mere hundred yards. They stampede to the next country and crush everything in their path. So how do you protect your country from this? Answer: You cut the grass, and clear away the brush, so that the next time the wildebeest sees something rustle in the grass it thinks, "No problem, I see what it is. It's just a bunny rabbit." Or if there is a lion approaching, the wildebeest has time to see it from afar, and to move away gradually without causing a huge stampede. If not, at least it will have time to get the herd to come together in a way that will scare off the lion. What transparency does is get more information to the wildebeests faster, so whatever they want to do to save their skins they can do in an orderly manner. In the world of finance this can mean the difference between having your market take a little dip and having it nosedive into sustained losses that take months or years to recover from.

When South Korea's economy got into trouble in December 1997, it was telling everyone that its foreign currency reserves were $30 billion, when in fact they were only $10 billion. And when the herd found that out, it just took off. At the same time, the Seoul government told the IMF that its total short-term borrowings from overseas were $50 billion. A week later it announced that they were $100 billion. Oops.

This sort of lack of transparency, notes Richard Medley, who does political risk analysis for finance houses, is what causes some of the worst stampedes. Lack of transparency, he argues, "is precisely what allows optimistic illusionists and paranoid illusionists the maximum freedom to roam." Think of Thailand, Korea or Russia in the early 1990s. In good times, the lack of transparency of their economies encouraged the optimistic illusionists to create a bubble, by pumping more and more money into these countries, confident that they could provide the same high returns they did the year before, even though the early money may have gone into productive factories and the later money was going into luxury condos and factories for which there was no demand. "You can't really do serious analysis on opaque systems," argues Medley. "You get [the Electronic Herd] into that sort of optimistic illusion about your country and it will bid prices through the roof. The optimistic illusionist says, 'Close your eyes and buy, and surely there will be water in the pool when you land.' But that is very dangerous. Because the same opaqueness that drives the optimistic illusionists to bid up prices to exaggerated levels also empowers the paranoid illusionists to bid them down to exaggerated levels when sentiment shifts. Because on the way down all of the stories that you as an optimistic illusionist told yourself, all the assumptions you made about the country's foreign currency reserves or forward obligations, collapse."

You go from believing everything to believing nothing. In fact, the paranoid illusionist believes more than nothing—he believes that there are hidden debts and off-the-books liabilities all over the place. Every herd has optimistic and paranoid illusionists, and if you give them the opportunity they will exacerbate stampedes in and out.

The Electronic Herd has taught that lesson to several countries in recent years. Today, South Korea's Ministry of Finance sends out an E-mail to global investors detailing its currency reserves at the end of each business day, including, as best it can, private capital flows. "The Koreans went from thinking that transparency is nothing to transparency is everything," one Wall Street fund manager told me. "They would send us a daily weather report if we asked for it." Rick Johnston, who heads up Latin American investing for Offitbank, a private New York bank, told me: "When I go down to Brazil I tell them, 'I need to see everything.' I tell them quite frankly, 'It's not for me. I'm your friend. I believe in you. But how can you help me convince the unbelievers?' And the unbelievers now tell us: 'Unless you strip down and let me look everywhere, I am not going to give you any money, because you have a historical propensity to disappoint. No transparency, no money. Show me the money. I want to see your books upside down, in the sunlight and then in the moonlight.' Every day now I get polling data about all aspects of the Brazilian economy, and I get a fax at the end of the day with all the capital flows of Brazil on that day. I know what went on in their commercial account, what went on in their financial account, what went through at the official Central Bank rate and what went through the parallel market for tourist transactions. This sheet comes from a local private firm, with data provided from the Brazil Central Bank. I will invest more if I know what is in their piggy bank at all times—even though there are still risks. Because with the right data, I have the ability to price the risks and I can change my mind if those flows turn negative; otherwise I would be guessing about rumors, and that's how you go broke."

And once you have committed yourself to that level of scrutiny by the herd, there is no going back, except at a huge price.

Standards

"If you were writing a history of the American capital markets," Treasury Secretary Larry Summers once observed, "I would suggest to you that the single most important innovation shaping that capital market was the idea of generally accepted accounting principles. We need that internationally. It is a minor, but not insignificant, triumph of the IMF that in Korea somebody who teaches a night school class in accounting told me that he normally has 22 students in his winter term, and this year [1998] he has 385. We need that at the corporate level in Korea. We need that at the national level."

One reason why that Korean accounting class exploded in size might be that the herd, in the wake of the 1997–98 financial crisis in Southeast Asia, began demanding better, more uniform accounting standards everywhere. When the herd started looking more closely at many of the companies in South Korea, Thailand or Indonesia, it found it could not make sense of them, because there were no unified balance sheets that aggregated all the units and subunits of companies, so that you could see *all* the assets and *all* the liabilities, not to mention *all* the off-book assets and liabilities.

The more the herd goes around investing in factories or markets in different countries and the more those countries want to enlist investment from the herd, and the more companies in those countries want to be listed on the stock exchanges of one of the major Supermarkets, the more pressure they will all come under to abide by international financial reporting standards.

Consider an example I came across in the December 1997 issue of United Airlines' *Hemispheres* magazine, which carried a story about one of the fastest-growing software companies in the world, India's Infosys. The article noted the following: "The key to their success has been abandoning the Third World policies and practices that hobble many subcontinent companies and forging a connection to the First World that permits the utmost in customer convenience. 'We decided from the outset that there would be no blurring of corporate and private resources,' says Narayana Murthy, the company's visionary founder and chairman. This means that no one uses a company car for a personal errand—a radical break from traditional Indian business culture. Frequently in India corporate officers make personal use of company assets. Company electricians work in executives' homes. Employees pick up their supervisor's

children from school and babysit them. Corporate accounts finance purchases of homes. Employees put up with such practices because they
have no choice. Nevertheless, they lead to growing alienation and a re-
bellious withdrawal of creative input. That doesn't happen at Infosys . . .
Infosys is the first Indian company to announce audited annual results
within a week of the close of the financial year, the first to publish quarterly audited financial statements, and the first to publish statements in
compliance with U.S. Generally Accepted Accounting Principles and the
disclosure requirements of the U.S. Securities and Exchange Commission. 'Its disclosure norms and accounting practices have set standards for
others to emulate,' states one analyst's report."

This trend is being enhanced by Internet brokerage. Online trading,
said John T. Wall, president of NASDAQ International, "definitely inten-
sifies the scrutiny on governments and companies for better governance.
Once people can invest overseas or from overseas and are able to execute
the trade through online trading, they want to know more about the companies, then they want to know whether they can trust the information
about the companies. Is [the financial data] compiled according to the international accounting standards? What is the quality of their corporate
governance? This is going to drive the harmonization of tax and legal systems."

Indeed, one of the things that was revealed by the 1997–98 Asian economic crisis was that most of the Big Five American accounting firms had
audited the books of the big Asian financial houses that had failed in the
crisis—audited them without raising any red flags about their troubles, according to a study by the United Nations Conference on Trade and Development. The main reason for this lapse, according to a November 17,
1998, story in *The New York Times*, was that the Big Five firms did not
apply the same detailed accounting rules and standards in Asia that they
use in America. And the main reason for this was that most of the big accounting firms—such as PricewaterhouseCooper or Ernst & Young—
moved into Asia by taking over local accounting firms, whose local clients
insisted on weaker local accounting rules. Not anymore. The World Bank
has asked the Big Five not to sign their names to any audit not done according to the Big Five's international accounting standards. If it was done
by one of their local subsidiaries by local rules it should be signed only by
the local firm—and investors beware. The UN study said poor auditing
did not cause the Asian economic crisis, but better auditing would have
detected the rising problems sooner and made the crisis less severe.

As we increasingly move into a world where the Internet defines commerce, this push for common global standards is going to become hugely intensified, for one very simple reason: from the minute you decide to do business on the Internet as a retailer or service provider, from the first moment you open your Web site, you are a global company—whether you are in India, Italy or Indianapolis. To do business on the Internet is by definition to be global. Therefore, you have to think globally and you have to think about what will appeal to and attract global buyers of whatever you are selling. And you'd better be able to assure customers that you can ship your goods in a timely and safe fashion, that their credit card number will be safe in your site, that money can be transferred according to international standards, laws and best practices and that all accounting and commercial issues will be dealt with according to international norms. "The more business that is conducted over the Internet by more people from more different corners of the globe, the more it is going to harmonize how people do business in every corner of the globe," argues Bob Hormats, vice-chairman of Goldman Sachs International.

I got a taste of this on several levels while visiting Sri Lanka in late 1999. The morning I arrived I drove from the airport two hours out of Colombo to visit one of Sri Lanka's top textile factories. The road to the factory was a single lane, where passing other cars and cows was a harrowing experience. The landscape was that of a tropical rainforest. Eventually, though, we reached the village of Pannala, outside of which was this very modern textile factory, with freshly painted buildings, manicured lawns and satellite downlinks. It looked like it had descended from Mars. The factory belonged to a Sri Lankan firm, named Slimline, that manufactured clothes for Victoria's Secret and Marks & Spencer. The factory was completely computerized and was soon to be linked by Internet to the Victoria's Secret chain to handle E-commerce. About 1,400 employees, mostly women ages eighteen and older, worked on rows and rows of pneumatic sewing machines. Everyone wore a uniform, and pregnant women were identified by a red cap, and expected to keep a slower pace. The factory was air-conditioned and was clean enough to eat off the floor. The workday was eight hours, but intense, as each woman had to stitch so many garments per minute. Each assembly line was tracked by computer and a certain average production had to be reached for the women to get their monthly bonuses. Wages were about $80–$100 a month, including breakfast, and there was a waiting list for jobs. In terms of working conditions, this factory was world-class. Wages aside, I would let my own daughters work there.

I asked the plant owner, Mahesh Amalean, why the fancy factory? Why not a sweatshop? Wouldn't that be more lucrative for him? No, he explained, it wouldn't—because of globalution. The only way Sri Lanka can survive in the textile business, against even lower-wage countries such as China and Brazil, is if it moves up the quality ladder, and produces better goods for big, global, brand-name retailers. Racing to the bottom with Bangladesh is a no-win game, he explained. The only way to build long-term relationships with the big global brands is to produce higher- and higher-quality products under better and better working conditions. "Those brand retailers are now demanding not only better prices and quality, but better conditions for workers," explained Amalean. This is not because Victoria's Secret has suddenly become socially conscious, but because American consumers and college students have become more socially conscious as a result of some very high-profile antisweatshop campaigns. And these consumers are now telling stores that they do not want to be wearing goods made under sweatshop conditions. In other words, one of the big reasons working conditions have improved in Sri Lankan textile factories is not because Sri Lanka put up walls against globalization, but because in today's global economy Sri Lankan manufacturers must tie themselves to big Western retailers to survive, and the more they do that the more their factory standards have to meet the workplace norms being demanded by Western consumers. "When the buyers from Victoria's Secret and the other big brands come through now, [working conditions are] one of the first things they ask about," said Amalean. "They have to, because they have customers asking them about it."

A few days after visiting the Slimline factory, I attended a breakfast with a group of young Internet entreprenuers, several of whom complained that one reason their infant companies were not developing much software of their own yet was because there was no effective local copyright law to prevent anyone from stealing it. They also complained that Microsoft had refused to enter the Sri Lankan market because of the lack of an intellectual property law. At that point, Lalith B. Gamage, who headed Sri Lanka's state-run Institute of Information Technology, said bluntly that in order to attract Microsoft and other big global technology companies to Sri Lanka the government was pushing through a new, rigorous intellectual property law. And he promised the others at the table that it would be ready within a year. All I could think of as I listened to this discussion was that Bill Gates had no idea of the impact his company was having on this small country.

Such globalution is not only happening in the developing world. Maybe the biggest example in the world today of globalution imposing standards from beyond was the European Union's decision to impose a single currency and financial standards—a single Golden Straitjacket—on all its members, under a single central bank. For a country like Italy, which was renowned for its corrupt and inefficient government, the European Monetary Union, begun in 1999, was a godsend. It forced Italy to stay inside the Golden Straitjacket by subcontracting key government operations to the European Central Bank in Frankfurt. National Public Radio ran a report from Italy in 1997 about how Italians—after a generation of inept governments had mismanaged their currency into Monopoly money—were eager to let the EU run their country. An Italian corporate lawyer, Mario Abate, was quoted as saying, "One of the immediate effects of joining the Euro is that of doing what I call 'in-house cleaning'—it really is forcing the government to come to grips with its huge deficit, with its inflation and spending. They are forced to do so. And in doing so, naturally, there will be advantages to the economy and I am very much in favor because of this." Abate added that most Italians would probably be quite happy to have their whole country run by European Union officials. There's little resentment in Italy toward the centers of European power in Brussels, Frankfurt and Strasbourg. "There's much more hostility toward Rome," concluded Abate, "because Rome has been the center of crime for us. They've been stealing our money. We consider it stealing, because they take it and don't give it back." Italy's Finance Minister, Vincenzo Visco, told the Italian newspaper *La Repubblica*, on the day the single European currency came into being at the start of 1999, that the Euro means that there will be "less malevolent buffoonery" on the part of Italian politicians and businesses, who in the past had exhibited "an abnormal quantity of illegal behavior." Monetary union, he added, "means that we will no longer be able to settle for lower standards simply because it pleases us."

Now that's a globalutionary talking.

Corruption

If you want to see how the globalization system can affect corruption in a positive way read the stories about the October 12, 1999, military coup in Pakistan. What happened? The coup was a classic power struggle among elites, driven in large part by politics. General Pervez Musharraf had been emboldened to make an incursion into Indian-controlled Kashmir, probably hoping that since both Pakistan and India had acquired nuclear weapons the world would step in and compel some sort of settlement in Kashmir. He miscalculated. The world did not step in and Pakistani forces got hammered by India. Prime Minister Nawaz Sharif backed out of the Kashmiri conflict and sought to blame the fiasco on the military and to fire Musharraf. In the ensuing power struggle, Musharraf and the army ousted Sharif instead. An old story.

What was new was what happened once Musharraf actually took over the reins of power. It was then that he had to face what was actually important to his own people, which, guess what, wasn't Kashmir but corruption—the massive corruption that had been tolerated by the Sharif government. So General Musharraf, instead of trying to legitimate himself as Pakistan's next leader by presenting himself as a Moslem nationalist standing up for Pakistan's territorial integrity, went a totally different route. He justified his takeover by presenting himself as Mr. Clean who would root out corruption in Pakistan once and for all. General Musharraf even offered to disclose his tax returns to prove he was clean! He knew that he had to address two audiences—those in Pakistan who were fed up with all the sleaze and those in the Electronic Herd who now controlled the resources he needed to get Pakistan growing again. When in the history of the world did a general take power and the first thing he vowed to do was disclose his tax returns! Instead of a purge of the left or the right, he pledged that his government was going to go after all debtors, tax evaders and other financial scoundrels. *The Washington Post* reported (Oct. 21, 1999) that a few days after the coup, Pakistan's largest private bank took out a front-page newspaper ad that read: "ATTEN-TION ALL LOAN DEFAULTERS! LAST CHANCE—PAY UP OR FACE THE CONSEQUENCES." I kept asking myself: Was this a coup by Pakistan's military, or was this a coup by Pakistan's IRS?

This was no anomaly.

Globalution is creating a much higher cost for any country that tolerates corruption, if for no other reason than that in a world where people have so many investing options, why bother investing in country X, where you have to pay off everyone and his uncle, when you can go to country Y, get the same labor rates and not have to pay off anybody? The Electronic Herd says to every country: "If you cannot provide us a stable pool of customers, and a secure set of opportunities for investments, fine, we will go elsewhere, and in a world without walls there are now a lot of places to go. For the herd, corruption is just another name for unpredictability, because any deal can be undone by someone bribing someone, and there is nothing the herd hates more.

Derek Shearer, who served as U.S. ambassador to Finland in the mid-1990s, saw firsthand how globalution is increasingly forcing Russians to choose between getting their corruption under control or remaining poor and underdeveloped forever. "As U.S. ambassador in Finland it was my job to go around to Finnish business leaders and encourage them to invest in Russia on the argument that this was the best way to produce stability across the border from them," said Ambassador Shearer. "But these Finns would say back to me: 'Sure, we'll do business with the Russians. They can bring their trucks in here and fill them up with whatever they want, as long as they bring a bag of cash to pay for it. But we're not going over there to do business. It is way too corrupt and dangerous. And why should we? We can go to Hungary, or Estonia, or the Czech Republic and make money and be assured of being able to get our profits out. Why should we bother with Russia in the condition it's in?' I would say, 'Yes, yes, but you should think about investing there for regional stability.' And they would just give me a blank stare. Well, now I'm out of government and I am advising several investment firms on Wall Street. They were asking me the other day about investing in Russia and I just told them, 'No way.' If I look at it not from a policymaker's point of view, but from a businessman's point of view, you would be crazy to invest in Russia now. The Finns had it right."

Sometimes, the herd's imposition of higher standards can come as a huge shock to even the most advanced economies. Consider the February 20, 1998, *Washington Post* article from Tokyo headlined "Japanese Lawmaker Hangs Self in Hotel." The lead of the story explained that Shokei Arai, the Japanese lawmaker at the center of a growing corruption scandal, committed suicide in his Tokyo hotel room, just hours before he was about to be arrested. Deep in the story, though, were buried two very telling points: "There is concern among some politicians that Arai may have left evidence incriminating others . . . There was no indication that

Arai had left such documents, but at a press conference on Wednesday evening, he did complain that he had been unfairly singled out by prosecutors. Arai told reporters that Nikko Securities assured him it had provided profits in a similar way to hundreds of other customers. *Japanese businessmen say privately that they are stunned by the swift way in which what is permissible in the business culture here has changed.* Once bureaucrats expected to be lavishly wined and dined, and companies openly participated in such activities, where it was said that bureaucrats and businessmen could informally exchange necessary information. 'VIP accounts' and racketeer payoffs were also an open secret, say businessmen, and prosecutors ignored those activities until recently. [Political commentator Minoru] Morita *attributes the tougher attitude to a new group of younger, more aggressive prosecutors who were trained overseas.* 'They are beginning to think like Westerners, and see the Japanese tradition of lavish entertainment of government officials as way beyond internationally accepted standards,' Morita said." (All italics mine.)

Robert Shapiro, chairman of Monsanto, once remarked to me that his company is not on a crusade for spreading anticorrupt practices. But not paying bribes is how it does its own business, and he is keenly aware that in so doing Monsanto is helping to seed the world with people who share its values. "We hire a lot of people now in a lot of foreign countries, and we become kind of a finishing school for them," remarked Shapiro. "A lot of people who join us abroad have trouble believing that we are serious about this anticorruption stuff, and that we really are not going to make a contribution to the local warlords."

To be sure, there have been and always will be exceptions, especially as global competition becomes more intense and therefore the temptation to chase after questionable business will increase. According to a U.S. congressional study, Citibank was so eager to do business with Raúl Salinas de Gortari, brother of the former President of Mexico, that the bank ignored its own safeguards and helped him move some $100 million in illicit funds out of Mexico, in a way that disguised the destination and origin of the funds. For now, though, these cases remain just that, exceptions. The dominant international trend is clearly in the other direction. The Foreign Corrupt Practices Act, passed in 1977, makes it illegal for American companies to pay bribes to advance foreign business deals. On November 20, 1997, the twenty-nine-nation Organization for Economic Cooperation and Development (OECD), which comprises the world's leading industrial democracies, agreed to adopt much of America's anticorruption legislation. Under the new OECD regulations European and Japanese firms will be banned from bribing foreign officials to win contracts, and it should also be harder for these firms to write off bribes as tax deductions, which was legal in both France and Germany. While there are still some loopholes in this new legislation, it marks a victory for the American bulls in the Electronic Herd, who argued that they were losing billions of dollars in contracts because of payoffs by Europeans and Japanese.

Free Press

China's going to have a free press. Globalution will drive it. Oh, China's leaders don't know it yet, but they are being pushed straight in that direction. Just look at what happened in the last two weeks of December 1996. During 1996 the two hottest stock markets in Asia were in China—the Shanghai and Shenzhen stock exchanges. Between April 1 and December 9, Shanghai's composite index was up 120 percent, while Shenzhen's was up 315 percent. One reason these two stock markets were so hot was that they were virtually unregulated, and one reason they were so unregulated was that China has only the most rudimentary securities and exchange system, and it has virtually no independent, responsible, uncorrupted financial press that can credibly highlight the quality stocks and brutally expose those flimflam Chinese companies that don't report timely, accurate or transparent financial data. *Barron's, Fortune, Business Week,* the *Far Eastern Economic Review, The New York Times* and *The Wall Street Journal* play that watchdog role all the time. In December 1996, China's government realized the Shanghai and Shenzhen markets were out of control—because of all sorts of wild speculation and unsavory trading practices—but its tools for dealing with this were limited to one sledgehammer: the state-owned press. So, on December 16, 1996, *The People's Daily,* China's official paper, published a blaring editorial warning that stock prices had been pushed to "irrational" and "abnormal" levels.

Guess what happened? Everyone tried to sell at once, both markets plunged and a lot of little investors got hurt—so many that police had to keep order among furious investors who staged protests outside brokerage houses in several major Chinese cities. The Asian *Wall Street Journal* reported that "outside a brokerage house in Beijing, a worker groused that he'd lost 20,000 yuan [about $2,400] so far this week. 'Before *The People's*

Daily opened its mouth, there was a balance between buying and selling,' a man in a leather jacket declared, to shouts of approval from dozens of other investors. 'After that, nobody has dared buy. The market is sinking.' "

The angriest person in the world is not someone who has lost his job. The angriest person in the world is someone who feels cheated out of the savings earned from his job. Over time, China's leaders simply can't control and monitor their bursting free markets, or prevent little people from getting cheated and then rioting against the government, without the other institutions that must go with free markets—from an effective SEC to a free and responsible press backed by the rule of law. In a word, globalution. It is not an accident that the Southeast Asian nation that has the freest press, Taiwan, was also the Southeast Asian nation that suffered the least economic setback in the 1997–98 Asian downturn.

Already 30 million Chinese own stock. With so many new shareholders, lots of underground stock-oriented newspapers and magazines have sprung up, because investors are demanding real economic news. "They start out as sort of tip sheets put out by the research offices of various brokerage houses, and then are faxed around town," explained Seth Faison, the *New York Times* bureau chief in Shanghai. "It is all market-oriented news about different companies or stocks, or it may be a tip about what a ministry in Beijing is going to do. A lot of it is just rumors, some of which turn out to be true. It is geared for an audience of people who are playing the markets, but don't feel they are getting enough news out of the daily papers." But what happens is that once the Chinese government tells the press they are free to write about business, newspapers like China's *Southern Weekend* use that opening to cram in all sorts of quasi-political news and criticism about corruption and political abuses by officials on the business pages. That is how a free press will get born in China.

Bond and Stock Markets

There are essentially three ways that businesses can raise money: by borrowing from a bank, by selling shares on a stock market and by issuing bonds on a bond market. It is very important for a country to have all three options, so if your banks get into trouble entrepreneurs can turn to the bond and stock markets. And if the bond market tanks, they can turn to the stock market and banks. This so-called "three-legged" approach disperses risks more widely and enhances any financial system's ability to cope with shocks. All too often, though, developing countries just have one or at best two legs of this three-legged stool, and that makes their financial systems less than stable.

Look at the Asian tigers. What they had in common when their economic crises hit was that each had very high levels of savings and very low levels of government debt. The people didn't spend and the government didn't borrow. Good news, right? Not necessarily. While these countries had all these people who loved to save, the only place they could put their money, for the most part, was in local banks, because mutual funds, pension funds and local bond markets were either nonexistent or highly underdeveloped. So what happened was that local banks built up huge cash balances. The only thing they could do with all these savings was lend them back to local companies. This led to fierce competition between local banks, and contributed to banks throwing money at less and less qualified borrowers for less and less qualified projects. Moreover, when the banks went bad or had to be restructured in a country such as Thailand, it was very difficult for businesses to raise fresh capital because it had no bond market and its stock market was in the tank. No wonder that Singapore and Hong Kong deliberately created bond markets—even though there was plenty of local capital around through bank savings—because they wanted a local bond market that would provide "patient capital," that is, long-term financing for corporate borrowers so that they would not be subject to the vagaries of short-term lending from banks. In addition, a bond market also gave Singapore and Hong Kong savers the chance to buy higher-yielding mutual funds, and pension funds, as an alternative to bank savings accounts for investing.

The Electronic Herd has long encouraged the creation of bond markets, both for its own appetites and because of how well-regulated bond and stock markets contribute to greater financial democratization and transparency. Bond and stock markets liberate entrepreneurs from having to cultivate relationships with just a handful of bankers in order to raise cash. Also, when companies are totally dependent on borrowing from banks—particularly in crony capitalist operating systems where the bankers are tied in with the companies and high bureaucrats—they can avoid a lot of the scrutiny that they would have to undergo if they were issuing bonds or stocks. Companies that issue stocks and bonds have their performance judged every day: their bonds are held by a diverse public and rated by independent rating agencies, while the stocks are traded by anonymous investors on an open market. The only way your corporate bond can be rated or your stock listed, in a properly regulated market, is through proper disclosure. And if you are appealing to international investors, and want to be rated by a Moody's or Duff & Phelps Credit Rating Co. or Standard & Poor's, that disclosure will have to be based on international norms. Punishment is swift for any deviants.

Consider this November 15, 1998, *Washington Post* report from Paris: The story begins with Serge Tchuruk, one of the best-known business executives in France, telling a breakfast meeting of big international investors that profits for his company, Alcatel, the French telecommunications giant, would be considerably lower than the company had forecast just a few weeks earlier. The herd does not like such surprises. Between the end of that breakfast and the close of business that day, Alcatel stock fell 38 percent—the largest one-day decline ever on the French stock exchange—as primarily American and British pension and mutual funds left Alcatel for dead. The *Post* reporter, Anne Swardson, then went on to note how the herd was reshaping the old ways of Europe, Inc.: "In the past few years, foreigners have pushed many companies to change management, reform accounting systems, initiate international mergers, inject English—the language of international commerce—into the boardroom. In general, European management, historically uninterested in shareholders' demands, has become more responsive and attentive."

What I enjoyed most, though, was reading that the day after the herd stampeded Alcatel stock, Tchuruk got on a plane and flew to London, then hopped the Concorde for New York to meet with his American mutual fund investors, to try to explain to them what went wrong and win back their confidence.

"He was apologetic, but it didn't matter," one U.S. participant told the *Post*. "By then we had sold all our shares."

Democratization

The Electronic Herd will intensify pressures for democratization generally, for three very critical reasons—flexibility, legitimacy and sustainability. Here's how: The faster and bigger the herd gets, the more greased and open the global economy becomes, the more flexibility you need to get the most out of the herd and protect yourself from it. While one can always find exceptions, I still believe that as a general rule the more democratic, accountable and open your governance, the less likely it is that your financial system will be exposed to surprises. And when it *is* exposed to shocks and surprises, the more quickly it can adjust to changing circumstances and demands. Also, the more open and democratic your society, the more feedback you are always going to be getting, the better chance you have to make midcourse corrections before you go over a cliff, and the easier it is to bring in new managers and to kick out inept ones.

Moreover, as your country has to make these often painful midcourse corrections, the more democratic it is, the more legitimacy your government will have to share the pain of reform with the whole population. "Think of what the Southeast Asian leaders were telling their people for most of the post–World War II era," says democracy scholar Larry Diamond. "They were telling their people: 'You give me your freedom and keep your mouth shut, and I will give you the opportunity to get rich. It was easy for people to be apolitical when all boats were rising, and people felt that they could leave political management to someone else without harming their economic well-being. Well, that worked fine for about thirty years, but then the growth collapsed and the distribution of riches, welfare and benefits collapsed too. And people realized that they could not leave politics to someone else. So the bargain breaks down. As a result, what the people have said to their governments in Thailand, Indonesia, Korea, and soon will in China, is that if you have taken away our growth, if the state cannot deliver on the previous bargain, then we want a new bargain and in this bargain we are going to have a much bigger say in how the system operates. But because we have a bigger say, we will be ready to make bigger sacrifices while the system is reformed and gets up to speed. And that is why they are ready to exhibit considerably more patience in the face of economic suffering than many people expected. Because their politics has been opened and democratized, they at least have more of a feeling that they are working through these problems with a degree of equality. They become part owners of the game."

Of those Asian nations that were fully plugged into the Electronic Herd (China, without a convertible currency and open capital markets, is not fully plugged in yet), those with the most noncorrupt and democratic systems—Taiwan, Hong Kong, Singapore, Australia—were hurt the least by the 1997 downturn. Those countries which had democratic but corrupt systems—Thailand and Korea—were hurt the second worst, but because they were democracies they were able to respond quickly to the crisis, without popular uprisings, by voting in better governance and software. After having been just hammered by the Electronic Herd in the fall of 1997, Thailand elected the cleanest, most democratic party in the country and passed a radical new anticorruption constitution. The new Thai constitution mandated for the first time that Thai politicians would have to declare their personal assets before and after leaving office and would be subject to impeachment if more than 50,000 voters signed a petition seeking a corruption investigation into their affairs. Thailand also passed the First Freedom of Information Act in Asia, which the Thai press is now aggressively using to monitor Thai ministers as never before. As a World Bank official in Bangkok observed to me: "The new constitution never would have been passed through Parliament without the banking crisis. Never. The banking crisis got both the King and the army to push it, after they had been hesitant [before]." How did Korea react? By electing the most liberal democrat in the country, Kim Dae Jung, a man who could not get elected dogcatcher before Korea's financial crisis.

The Southeast Asian country that was the most authoritarian and the most corrupt, Indonesia under Suharto, was the one that was least flexible, least capable of adopting new software, and the one that eventually melted down—because the Indonesian masses were not ready to share the pain of reforms, because they did not feel the government was their own. When the Indonesian currency got hammered in 1998, and the IMF would give bailout loans only if Indonesia cut spending, President Suharto had to say to his people: "Friends, we've got to tighten our belts. We're all in this together." And when he tried that, the answer he got back from his own people in an explosion of rage was: "Mr. President, we all weren't in the toll roads, and hotels, and airlines and taxi companies you and your children own together. So screw you."

Finally, it is one thing for a government to improve its operating system and software on paper, but the only way to make sure those improvements are sustainable is to firmly locate them within a democratic or democratizing system. As Diamond puts it: "Nations that try to plug into the herd with good software, rule of law, and accountability—but with no regular free elections—will not be able to keep up with the herd in the long run. Because you cannot sustain good software with an authoritarian regime that is not itself accountable, does not permit the free flow of information, does not permit an independent judiciary to pursue corruption, and does not permit free elections so that the political management can be changed."

Elections alone will never be enough to ensure good governance; Russia and Pakistan are proof enough of that. At the same time, just installing modern operating systems and software in a country, without holding regular elections that can remove corrupt leaders, will never be effective either. That is why the wisest leaders in developing countries will be those who understand quickest that without the herd there will be no growth, and without better software and operating systems there will be no herd, and without regular elections there will be no long-term better governance.

While the logic of globalution leaves me an optimist that the herd will make an increasingly important contribution to democratization, the reality of how it will unfold has to leave you cautious. You don't just plug into the herd and get better software, operating systems and democracy on the other end. You have to work at it. Building software is an inherently political process, involving real human beings, that often runs into political, economic, historical and cultural resistance. There are no shortcuts and people almost always have to learn the hard way. America got where it is today thanks to two hundred years of boom and bust cycles in the railroad business, endless bank failures, huge bankruptcies, monopolies created and busted up, the stock market crash of 1929 and the savings and loan crisis of the 1980s. We weren't born this way.

I once asked Anatoly Chubais, the architect of many of Russia's halting economic reforms, about how difficult it was for Russia to move to a free-market system.

"We did not have enough people with experience in modern governing or technologies or markets, because we had no markets," he answered. "The very word 'market' was prohibited in the Soviet Union. I am not an old man, but I do remember a friend of mine, an economist, who in 1982 lost his job for writing an article in a scientific journal where he used the word 'market.' "

And here's what's really scary. Even when you figure out what a market is, even when you build better software, improving it is a never-ending task. What happens when you get DOScapital 6.0?

You get to start working on DOScapital 7.0.

Julia Preston, the *New York Times* correspondent in Mexico City, once told me of an unusual meeting of the Zapatista guerrillas, the peasant group that has been fighting the effects of free trade and globalization on Mexico. The Zapatistas held a convention in the jungle of southern

Mexico entitled "The Intercontinental Forum in Favor of Humanity and Against Neoliberalism." The closing session met in a steamy mudhole amphitheater and was presided over by Zapatista leader "Subcommander Marcos"—a Mexican combination of Robin Hood and Ralph Nader. The session ended with the Zapatistas doing a kind of drumroll and announcing the most evil, dangerous institution in the world today. To a standing ovation, the Zapatistas declared the biggest enemy of mankind to be the WTO—the World Trade Organization in Geneva, which promotes global free trade and an end to protectionism.

That story always reminded me of the fact that while the Electronic Herd and the Supermarkets will be important contributors to democratization, they will also create the opposite effect. They will contribute to a widespread feeling, particularly within democracies, that even if people have a democracy at home they have lost control over their lives, because even their elected representatives have to bow now to unelected market dictators.

The bigger, faster and more influential the herd becomes, argues Wharton School globalization expert Stephen J. Kobrin, "the more individual citizens start to feel that the locus of economic control and political decisionmaking on economic matters is shifting from the local level, where it can be controlled, to the global level, where no one is in charge and no one is minding the store. When all politics is local, your vote matters. But when the power shifts to these transnational spheres, there are no elections and there is no one to vote for."

There is no question that in the globalization system, where power is now more evenly shared between states and Supermarkets, a certain degree of decision-making is moved out of each country's political sphere into the global market sphere, where no one person, country or institution can exert exclusive political control—at least not yet. Think how many times you've heard the expression "The markets say . . . ," "The markets are demanding that . . . ," "The markets were not happy . . ."

As Israeli political theorist Yaron Ezrahi notes: "The most arbitrary powers in history always hid under the claim of some impersonal logic— God, the laws of nature, the laws of the market—and they always provoked a backlash when morally intolerable discrepancies became glaringly visible. The Enlightenment was really the globalization of science and rationality and the backlash came when every thief, crook, exploiter and fraud claimed that whatever he was doing was necessitated by science and logic. The same could happen with globalization. Many will see it as little more than a mask used by certain economic elites for taking away the voice of the individual citizen. That is why some argue that the globalizers in each society want to buy the media first, because they want to turn potentially aggrieved and assertive citizens into conforming consumers. Turning politics into a spectator sport is one of the subtle processes which supports globalization. It converts or transforms the citizen from an actor to a spectator, with illusions of participation."

The more citizens begin to feel that in this new system of globalization things are controlled from afar, not from at home, the more the globalizers in these countries will be exposed to attacks. Egypt's Minister of Economy, Yousef Boutros-Ghali, once observed: "The whole process of globalization is very easy to demagogue. Those who want to resist change point to anyone who wants to open the economy for foreign investment and say, 'Look, here is a man who is a traitor to our cause, because he wants to open the system to foreigners.' And then you say, 'Yes, but it is more efficient to let markets determine prices,' and they come back at you and say, 'Are you crazy? Markets are determined by foreigners. How can we let our markets determine prices when markets are controlled by foreigners?' "

Clearly, one of the biggest challenges for political theory in this globalization era is how to give citizens a sense that they can exercise their will, not only over their own governments but over at least some of the global forces shaping their lives. "Because market forces and institutions are ethically indifferent, they require a deliberative, communal intelligence to prevent extreme injustices," says Ezrahi. "That deliberative role is the essence of citizenship and democratic governance—guarding and shaping the public space and collective life. And you really have a problem if your public space and collective life are being shaped by forces beyond your own politics." Our children's civics classes will have to go beyond the study of local, state and national governments, into the realm of studying what is acceptable conduct in the relations between states and Supermarkets, between states and Super-empowered individuals and between Super-empowered individuals and Supermarkets. How do we deal with a world where the Electronic Herd gets to vote in all kinds of countries every day, but those countries don't get to vote on the herd's behavior in such a direct and immediate manner? Who will govern relations between me and my Internet, and between the Supermarkets and me, and between my government and the Supermarkets? To paraphrase Larry Summers, this is "the globalization trilemma."

The one thing you can say in favor of the globalization system is that it doesn't discriminate—it leaves both the weak and the powerful feeling a loss of control and under the thumb of unelected and at times uncontrollable forces. I went to see Mexico's Finance Minister, Guillermo Ortiz, immediately after the 1995 crash of the Mexican peso. He was sitting at his desk, tied to his computer screens, which were charting the second-by-second fall of the peso like an EKG heading for a heart attack.

"Give us a truce," said Ortiz, addressing the global markets. "You have pounded us to death. Stop selling us short." When I asked him what it was like to be caught in the maw of the global markets, which were chasing him with a Golden Straitjacket, Ortiz gestured to the three computer screens next to his desk that track the peso, second by second: "I have days when I feel absolutely powerless. Sometimes I have to go work in the other room so that I can concentrate away from the screens."

10

Shapers, Adapters and Other New Ways of Thinking About Power

REDMOND, Wash., October 21, 1997—In direct response to accusations made by the Department of Justice, the Microsoft Corporation announced today that it will be acquiring the Federal Government of the United States of America for an undisclosed sum. "It's actually a logical extension of our planned growth," said Microsoft chairman Bill Gates. "It really is going to be a positive arrangement for everyone."

Microsoft representatives held a briefing in the Oval Office of the White House with U.S. President Bill Clinton, and assured members of the press that changes will be "minimal." The United States will be managed as a wholly owned division of Microsoft.

An initial public offering is planned for July of next year, and the Federal Government is expected to be profitable by "Q4 1999 at the latest," according to Microsoft president Steve Ballmer.

In a related announcement, Bill Clinton stated that he had "willingly and enthusiastically" accepted a position as a vice president with Microsoft, and will continue to manage the United States Government, reporting directly to Bill Gates. When asked how it felt to give up the mantle of executive authority to Gates, Clinton smiled and referred to it as "a relief." He went on to say that Gates has a "proven track record" and that U.S. citizens should offer Gates their "full support and confidence." Clinton will reportedly be earning several times the $200,000 annually he has earned as U.S. President, in his new role at Microsoft.

Gates dismissed a suggestion that the U.S. Capitol be moved to Redmond as "silly," though he did say that he would make executive decisions for the U.S. Government from his existing office at Microsoft headquarters. Gates went on to say that the House and Senate would "of course" be abolished. "Microsoft isn't a democracy," he observed, "and look how well we're doing." When asked if the rumored attendant acquisition of Canada was proceeding, Gates said, "We don't deny that discussions are taking place." Microsoft representatives closed the conference by stating that United States citizens will be able to expect lower taxes, increases in government services and discounts on all Microsoft products.

About Microsoft: Founded in 1978, Microsoft (NASDAQ 'MSFT') is the worldwide leader in software for personal computers and democratic government. The
company offers a wide range of products and services for public, business and personal use, each designed with the mission of making it easier and more enjoyable
for people to take advantage of the full power of personal computing and free society every day.

About the United States: Founded in 1789, the United States of America is the
most successful nation in the history of the world, and has been a beacon of
democracy and opportunity for over 200 years. Headquartered in Washington,
D.C., the United States is a wholly owned subsidiary of Microsoft Corporation.
                         —*anonymous spoof of Microsoft that appeared on the Internet*

I was reading the *Financial Times* one day in the fall of 1995, when a
front-page picture jumped out at me. It showed Bill Gates, the chairman of Microsoft, holding talks with Jiang Zemin, the President of
China. The caption was written as though this were a standard summit
meeting between two world leaders. It said the two men held "very cor-
dial" talks, in contrast with their frosty meeting eighteen months earlier. I
thought to myself, Bill Gates has met Jiang Zemin twice in eighteen
months. Hmmm, that's once more than Bill Clinton has met the Chinese leader. That was no accident. The Chinese seemed to believe at the
time that they needed Bill G. more than they needed Bill C. And who
could blame them? The Chinese were upset that the Chinese-language
translation of Windows 3.1 was done by Taiwanese computer linguists—
using Taiwanese-style Chinese characters and computer codes. Nothing
could possibly enrage China more than the thought of Taiwan shaping
the software and operating systems for every Chinese computer. As a result, the Beijing authorities were blocking market access for Windows 95
until Microsoft agreed that the Chinese version of that software would be
jointly produced by Microsoft and a Mainland Chinese company.
    Reading that story, and studying that caption, started me wondering
whether the attributes of countries and companies weren't starting to converge. After all, if it's right that when you link your country up with the
global economy, it's like taking your country public—like turning your
country into a public company with shareholders all over the world—this
alone is giving countries more of a corporate feel. Citizens are behaving

more like shareholders, leaders more like management and foreign policy analysts more like credit-rating agencies.

At the same time, the more widespread the Internet becomes in the lives of citizens, the more they are going to put pressure on their governments and legal systems to operate at Net speed. In the Cold War system the gap between companies and governments existed, but it wasn't huge. IBM and General Motors operated a lot like the federal government or even the Kremlin. Not anymore—which is why the demand for E-government is rising. Why should you wait in line for six hours at the county license bureau to get your license renewed, when you can buy the whole bloody car online? More and more, citizens will expect the same ease of service from the United States of America as they get from America Online. When we all know how each other lives, governments increasingly have to promise the same things. And when we all know how each other shops, governments increasingly are going to have to *deliver* the same services with the same ease. And the only way governments will be able to do that is by operating more like good companies. To put it another way, the more people want government to become as quick and efficient as Amazon.com, the more government *has* to operate like Amazon.com.

Moreover, countries are under pressure to behave more like companies because in the globalization system countries, more than ever, can choose prosperity—depending on the policies they adopt—and their citizens will start to catch on to that and demand better management accordingly. As people become increasingly aware that their government is running DOScapital 1.0, while the government next door is running DOScapital 6.0, they will start to ask: Why? People will learn that unlike in the Industrial Revolution, countries today don't have to be prisoners of their natural resources, geography or history. In today's globalization system any country can plug into the Internet, import knowledge and develop its own educational base; any country can find shareholders from any other country to invest in its infrastructure; any country with the right leadership can implement DOScapital 6.0 over a period of time. "Which will be the world's fastest-growing economy this year?" Asked *The Economist* Intelligence Unit in early 2000. "Mozambique. Mozambique has been one of the world's fastest-growing economies for the past four years. GDP growth there has averaged 10 percent. Botswana has enjoyed average growth of 7 percent over that period. Despite Africa's disadvantages, such as climate and disease, some political stability, prudent fiscal policies and business-friendly reforms can work wonders, even in desperately poor countries." Mozambique and Botswana chose prosperity. As Harvard Business School professor Michael Porter once put it: "A nation's wealth is [now] principally of its own collective choosing. Location, natural resources and even military might are no longer decisive. Instead, how a nation and its citizens choose to organize and manage the economy, the institutions they put in place and the types of investments they individually and collectively choose to make will determine national prosperity."

If countries can now choose prosperity just like companies, what are the policies and skills countries should adopt in this era of globalization? What follows—over this chapter and the next—is my own checklist, developed from looking at the best global companies and countries. When I come into a country today these are the first two questions I ask when trying to assess its economic power and potential.

How Wired Is Your Country or Company?

In October 1995, I flew out to Redmond, Washington, to interview Microsoft's number-two man, president Steve Ballmer, in order to ask him one simple question: Microsoft is the most important company in America today, so how does Microsoft measure power in its universe? When it looks out on the world, which countries strike it as powerful today and why? Ballmer had a simple answer back in October 1995: "We measure power in one ratio—PCs per household," he said. O.K., I answered, then give me your power map of the world. Well, he said, the fastest-growing region for Microsoft was Asia, where South Korea had the highest density of PCs per household. Japan was just taking off, he said, but Microsoft was most excited about China.

"How can you like China?" I asked. "People make fifty dollars a month there."

"Oh, you don't understand," Ballmer answered. He then went over to a blackboard and drew two short lines together on one side, two short lines on the other side, two short lines under both of them and one line at the bottom. "What's that?" I asked. He then circled each pair of lines at the top and then the pair of lines under them and then the last line at the bottom, and said: "That is two Chinese maternal grandparents and two Chinese paternal grandparents and two Chinese parents all saving for the

Windows 95 for one Chinese kid." Yes, even birth control in China works for Microsoft.

"Keep going around the world," I said.

Brazil and India were both hot, with a rapid growth in PCs per household, Ballmer said. But the Middle East was pretty much a black hole for Microsoft from Morocco to the border of Pakistan, with the exception of Israel, which had its own Microsoft development center—a whole different level of power—and Saudi Arabia, where Egyptians were running Microsoft for multinationals. Western Europe was strong everywhere, Ballmer indicated, except one country—France. "I don't want to say [France] has fallen behind," said Ballmer, but "the penetration of PCs relative to population was quite high in France. That's not true anymore."

I called Ballmer's power map "Foreign Policy 3.1." Three years later, in 1998, I decided I should update it. This time, though, I decided to go to Silicon Valley and ask the top managers at the leading companies there—Intel, Sun and Cisco—as well as professors at the Stanford University School of Engineering, how they measured power. Interestingly, I discovered things had evolved considerably. Silicon Valley, they explained, measured power in 1998 not just by PCs per household anymore but by "degree of connectivity."

The important thing now, they said, is how broadly and deeply your country has taken its PCs and linked them together into networks within companies, schools and entertainment sources, and then tied those intranets into the Internet and the World Wide Web. Degree of connectivity is usually measured by how extensive is a country's bandwidth: the capacity of its cable, telephone lines and fiber optics to carry digital communications—all those packets of 1's and 0's—from point to point within networks. If the mantra of the PC decade, the 1980s, was "You can never have too much memory in your computer," the mantra of the post-PC decade, the network era, is "You can never have too much bandwidth in your country."

The more installed bandwidth your country has, the greater its degree of connectivity. If you want to know just how connected a country is, you measure its "megabits per capita"—how much installed bandwidth it has, divided by the number of its potential users. Megabits per capita has now joined PCs per household as a key yardstick of power in the silicon universe. It will tell you the rate of information dissemination within the population and to and from decisionmakers. Jobs, knowledge use and economic growth will gravitate to those societies that are the most connected, with the most networks and the broadest amount of bandwidth—because these countries will find it easiest to amass, deploy and share knowledge in order to design, invent, manufacture, sell, provide services, communicate, educate and entertain. Connectivity is now productivity.

As Brian Reid, a Digital Equipment Corporation executive who did some of the pioneering work on the Internet, once told *The New York Times* (Dec. 8, 1997): "Bandwidth is the delivery system by which companies sell their goods in the information age. Bandwidth in the late 1990s is important for commerce in the same way that railroads were important in the 1890s and seaports were in the 1790s. It's the way you sell your product."

John Chambers of Cisco likes to say that the companies and countries who will thrive in this Internet economy are those who will grasp its importance first, and get wired before the rest of the world realizes that they have to change. If you do that faster than your competitors, says Chambers, there's only one thing you'll have to say to them: "Game over."

Because as we rapidly move into a world in which the Internet will define commerce, education and communication, there will be just two kinds of businesses: Internet businesses and anti-Internet businesses. Internet businesses are those that can either be done over the Internet, everything from book selling to brokerage to gambling, or be significantly enhanced by the Internet, which applies to everything from management consulting to inventory control. Anti-Internet businesses are those that cannot be done over the Internet—such as preparing food, cutting hair or making steel—and those that are in some ways a reaction against the Internet. This would include things like shopping centers and Starbucks coffeehouses. Starbucks and the shopping center are anti-Internet businesses because they benefit from the fact that the more people are home alone with their computers, surfing the Net, the more these same people will want to get out of the house, go to the mall or Starbucks or Main Street and touch someone, smell something, taste something or feel something. Products will always need exposure in a way that people can touch or feel; people will always seek community, whether on Main Street or in the mall.

As the Internet becomes the backbone of global commerce, education and communication, the quality and scope of the networking within countries will be decisive in determining their economic strength. So who's hot and who's not today according to this new networking power standard? Taiwan is feared in Silicon Valley for its innovative prowess, connectivity and dynamic capitalist business culture that deftly exploits all this technology. If Taiwan were a stock, I'd buy it. The United States, Britain, Canada, Australia, Scandinavia, Iceland, Israel, Italy, Singapore, Costa Rica and India also fall into this category. Costa Rica is implementing a plan to give every high school student an E-mail address. Japan, Korea and China are all coming on strong, after falling behind early. Soon Singapore won't be the only country in the world that holds an annual "Miss Internet" pageant. A caption in USA Today (Jan. 19, 1999), beneath a picture of a young Singaporean woman being crowned Miss Internet, reported: "Singapore is so serious about the digital age that it has a Miss Internet contest. Stella Tan, seated, won in August. Categories in the competition include business wear and Web design."

From Bert Parks to Bill Gates: waistwidth is out, bandwidth is in.

But here's the big question: what comes next, after PCs per household and networks per capita, as the key metric of economic power?

The answer to that is twofold: Physically what comes next is the "Evernet," a world in which we will all be able to be online all the time — through some information appliance, be it your television, PC, pager, faxer, toaster or E-mailer. Anything that runs on electricity is now being fitted with software and linked to networks that run through your home or office. The more the Internet breaks free from your desktop computer and becomes accessible from all sorts of information appliances, the closer the Evernet comes. How you choose to surf it, through your watch, cell phone or PC, will be your business.

As more and more countries go down this road, countries will increasingly be measured by how close they are to universal connectivity. They will be measured by how close they are to having all their people online, or able to get online, all the time everywhere they go, and by how rich a variety of services they can offer on this Evernet. For instance, how many of your households will have speech-to-text transcription services through the Evernet, so people can just dictate anything to anyone on their home computers? How good will the video-conferencing services offered by your Evernet be, so that people can transmit images and talk face to face through the Evernet at virtually no cost? How many of your educational institutions will be offering courses online, so people can study and learn whenever they want, from wherever they want? How well encrypted will your Evernet be, so that data can be stored safely and all credit card commerce can be conducted without worry of cybertheft? How convenient and multidimensional will be the information appliances that your people carry around with them at all times so that they can always be on-line?

Is Your Company or Country a Shaper or an Adapter?

But while having your companies and population linked to the Evernet will be a necessary component of economic power, it will not be sufficient. It's only going to be half the power story. The other half will be about how well, and how creatively, your country or companies learn to exploit this Evernet. Power will flow not simply to those who are the most wired, but to those who are the most creative at bringing together firms, governments, capital, information, consumers and talent in networked coalitions that create value. Some will be corporate-led coalitions to create commercial value. Some will be government-led coalitions to create geopolitical value. And some will be activist-led coalitions to create, or preserve, human values—such as worker rights, human rights or environmental preservation.

In this system companies, governments or activists will either be what John Hagel III of McKinsey originally called "shapers" or "adapters." The shapers are those companies, countries or activists who define the rules and interactions that will govern a certain activity in this Evernet world—whether that activity is making a profit, making a war or making a government or corporation respect human rights. The adapters are those companies who adapt themselves to the rules and interaction frameworks shaped by others and learn to profit from them by carving out their own niches. The more consumers, companies and countries are all connected into a single Evernet, the more power will accrue to the great shapers. Already, you can see all over the world struggles emerging over which country, or company, or consumer activist group, or Super-empowered individual is going to be the shaper of various rules or standards—because once you shape a new standard in such a wired world, in such a world without walls, its reach can be enormous. It can influence the behavior or buying habits of a huge number of people from one end of the globe to the other.

A good example of a shaper in the economic realm is eBay, the online auction site. It came out of nowhere and within three years created a new set of rules and forms of interaction by which consumers would buy and sell things on the World Wide Web. eBay brought together buyers and sellers on the Internet to create a whole new marketplace for doing this, outside conventional newspaper classified ads or other traditional barter centers, and also to create its own set of rules. Each person selling things on eBay is rated by people who do business with him or her, and if you cheat people even once your eBay rating will be affected in a way that could make it impossible for you to do business in the future, because everyone on the World Wide Web can find out that you have been rated a cheater. Once a standard such as eBay's emerges, the competition then moves to other areas or to see who can adapt eBay's innovation the best. So now you don't just have individuals quaintly buying and selling and trading goods through eBay, but you have people who have set up whole companies to do so. You want a lot of people adapting to your standard, and profiting from it, because that stabilizes it and locks it in. It also creates a lot of innovation around your standard that is bound to improve it. The emergence of the Evernet is making it possible for people to develop eBay-like exchanges in a variety of industries—from home building to construction to the selling of steel or plastics. These exchanges bring buyers and sellers together in a particular industry in a way that is allowing much more efficient trading, selling and bartering of goods on a global scale—as well as a sharing or selling of expertise. If your company or country can become the shaper of one or more of these exchanges— E-steel, E-rubber, E-cement—in the great Evernet land grab that is now under way, it will be a real source of power. Because the reach of these exchanges will be global, and once one gets established, such as eBay, it is difficult to knock off. There will be one or two in every industry, and that's it.

Microsoft is another shaper. It has brought consumers and companies together into a value net based around its technologies, standards, software and operating systems. To be an effective shaper you have to be able to attract a lot of adapters. But the key to having a lot of adapters to your standard is that it be able to create a lot of value for other people too— whether it is a product, a human value or a set of geopolitical rules. If people become reluctant members of your value network, eventually they will rebel against it by seeking a different standard. So one thing a shaper always has to be aware of is whether he is leaving room in his value chain—some food on the table—so that others will have an incentive to adapt to his standards. Or, is he trying to gobble up every crumb of profit potentially created by his standard. If eBay not only shaped a whole new marketplace for doing business, but also tried to run all the most profitable exchanges under its umbrella, fewer and fewer people would have an incentive to adapt to the eBay system and eventually it would collapse. Microsoft's greed, and its reluctance to make room for others, such as Netscape, to adapt its operating system for easy browsing of the Internet, ultimately led to the Justice Department's antitrust suit against Microsoft—as well as provoking others to try to shape a different Internet standard from Microsoft's. The key to being an effective shaper is not to be a pig, which Microsoft was.

Not all successful shapers start out as shapers. Dell, for instance, started out as an adapter. It took an existing technology, the IBM PC, and brilliantly adapted it through creative manufacturing techniques. Dell became part of IBM's value chain. Then Dell, in turn, became a shaper. In its effort to become the best adapter of the IBM PC, Dell shaped innovative new ways to use the Internet to reach customers and manage suppliers and inventories. In doing so, it created its own value chain, and IBM turned around and became an adapter of Dell's Internet-based manufacturing and inventory techniques.

The same principle applies in geopolitics. The United States today is the world's great geopolitical shaper. While it would be too much to say that the United States is in charge of globalization, it is the country with the greatest ability, for the moment, to shape the coalitions that can manage globalization geopolitically. For instance, in this more connected world, the United States defined how capital, information and military might were to be brought to bear to rescue the Kosovar Albanians evicted by Yugoslavia in 1999. It was the United States that shaped many of the key rules by which the World Trade Organization would operate and the terms under which China would be admitted. It was the United States that shaped the United Nations' response to Iraqi President Saddam Hussein. The other NATO countries, the Chinese and the Russians, were usually adapters, sometimes reluctant adapters.

The United States and Great Britain were the key shapers of the Golden Straitjacket, along with the Supermarkets. In this interconnected world the rules of the Golden Straitjacket have become the widely adopted standard for creating growth. The Golden Straitjacket has also created a global value chain for how business and trade are conducted—from which countries such as the United States and Great Britain greatly benefit. But there are now a lot of countries who see benefit in adapting to it and coming up with their own variations—thus reinforcing the influence of the Golden Straitjacket.

As in the business world, the key to being a successful geopolitical shaper is being generous and not too overbearing, so other countries see benefit—to themselves or to the stability of the region around them—from adapting to your standard and geopolitical rules. America would be a greedy shaper if it were to say to the rest of the world: "You must adopt the Golden Straitjacket and open your country to free trade. But as you do, we're going to export everything we can to your country and we're only going to let you export a few things to America." That wouldn't give countries much incentive to put on the Golden Straitjacket, and would give them instead a great incentive to write their own new standard. The geopolitical shapers who don't last long are those who try to capture too much for themselves and don't leave anything on the table for others to have an incentive to adapt and create around.

What is least understood and in many ways most interesting is how the same principle of shapers and adapters can be applied when thinking about human rights, social activism, charity and environmentalism. All sorts of private groups, governments, Super-empowered individuals and companies can now become shapers of rules and coalitions to produce better governance in all these areas—much more than ever before. But many activists don't understand this opportunity for social entrepreneurship.

Here's how to think about this: When America, beginning in the late nineteenth century, moved from a collection of semiautonomous regional economies to a more integrated national economy it really gave birth to the federal government as we know it today. The Federal Reserve, the Securities and Exchange Commission, the Federal Communications Commission and other such institutions all came out of this era. A national economy needed a set of national institutions that could cover it, monitor it and regulate it. The natural tendency is to assume that the same will, or should, happen with globalization. That is, as we move from a collection of semiautonomous national economies to a more integrated global economy we will develop a kind of global government to cover it, monitor it and regulate it.

But making the leap from regional institutions to national institutions within countries is much easier than making the leap from national institutions within each country to global institutions that will oversee every country. You bump into two problems when you go global: One is sovereignty—the sheer reluctance of people to be ruled by politicians and bureaucrats from the other side of the world, over whom they have no democratic or other control. And the other is the very nature of the globalization system itself. In a world without walls, increasingly built around an Evernet, the ability of any global governing institution to actually get its arms around a problem and enforce certain taxes or behaviors is limited—whether it is Interpol trying to track criminal financial transfers over the Internet from the Cayman Islands to the Channel Islands, or the World Trade Organization trying to figure out how to regulate trade in cyberspace. Every day there are more and more places that traditional government institutions find it hard to reach into.

Therefore, when it comes to enforcing global norms—for the environment, human rights, financial interactions or worker conditions—the shaper is not going to be a global government, at least any time soon. But what then do we do? We can't ignore these problems and we don't want to just leave them to the marketplace to solve. So now we come to the key question: How do we get better global *governance*, in areas such as environment, human rights, financial interactions and worker conditions, without having global *government*? How do we manage and regulate issues that we really value as human beings and communities, but without some global cop to do it for us?

The answer is to understand that in a world of networks, individuals, companies, communities, consumers, activist groups and governments all have the power to be shapers—to shape human value chains. And when you are the shaper of a coalition in support of a certain human value, you would be amazed what you can do without global government to create better global governance. It requires a radical new way of thinking about how to mobilize power, though. It requires thinking about how one can exploit the Internet, the power of consumers, and the exposure of multinational companies who need to do business all over the world and therefore need to protect their brand names all over the world.

Let me give a few examples. One of the biggest questions to arise in the age of globalization is how we deal with the important issue of workers' rights and sweatshops in the developing world. In this postcommunist era, while many human rights activists are still focused on promoting issues of free speech, elections and the right to write an op-ed piece, people in the developing world are increasingly focused on workers' rights, jobs, the right to organize and the right to decent working conditions. Quite simply, for many workers around the world, oppression by the unchecked commissars has been replaced with oppression by the unregulated capitalists, who move their manufacturing from country to country, constantly in search of those who will work for the lowest wages and lowest standards. To some, the Nike swoosh is now as scary as the hammer and sickle.

These workers need practical help. But there is no global government to turn to that can legislate better working conditions for all. For years, U.S. manufacturers have used their clout in Congress to block any attempt to impose U.S. working standards on their factories abroad. Meanwhile, when these shirt makers from South Carolina shift production to Guatemala, there are no local standards that are enforced there, and the International Labor Organization has no clout. So you end up with neither local nor global enforcement, which was highlighted in 1996 with the exposure of the appalling working conditions in a Honduran factory producing Kathie Lee Gifford brand clothing. Therefore, to wait for global government to fix the problem is to wait forever.

In the face of such a challenge the human rights community needs to retool in this post–Cold War world, every bit as much as the old arms makers have had to learn how to make subway cars and toasters instead of tanks. "In the Cold War," argued Michael Posner, head of the Lawyers Committee for Human Rights, "the main issue was how do you hold governments accountable when they violate laws and norms. Today, the emerging issue is how do you hold private companies accountable for the treatment of their workers at a time when government control is ebbing all over the world, or governments themselves [such as in China] are going into business and can't be expected to play the watchdog or protection role."

In such a world, activists have to learn how to use globalization to their advantage. They have to learn how to compel companies to behave better by mobilizing global consumers through the Internet. I call this the "network solution for human rights," and it's the future of social advocacy. It is bottom-up regulation, or side-by-side regulation—not top-down regulation. You empower the bottom, instead of waiting for the top, by shaping a coalition that produces better governance without global government.

Precisely such an experiment was initiated in late 1999. Out of the Kathie Lee Gifford controversy a new coalition was born, called the Fair Labor Association. It brought together the U.S. government, workers' rights activists such as the Lawyers Committee, apparel makers and American college students. It works like this: Most of the major global apparel companies and human rights groups agreed on a minimum standard for working conditions in their factories, including restrictions on child labor and working hours. They also agreed on a uniform system of monitoring whereby independent external monitors are being allowed to make surprise visits to factories. The monitors are accredited by the FLA and range from church groups to PricewaterhouseCoopers. The FLA issues annual reports on each company's compliance, which are broadcast on the Internet and eventually should be published by *Consumer Reports*. If a company meets the standards, it is allowed to attach a special "FLA" label on its clothes, so consumers have credible information to differentiate among brands—that is, to buy those that support worker rights and shun those that don't. More than one hundred universities joined the coalition and have insisted that their bookstores, which sell huge numbers of sneakers, T-shirts and sweatshirts, sell only FLA-labeled products. The hope is that eventually all major retailers will do so as well.

This program is not going to revolutionize working conditions overnight. But it's a start—a start at shaping a new set of norms and rules for the global garment industry. And it is being done without global government, but instead by putting together a coalition that has the potential to make every consumer a human rights enforcer and to deprive global corporations of anywhere to hide.

"It's amazing how caught up some activists are in the old world," said Paul Gilding, the former head of Greenpeace who now advises multinationals on sustainable development. "The old model is you go into the streets, raise the outrage of the community, get the government to pass a law, the companies resist, eventually a compromise is reached and in five years things change. We don't have time for that anymore."

The groups making the biggest difference today are those that harness the economic self-interest of companies and consumers and make that a force for environmental protection, for upgrading workers' rights, for promoting human rights—rather than a force working against such values. That means working with multinationals and consumers and basically showing the companies how they can be both green and profitable at the same time, and making clear to them that if they don't upgrade their environmental practices or their labor standards abroad, the activist community will mount a campaign against them through the Internet with consumers all over the world. Economic self-interest is the big force at work in the world. It isn't the only one. Laws and norms still matter. Government still matters. Government still needs to pass laws and regulate in ways that protect society as a whole and not just the interests of one particular group of consumers or activists. But often the best way to win adherence to laws and norms is by trying to channel economic self-interest—the very metabolism of the globalization system—in a way that makes it restorative rather than destructive.

In the early 1990s, the World Trade Organization ruled that American laws banning tuna caught in nets that also catch dolphins were a trade barrier. This, understandably, upset many environmentalists. Some chose to attack the WTO, particularly at its meeting in Seattle in late 1999. But others decided to get organized and become shapers of the value they wanted to uphold—that fishermen shouldn't kill dolphins simply to catch tuna on the cheap. As a result of their actions it has become virtually impossible to buy a can of tuna in an American grocery store that isn't labeled "Dolphin Safe." But how could that be if the WTO said our law was a trade barrier? Because the smart activists just went around the WTO ruling and sought to shape new behavior in another way. They mobilized consumers and the Internet to pressure the tuna companies into going dolphin-safe; the tuna companies pressured the fishermen into using dolphin-safe nets because they didn't want to lose their customers; and, as a result, many dolphins got saved. The dolphin-safe standard is still not perfect; some fishermen still cheat and companies look the other way. But it's a vast improvement on the free-for-all that existed before, and that improvement is the result of environmental activists shaping a new standard by using a network solution, with no real government involvement. "Our decision to go dolphin-safe was purely based on consumer feedback," Michael Mullen, spokesman for StarKist tuna, told me. "We probably get about a thousand calls and three hundred consumer E-mails a week."

(In chapter 13, "Demolition Man," I will explore in greater detail how this approach is being applied in the environmental arena by organizations such as Conservation International to help save everything from the Brazilian rainforest to the world's biggest wetland.)

Consider one more example of this strategy from a whole different area—the war on poverty. Let me introduce the Web site www.planetfinance.org. It is the brainchild of French banker Jacques Attali, who decided that globalization empowered him to become a shaper of strategies for combating global poverty—without waiting for some global government to do it. PlaNet Finance works like this: Roughly 1.3 billion people live on a dollar a day. One thing we know is that one of the most effective tools for combating their poverty is microlending. Microloans range from $100 to $1,000. They go mostly to women and are given without any collateral. Microloan recipients use them to buy everything from sewing machines, to bicycles to get their vegetables to market, to beauty supplies to start a salon in a Bangladesh slum. These people have the will to better themselves, they just don't have the basic cash, and that's what microloans provide. While people who need microloans are not online, many of the microbanks and aid organizations that work with the poor do have phones and computers and can get online. What PlaNet Finance is doing is wiring these 7,000 microfinance groups around the world into a network that holds huge possibilities.

"First," explained Mr. Attali, "PlaNet is connecting as many microbanks as possible so they can share solutions. Second, we are helping those that are not online get online, as we did in Benin. Third, we are creating a system, like Moody's, that is rating microbanks according to their ethics, how well they serve the poor and financial efficiency. Fourth, we are setting up a university online to teach best practices to microbanks, and an online marketplace for microloan recipients to sell their crafts. Finally, we are creating PlaNet Bank, which is extending lines of credit to microbanks and will enable anyone to come to our Web site, donate money to selected projects offered by the best microbanks and then track who that money went to and how it is used."

Once PlaNet can rate and link all the microbanks through the Internet, it can help them lower their biggest cost—tracking and processing all these little loans. The hope is that a single microbanker, armed with the sort of information device that FedEx uses to track your packages, could keep track of hundreds of loans and interest payments at a time. If the processing and transaction costs of these microloans can be reduced, they can be bundled together and sold on a commercial basis to the Citibanks of the world. Microbanks usually charge 4 to 5 percent interest a month in order to cover costs and get people to pay them back quickly so that the money can be recycled to someone else. So this market, with those sorts of interest rates, would appeal to big banks—if the processing costs were cut. And that would change everything, because right now there is great demand for microloans, but the money pool for them is limited to donations by individuals and governments. By contrast, with $20 billion in commercial loans from big banks you could provide microloans to 100 million people living on a dollar a day.

That's how you change the world—by using globalization against it-self, by becoming a shaper who doesn't just wait around for global government to alleviate poverty but instead uses the new system to mobilize the big, cold, selfish market players to do the right thing for the wrong reason—greed. By getting the big banks to become adapters of the new concept shaped by PlaNet Finance, and giving them an economic incentive to do so, a whole new set of possibilities for combating poverty are opened up.

"There's an old saying, 'Feed a man a fish and you've fed him for a day. Teach a man to fish and you've fed him for a lifetime,'" said Mr. Attali. "Well, we have millions of poor people who know how to fish. They just don't have a pole. Through PlaNet we might be able to get poles for a lot more of them."

In a wired world without walls, the future belongs to the shapers and adapters—and they can be companies or consumers, superpowers or Super-empowered individuals.

11

Buy Taiwan, Hold Italy, Sell France

While getting wired and learning to become a shaper or adapter are going to be critical in determining a country's or company's clout in the Internet age, other factors will also be important—factors that will determine just how good a shaper or adapter you will be. This chapter explores what those factors are, and why countries or companies that have them are ones you would want to buy or hold and why countries that don't have them are ones you would want to sell. I call this checklist The Nine Habits of Highly Effective Countries.

In the Cold War system regions tended to develop together. Western European countries developed at their own pace, Latin America at its own pace, the East Asian tigers at their own pace, Eastern Europe at its own pace and Africa at its own pace. The big differences tended to be among regions. East Asia made it; Latin America walked ahead; the Middle East stagnated, except for the windfall profits of oil; and Africa fell through the floor. Egypt and South Korea started at the same level of per-capita income back in the 1950s, but by the 1990s there was a huge gap between them.

What we are going to see in the globalization system is a continuation of this trend, only now the differentiation is going to be increasingly *within* regions and *within* countries of the same region—as some choose prosperity, get wired, become shapers and adopt the habits of effective countries, and others do not. For instance, you will see a gap emerge in the Middle East between Tunisia—which in the 1990s put on the Golden Straitjacket, signed a free-trade agreement with the European Union and adopted many of the habits of effective countries—and some of its Arab neighbors, which have not. And you will see "hot zones" emerge within countries, such as coastal China around Shanghai, or Bangalore in India, where incomes and lifestyles will far outstrip other regions right next door in the same country—so much so that it will feel like they are in a different country. The gaps between developed countries, and within developing countries, may become politically the most sensitive for world politics. Who is in the Fast World within a particular region or country will be much more important than whether that country was in the First World or Third World during the Cold War.

As I noted in the previous chapter, the best countries and companies will mirror one another's habits. So, after asking the two most basic questions—how wired is your country or company and is it a shaper or adapter—here are the other nine questions I ask to measure its economic power and potential.

How Fast Is Your Country or Company?

Klaus Schwab of the Davos World Economic Forum once observed: "We have moved from a world where the big eat the small to a world where the fast eat the slow." And he is right. Because of the three democratizations, the barriers to entry into virtually any business today have been dramatically lowered, and this means that the speed by which a product goes from being an innovation to being a commodity has become turbocharged. If your company or country, for social, cultural or political reasons, is not willing to let Schumpeter's creative destruction work as fast as today's turbomarkets, it will fall behind. It is not for nothing that Bill Gates likes to say that at Microsoft they know only one thing: In four years, every product they make will be obsolete. The only question is whether Microsoft will make it obsolete or one of its competitors will. If Microsoft makes it obsolete, the company will thrive. If one of its competitors makes it obsolete, Microsoft will be in trouble. Bill Gates almost made Microsoft obsolete by initially concluding that the Internet was not the future of computing. Lucky for him, he came around before his four years were up.

No one has to explain this speed issue to the senior managers of Compaq Computer—they thrived by it and they died by it. Compaq got its start by being quicker than IBM at creative destruction. It almost creatively destroyed IBM in the process. What happened was that in 1985

Intel developed a new 386 microprocessor, offering roughly double the speed of its 286 chip. Compaq's whole business strategy was to become the technology leader in clock speed. That meant that every time Intel came out with a new, faster chip—not just from 286 to 386, but even within each chip model, when it increased the speed by even 5 MHz— Compaq wanted to be the first to market with that faster chip in its desktops and laptops.

In the 1980s, when a new personal computer was launched, it would be phased in first in the United States and a few months later in Europe, and eventually it could hit India and the Middle East. It was assumed that the European and Asian markets were somehow shielded from what was happening in America. Compaq was the first to understand that this was not the case—that a new product had to be released at absolutely the same moment across the world. And, therefore, if Intel announced a new chip and people read about it in their newspaper or on the Internet, they expected to find it installed in the PC or laptop they went out to buy the next day. "That day you want to be on the dealer's shelf," said Enrico Pesatori, Compaq's senior vice president for corporate marketing. "And if you are just two weeks late, you are considered to be slow, you are rated by the analysts as a slow company, you will be seen as not capturing the early gross margin which comes from being the first to market."

As such, Compaq perfected a very fast development cycle for installing new chips. The company had an intimate relationship with Intel, so that Compaq's engineers were able to incorporate the latest new chip into their designs with the minimal modifications to their basic computer box, and then get that basic PC box and its faster chip out the door before any of the other large manufacturers. Compaq was able to stay at the cutting edge because, for as long as possible, it kept most everything else about its basic PC models the same—except the speed of the microprocessor chip and the programming needed to run it. As a result, Compaq was constantly driving down the cost of its basic PC box and its components by using the same design over and over again (rule: the longer any product is on the market the cheaper its components become) and just installing the latest, fastest microprocessor. And since the microprocessor speed was driving the market price of computers, Compaq was able to quickly grow its profit margins—making cheaper and cheaper boxes, for which they could charge more and more because they always had the fastest new chip. And then doing it all quicker and quicker. These rising profits also gave Compaq the ability to discount, and therefore eat into IBM's lunch coming and going.

IBM, by contrast, wanted to take its time. It always preferred to introduce any new leap in technology all at once, with a whole new computer model. That's why when Intel came out with the 386 chip and invited IBM to run with it, IBM didn't want to introduce that faster chip into its already existing model—the IBM AT, which stood for Advanced Technology and was based on the 286 chip. IBM basically wanted to wait until it sold all its ATs so that it could introduce the 386 into a whole new PC system—the PS\2. Why not? IBM was the biggest, baddest company on the block, and in a world of walls IBM figured it had plenty of time to do things its way.

IBM, under its chairman at the time, John Akers, was incredibly arrogant, and really did resemble the Soviet Union in many ways. The whole company was set up to meet the revenue and profit numbers dictated by the chairman's "plan." So, internally the whole company got focused not on what the market was demanding by way of products—in this case, incrementally faster computers as soon as the new technology was available—but rather on what the politburo of IBM wanted by way of profit numbers in order to grow the company at a certain rate. What IBM didn't understand at that time was that the barriers to entry into its business were falling and that the key to success was an ability to limit your product line— keeping as many components and factors of design constant for as long as possible—in order to ride down the cost curve and focus on what the public really wanted, which was a computer that didn't take all morning to boot up. But IBM was still caught up in its old culture. Its primary business, up until the 1970s, was leasing large mainframe computer systems to companies. And if IBM could come up with a whole new large system every couple of years, it would just install it for all those customers and charge them more. But the PC was a whole different animal. Customers didn't want to have to adopt a whole new system every couple of years. They just wanted it faster. Compaq, listening to its customers, understood that—and got fast. IBM, listening to itself, didn't—and stayed slow.

"IBM was working on an old business model. It did not understand that for this new category completely different rules applied," Eckhard Pfeiffer, Compaq's president from 1991 until early 1999, told me. "So Intel came out with the 386 chip and they said to IBM, 'Go with it,' and IBM said 'No.' So Intel came to Compaq and we said, 'We'll do it.' We struck the deal with Intel."

Game over—at least for a while. Compaq took a huge bite out of IBM's PC business. "I'd say ten to fifteen years ago it was not critical not to be out on the starting line when Intel put their next microprocessor out," added Pfeiffer. "Because people didn't have that sense of urgency. They said, 'Fine, I'll wait a month or two. Maybe that will get me a few more bucks out of the system I'm selling.' But today it's an absolute must to be ready to take that next microprocessor and run with it from day one."

In the late 1980s and early 1990s, Compaq could design products faster than its competitors, so it could provide solutions for its customers faster than its competitors, so it could collect profits faster than its competitors. Earl Mason, Compaq's then chief financial officer, told me in 1998: "If you can continuously reduce the time from when you pay a dollar out [to a supplier] to the time when you collect a dollar in [from a customer] your total asset turns will start to accelerate to a point where you are able to draw in tremendous amounts of cash . . . From the end of 1985 to the first quarter of 1998, our cash-to-cash acceleration has allowed us to grow our cash account from nine hundred million dollars to seven billion dollars. If you're successful at being fast, by definition you'll get big. But if you're just big, and not fast, you're goin' down."

Alas, that is eventually what happened to Compaq less than a year after I interviewed Mason. Compaq reached a point where it got bigger without getting faster—because it missed the next revolution. By failing to understand the full meaning of the Internet, and evolve its marketing and manufacturing model accordingly, Compaq fell behind its main competitor, Dell. Dell pioneered the use of telephone sales to tie marketing to manufacturing and make every PC box a custom-built box that each caller to Dell could design to his or her specifications. By selling directly to customers, and avoiding the dealers and their markups, Dell was always able to give customers a little bit more speed and power for their money. Then, when the Internet came along, Dell was the first to absorb it and integrate it into every aspect of its business.

The Internet gave Dell even more control over its inventory, so, in effect, it didn't have to build a computer until it was ordered. Suppliers were connected via the Internet, so they could see just when a customer was ordering a computer and therefore parts didn't have to come from the suppliers until they were needed. Dell could synchronize raw materials coming into its factories from all over the world and operate with just six days of inventory on hand, which saved it huge amounts of money. This made it easier to do even more customization for consumers and to do it faster and cheaper. Dell didn't just use the Internet. It made it the backbone of how it related to itself, customers and suppliers, and in doing so it got very, very fast. Compaq, by contrast, stuck too long with its more traditional manufacturing model and in-store and dealer sales channel, ignoring the role of the Internet. So Dell did to Compaq with the Internet what Compaq did to IBM by installing faster chips faster.

And it all happened so fast. Boy, do I know. I was writing the first edition of this book at the time. I had gone down to Houston to interview the Compaq leadership in August 1998. On the wall of the management suite at Compaq was the *Forbes* magazine cover story naming Compaq the best-managed company in America in 1997. A month later I was at a conference at Stanford and ran into John Chambers from Cisco. He asked me what I was doing and I mentioned to him that I was using Compaq as an example of a fast company for this chapter of my book.

"Big mistake," said Chambers. "You should be using Dell." My heart sank. But it was too late. I was already locked into Compaq. I had just interviewed its whole leadership. But Chambers, because his company makes the black boxes that connect firms to the Internet, knew the difference between Dell and Compaq, long before the market did. He could see that Compaq was falling behind, and in a fast world it wouldn't be long before the gap would be there for all to see. Well, the first edition of this book was published on April 21, 1999. The week before the book hit the stores Compaq's top leaders, including Pfeiffer and Mason, were ousted by the company's board after that year's first-quarter profits were half of what analysts had expected.

As the Compaq case illustrates, the Internet is creating a whole new level of speed, which has come to be known as "Net speed." No one can tell you how fast Net speed actually is, but what they can tell you is that the Internet, as it moves into business, is forcing every company to speed up everything it does—from design to production to marketing. "The word from the Silicon frontier is that you can kiss your five-year plan goodbye. Or, for that matter, any plan that ends in year," reported *Business Week* (Nov. 1, 1999). "And that goes for the rust belt too. Some companies are writing and rewriting strategy every quarter, or even every week—or else . . . Net speeds force all sorts of cultural changes. Hierarchies flatten out. Budget-cycles get compressed. Decision-making gets pushed out to the front lines. And customer expectations, not the executive board, guide the next big project. What's driving all this? Certainly

Web economics is a factor. As costs plummet for new entrants in business such as retailing or finance, new competition springs up faster and forces everybody to counter-punch constantly. But a bigger factor is how the Net puts companies in closer touch with customers, both through direct sales and by soliciting regular feedback. 'Strategic planning used to be based on a build, then sell model,' says John M. Jordan, director of E-commerce research at Ernst & Young. Now, he says, that's out the window. 'Customers are calling the shots, telling companies what they want, and companies have to respond to those desires or lose out. It's a whole new way of thinking about strategy.' "

Countries need to take heed of such sagas. So when I come into a country now, one of the first questions I ask is: How quickly does your government and society evaluate, innovate, decision-make, deregulate and adapt? That is, to what extent have you restructured your economy to increase the speed of government approvals, transactions, investment and production? How fast can one of your citizens move an idea from his garage to the market? How quickly can you raise capital for a crazy idea, and how quickly can you come up with new ideas? And how quick are you at destroying, through bankruptcy, inefficient firms?

Some countries or regions are fast at capitalist creation because their governments have learned how to speed things up. "Before, nobody was really producing in Scotland," said Enrico Pesatori, Compaq's senior vice president for corporate marketing. "Now, you can't afford not to be there. Why? Because they have constructed an infrastructure. If you go to Scotland everything is ready—the regulatory system, the tax environment, the transportation, the telecommunications—for you to set up your manufacturing facility as fast as you can."

And some countries are fast because their people—for reasons of culture, history or sheer DNA—are naturally agile, and they have gotten even faster as their governments have provided them with the basics and then just gotten out of the way. Regions such as northern Italy, Tel Aviv, Shanghai, South Korea, Beirut and Bangalore are naturally fast and are taking off these days, separating themselves from other parts of their own countries. These regions are the "hot zones," and they will be incredible engines of growth for their countries. When you take one of these hot zones, equip it with the Internet and connect it with a diaspora community spread out all over the world—such as overseas Chinese, Jews, Italians, Lebanese, Indians or Koreans—you have what I like to call a "cybertribe." These cybertribes combine speed, creativity, entrepreneurial talent and global networking in ways that can generate enormous wealth.

In fact, northern Italy today is the richest region of Europe. Reginald Bartholomew, a former American ambassador to Italy, explained why, saying: "Let's say you come to France, Germany and Italy and tell them, 'I want to buy some purple cheese.' What happens? Well, the French will tell you, 'Monsieur, cheese is never purple.' The Germans will tell you, 'Purple cheese is not in the catalogue this year.' But the Italians . . . Ah, the Italians will say to you, 'What shade of purple would you like? Magenta?' "

If northern Italy were a stock, I'd hold it.

Is Your Country or Company Harvesting Its Knowledge?

We have moved from a world where the key to wealth is how you seize, hold and exploit territory to a world in which the key to wealth is how your country or company amasses, shares and harvests knowledge. As former Citibank chairman Walter Wriston observed in an essay in *Foreign Affairs* (Sept. 1997): "The pursuit of wealth is now largely the pursuit of information and its application to the means of production. The rules, customs, skills and talents necessary to uncover, capture, produce, preserve and exploit information are now humankind's most important assets. The competition for the best information has replaced the competition for the best farmland or coalfields. In fact, the appetite to annex territory has already attenuated, and major powers have withdrawn from previously occupied territories . . . In the past when the method of creating wealth changed, old power structures lost influence, new ones arose, and every facet of society was affected. As we can already see the beginning of that process in this revolution, one can postulate that in the next few decades the attraction and management of intellectual capital will determine which institutions and nations will survive and prosper, and which will not."

"How Wired Is Your Country?" is a measure of how broad and deep are its networks. "Is Your Country Harvesting Its Knowledge?" is a measure of how well a country and its companies are using those networks. Being wired is necessary, but not sufficient. A country also needs to amass knowledge effectively and deploy it effectively. It needs to be more wired than ever and more educated than ever.

That is why I like to look at two tables when I come to a country. One is the table that Hewlett-Packard puts together showing which countries in the world today are the most wired. The other is the annual OECD table that lists which of the twenty-nine richest countries in the world are producing the highest percentages of high school graduates and spending the highest percentages of their national income on teacher salaries. If you see which countries top both lists—megabits per capita and high school grads per capita—you will have a good indication of who is on the right track and who is not. It is no accident, for instance, that Finland, which now has one of the world's highest standards of living, sits near the top of both lists.

The same is true for companies. German electronics giant Siemens is a very wired company, but it has a reputation for being weak at tapping its own knowledge. I once heard a management consultant who worked with Siemens remark: "If Siemens only knew what Siemens knows it would be a rich company." The same is true of countries. "If France only knew what France knows . . . If China only knew what China knows . . ."

The companies and countries that learn to use their networks most efficiently are those that will thrive. At General Electric the notion of sharing ideas has been so deeply imbedded into the company's culture that pay and promotions are based, in part, on an executive's "boundaryless behavior"—his or her ability and willingness to synthesize ideas, cross-fertilize the company and bring disparate knowledge threads together to produce value-added products.

You can understand this principle best when you apply it to a company that you normally would not associate with being in the knowledge business—say, for instance, the Chevron oil company. I was in Kuwait in 1997 talking with H. F. Iskander, the general manager of Chevron's Kuwait office and one of the sharpest oilmen in the Gulf. We were chatting about how Chevron was trying to get back into oil exploration in Kuwait. As Iskander was ticking off Chevron's strong points and why they should be attractive to Kuwait, he mentioned in passing that "Chevron is not an oil company, it's a learning company."

"What do you mean 'a learning company'?" I asked. Oil companies are drilling companies. They're guys in hard hats, with their hands and faces smeared with crude oil. What's this "learning company" stuff?

Iskander explained: In the 1970s, virtually all the oil-exporting countries in the Middle East kicked out the major multinational oil companies in order to pump their own oil. It was partly an economic decision and partly a political decision reflecting the broad assertion of independence by postcolonial countries during the Cold War. But twenty years later, many of those oil-exporting countries are now reconsidering what they did, and are looking to invite the multinational oil companies back in. In part, it's because, as oil reserves diminish and they need to start looking for more hard-to-find reserves, oil exploration becomes more expensive and requires more capital. But in part it's because, as oil reserves diminish and they need to start looking for those hard-to-find reserves, oil exploration requires more knowledge.

"Chevron is pumping oil in different locations all over the world," explained Iskander. "There is no problem we have not confronted and solved somewhere. There isn't a rock we haven't drilled through. We centralize all that knowledge at our headquarters, analyze it, sort it out, and that enables us to solve any oil-drilling problem anywhere. As a developing country you may have a national oil company that has been pumping your own oil for twenty years. But we tell them, Look, you have twenty years of experience, but there's no diversity. It is just one year of knowledge twenty times over. When you are operating in a multitude of countries, like Chevron, you see a multitude of different problems and you have to come up with a multitude of solutions. You have to, or you won't be in business. All those solutions are then stored in Chevron's corporate memory. The key to our business now is to tap that memory, and bring out the solution that we used to solve a problem in Nigeria in order to solve the same problem in China or Kuwait. In the old days, it might have taken us two years to find the person in the company who actually found that Nigeria solution and to get him to China, where he could apply it. Now, with E-mail and the globalization of our workforce, where people move around the world to different assignments much more frequently, we can get that solution out of Chevron's memory very quickly."

This is why companies today protect their internal knowledge networks the way ancient kingdoms used to build walls and moats around their territory and farm fields. I went to visit Sun Microsystems at their headquarters outside Palo Alto. Before I could get inside to see the executive I was scheduled to interview, the receptionist handed me a one-page legal form to sign, entitled "Confidential Nondisclosure Agreement." At the top of the form there were two boxes to check: "Confidential Visit" or "Unclassified Visit." Among the things I had to agree to on this document before I could enter Sun's offices was that the "Signatory agrees not to disclose the Proprietary Information to any third party. Signatory agrees to use the Proprietary Information only for purposes expressly authorized in writing by Sun and not to use it for signatory's own use." You can get into the CIA today with less paperwork.

This is also why all major companies now, and many minor ones, have added the job of CIO—chief information officer. Companies have found that there is a material benefit and much improved effectiveness from making sure they are using their knowledge and information well at every stage of production and development. How long will it be before every country has a "Minister of Information," whose job it is not to tell the outside world what's going on inside that country, as it was in the Cold War, but to help that country understand what it knows and to make sure it is harvesting its own knowledge in the most efficient manner.

T. J. Rodgers, founder of Cypress Semiconductor, says: "The winners and losers in the information age will be differentiated by brainpower. It takes two percent of Americans to feed us all, and five percent to make everything we need. Everything else will be service and information technology, and in that world humans and brains will be the key variable."

How Much Does Your Country or Company Weigh?

We are moving from a world where the heavy eat the light to a world where the light eat the heavy. So when I come to a country now, one of the things I ask is how much does it weigh—or actually, how much does an average container of its exports weigh?

Alan Greenspan taught me the relevance of this question. It has to do with what economists call "the substitution effect," whereby ideas, knowledge and information technologies are increasingly substituted for bulk weight in the creation of economic value. The more knowledge and information technology, such as miniaturized microchips, are designed into a product, the less it tends to weigh, the more productive it tends to be, the more it tends to sell for and the richer it will make your company or your country. By substituting transistors for vacuum tubes, we have made radios smaller. Hair-thin fiber-optic cable has replaced heavy copper wire. Digital tape recorders now offer voice-quality recording with no tape at all, just microchips and digits. Your dad's old desktop adding machine is now a handheld calculator. Advances in architecture and engineering, as well as the development of lighter but stronger building materials, now give us the same working space, but in buildings with significantly less concrete, glass and steel tonnage than was required in an earlier era. Your 125-pound receptionist behind a 200-pound desk has probably already been replaced by a tiny voice-mail device in your phone that weighs less than a feather.

Therefore, one measure of the strength, vitality and power of a country today has to be how light is its GDP. There is less weight today in each dollar of U.S. GDP than ever before. As recently as the middle of this century, Greenspan explains, the "symbols of American economic strength" were still our output of such weighty products as steel, motor vehicles and heavy duty machinery—items for which sizable proportions of production costs reflected the value and weight of the raw materials and the manual labor required to manipulate and craft them. So ingrained was this notion of "weight equals value" that legend has it that when Apple Computer came out with the Apple II, the first real home computer, in 1977, Apple folks actually considered adding some artificial weight to it because it was so light they feared people would not take it seriously. Since then, though, Greenspan points out, trends have focused on "downsized, smaller, less palpable evidence of output." Today, a country that exports primarily raw materials—commodities, iron ore, crude oil—is going to weigh a lot. A country that specializes in information technologies and services is going to weigh a lot less and is probably providing a higher standard of living for more of its people.

So it is with companies. DuPont now demands that each of its divisions provide an annual measurement called "shareholder value per pound." DuPont takes every product that a division makes and tries to ensure that it is constantly creating more profit out of less materials each year for each manufactured product.

The 1983 prospectus for Compaq, when the company first went public, boasted: "The Compaq Portable Computer . . . is a 16-bit personal computer in a self-contained, portable unit that is 20 inches wide, 8.5 inches high and 16 inches deep. The standard configuration weighs approximately 28 pounds, [and] is light enough to carry from office to office, home for the weekend, or on business trips . . ."

That 28-pound "laptop" was known at Compaq as the "luggable," because the only way to get it around was by lugging it around. Its retail price for a standard configuration was $2,995. By 1999, Compaq's latest laptop, the Compaq Armada 3500, weighed only 4.4 pounds, with five hundred times the memory. It cost $3,299 to $4,399, depending on the configuration. Since Compaq as a whole operated in 1983 on a gross profit margin of 27.6 percent and by 1997 on an almost identical margin of 27.5 percent, it is now making more money by learning how to pack more brainpower into a product that weighs one-seventh of what it did in 1983. Compaq got richer (for a while at least) by getting lighter by getting smarter.

Does Your Country or Company Dare to Be Open on the Outside?

We've moved from a world where the closed think they can survive better than the open to a world where the open thrive far, far more than the closed. Again, look at the computer world. Those computer manufacturers that tried to compete by having their own monopoly standards have had the most trouble surviving, while those that opted to compete on the basis of the open industry hardware standard—which was pioneered by IBM, with help from Intel—have thrived. The so-called IBM PC clones—Compaq, Dell, Gateway, HP, Micron, Acer—adopted the IBM-established standard and then proceeded to try to kill IBM and one another by building computers that could run that open standard better, cheaper and with more technological backup. The computer companies Data General, Commodore, Wang, Prime and Apple all tried to have their own proprietary standards. They thought, as Nicholas Negroponte pointed out in his book *Being Digital*, that if they could come up with a system that was both popular and unique, they could dominate and lock out all the competition. The only one of them to thrive was Apple, and that is only because it managed to build up a network of fiercely loyal niche users rather than appealing to the broadest mainstream.

"In an open system, we compete with our imagination, not with a lock and key," Negroponte observed. "The result is not only a larger number of successful companies, but a wider variety of choice for the consumer and an ever more nimble commercial sector, one capable of rapid change and growth."

That strategy was key to Compaq's becoming both an effective adapter of IBM's technology and shaper of its own. Earl Mason explained: "Compaq's strategy [was to be] the leader in open standards computing because the more people write applications and software for our hardware, the more we can grow our hardware sales, service sales and solution sales. In the old paradigm, the thinking in the computer industry was that if I had my own operating system, if I had my own independent software vendors working just for me, then I would control this whole thing. I would be independent, not interdependent, and have something that nobody else has. It didn't work, because software writers wanted to write for bigger and bigger audiences and therefore, as a computer maker, if you adopted the open standard of the industry, you got to sell to bigger and bigger audiences. Apple, when it first started, wouldn't share its standards in an open way. So the software guys said, 'Hey, this is no fun. If I work on Apple software, I'm only going to be able to write so many applications and I'm only going to be able to sell so many, and I'm going to be dependent on Apple for all my volume. But if I work with companies operating on the open standard, I will be interdependent with a lot of different companies, like Compaq, IBM and Dell, and that will really allow me to grow my sales.'"

If you can get the meat and potatoes right—learning how to adapt faster, learning how to engineer smarter, learning how to relate to customers better, learning how to manage knowledge better, learning how to control costs more effectively and learning how to manufacture more reliably—you can always compete with anyone on any standard. Indeed, the only knowledge that you want to protect and keep secret is the techniques you develop for being a better shaper or adapter than anyone else. "There are things we don't share," Mason explained. "The reason we don't want you to see some things we do on the manufacturing floor is because there are things we do down there that constitute our real business edge, and if you as a competitor saw it and walked out with it, you could easily implement the same thing."

One reason that the Internet has grown so far so fast is that it is an open standard. The best solutions win out quickly, and the dead are removed from the battlefield quickly. There are no funerals. Relatively little time is spent by companies on securing patents, and more time is spent on just winning out in the open.

Robert Shapiro, chairman of Monsanto, likes to say that there are always a few things that it pays to keep secret. But the culture you create around secrecy is a slower culture suited to a slower world. As a company you always end up overvaluing what you know and undervaluing what is out there in plain sight. As Shapiro puts it: "I would much rather say, 'Look, I will tell you everything I know about how this system works, and still beat your brains out building it.' Because the truth is you cannot rely on monopoly information for long. In the end, what matters and what lasts is what makes you better as a competitor in a wide-open race. The way you manage and exchange information and the way you learn as a company—those are your only sustainable advantages."

And so it is with countries as well. "All I can say," said Mason, "is that being open, the chance of you becoming a victim of what you think you know is a lot less than if you're closed. Look at Japan's banking industry. Why is it technically bankrupt? Because it's very closed. They became victims of what they thought they knew."

Indeed, there is a direct correlation between the openness of a country's economy and its standard of living. A study carried out by economist Jeffrey Sachs and the Harvard Institute for International Development found that openness was decisive for rapid growth. Open economies, Sachs reported, "grew 1.2 percentage points per year faster than closed economies, controlling for everything else, because the more open you are, the more integrated you are into today's world network of ideas, markets, technologies and management innovations."

When I was visiting Jilin province in northern China, monitoring village elections, one of the villages we toured was Kai An, where we were able to see many villagers in their homes. Most of them were three-section homes. The first section was a small mud-brick hovel where the family lived under Mao, the second was a larger red-brick structure, where the family lived under Deng Xiaoping, and the third, which was always the newest, was a white-brick structure, with painted tiles around the front door, and it was built in the Jiang Zemin era. You could literally see how as China became more open as a country, the length of each villager's home grew.

In the future, the virtues of keeping your economy as open as possible will only multiply, because in the era of globalization knowledge is the key to economic growth, and if you close your country off in any way to either the best brains in the world or the best technologies in the world, you will fall behind faster and faster. That's why the most open-minded, tolerant, creative and diverse societies will have the easiest time with globalization, while the most closed, rigid, uptight, self-absorbed and traditional companies and countries, which are just not comfortable with openness, will struggle.

University of California at Berkeley urban studies expert AnnaLee Saxenian has done a fascinating study entitled "Regional Advantage," explaining what makes Silicon Valley so distinctive from most other high-tech beehives. What makes Silicon Valley unique, she concluded, are the extremely open boundaries that exist there among technology firms, and between these firms and the venture capital community, the banking community, the university research community and the local government. Saxenian points out that the Silicon Valley of the East Coast, Route 128 in Boston, has always lagged behind the real Silicon Valley, because Route 128 was dominated by a culture of secrecy and self-sufficiency within firms and risk aversion within both the business and financial communities.

Some small countries are catching on to the virtues of openness. *The Washington Post* reported (Oct. 17, 1997) that while immigration was becoming a flash point between conservative and liberal ideologues in the United States, "other countries have decided to take a leaf out of the book of the American immigrant experience." Singapore's ambassador in Washington, Heng-Chee Chan, has unveiled an initiative to attract immigrants to Singapore, urging them to "Go West" — really west, far west — "farther and farther west until they hit Asia." The ambassador was quoted as saying: "We recognize that we need more people to contribute to our vision for an intelligent city, a city of the future." The idea of seeking immigrants, she explained, stemmed from a survey of thriving societies, such as the United States and Britain, which prosper because of their openness and diversity.

"We discovered that societies that are open remain innovative and move on," said the ambassador. Therefore, Singapore was seeking "cross-fertilization" in the fields of information technology, engineering, pharmaceuticals, and research and development, as well as banking. "You will continue to see growth in these [diverse] countries," she said. "That is why Singapore is quite confident in recruiting talent." Singapore's labor-recruiting program, called "Contact Singapore," has already attracted young Europeans and Australians. The Singaporean ambassador said the salaries being offered are high and competitive with Silicon Valley, and, yes, Singapore "does have Brooklyn Bagels."

Singapore had Brooklyn Bagels, but it didn't have the atmosphere of intellectual openness to really develop its own bagel — let alone cutting-edge software or Internet-enabling technologies. Prime Minister Goh Chok Tong even declared in a national address in August 1999 that "We have to create a Silicon Valley state of mind in Singapore — creative and willing to take risks." His government started to loosen up on its censorship of Internet sites as a symbolic gesture in that direction. But the ruling party in Singapore still maintained a tight grip on information and politics in the country, one that created an atmosphere unlikely to attract and hold the best bagel or chip makers.

Still, it is worth watching Singapore because of the way it has made the connection between intellectual freedom and openness and the ability to thrive in the Internet age. That is a hopeful sign. As Lyric Hughes, the founder of China Online, once observed, "If formerly restrictive regimes can be persuaded to see the free flow of information not as a threat to the power of sovereign states, but as the creator of a viable economic infrastructure and a population incentivized to take advantage of the new economy, the next century will be promising indeed."

You will not only attract more brains when you are open, but also more technology transfers from the Electronic Herd. When a country has lower tariffs and trade barriers it is a very important signal to the Electronic Herd, especially to the multinational companies, the long-horn cattle. Let's say you are Xerox and you have decided to build a plant in Brazil to make copiers. If Brazil keeps its copier market open, and does not try to protect its own copier factories, Xerox will have a great incentive to transfer its top-of-the-line copier technology to its new Brazilian factory, because it can get competition in the Brazilian market from anywhere in the world, including the best Japanese and European copiers. But if Xerox knows that Brazil intends to maintain high tariff barriers to protect its own copier factories, Xerox may still open a factory there to compete in the Brazilian market, but it will be under no pressure to install its most cutting-edge technology in that Brazilian factory. Why should it, when it only has to compete against fledgling, protected Brazilian companies? So Brazil ends up losing. Its workers, its market and its consumers are deprived of exposure to the best technologies available.

This is a true story: Brazil and Taiwan had roughly the same per-capita income in the early 1980s, with lots of serious domestic companies, abundant capital, skilled workers and well-trained middle management. They each decided they wanted to dive into the international electronics business in a big way, and in particular the market for making fax machines. The problem was that the source of the best fax technology for both countries was the same, the Japanese company Fujitsu. The Brazilian Congress in 1988 imposed a broad range of tariffs on electronic products, including fax machines, in an effort to protect Brazil's infant fax industries. As a result, no one had an incentive to transfer to the Brazilian market their best fax technology. Taiwan announced zero tariffs and open competition for who could make the best fax machines. According to a

World Bank study, by 1994 Taiwan was the leading manufacturer of fax machines in the world, while Brazilian fax machines cost far more than the world average and were on the verge of extinction. In 1995, the Brazilian Congress rescinded the tariffs on fax machines and decided to compete on an open standard.

When China was accused in 1999 of having stolen some American nuclear warhead secrets, I was as upset as anyone—but not that upset. Because America's most important secret is one that the Chinese can never steal. It is how we live. It is how we live as an open society. When you live as a closed society there is always one more secret you have to steal to stay in the game, because there is always one new innovation you have to catch. It is not that closed societies can't innovate, it is simply that the chances of their doing it consistently are much, much lower. When you live as an open society your strength comes precisely from that openness and the undying spirit of innovation and entrepreneurship it constantly nurtures. When the Chinese photocopy *that*, I will start to worry about them as competitors.

Does Your Country or Company Dare to Be Open on the Inside?

It is not only critical in this era of globalization to learn how to compete without walls on the outside of your country, it is also critical to learn how to remove the walls inside. The more transparent you are inside, the more your government is grounded in the rule of law, the more you are willing to share how and where decisions are made, the less likely it is that corruption will remain hidden, and the more likely others will be willing to stick with you. An efficient, transparent and honest legal system— where citizens can get an accurate picture of how their government's policies are performing and investors can be assured that private property and intellectual innovation will be respected and the playing field will be relatively level—is essential for sustainable growth. Which is why Lyric Hughes, the founder of China Online, rightly argues that in the coming years we will no longer refer to developed and underdeveloped countries, or emerging markets and nonemerging markets. Instead we will refer to "transparent countries" and "nontransparent" countries.

"Every economic decision will be global in the twenty-first century," argues Hughes. "In a world of global capital markets, investment will flow to the regions that are transparent to the international financial community. The very term 'emerging market' will soon be viewed as a quaint twentieth-century term to be replaced by a new worldwide paradigm of transparent and nontransparent economies. Looking into the future, developed markets such as Japan, which fail to create a free flow of information, and whose economic structures remain opaque to the outside world, will find themselves competing against formerly poor nations, whose public policy environment favors transparency."

Does Your Country's or Company's Management Get It and Can You Change Management If They Don't?

Several years ago I was interviewing the leader of an Arab country and, in the course of the interview, I complimented him on the fact that Moody's credit-rating agency had just re-rated his country and boosted its credit rating from below investment grade to investment grade. This Arab leader thanked me for my congratulations and then turned to an adviser seated next to him, and said in Arabic: "What is Moody's?"

Management always matters, but in this more complex and fast-paced system, management and strategic vision matter a lot more. When I look at a country or company today I ask: Can the boss do information arbitrage, can he or she be constantly synthesizing six different dimensions at once, does he or she understand the three democratizations and have a strategy for how to take advantage of them? Because if you can't see the world, and you can't see the interactions that are shaping the world, you surely cannot strategize about the world. And if you are going to deal with a system as complex and brutal as globalization, and prosper within it, you need a strategy for how to choose prosperity for your country or company.

Craig Barrett, the president of Intel, once remarked to me: "We are the biggest investor in Ireland and, I believe, the biggest employer. We are there because Ireland is very probusiness, they have a very strong educational infrastructure, it is incredibly easy to move things in and out of the country and it is incredibly easy to work with the government. I would invest in Ireland before Germany or France. France is the one country in the world that has outlawed the use of encryption for Internet commerce." Encryption technology, which Intel is now building into its chips, is critical for Internet commerce to prevent criminals from stealing credit card numbers and other personal data. "France is the only country in the world where we can't take orders over the Internet from our customers, because we can't use encryption technologies," said Barrett. "I was just in Paris to show off some new Intel products and we had to get a special, twenty-four-hour written waiver from the French government just to demonstrate our encryption technology for this single marketing event."

Most countries in the world would be terrified to know that the head of Intel thinks they're out of step. France thought Intel was out of step. "You put in a silly rule outlawing encryption—encryption that you can already download from the Internet—and you end up inhibiting the growth of your commerce and your economy," said Barrett. "Either you allow me to encrypt at the cutting edge or I go away."

In the late 1980s, Intel was holding a Europe-wide marketing meeting, deciding where to put resources and figuring out which countries would be hot and which would not. The head of European marketing for Intel showed up at the meeting with a map of Europe—only he had cut France out of his marketing map with a razor blade.

It was such obtuse behavior that started me thinking that if France were a stock, I'd sell it. France is changing, though, and eventually I expect it will make an appearance on the buy list. While certain French government officials and intellectuals say a lot of silly things about and against the globalization system, French industrialists and entrepreneurs are putting on the Golden Straitjacket with a vengeance. (France has even loosened up on encryption controls since Barrett was in Paris in 1998.) When it comes to globalization, the French are like the driver who always signals left and then turns right. If you only read the French pundits in Le Monde, you would think France is never going to get it; but if you read the French business news in the European Wall Street Journal, you realize that their private sector elites get it quite well and are pushing France into the globalization system.

"Potent forces are fast undermining the French government's traditional influence on the economy," The Wall Street Journal Europe reported (Nov. 19, 1999). "Privatized companies no longer exist to serve the state and provide jobs; they answer to a demanding bunch of international investors whose main concern is profits. At the same time, the growing clout of the European Union makes it increasingly difficult for French rule-makers to get their way . . . Unlike in the past when government bureaucrats pulled many of the French economy's strings, a majority of today's mergers are cooked up by independent-minded corporate managers and ratified by investors scattered around the globe."

There will be a steady backlash within France against this sort of corporate adjustment to the globalization system, but eventually the backlashers will lose. Not without a good fight, though. A friend of mine went to Paris in the summer of 1999 and she had to use the public Internet facility at the central post office in Paris to send some E-mail. She arrived around lunchtime and when she got there she found the Internet room was closed. It was manned by a French bureaucrat and when he went out to lunch each afternoon he locked the door and put up a sign that said he was out to lunch. So the good news is that the Paris post office is now offering Internet services to the public. The bad news is that the room in which it is located still operates on two-hundred-year-old French business hours and closes for two hours at lunch, as though it were a butcher shop.

Another major country that is on my temporary sell list is Russia, which still has not put in place the operating systems and software to choose prosperity. The most graphic demonstration of that came in October 1999 when Russia's top stock-market watchdog quit after declaring that Boris Yeltsin's government was simply not interested in enforcing laws to protect shareholders in Russia. Imagine if you picked up an American newspaper and found that Arthur Levitt, the head of the U.S. Securities and Exchange Commission, had quit, saying that the New York Stock Exchange, and American commercial courts, were so corrupt that you were better off going to Las Vegas and putting your money on red or black than investing in the market.

"You need a whole different group of people at the top in Russia," remarked Bill Lewis, who heads the McKinsey consulting firm's Global Institute, which conducted a massive study of the Russian economy in the fall of 1999. "Many people have pointed to the fact that Russia has consistently held free elections as a sign that it is basically going in the right direction. But the real question is, Do Russians have people to vote for? Do they have politicians who understand what Russia needs today and are ready to implement it? The answer is no. What Russia needs most is their version of our Roosevelt. They need a shrewd, honest, savvy pol who can attract the right technocrats around him and lead a democratic process to put in place the social policies and limited, but enforceable, regulations that are the necessary foundation for growth."

I remain hopeful that, as in France, a new generation is slowly coming of age in Russia that understands the globalization system and will demand the instruments and governance to succeed within it. In November 1999, I attended a seminar on competitiveness in Colombo, Sri Lanka, organized by USAID. The audience was made up of Sri Lankan, Indian, Pakistani, Bangladeshi and Nepalese business leaders and economists. One of the keynote speakers was former Costa Rican president José María Figueres, who gave the audience an hour-long, spellbinding description of how Costa Rica got Intel to set up a factory in its country and successfully adapted to the Information Revolution. The audience of South Asians was awed, and when it came to question time, one questioner after another stood up and asked: "Would you run for president in our country?"

It was the most striking scene. People from several different countries standing up and asking the former president of another to run for office in their homelands—and not being at all embarrassed. What this tells you is that as we enter this era when everyone increasingly knows how everyone else is living—especially the thirty- to forty-year-old, educated generation coming of age today in many countries—they are not going to tolerate bad political management forever. A forty-six-year-old Sri Lankan woman banker who attended the seminar with me expressed quite beautifully her frustration: "We have lost twenty-five years," she said. "In 1964 Lee Kwan Yew [the leader of Singapore] came to Sri Lanka and said Singapore should become like Sri Lanka. We were his model—on literacy, on health care, on education. But now Singapore is the model and [ours is] a destiny we never achieved. So when people listened to Figueres, they said, 'Why can't we get leaders like this?' 'Where did he come from?' 'How did he happen?' 'Is it that people get the leaders they deserve?' 'Have we done something wrong?' We need to take all these leaders who are corrupt and bumbling and ostracize them, but we never do. There are so many people whose heads haven't rolled who should have." No wonder, she added, that "so many people walked out [after Figueres's speech] and said, 'If we don't have that kind of competence within our own country, why can't we hire it?' One of the big Sri Lankan businessmen said, 'I wouldn't even mind paying his salary myself.' The brains are here. Look at the number of companies that Sri Lankans or Indians have started [in Silicon Valley], but we don't have the necessary leadership here to manage our own ship."

Is Your Country or Company Willing to Shoot Its Wounded and Suckle the Survivors?

In a world without walls your company or country has to have a culture that encourages the destruction of established businesses, even while they still seem to be successful, otherwise somebody else will. Compaq got created precisely because IBM was not willing to destroy one of its own computer innovations, the IBM AT, based on the 286 chip, and jump ahead for a faster PC based on the 386 chip, as soon as that microprocessor was available. So Compaq came along and built the 386-based PC instead, and dealt a serious blow to Big Blue.

As MIT economist Lester C. Thurow points out in his book *Building Wealth*, old big firms understand, and often even invent, the new technologies that transform the world, but they have a structural problem that is almost impossible to solve. "When breakthrough technologies come along, such firms must destroy the old to build the new. Four of the five makers of vacuum tubes, for example, never successfully made transistors after transistors emerged to replace the vacuum tube—and the fifth today is not a player," notes Thurow. "When the microprocessor allowed the personal computer to replace the mainframe as the dominant growth market in the computer industry, the old industrial leader, IBM fell off a cliff."

Business Week (Dec. 13, 1999) profiled Edward Zander, the hard-charging president of Sun Microsystems. One paragraph in the story jumped out at me. It read: "Having watched former employers Data General and Apollo Computer get creamed at the height of their success, Zander is launching his second makeover of Sun in five years. He's trying to create a new kind of company, designed to be less about selling stand-alone computers and more about making Web sites, corporate networks, and hand-held gizmos work without a glitch . . . 'We're going to break the company again,' he says. 'I want Sun to be the IBM of the Internet Age.' "

What goes around comes around—because IBM also wanted to be the IBM of the Internet age, the industry leader. And interestingly enough, this time IBM is making the transition. IBM has not only transformed itself into more of an Internet-based company, but it transformed its business into a full-service Internet clinic—where any company, large or small, can come to acquire the technology, support services and advice for becoming an E-company or doing E-business. In other words, IBM went from being the industry leader to being the corporate equivalent of the Soviet Union to being one of the leaders again, by first inventing it-self, then being unwilling to reinvent itself and then by radically reinvent-ing itself. By the year 2000 IBM was one of the leading Internet doctors and E-business-solutions providers, giving Sun, Compaq and all the oth-ers who seemed to overtake IBM in the 1980s and early 1990s a run for their money.

Countries need the same culture of reinvention to thrive. As Thurow again notes, "Societies that aren't ready to break with the past, aren't will-ing to let entrepreneurs come into existence. Europe provides a good ex-ample of the importance of entrepreneurship. Europe saves and invests more than the United States, has a better-educated populace, and has a basic understanding of science that is just as good as in the United States, yet it has created none of the new brainpower industries of the twenty-first century. Last year (1998), the production arm of the last indigenous European computer manufacturer, Siemens Nixdorf, was sold to Acer of Taiwan. How can a region be a leader in the twenty-first century and be completely out of the computer business? The European entrepreneurs that should exist don't. Sociology almost always dominates technology. Ideas often lie unused because people do not want to use them. The fact that something is possible does not mean that it will happen."

A society that welcomes, or at least tolerates, creative destruction has to be in place for revolutionary products to emerge. This is particularly crucial in a world without walls in which it is much harder to protect the old from the new. A country should worry about the loss of jobs, but not the loss of firms. That may seem contradictory, but it is not. If you worry about the loss of firms, you will end up losing a lot more jobs. You should have safety nets for people who lose their jobs, but not for firms that lose their edge.

It is not an accident that Taiwan survived the Asian economic crisis of the late 1990s to a much greater degree than all its neighbors. The most important reason for this, argues Chi Schive, vice-chairman of Taiwan's Council for Economic Planning and Development, was the willingness of Taiwan's government to tolerate a culture of creative destruction. Part of this was an accident of history. When the nationalists came to Taiwan from the mainland during the civil war in China in 1948, they took over the reins of government, but they did not take a great deal of interest in business. This was because they didn't plan on staying in Taiwan long. They assumed they would be going back to the mainland. So, from the beginning, Taiwan's government had much more of a hands-off approach to business than others in Southeast Asia. Instead of nurturing huge conglomerates, as in Korea or Japan, the Taiwanese government, relatively speaking, stayed out of the business world. The result was the emergence of a beehive of small and medium-sized enterprises that often began with one family working out of its living room. These businesses could only survive by being highly flexible and highly efficient, and by being ready to jump from business to business and market to market at a moment's notice.

And because the Taiwanese government opened its economy in the 1980s, and did not try to protect these small businesses, they were constantly exposed to the most competitive markets and technologies in the world, so they steadily accelerated automation, improved their product quality, moved into higher value-added goods and relocated manufacturing overseas, even though it temporarily cost some jobs at home. Those who couldn't keep up were left as roadkill or absorbed by better firms. Indeed, the Ministry of Economic Affairs in Taiwan proudly offers a statistic entitled "Births and Deaths of Companies in Taiwan, 1986–98," which shows a steady balance of new companies being created and old companies killed off, even during the Asian economic downturn.

It isn't enough, though, to be willing to shoot your wounded, and let the Darwinian process work in the marketplace. Successful countries, notes Schive, are also those that have a venture-capital mentality and community that can help identify winners and nurture them so that they can commercialize their innovations. Having a gambling culture, such as Taiwan's, really helps, because when an innovator comes up with a new idea in his garage, he usually finds it difficult to develop that idea because of the high risks involved. That is why small and medium-sized businesses, such as those in Taiwan, need venture capitalists, ready to take high risks for high rewards. Taiwan's venture-capital industry emerged in the early 1980s and by all measures has been a huge success, spawning hundreds of profitable firms. In Silicon Valley today some of the most successful companies, such as Cisco and Intel, were initially nurtured by gambling venture capitalists.

How Good Is Your Country or Company at Making Friends?

We have moved from a world where everyone wants to go it alone — where the rugged individualist is the executive role model and the vertically integrated company that does it all is the corporate model—to a world where you can't survive unless you have lots of allies, where the Churchillian alliance maker is the executive role model and the horizontally allied company is the corporate model.

In a global economy, you cannot survive in certain industries unless you are able to compete on a global basis and you cannot do this without alliances. It is easy to see why. In a number of industries, such as semiconductors, aerospace, telecommunications and pharmaceuticals, notes Stephen J. Kobrin, the Wharton School expert on globalization, "the scale of technology has grown to the point where even industry leaders may not have the resources to mount a competitive R&D effort alone, given the enormous costs involved, the uncertainty of outcomes, and, importantly, shortened product life cycles." Also, the sheer amount of scientific and technical knowledge required to develop certain complex products in today's world increasingly requires several firms to pool their resources. Moreover, the only way these firms can ever recover their huge investments in research and development is by selling not just to their national markets, which are too small, but to the whole wide world, and this also requires allies. This increased pressure for alliances, concludes Kobrin, "is one of the features of this era of globalization that is not only new in degree but also new in kind. It is one of the features subtly knitting the world together, and promoting more globalization, in ways that are not always apparent."

Alliances are not mergers. They involve two companies keeping distinct identities, but agreeing to work together in a very intimate way, and they are now forming all over the world at a pace never seen before. One place where alliances are most obvious to the naked eye is in the airline industry. Look at the ads for the "Star Alliance"—which is an alliance of six airlines to book seats on one another's flights, through reservation code sharing, and to honor one another's frequent flyer programs. This enables the member airlines, by partnering, to offer their customers one-stop shopping for travel anywhere on the globe. They know that in today's world they have to be able to offer such service, but they can only do so through an alliance, because no one of them could possibly cover the world alone. Their ad shows an elongated airplane in which the nose section is from United, the front cabin Air Canada, the midsection SAS, Varig and Thai Airways and the tail section Lufthansa—all next to the revealing headline: "Star Alliance: The Airline Network for Earth." And now who's their competitor? Another airline alliance, of course. It's called "One World," and its ads boast: "Now you can look forward to recognition on seven of the world's finest airlines. With access to even more lounges. Smoother transfers. And the ability to earn and redeem frequent flyer miles to even more destinations."

Having a CEO who knows how to forge and manage alliances—to build trust and transparency with other companies—is a critical asset for surviving in the globalization system. It can get very complicated. Compaq, by forging a strategic partnership with Intel to make its microprocessors, and with Microsoft to provide Windows operating systems and software, was able to immediately integrate the newest technological advances in both semiconductors and operating systems into each new computer to stay right at the cutting edge. Compaq's 1997 annual report stated that "customers are increasingly recognizing that the best computing comes from the company that partners the best." *Forbes* once quoted a management consultant describing the relationship between Intel's Andy Grove and Compaq's Eckhard Pfeiffer this way: "From Andy's mouth to Eckhard's ear. It's kind of like a marriage."

As with companies, so with countries. In terms of economic security, America has always needed allies in the international economics realm. We have never been an island unto ourselves. We just need more allies now in more ways at more times. "I can't imagine that twenty or twenty-five years ago my predecessors would have been worried about an economic crisis in Thailand or Indonesia, or even Korea," former U.S. Treasury Secretary Robert Rubin said to me. "England you worried about. Japan you worried about. But not Thailand. But today so many more countries are part of what is for practical purposes considered the global economy. Their performances can affect our country, and it takes a lot of my time and energy to deal with the ramifications of that."

On the national security side, many of the same pressures to find more partners and allies apply. For one thing, in the absence of an all-dominating Cold War, with an all-threatening enemy, nobody's public wants to pay a heavy price in either blood or treasure to beat back the smaller rogues—even though they can be enormously dangerous. Even when a Saddam Hussein comes along, threatening oil routes and brandishing weapons of mass destruction, the Bush Administration had to spend six months putting together a coalition of partners, not just to wage war on Saddam but, more important, to pay for it. I was covering Secretary of State Baker when he went out on his fund-raising trip for the first Gulf War. All the reporters on the plane pitched in and bought him a tin cup.

But besides needing more allies to face down the rogues, there are a whole host of transnational issues that are now more threatening than ever in a world without walls. When there are no walls to protect you, the only way to protect yourself from internal or external threats is by getting the quality of your own governance and oversight up and by building alliances with others to do the same—whether it is to combat terrorists, the Mafia, weapons proliferators or El Niño.

Throughout the late 1990s, the United States tried to get a weak Russian government to restrain the sales of nuclear and missile technology to Iran by *private* Russian companies. In the Cold War world of walls, the United States never had to worry about private Russian firms acting on their own. There was no such thing. There were just official Russian arms sales that could be deterred by the threat of official American arms transfers or by other state-to-state means.

But this is not the case anymore. Russian arms manufacturers are now increasingly autonomous actors, desperate for cash. The United States cannot, on its own, impose export restrictions on private Russian companies. Instead, America has to try to create tacit walls against such exports by using its leverage to shape a coalition and try to get others in the public and private sector to join it. In the case of the Russian arms transfers to Iran, the Clinton Administration imposed economic sanctions on a Russian university and two technical institutes, and then tried (with mixed success) to get the Europeans to do the same, because the Russian experts at these schools were suspected of working with Iran, and the Russian government would not or could not do anything about it. In the Cold War, America could stop such Russian transfers as a soloist. Now it can stop them only by acting like an orchestra conductor.

That is why in the system of globalization the biggest challenge for American leadership is to sort out which problems it can still shape alone, through classical state-to-state military deterrence, and which problems it can shape today only with partners. There are unilateralists in American politics who believe we should shape every issue alone; there are multilateralists who believe we should shape every issue with our allies and those whom we want to become our adapters. The truth is there has to be a combination of the two approaches. If America is not prepared to do certain things alone, no one will follow. But if it seems as though it wants to do everything alone, no one will follow either.

Monsanto chairman Robert Shapiro, whose company had to manage a lot of global strategic alliances with farmers, seed distributors and food buyers, in order to get the most value for its products, once talked to me about how complicated this can get. He sounded at times like the President of the United States trying to figure out how America should shape the bailout of Mexico or what coalition, if any, to use when confronting and containing Iraq. Shapiro said: "This new world of alliances is terra incognita. Everyone has a model in their head but no one knows how it works: How do you balance shared interests and self-interests, short-term gains and long-term gains? Where do you have things in common and where do you really want to preserve separate identities? Mergers we know how to do, but alliances between equals are different. I have to count on your capabilities as an important part of my life. And the real challenge is that you are not going to just have one of these alliances. You are going to have a bunch going all at the same time if you are competing globally. And then it comes down to how do I make trade-offs between you and me, you and Fred, and Fred and me? It's really complicated."

How Good Is Your Country's or Company's Brand?

In today's globalized world, both a powerful global company and a powerful country need to have "strong" brands that can attract and hold consumers and investors. What is a brand name? A team from the McKinsey consulting firm defined it well in 1997 in their company's journal: "A name becomes a brand," the McKinsey team wrote, "when consumers associate it with a set of tangible or intangible benefits" that they obtain from that product or service. "As this association grows stronger, consumers' loyalty and willingness to pay a price premium increase . . . To build brand equity, a company needs to do two things: first, distinguish its product from others in the market; second, align what it says about its brand in advertising and marketing with what it actually delivers. A relationship then develops between brand and customer . . . As the alignment grows stronger, so does the brand."

In other words, to build a strong brand, a company has to demonstrate how relevant the particular strengths of its product are and how different they are from others. And brands are so much more important in today's globalization system because consumers and manufacturers are now meeting one another so much more directly in a world without walls or middlemen. When people can go online and buy whatever they want— rather than going to Saks, Sears or Circuit City and having a store and salesperson mediate for them and help them choose—having a strong brand that conjures up a strong image with customers is essential.

Compaq ran into a serious branding problem in the mid-1990s when, in effect, it got "outbranded" by its components and alliance partners— Intel and Microsoft. Consumers stopped caring very much about the box, and whether it was called Dell, Gateway, HP, IBM or Compaq. All they cared about was whether it had Intel microprocessors inside and ran Windows operating systems and software. No wonder Compaq executives started to grumble, "We're tired of being distributors for Andy Grove."

One reason Compaq got outbranded by Intel and Microsoft was that it saw itself in a very limited way, and its advertisements reflected this. Compaq saw itself as a purely product-oriented company, a maker and marketer of computers. It made good computers and its advertisements were little more than pictures of each one of its desktops, laptops and servers. In June 1998, just after Compaq acquired Digital Equipment Corporation, it launched a new global campaign to rebrand itself. The strategy was to create a real bond between Compaq and its customers, from the smallest desktop buyer to the largest corporate or government user. It did this in three ways. First, by changing how it delivered its products. Compaq had always sold its computers through retail outlets and other third-party resellers. As a result, it did not have a direct relationship with most of its customers. So it moved instead to a hybrid distribution strategy which would allow Compaq to do sales over the phone and over the Internet, as Dell did, in order to build its own direct partnership with customers. Second, it beefed up its customer technical service department so anyone with a Compaq computer could call anytime, from anywhere, with any problem—whether it was related to the computer, the software or the New York Times Sunday crossword puzzle—and a Compaq service representative would help them solve it. Lastly, Compaq redesigned its ad campaign to reinforce this new approach, by publishing ads that evoked a feeling of partnership rather than displaying a product. Compaq bought a twelve-page spread in The Wall Street Journal to unveil its new brand and that twelve-page spread did not include a single picture of a computer. Instead, it contained pictures, like that on the final page, showing two little kids walking through the forest, hand in hand, above the logo: "Compaq. Better Answers."

Countries now face the same challenge vis-à-vis their customers in the global marketplace—the members of the Electronic Herd. Countries used to just brand for tourism. But that is not enough anymore. As we move into a world where everyone has the same hardware and everyone is being forced to get the same software to go with it, a country's brand, and the unique bond it can build with its foreign investors, becomes even more important. Think of Europe after the European Monetary Union is in place. Why would you put your factory in Italy rather than in Scotland? It may come down to the weather or the food or the fact that the Italian brand seems to evoke a little more fun, style and pizzazz.

My colleague Warren Hoge, the *New York Times* London bureau chief, captured Britain's efforts to rebrand itself into "New Britain." In the newly rebranded Britain, Hoge wrote on November 12, 1997, "out are scenes of village cricket, tea and scones, baronial castles, Beefeaters, grouse hunts on heathery moors, ceremonial celebrators in wigs and tights, tepid amber ale and Union Jacks fluttering triumphantly. In are images of pulsing telecommunications, global business transactions, information technologies, buccaneering entrepreneurs, bold architecture, cheeky advertising, daring fashion, Britpop music, nightclubbing—anything, in short, that is youthful, creative and, in the word most uttered by the leaders of this updated land, 'modern' . . . The style offensive is being undertaken by the new Labour Government at the suggestion of Demos, a social policy research center close to Mr. Blair, which recommended last month that it was time to 'rebrand' Britain as 'one of the world's pioneers rather than one of its museums.' 'I'm proud of my country's past but I don't want to live in it,' said Tony Blair. The British Government tourist agency got it just right when it decided in 1997 to change the country's logo from 'Rule, Britannia!' to 'Cool Britannia . . .' "

A country can also tarnish its brand. Malaysia in the 1990s developed a wonderful brand image, that of a multiethnic Muslim state that was embracing the technological revolution and making its name synonymous with information technology, even building something called the Information Technology Super Corridor, a high-tech industrial park around Kuala Lumpur. But when the Asian currencies collapsed in the summer of 1997 and Prime Minister Mahathir went on his tirade, accusing the Jews, George Soros and his own Deputy Prime Minister, Anwar Ibrahim, of conspiring to wreck Malaysia's economy, he soiled the brand of Malaysia, Inc., and undermined international confidence in his country.

These days, every country has to care about its brand and even the petty thieves understand that. John Bussey, a reporter with *The Wall Street Journal*, wrote a remarkable story (Feb. 27, 1998) about what happened to him and his girlfriend when they got into a cab in Mexico City

one night and were, in effect, kidnapped by the cabdriver and some co-
horts: "The fellow holding a gun to my head Saturday night in Mexico
City had discovered I worked for a newspaper. We had been riding
around in a taxi for an hour, me face down on the cab floor, he seated
above me. An accomplice was sandwiched in the seat next to him, half
sitting on my dinner guest, pinning her in place.

" 'You work for an American newspaper?' the robber with the gun
asked again.

" 'Yes, I'm on a business trip from the U.S.,' I answered, wondering if
this was a good thing or a bad thing. Maybe he didn't like journalists.
Maybe he hated gringos.

" 'Well,' the man said, 'don't write anything about what happened
tonight. It would be embarrassing for my country.'

" 'Embarrassing for my country'? If these had been slightly different
circumstances, if the barrel of the .45 hadn't been three inches from my
head for the last hour, if the robbers hadn't emptied my wallet, taken my
watch, and now been trying to crack my bank account with my ATM
card—well, I might have found the thought endearing. A little national
pride, a kind of patriotic World Cup enthusiasm. His heart belongs to
Mexico.

" 'No, don't worry,' I assured our robber from the floor of the cab. 'It's
a business newspaper, stocks and bonds. Wouldn't be able to get a story
like this into the paper—just another robbery in Mexico.' " If Mexico
were a stock . . .

As more and more people start to realize that their country can actually choose prosperity, if it puts the right policies in place, and as more
and more people come to understand fully how other people, particularly
successful nations, live, they are going to start asking why their own political management hasn't chosen prosperity. In the Cold War system, a lot
of countries could get by on *where* they were and *who* they were. Egypt
was hugely elevated in the Cold War by the fact that it was the pivotal
state in the Middle East between Americans and Soviets and later between Arab states and Israel. And it had a grand history and pyramids to
boot. France was elevated in importance by its ability and willingness to
maneuver between the United States and the Soviet Union. And it had
an illustrious history to boot.

In the globalization system, *where* you are doesn't matter much anymore. And it also doesn't matter *who* you were. While countries should be
encouraged to preserve their culture and heritage, they can't ride on it.

What matters now is *what* you *are*, and that depends on whether you make the choices for prosperity available in this system. Derek Shearer told me a useful story along these lines. In the mid-1990s, when he served as the U.S. ambassador to Finland, he was accompanied by his wife, Ruth Goldway, who served as mayor of Santa Monica in the 1980s and presided over that city's revitalization. One day Ambassador Shearer and his wife went from Helsinki over to the great Russian city of St. Petersburg, to meet with the city fathers, along with the U.S. consul general there. Shearer said: "So we were meeting with the deputy mayor of St. Petersburg and the chief city planner and some other city officials at a dinner hosted by our consul general. And these city officials are going on and on about what a grand city St. Petersburg is and how it has all these great cultural offerings. But we had come in from the airport that day and the road from the airport to town was so full of potholes you could barely drive on it. And we had been to the Hermitage Museum that day and it was sad to see that the place was crumbling—none of the art was properly lit. It doesn't have a restaurant or proper gift shop. The place was a mess. It may have a great history, but it could never compete today with other cities with great museums. Meanwhile, these Russian city officials were arguing over what to rename the streets. [St. Petersburg had been Leningrad in the days of the Soviet Union and the street names were all from the Communist era.] So Ruth says to them, 'I have a small suggestion for you. Instead of arguing over what to name the streets, why don't you repair them.' They said, 'You know, that's a good idea.' "

12

The Golden Arches Theory
of Conflict Prevention

E very once in a while when I am traveling abroad, I need to indulge in a burger and a bag of McDonald's french fries. For all I know, I have eaten McDonald's burgers and fries in more countries in the world than anyone, and I can testify that *they all really do taste the same.* But as I Quarter-Poundered my way around the world in recent years, I began to notice something intriguing. I don't know when the insight struck me. It was a bolt out of the blue that must have hit somewhere between the McDonald's in Tiananmen Square in Beijing, the McDonald's in Tahrir Square in Cairo and the McDonald's off Zion Square in Jerusalem. And it was this:

No two countries that both had McDonald's had fought a war against each other since each got its McDonald's.

I'm not kidding. It was uncanny. Look at the Middle East: Israel had a kosher McDonald's, Saudi Arabia had McDonald's, which closed five times a day for Muslim prayer, Egypt had McDonald's and both Lebanon and Jordan had become McDonald's countries. None of them have had a war since the Golden Arches went in. Where is the big threat of war in the Middle East today? Israel-Syria, Israel-Iran and Israel-Iraq. Which three Middle East countries don't have McDonald's? Syria, Iran and Iraq.

I was intrigued enough by my own thesis to call McDonald's headquarters in Oak Brook, Illinois, and report it to them. They were intrigued enough by it to invite me to test it out on some of their international executives at Hamburger University, McDonald's in-house research and training facility. The McDonald's folks ran my model past all their international experts and confirmed that they, too, couldn't find an exception. I feared the exception would be the Falklands war, but Argentina didn't get its first McDonald's until 1986, four years after that war with Great Britain. (Civil wars and border skirmishes don't count: McDonald's in Moscow, El Salvador and Nicaragua served burgers to both sides in their respective civil wars.)

Armed with this data, I offered up "The Golden Arches Theory of Conflict Prevention," which stipulated that when a country reached the level of economic development where it had a middle class big enough to support a McDonald's network, it became a McDonald's country. And people in McDonald's countries didn't like to fight wars anymore, they preferred to wait in line for burgers.

Others have made similar observations during previous long periods of peace and commerce — using somewhat more conventional metaphors. The French philosopher Montesquieu wrote in the eighteenth century that international trade had created an international "Grand Republic," which was uniting all merchants and trading nations across boundaries, which would surely lock in a more peaceful world. In *The Spirit of the Laws* he wrote that "two nations who traffic with each other become reciprocally dependent; for if one has an interest in buying, the other has an interest in selling; and thus their union is founded on their mutual necessities." And in his chapter entitled "How Commerce Broke Through the Barbarism of Europe," Montesquieu argued for his own Big Mac thesis: "Happy it is for men that they are in a situation in which, though their passions prompt them to be wicked, it is, nevertheless, to their interest to be humane and virtuous."

In the pre–World War I era of globalization, the British writer Norman Angell observed in his 1910 book, *The Great Illusion*, that the major Western industrial powers, America, Britain, Germany and France, were losing their taste for war-making: "How can modern life, with its overpowering proportion of industrial activities and its infinitesimal proportion of military, keep alive the instincts associated with war as against those developed by peace?" With all the free trade and commercial links tying together major European powers in his day, Angell argued that it would be insane for them to go to war, because it would destroy both the winner and the loser.

Montesquieu and Angell were actually right. Economic integration was making the cost of war much higher for both victor and vanquished, and any nation that chose to ignore that fact would be devastated. But their hope that this truth would somehow end geopolitics was wrong. Montesquieu and Angell, one might say, forgot their Thucydides. Thucydides wrote in his history of the Peloponnesian War that nations are moved to go to war for one of three reasons—"honor, fear and interest"—and globalization, while it raises the costs of going to war for reasons of honor, fear or interest, does not and cannot make any of these instincts obsolete—not as long as the world is made of men not machines, and not as long as olive trees still matter. The struggle for power, the pursuit of material and strategic interests and the ever-present emotional tug of one's own olive tree continue even in a world of microchips, satellite phones and the Internet. This book isn't called *The Lexus and the Olive Tree* for nothing. Despite globalization, people are still attached to their culture, their language and a place called home. And they will sing for home, cry for home, fight for home and die for home. Which is why globalization does not, and will not, end geopolitics. Let me repeat that for all the realists who read this book: *Globalization does not end geopolitics.*

But it does affect it. The simple point I was trying to make—using McDonald's as a metaphor—is that today's version of globalization significantly raises the costs of countries using war as a means to pursue honor, react to fears or advance their interests. What is new today, compared to when Montesquieu and even Angell were writing, is a difference in *degree*. Today's version of globalization—with its intensifying economic integration, digital integration, its ever-widening connectivity of individuals and nations, its spreading of capitalist values and networks to the remotest corners of the world and its growing dependence on the Golden Straitjacket and the Electronic Herd—makes for a much stronger web of constraints on the foreign policy behavior of those nations which are plugged into the system. It both increases the incentives for not making war and it increases the costs of going to war in more ways than in any previous era in modern history.

But it can't guarantee that there will be no more wars. There will always be leaders and nations who, for good reasons and bad reasons, will resort to war, and some nations, such as North Korea, Iraq or Iran, will choose to live outside the constraints of the system. Still, the bottom line is this: If in the previous era of globalization nations in the system thought twice before trying to solve problems through warfare, in this era of globalization they will think about it three times.

O f course, no sooner did the first edition of this book come out, in April 1999, than nineteen McDonald's-laden NATO countries undertook air strikes against Yugoslavia, which also had McDonald's.

Immediately, all sorts of commentators and reviewers began writing to say that this proved my McDonald's theory all wrong, and, by implication, the notion that globalization would affect geopolitics. I was both amazed and amused by how much the Golden Arches Theory had gotten around and how intensely certain people wanted to prove it wrong. They were mostly realists and out-of-work Cold Warriors who insisted that politics, and the never-ending struggle between nation-states, were the immutable defining feature of international affairs, and they were both professionally and psychologically threatened by the idea that globalization and economic integration might actually influence geopolitics in some very new and fundamental ways. Many of these critics were particularly obsessed with the Balkans precisely because this old-world saga, in which politics, passion and olive trees always take precedence over economics and the Lexus, is what they knew. They were so busy elevating the Balkan war into a world historical issue, into the paradigm of what world politics is actually about, that they failed to notice just what an exception it was, and how, rather than spreading around the world, the Balkans were isolated by the world. They were so busy debating whether we were in 1917, 1929 or 1939 that they couldn't see that what was happening in 2000 might actually be something fundamentally new—something that doesn't end geopolitics but influences and reshapes it in important ways. These critics, I find, are so busy dwelling on what happened yesterday, and telling you what will happen someday, that they have nothing to say about what is happening today. They are experts at extrapolating the future from the past, while skipping over the present. It's not surprising this group would be threatened by the McDonald's argument, because, if it were even half true, they would have to adapt their worldviews or, even worse, learn to look at the world differently and to bring economics, environment, markets, technology, the Internet and the whole globalization system more into their analyses of geopolitics.

My first reaction to these critics was to defensively point out that NATO isn't a country, that the Kosovo war wasn't even a real war and to the extent that it was a real war it was an intervention by NATO into a civil war between Kosovo Serbs and Albanians. And I pointed out that when I posited my orginal McDonald's theory I had qualified it in several important ways: the McDonald's theory didn't apply to civil wars, because, I explained, globalization is going to sharpen civil wars within countries between localizers and globalizers—between those who eat the Big Mac and those who fear the Big Mac will eat them. Moreover, the theory was offered with a limited shelf life, because, I said, sooner or later virtually every country would have McDonald's, and sooner or later two of them would go to war.

But I quickly realized that no one was interested in my caveats, the fine print or the idea that McDonald's was simply a metaphor for a larger point about the impact of globalization on geopolitics. They just wanted to drive a stake through this Golden Arches Theory. So the more I thought about the criticism, the more I told people, "You know what, forget all the caveats and the fine print. Let's assume Kosovo is a real test. Let's see how the war ends." And when you look at how the war ended you can see just how much the basic logic of the Golden Arches Theory still applies.

Here's why: As the Pentagon will tell you, airpower alone brought the 1999 Kosovo war to a close in seventy-eight days for one reason—not because NATO made life impossible for the Serb troops in Kosovo. Indeed, the Serbian army ended up driving most of its armor out of Kosovo unscathed. No, this war ended in seventy-eight days, using airpower alone, because NATO made life miserable for the Serb civilians in Belgrade. Belgrade was a modern European city integrated with Western Europe, with a population that wanted to be part of today's main global trends, from the Internet to economic development—which the presence of McDonald's symbolized.

Once NATO turned out the lights in Belgrade, and shut down the power grids and the economy, Belgrade's citizens almost immediately demanded that President Slobodan Milosevic bring an end to the war, as did the residents of Yugoslavia's other major cities. Because the air war forced a choice on them: Do you want to be part of Europe and the broad economic trends and opportunities in the world today or do you want to keep Kosovo and become an isolated, backward tribal enclave? It's McDonald's or Kosovo—you can't have both. And the Serbian people chose McDonald's. Not only did NATO soldiers not want to die for Kosovo—neither did the Serbs of Belgrade. In the end, they wanted to be part of the world, more than they wanted to be part of Kosovo. They wanted McDonald's re-opened, much more than they wanted Kosovo re-occupied. They wanted to stand in line for burgers, much more than they wanted to stand in line for Kosovo. Airpower alone couldn't work in Vietnam because a people who were already in the Stone Age couldn't be bombed back into it. But it could work in Belgrade, because people who were integrated into Europe and the world could be bombed out of it.

presented by NATO with the choice—your Lexus or your olive tree?—
they opted for the Lexus.

So, yes, there is now one exception to the Golden Arches Theory—an
exception that, in the end, only proves how powerful is the general rule.
Kosovo proves just how much pressure even the most olive-tree-hugging
nationalist regimes can come under when the costs of their adventures,
and wars of choice, are brought home to their people in the age of globalization. Because in a world where we all increasingly know how each
other lives, where governments increasingly have to promise and deliver
the same things, governments can ask their people to sacrifice only so
much. When governments do things that make economic integration
and a better lifestyle—symbolized by the presence of McDonald's—less
possible, people in developed countries simply will not tolerate it for as
long as they did in the past. Which is why countries in the system will
now think three times before going to war and those that don't will pay
three times the price. So let me slightly amend the Golden Arches Theory in light of Kosovo and what are sure to be future Kosovos. I would re-
state it as follows: People in McDonald's countries don't like to fight wars
anymore, they prefer to wait in line for burgers—*and those leaders or
countries which ignore that fact will pay a much, much higher price than
they think.*

On July 8, 1999, *USA Today* ran a story from Belgrade that caught my
eye. It was about the economic devastation visited on Yugoslavia as a result of the war. It contained the following two paragraphs; had I written
them myself, I would have been accused of making them up.

"Zoran Vukovic, 56, a bus driver in the city of Niš, earns the equivalent of $62 a month, less than half his salary before the war. The [Serb]
government laid off almost half of the roughly 200 drivers last month.
The rest had their salaries slashed. With the state controlling the price of
food, Vukovic and his eight dependents can survive. But most extras are
simply out of the question.

" '... now only a dream,' says Vukovic, who used to take
... en to the Belgrade outlet. 'One day, maybe, every-
... st don't think it will be in my lifetime.' "

... everything you need to know about the differ-
... e Cold War system shaped geopolitics and how
... apes geopolitics by studying Albania.

When Albania was engulfed in civil war in early 1997, I happened to be watching CNN to stay abreast of the story. CNN had no live footage from Albania, so it kept showing a map of the Adriatic Sea, off the coast of Albania. On this map were little ships, each representing one of the American, European and other countries' naval vessels that had rushed to evacuate their citizens from Albania. As I looked at that map, the first thought that occurred to me was that if this were still the Cold War, the ships on that map probably would have been U.S. and Soviet warships, each competing to see which one could fill the vacuum in Albania, which one could support their proxies there most effectively and which one could pull the Albanian pawn the fastest onto their side of the Cold War chessboard. In short, the two superpowers would have been competing to see which could get into Albania the first, the farthest and the deepest. But that is not what was happening on CNN that day. This was now the globalization system, and in this system the different powers were actually competing to see which could get their people *out* of Albania *the first, the farthest and the fastest.* The country that got its people out of Albania the first, the farthest and the fastest was the winner in Albania and the loser was the outside power that got stuck with responsibility for managing Albania—which turned out to be Italy.

What is this telling us? It is telling us that the Cold War system was characterized by two fundamental features: the chessboard and the checkbook. That is, the Cold War system was dominated by two superpowers, the United States and the Soviet Union. And they were engaged in a global competition for strategic advantage, resources and honor, in which each side's gains were the other's losses and every corner of the world was at stake, in play, and counted as much as any other corner. As Michael Mandelbaum put it: "In the Cold War system, the world was like a single integrated chessboard. Every move the Soviets made affected us and every move we made affected them. We were white and the Soviets were black. If they moved onto a white square, we moved onto a black square. If they moved black pawns in Albania, we moved white pawns. Every pawn was important because it was protecting your king. So if they took a pawn, they were that much closer to your king and therefore you were that much closer to defeat. And that is why you had to protect every pawn. Defending pawns was a way of defending your king. And that is why we ended up getting involved in places of no intrinsic importance, such as Vietnam, Angola or El Salvador."

In other words, the Cold War system had a certain built-in incentive for encouraging regional conflicts and for elevating them into an integral part of the global superpower competition and into a matter of global concern. Because there was a global competition on this chessboard, neither superpower ever wanted to concede a loss of a black or white square anywhere, for fear that it would lead to other losses and ultimately to global domination by the other side. This fear became known as the "domino theory" of geopolitics.

In addition to this chessboard, the Cold War system was also defined by the checkbook. As noted earlier, in the Cold War system it was much easier for a developing country to get by economically, despite a poor operating system and software. Some developing countries could underperform for long periods of time, because they could suck in funds from the competing superpowers by simply pledging allegiance to one side or the other in the Cold War. The U.S. government and the Soviet government, and to a lesser extent the Chinese government and the European Union, were ready to go to their taxpayers, take their money and then write big checks to foreigners in order to buy influence on different squares of the chessboard. This checkbook diplomacy was called "foreign aid." America dunned its taxpayers to pay the salaries of the Contras in Nicaragua or the Mujahideen in Afghanistan, and the Soviets did the same for the Sandinistas in Nicaragua and the Vietcong in Vietnam. America dunned its taxpayers to subsidize the Israeli Army, and the Soviets dunned their taxpayers to rebuild Syria's air force after Israel shot down ninety-seven Syrian fighter jets on the first day of the 1982 Lebanon war. The superpowers bought allegiance not only with guns but also with butter. They opened their checkbooks to subsidize roads, dams, cultural halls, imports—anything to bind a Third World country to their side in the global struggle. Moscow and Washington wrote those checks without, in most cases, making any demands on how these countries actually ran their economies, because both Moscow and Washington worried that if they pressured their pawns too tightly on issues of internal reform, they would bolt to the other side. So venal, inefficient, corrupt regimes, such as that of Ferdinand Marcos in the Philippines or Anastasio Somoza in Nicaragua, got their checks from Washington, and Cuba, Angola and Vietnam got their checks from Moscow, purely on the basis of whose economic hardware—capitalist or communist—they supported, not whether they actually operated those systems efficiently.

The superpowers just were not that interested in the economic wiring of these countries, because at that time they wanted to buy their allegiance, not their telephone companies. Even in the case of Japan, America tolerated absurd levels of protectionism by Tokyo, because it needed Japan's support in the Cold War and the Pentagon and State Department would never let the Commerce Department or the Trade Representative's office squeeze Japan very hard on trade matters, for fear of losing it on security matters. But precisely because the superpowers were ready to write blank checks, a lot of Cold War regional conflicts smoldered on much longer than they should have. What incentive did the PLO have for recognizing Israel during the 1960s and 1970s, when the Soviet Union was there to provide scholarships for Palestinian youths and guns for Palestinian guerrillas, no matter what the PLO did?

So not only did this Cold War system provide *incentives* for regional conflicts to flourish and get globalized; it also provided the *resources* for these regional conflicts to flourish and become globalized—with Ivan and Uncle Sam both furiously writing the checks.

N ow sweep this world away.
Enter globalization. Once it became the dominant international system with the end of the Cold War, globalization put a rather different frame around geopolitics. While the globalization system does not end geopolitics, to think that it doesn't affect it in some fundamental ways is flat out stupid.

To begin with, in the era of globalization there is no more chessboard, on which the entire world gets divided up into white or black squares. Since the Soviet Union has collapsed, there is no black anymore, so there is no white anymore. There are no "their guys," so there are no "our guys." Therefore, the inbuilt Cold War incentive for every regional conflict to escalate into a global conflict is gone. And so too are the resources. In the era of globalization, someone new is holding the checkbook. The Electronic Herd is the only entity now with cash to throw around. The Soviet Union doesn't exist anymore to write big checks, and the United States has put on the Golden Straitjacket and won't write big foreign aid checks anymore.

The only place a country can go to get big checks is the Electronic Herd, and the Electronic Herd doesn't play chess. It plays Monopoly. Where Intel, Cisco or Microsoft builds its next factory, or where the Fidelity global mutual fund invests its cash, is what determines who gets funded and who does not. And the bulls of the Electronic Herd do not write blank checks to win a country's love and allegiance; they write investment checks to make profits. And the Supermarkets and the Electronic Herd really don't care what color your country is outside anymore. All they care about is how your country is wired inside, what level of operating system and software it's able to run and whether your government can protect private property.

Therefore, not only will the herd not fund a country's regional war or rebuild a country's armed forces after a war for free—the way the superpowers would, just to win its allegiance—the herd will actually punish a country for fighting a war with its neighbors, by withdrawing the only significant source of growth capital in the world today. As such, countries have no choice but to behave in a way that is attractive to the herd or ignore the herd and pay the price of living without it.

Obviously, some countries have chosen to live without the herd so that they can pursue their own political agendas, and some always will. Iraqi President Saddam Hussein would rather pursue his own megalomaniacal ambitions, gas and pillage his neighbors, than subject himself to the discipline of the herd, and through his oppressive regime he is able to impose his will on his people. The same is true of regimes in North Korea, Afghanistan, Sudan and Iran. The Golden Arches Theory does not apply to them because they have chosen not to plug into the herd and the Supermarkets, and they have either enough oil or enough ideology to live without the herd for a while. But this is true of fewer and fewer countries today. If you look at both Russia and China, for example, and ask why it is that they don't more aggressively challenge the United States in their respective regions, the answer is not only because they are weaker than the United States, but also because it is not in their interests. A whole different web of interests and countervailing incentives has been spun by globalization, and this has become constraining for countries like China and Russia.

In 1979, China had no McDonald's. Deng Xiaoping was just opening up China to the world. When Deng came to America for a summit with President Carter he mentioned, in passing, that when he got back home he was going to invade Vietnam, because the Vietnamese were getting too uppity and arrogant. Carter tried to talk him out of it, using the argument that it would be bad for China's *image* (not its economics), but Deng was not persuaded and he invaded Vietnam.

Now fast-forward to 1996. China has over 200 McDonald's franchises. I am in Beijing observing the tension between China and Taiwan. I am interviewing a senior economist from the Chinese Academy of Sciences just prior to Taiwan's first fully democratic election, which many officials in Beijing feared would be a prelude to Taiwan declaring total independence from China. China is threatening to invade Taiwan if it goes off on its own. As we slurp down noodles in a rooftop restaurant in Beijing, I pose a simple question to this Chinese economist: Can China afford to attack Taiwan? His unhesitating answer was: "No—it would stop investment in China, stop growth, stop our last chance to catch up with the rest of the world."

Like everyone else I had spoken to in the Chinese government at the time, this economist felt China would be fully justified in blasting Taiwan to smithereens to prevent it from ever becoming independent. But unlike others, he was also ready to express what every senior Chinese leader knew but would not say aloud—that China could not attack Taiwan without devastating its own economy.

In the era of globalization, China and Taiwan had mutual assured economic destruction, and both knew it. In 1995–96, when China threatened Taiwan, the Taiwan stock market crashed, but China's little markets were unaffected. In the 1999 crisis between the two countries, when China rattled its saber at President Lee, it knocked down Taiwan's stock market, the TAIEX, by 20 percent. What people didn't notice, though, was that the Shanghai Stock Exchange B-share index plunged 40 percent! Two countries, one stock market.

From Beijing's perspective, China is no longer the isolated, peasant-based economy of the Mao and early Deng eras. It is now partially connected to the Electronic Herd, and the only ideology of the Chinese leadership today is: "To get rich is glorious." China's leaders cannot deliver on that ideology without the billions of dollars in foreign investment that pours into China each year. According to the *Far Eastern Economic Review*, Taiwan's total contracted investment in China by 2000 was $46 billion in roughly 46,000 different factories and firms. And Taiwanese businessmen know it, and are not afaid to remind China of it. "Taiwan is China's biggest capital supplier today, because [Taiwanese businessmen] are ready to play by the local rules, but this may not last forever," Douglas Hsu, chairman of Far East Textile, one of Taiwan's biggest conglomerates, remarked to me one afternoon in Taipei. "I am torn right now. China is a big market. Where am I going to find an alternative to this market? But I am living under this cloud of uncertainty with them. I am an industrialist. I have enough problems building plants and finding customers. I can't be worried about missiles flying back and forth. This is a cloud, and if it stays there, [China] is going to pay a price."

China is also constrained in dealing with Taiwan militarily by the fact that the U.S. Congress would surely retaliate by blocking many Chinese imports into America—which account for 40 percent of China's total exports. Between 1990 and 1999, China earned $65 billion from trade with the United States—half of its total foreign reserve growth in that period. Wang Shougeng, a director of Shanghai's Foreign Investment Commission, probably best summed up China's vulnerability to a war with Taiwan when he declared at the height of the 1996 China-Taiwan crisis that even if China had to attack Taiwan, "there will be no big change in our attitude toward Taiwan investors." I loved that statement. Even if we invade you, we sure hope your investors won't take it personally!

But this mutual assured destruction is indeed mutual. Taiwan can afford a loss of international investor confidence even less than China, which constrains its olive tree independence drive. It's not only that its stock market would crash and Taiwanese would lose all their wealth. It is much deeper. The Electronic Herd would stampede away. It is one of those little-known facts that PCs and laptops are made in a global supply chain and Taiwan, and Taiwanese-owned firms in China and Asia, are the key link in that chain. They make the most important parts that go into Dell, Compaq, Acer, Hewlett-Packard and IBM PCs, as well as into Cisco routers that keep the Internet flowing. Most U.S. computer firms have moved out of manufacturing. This has left Taiwanese firms as the world's largest supplier of thirteen critical computer components. We're talking about cases, screens, microprocessors, hubs, modems, LAN cards, keyboards, monitors, scanners, motherboards, power supplies, CD-ROMs and graphics cards. Many are sole-sourced in Taiwan. In its July 19, 1999, issue, *Electronic Buyers' News* asked some of these global computer manufacturers what their reaction was to the rising tension between Taiwan and China. "So far everything seems fine," said a spokesman for Compaq in Taipei. "But if there is a big reaction from China, we will consider a plan to shift our orders from Taiwan to Korea or Japan."

I have absolutely no doubt that if Taiwan were to go too far in its quest for a more independent profile on the world stage, China would use military force to stop Taipei—no matter what the economic consequences. No Chinese leader could survive if he let Taiwan become independent. The legitimacy of China's leadership would be undermined. But no Chinese leader can survive today without continued foreign investment and trade, either. Their legitimacy now depends even more on this. So China's leadership has had to make some very different calculations, now that they are partially plugged into the Electronic Herd, from those they made in the past.

Great wars happen only when great powers want to fight, and the first instinct of great powers within today's globalization system is not to jump into the fray. Instead of getting drawn into regional conflicts, such as Bosnia, Rwanda, Liberia, Algeria or Kosovo, today's great powers prefer to try to build iron curtains around these civil conflicts, and drive around them as though they were bad neighborhoods. And when they do get drawn in, as in Kosovo or Bosnia, they try to get out as fast as possible, because owning such places does not enhance their power, but diminishes it. That is why many regional military conflicts today, instead of automatically becoming globalized, as in the Cold War, tend to become ghettoized. This may be unfortunate, in that they become easier to ignore, but it is a fact. While regional military crises get ghettoized today, what gets globalized are the regional economic crises—like Mexico in the mid-1990s, Southeast Asia in the late 1990s and Russia at the end of the 1990s. It is these regional economic crises, and their potential to spread to other markets, that have rattled the globalization system in its early years. The domino theory, which once belonged to the world of politics, today belongs to the world of finance.

The Golden Arches Theory highlights one way in which globalization affects geopolitics—by greatly raising the cost of warfare through economic integration. But globalization influences geopolitics in many other ways. For instance, it creates new sources of power, beyond the classic military measures of tanks, planes and missiles, and it creates new sources of pressure on countries to change how they organize themselves, pressures that come not from classic military incursions of one state into another, but rather by more invisible invasions of Supermarkets and Super-empowered individuals.

The best way to see this is to take a region, such as the Middle East, and look at it from a multidimensional globalist point of view. You start to see some very interesting things.

In the fall of 1997, I was visiting Israel. The peace process was at a particularly low point, but I happened to notice a story in the business section of the paper reporting that foreign investment in Israel was as strong as ever. This intrigued me, so I went to see Jacob Frenkel, the governor of the Central Bank, and asked him the following question: "How is it that the peace process can be going down and foreign investment in Israel be going up?"

The answer that Frenkel and I came up with was that Israel today was rapidly moving away from its old economy of oranges, diamonds and textiles toward a high-tech economy that, in some ways, made Israel much less vulnerable to Arab political pressures, terrorism, boycotts and the ups and downs of the peace process, while making Israel much more vulnerable to a conventional war. Here's why: In the old days Israel grew oranges, Morocco grew oranges, Spain grew oranges. So if a country such as Japan or France was upset with some Israeli policy on the West Bank it could easily punish Israel by buying someone else's oranges. But what happens when an Israeli company, Galileo Technology, Ltd., is the inventor of the single-chip Ethernet switch used in many intranet data communications systems? You can't get those from Morocco. What happens when Israeli companies start to dominate a key high-tech sector, such as online encryption tools for Internet security, which are built around complex algorithms developed in the Technion and Israeli Army? You can't get those from Spain. What happens, as a result, is that everyone comes courting Israel, no matter what the state of the peace process. Every major American high-tech company has a branch in Israel—Intel just put in a $1.5 billion chip plant—or owns part of an Israeli computer company. Japan, which always shied away from Israel, fearing Arab retaliation, is now the second largest venture capital investor in Israel, after the United States. Japan is weak in software design and today is gobbling up Israeli software companies. I find this particularly amusing since, when I was the *New York Times* correspondent in Jerusalem in the mid-1980s, the only Japanese car you could buy in Israel was a tin-bucket Daihatsu or a low-end Subaru. Japan, Inc., would only sell its really good cars to the Arabs. Not anymore. You can get any Lexus you want in Israel today, because in economic terms, Israel today is a bigger energy exporter than Saudi Arabia. That is, by exporting software, chips and other high-tech innovations Israel is exporting the power sources of today's information economy, and every country wants that power, no matter what Israel is doing to the Palestinians, just as they wanted the oil in the 1970s no matter what the Arabs were doing to the Jews. This has real geopolitical significance. Just look at the numbers. In 1998, China had fifty-two scientists doing research at Israel's renowned Weizmann Institute. India also had fifty-two. Two countries that would not touch Israel in the 1970s are now dying to send their scientists there.

Another reason Israel is less vulnerable to low-level pressures is that high-tech knowledge exports tend to be very light and not easy to disrupt. Some are exported by modem. High-tech investment in Israel is also largely in people, and brainpower, not in factories that can easily be destroyed. Also, Israel's high-tech exports go not to its neighbors, with whom it is in tension, but to faraway markets in Asia, Europe and North America. In fact, most Israeli high-tech firms sell virtually nothing in the Israeli or Middle Eastern markets, so they are not that vulnerable to the region's politics. It is not an accident that the Tel Aviv Hilton decided in the 1990s to put in a sushi bar, not an Arab restaurant. Israeli high-tech companies also raise most of their capital on Wall Street or from venture capital firms in Silicon Valley and are not dependent on the Tel Aviv Stock Exchange. And the latest trend now is for Israeli high-tech companies to co-locate their operations, with a branch in Silicon Valley and a branch in Israel. Check Point, an Israeli company that controls about 50 percent of the Internet security market for firewalls to protect information, has an office and research arm in Israel and pays some taxes there, but now also has an office in Silicon Valley, close to the market. A Wall Street analyst I know who covers Israel's high-tech industry told me she now spends more time going to California to cover Israeli companies than to Tel Aviv.

For all these reasons, though, Israel is more vulnerable in another way. While Israel is developing a knowledge economy, knowledge workers are very mobile and like to live in nice places. If the key knowledge workers in Israel decide that the situation has reached an intolerable point—because of a never-ending conflict or religious discord—they will leave, or they will locate more and more of their operations outside Israel. Such a situation is still a long way off, but it is no longer unthinkable. With a $17,000-a-year per capita income, Israel today has a standard of living close to England's. Israel is a McDonald's country. If an Israeli Prime Minister ever called on Israeli boys to go back and recapture parts of the West Bank or Gaza in what appeared to be a war of choice but not survival, a lot of Israeli knowledge workers would be out the door.

Obviously, if someone who is not plugged into the herd, such as Saddam Hussein or some terrorists, gets hold of a nuclear weapon and drops it on Israel, it won't matter how high- or low-tech its economy is. Military power still matters. But I believe the nonmilitary power gap between Israel and the Arabs is going to grow wider and faster in the coming decade, if Israel is able to put the Israeli-Palestinian conflict behind it. When all you have to offer the world is cheap labor or oil, as tends to be the case with most Arab states, you are limited by the size of your labor pool and the price of oil. But when you have an economy that has chosen prosperity and is able to assemble knowledge, capital and resources from all over the world, you are not limited by your size anymore, and Israel is not limited by its size anymore. Historically there have been two river powers in the Middle East: Egypt on the Nile and Mesopotamia on the Tigris and Euphrates. In the twenty-first century, I believe, there will be a third river power emerging: Israel on the Jordan. Israel will be a high-tech locomotive that will pull Jordan and the Palestinians along with it. Already Siemens has linked up its Israeli factory, Siemens Data Communications, near Haifa, and a Siemens team of Palestinian systems engineers in the West Bank town of Ramallah, with Siemens headquarters back in Germany. It's just the beginning.

The same globalist perspective is useful in explaining the Arab-Muslim world today. In November 1997, I took a trip to the Persian Gulf. Let me share four stories from this trip:

Story #1: On my first stop in Kuwait I was about to go to bed one night in the Sheraton Hotel when at around ten o'clock my phone rang. It was a young Kuwaiti woman. She explained that she worked for the Kuwaiti News Agency (KUNA), had often translated my articles and would like to interview me. I was amazed by the call—a Kuwaiti woman journalist calling a Western reporter in his hotel at 10 p.m. I told her that I would be touring the oil fields the next day and if she wanted to ride along with me and talk that would be fine, but she had to meet me in the hotel lobby at 7 a.m. At 7 a.m. she was there waiting, her head covered conservatively with a veil. She turned out to be a very bright young woman. Along the way, I asked her if she had any siblings. "I have a brother," she said. "He just got married to a Kuwaiti woman he met on the Internet in a Kuwaiti chat room." What she did not tell me, but I found out later, was that this was a mixed marriage. One family were Sunni Muslims; the other Shiites. But the couple had met over the Internet, where none of the old conventions and restrictions of Kuwaiti society applied, and when they met in person it was love at first sight (or love at first "byte," as someone said). The girl's parents were very upset. But she told them she was getting married, like it or not, and eventually they relented.

"Their wedding cake was a computer and a keyboard," the young Kuwaiti woman journalist told me.

Story #2: While in Kuwait, I went to see Ibrahim S. Dabdoub, chief general manager of the National Bank of Kuwait, and one of the region's most respected bankers. When I came into his office in Kuwait City he was clearly agitated. What's wrong? I asked. Dabdoub explained that Kuwait Airways, the national carrier, had just put out to bid the financing of its purchase of two new Boeing aircraft. It was the sort of deal the National Bank of Kuwait got in the past as a slam dunk. Well, he explained, this time around his bank lost the bid to, as he put it, "something called NationsBank in Maryland," which offered to do the financing at a quarter point above the prime rate, an almost ridiculously low fee. "That's dumping," Dabdoub exclaimed to me. "It is like financial dumping." He was referring to the practice of countries who export their products for below the actual manufacturing costs just to get control of the market. "That is not a fair game after all. A large U.S. regional bank, not even a [global] money center bank, unknown to a lot of people, competed with the local Kuwaiti banks and was awarded the deal."

Story #3: I go from Kuwait to Qatar for a conference. As I'm packing my bags in my Sheraton hotel room to leave, the phone rings. It is a twenty-one-year-old Qatari woman journalist. She's read my book and would like to meet me. (I am not making this up, but my wife doesn't believe any of it!) I tell her that I am about to go to the airport, but if she wants to ride in the cab with me, we can talk. She takes me up on the offer. She is a lovely young woman, obviously intelligent and speaks good English. In fact, her English is so good I ask her if she has ever written a news story in English, because if she had maybe she could file for *The New York Times* as a stringer during the upcoming Middle East Economic Summit. Well, she says, "to tell you the truth, I write for a Gulf news Web site, and my government doesn't know about it."

I just loved that. Think how super-empowering it is for a young Arab woman to be telling the world about her country through the Internet, and her government doesn't even know she exists. That would have been unheard of just ten years ago, let alone a hundred. But now it's the future. Today, some of the most popular Arabic television programs and most widely read Arabic newspapers are broadcast and printed in Europe by privately owned companies, and are now outside any local government controls.

Story #4: Saudi Arabia is considering letting women drive, something it has always banned. This issue has been hotly debated inside Saudi Arabia for years, but lately has taken on a new urgency. Why? Because with the fall of oil prices, the Kingdom increasingly cannot afford to pay the 500,000 foreigners who come to Saudi Arabia to work as chauffeurs. Consider the interview published in the Arabic newspaper Al-Quds al-Arabi and translated by the Mideast Mirror on April 17, 1998. The interview is with Prince Talal bin Abdelaziz, probably the most liberal member of the Saudi ruling family. Talal is the half brother of both King Fahd and Defense Minister Sultan, and the father of Prince al-Waleed bin Talal, Saudi Arabia's most dynamic venture capitalist. Asked if he favored women being allowed to drive, Talal said absolutely, adding: "Saudi women used to drive camels and journey at night among men. What's the difference between a camel and a car? . . . Women driving has become an economic necessity. We transfer millions of dollars in hard currency to the home countries of expatriate chauffeurs. We can save ourselves that."

Prince Talal continued: "Political reforms are coming as part of globalization, and we must prepare ourselves for this new development from all aspects . . . Globalization is currently based on democracy, human rights and market economics. Someone once jokingly called globalization the 'fashion' of the age, which we must share in. If communist China is going along with the 'fashion,' what about the small states in the Arab world? They must appreciate that change is inevitable."

What are these stories telling us? They are telling us that what Saddam Hussein does or does not do, which neighbor he does or does not invade, will have a huge impact on the stability of the Middle East. And that his actions are likely to trigger more wars and more cease-fires before he's done.

But in the meantime, there is another, silent invasion going on in the Middle East—the invasion of information and private capital through the new system of globalization. For years the Arab world has been largely walled off from the information and financial markets revolutions that have transformed Asia and other parts of the globe. Oil allowed the Arabs and Iranians to escape many of the pressures for downsizing, streamlining and privatizing their economies. It enabled them to build fences against these pressures, and to keep these fences up even after the Berlin Wall came down. But no more. How Arab societies respond to this invasion of private capital and information—whether they adapt to it, adopt it, resist it or reject it—will have every bit as much impact on the geopolitics of this region as Saddam Hussein. And if you don't see this other invasion, you don't see the Middle East today, and if you don't take this other invasion into account you can't strategize properly about the Middle East today. And be advised: With this silent invasion, there will be no cease-fire.

I was once walking down the street in Teheran with the *New York Times* stringer there, a twenty-one-year-old Westernized Iranian woman. We were talking about what impact oil had had on Iranian politics, particularly the fact that oil had enabled the ayatollahs to stay in power longer than they otherwise might have, because oil revenues made up for Iran's generally weak economic performance under the Islamic regime. Oil, not just religious fervor, was the ayatollahs' real secret weapon. Without the financial lifeline that oil provided, the ayatollahs would have had to open Iran more to the world and put on the Golden Straitjacket, because its economy simply could not sustain its population growth without massive foreign investment. As we were musing about this, this young Iranian woman said something that I will never forget. She said of Iran: "If only we didn't have oil, we could be just like Japan."

I promised her one thing. One day Iran's oil wells will run dry, or the world will find an alternative, and when that happens, the ayatollahs will have to put on the Golden Straitjacket or be ousted. "Tell me the day Iran's oil wealth will start to dwindle," I told her, "and I will tell you the day that Ayatollah Gorbachev will appear on the scene here."

And also Ronald McDonald.

Over dinner in Morocco in 1996 an American diplomat friend of mine, whom I had first met in Moscow in the 1980s, was explaining to me how different his job was from the Cold War days and how the forces that seemed to be shaping the country he was working in, and world affairs in general, were now so hard to see, compared to the raw power clash between the United States and the U.S.S.R.

"When I joined the foreign service," he confided, "it was an institution where you knew where the goalposts were. You got your language training, you were sent into the game and you were sent to an embassy overseas. It was like the old tackle goes out and the new tackle goes in, and you knew what all the plays were and you knew what the game was and you knew where the goal line was. But now we're in the huddle and we're saying to each other, 'Where are we going and what kind of ball are we using and who's watching anyway?' Your ambassador comes to you and asks, 'What are you doing for me?' And you're not quite sure. So you start asking yourself, 'Why am I here?' [The fact that] the U.S. government could shut down [in 1996] and it didn't matter was a wake-up call for a lot of people . . . The more I'm here, the more I feel like I'm in that scene in *The Grapes of Wrath* when the banker comes to take away the tenant farmer's home and the farmer threatens to shoot the banker, but the banker says it's not his fault, he's just working for the big corporation. And the farmer asks, but where does it all stop? Who can we shoot? And the banker says, 'I don't know, maybe there's nobody to shoot.' "

My friend's lament is one you hear often these days in the foreign policy community. Why was he so confused? Because the Cold War system was a world divided, and everyone knew how to measure power, assess the threats, the deterrents and the incentives, and design strategies in that world. While there were many disagreements about what the strategy should be—hard containment, détente or arms control—everyone seemed to share a common vocabulary and perspective on what the elements of the strategy were. There was broad agreement that the Cold War was a conventional balance-of-power system built around states, armies and nuclear weapons. And being a strategist meant shuffling those pieces around in different configurations to make sure more of them were on our side than on the other.

But globalization geopolitics is much more complex. You still have to worry about threats coming from nation-states you are divided from—Iraq, Iran, North Korea. But increasingly now you have to be concerned with threats coming from those to whom you are connected—including over the Internet, through markets and from Super-empowered individuals who can walk right in your front door. Moreover, in this interconnected world states can be threatened, or sucked into conflicts, as much by the collapse of a neighbor or a traditional enemy (Yugoslavia) as they can in response to their rising strength or aggression (Iraq).

Most important, the preoccupation of states within this globalization system are incredibly diverse, with so many more agendas to think about than simply whose side you are on. You have a five-ring circus going on in the globalization system—with some states grappling with their shape, some their size, some their quality, some their equality, some their liberty and some all of the above. To measure power in such a system, and to predict or manage the behavior of states, the foreign-policy analyst or strategist has to think about all five of these issue areas at once.

Let's look at each one. To begin with, notes Michael Mandelbaum, once the Cold War walls fell "many states found themselves refocusing for the first time in 50 years on what shape they should be and who should be inside their borders and who not." You can see this everywhere from the former Soviet Union to Yugoslavia to Indonesia—with several nations trying to sort out who owns which olive tree along, and within, their borders now that the Cold War rigidities no longer applied. But those states that are already comfortable with their shape have other pre-occupations in order to survive in the globalization system. "Others are focused on getting their size right," says Mandelbaum, "that is, the size of their state apparatus." This would include, for instance, all the states of the European Monetary Union, which have been shrinking their governments in order to maintain a single currency and survive in the globalization era. They know the shape in which each E.U. member state is fixed. It's the size of their individual governments they are now focused on, as each needs to shrink in order to fit into the E.U. version of the Golden Straitjacket. Some other states are focused on getting the quality of their state right for the globalization era—for instance, Thailand, Korea and Brazil—all of whom have been focused since the Asian economic crisis on trying to upgrade the quality of their government and financial operating systems in an effort to root out corruption and cronyism. Still other states are focused on getting their equality right, because of the way in which globalization can hastily widen income and social gaps. Mexico and Venezuela, for instance, have been focused on this issue of equality and distributive justice—who gets what between the winners and losers from globalization. And, finally, still other states are working on getting their liberty right—because the demands of this globalization system are so intense that without increasing democratization, without a free press to watchdog business and without the option to change management when it messes up, countries will have a difficult time thriving. So nations as diverse as Pakistan, Peru and China are struggling with the issue of liberty.

What makes Russia and China so problematic, notes Mandelbaum, "is that they are facing all these issues at once." They are wrestling over their shape—who will be inside their states (Tibet? Taiwan? Chechnya?); they are trying to get the size of their states down in accordance with the demands of the globalization system; they are trying to get the quality of their states up in accordance with the demands of the globalization system; they are trying to manage the huge issues of inequality that arise when a communist country sheds the welfare state, plugs into the globalization system and certain oligarchs are able to steal state assets through privatization. And they are wrestling with the increasing demands for real democratization and participatory government.

As such, you cannot make policy toward Russia or China today without having a feel for all five of these challenges, without having an idea of where you would like Russia and China to come out on all five and without having a sense of how their ability or inability to manage them will affect their international behavior. What China and Russia do will depend in large part on what sort of countries they become and that will depend in large part on how they tackle these issues. All of these issues tended to get suppressed during the Cold War, because it was a war and the only question that statesmen really had to focus on was: Whose side are you on? If you were on our side you were by definition good—no matter what your shape, size, quality, equality or liberty. If you were on the other side you were by definition bad—no matter what your shape, size, quality, equality or liberty. We blithely assumed that once the Cold War ended everything would be O.K., but instead we have actually moved to this much more complex agenda, in which it is highly uncertain whether Russia, China and many other states will be O.K. But these are the issues statesmen have to tackle, and if as a statesman all you can speak about is the shape of countries and nothing else, you are not going to be very relevant in this new system.

In sum, let me stress again that the drama of international relations today is what is new—the pressures, incentives and complexities of today's globalization system—interacting with what is old, the olive tree passions in us all. One has to respect the power of the globalization system, with its Golden Straitjackets, Supermarkets, and, yes, Big Macs, to constrain the aggressive behavior of states, and one always has to respect the power of our olive tree urges and attachments to bring out the irrational in us at any time. My only claim is that the constraining pressures of today's globalization system, these Lexus pressures, have tended to trump the olive tree urges in most nations—even in Serbia in the end. Will this trend continue and will it guarantee a Long Peace? Impossible to predict. You never know what crisis or trend could come along and start to bring out the olive trees in us all in aggressive and ugly ways.

To illustrate this ever-present tension between today's globalization system and the olive trees in us all, I once tried to imagine how a discussion would go if a very decent American Secretary of State, such as Warren Christopher, were to try to explain globalization to a not so decent leader, such as Syrian President Hafez el-Assad—a man of olive trees and the Cold War. It would sound like this:

Warren Christopher: "Hafez—you don't mind if I call you Hafez? Hafez, you are yesterday's man. You're still living the Cold War. I know you've only traveled outside the Middle East a few times, so let me tell you a little bit about the new world. Hafez, Syria debated for years whether to allow its people to have fax machines. Then you debated for four years whether to allow them all to have the Internet. That's sad. That's why your per capita income is only 1,200 dollars a year. And you can barely make a lightbulb. Since 1994, your entire private sector has barely exported one billion dollars a year. We have dozens of companies no one has ever heard of that export one billion dollars a year. Now, Hafez, the reason I'm telling you all this is because during the Cold War, it didn't matter whether Syria made computer chips or potato chips, a Lexus or a lightbulb, because you could make a good living just by milking the superpowers for aid and blackmailing your neighbors. Yes, I see you smiling, Hafez. You know it's true. You milked the Saudis for billions by letting them know that there could be, as the Mafia would say, 'an unfortunate accident' in the Saudi oil fields if they didn't pay up. You milked the Russians on Monday, Wednesday and Friday, the Europeans Tuesdays and Thursdays and the Chinese on Sunday. The Soviets even bought that junk your state-owned factories produced and gave you arms and aid in return for your friendship. It was a good living, Hafez, a good living, and you played them all off against each other brilliantly. Chapeau. But, Hafez, those days are over. The Saudis can't pay your extortion anymore, your own oil supplies are running out, you will be a net oil importer within ten years, and you have the highest birthrate in the Middle East. That's not a pretty picture, Hafez. What's worse for you is that there is a new global architecture. There are no longer two superpowers to play off against each other. The Soviets are kaput and we're running a balanced budget. Instead of superpowers, Hafez, there are Supermarkets. And let me tell you, Hafez, you don't play the Tokyo bond market off against the Frankfurt bond market off against the Singapore bond market off against Wall Street. No, no, no, Hafez. They play you. They play Syria off against Mexico off against Brazil off against Thailand. Those who perform are rewarded with investment capital from the Supermarkets. Those who don't are left as roadkill on the global investment highway. And, Hafez, you are destined to be roadkill.

"By the way, Hafez, I noticed that you and Turkey have been skirmishing along the border lately, but I also notice you are desperate to avoid a real war with Turkey. We both know why, don't we, Hafez? It's because the Soviet Union doesn't exist anymore, and you know that any weapon you lose in a war with Turkey, or with Israel, or with anyone else, is a weapon that you will have to replace with your own money—cash on the table. Show me the money, Hafez! Show me the money! There is no more Soviet Union that is going to give you new weapons or barter them to you in return for the garbage you produce in your state-owned factories. And there are no Arab oil producers who are going to buy these weapons for you, because they're broke too. So you're screwed, Hafez. I always say there is no better constraint on the leader of a developing country than telling him that he has to pay cash for his weapons, especially in this day and age, when just one advanced fighter aircraft can cost fifty million dollars. Tell you what, Hafez, I'm going to leave you my cellular satellite phone. It's the latest model from Motorola, linked up with their new Iridium satellite system. You can reach me in Washington in seconds. Because, Hafez, I don't intend to make any more trips out here. These nine-hour history lessons on the Crusades that you put me through each visit are not an efficient use of my time. Why don't you digitize them, put them on a compact disc and just hand them out to every visiting Secretary of State, or put them on a Web site so my staff can download them. You see, Hafez, I've got too many other important places to be: Mexico, Thailand, China. Who should rule the Golan Heights is a fascinating question, but it's utterly irrelevant to American interests today. But, hey, we'd still love to hear from you. When you're ready to do business, just dial 001-202-647-4910, press SEND, and ask for Chris. Otherwise, Hafez, stay out of my life."

Here's what I think Assad would answer:

Assad: "Chris—you don't mind if I call you Chris? I hope you're comfortable in that overstuffed chair. I've had many Secretaries of State sink in there before you. Kissinger liked to regale me with stories about his dates with Jill St. John—such a lady's man that Henry. Baker was always snapping his notebook shut and telling me if I didn't accept his latest terms he would leave Damascus and never come back. Ah, but they always come back, don't they, Chris? And so will you. You've been here twenty-one times already, and you've been to Mexico once. I'm glad to see you have your priorities right. Now, Chris, you told me a lot about the world outside Syria. But let me tell you about my neighborhood. Politics and passion may have yielded to the bond market in America, but not in the alleyways of Damascus. Here tribal bonds, not corporate bonds, still rule the day. Here the iron fist of the ruling tribe, not the hidden hand of the marketplace, still dominates politics. We're into olive trees here, Chris, not Lexuses. I come from a minority tribe in Syria, the Alawites. That means that if I show any vulnerability, the Muslim majority here will skin me alive and leave my body as roadkill. I'm not just speaking metaphorically, Chris. Have you ever seen a man skinned alive? I think about that every morning, Chris—not about Amazon.com. I live in a real jungle, not the cyber version. That's why I may be poor, but I'm not weak. I can't afford to be weak, and my people don't want me to be weak. They appreciate the stability my iron fist brings. We have an Arabic proverb: 'Better a hundred years of tyranny than one day of anarchy.' It's true we don't have, how do you call it, McDonald's, here. And our per capita income is not as high as Israel's. But our currency is stable, nobody is starving or sleeping on the sidewalks, family ties are still strong and we are not stampeded by your greedy Electronic Herd. We're in the Slow World here, Chris, not the Fast World. I can be patient. Do my people look impatient to you, Chris? Not at all. I won my last election by 99.7 percent of the vote, Chris. My aides came to me afterward and said, 'Mr. President, you won by 99.7 percent of the vote. It means that only 0.3 percent of the people didn't vote for you. What more could you ask for?' And I said, 'Their names.'

"Ha, ha, ha!

"No, Chris, I can afford to be patient. I will make peace with the Jews only in a way that establishes me as the one Arab leader who knows how to make peace with dignity—who does not grovel the way those lackeys Arafat and Sadat did. I won't be another Sadat. I intend to be better than Sadat. I intend to give the Israelis less and get more. That is the only way I can protect myself from my own fundamentalists and domestic opponents and maintain the Arab leadership status that will always bring Syria money from someone. And if this means I have to use my proxies in Lebanon to make the Israelis bleed, no problem. It's a bad neighborhood, Chris, and the Israelis have gone soft. Too many of those kosher Big Macs, Chris. All these Israeli boys who come to fight in Lebanon carry their cell phones with them so they can call their Jewish mothers every night. Such good little boys. Do you think we don't notice that?

"So, Chris, if you want to forge a deal between me and the Jews over the Golan, you'll have to pay for it in my currency. I'm not going to just fall into your lap. But, Chris, I'm worried. As I have watched the parade of Secretaries of State sitting in that overstuffed chair I have seen not only the end of the Cold War but the end of America as a superpower. From where I sit it looks like we've gone from a two-superpower world to a one-superpower world to a no-superpower world. You come here with empty pockets and a rubber fist, Chris. I would be better off negotiating with Merrill Lynch. At least they deliver on their threats. You also come here not willing to impose any restraint on the Israelis, because your Administration is so politically weak you are afraid of offending even one Jewish voter. Look at the Israelis. They're still building settlements like crazy in the West Bank and you haven't uttered a peep, Chris, not a peep. One thing a Syrian President learns to smell is weakness, and I smell it all over America right now.

"You know what really bothers me about you Americans—you want to have it both ways all the time. You want to lecture everyone about your values, about freedom and liberty, but when those values get in the way of your political or economic interests, you just forget about them. So spare me the values lecture, Chris. You're the ones who need to decide whether you want to be a superpower that represents your super values or a traveling salesman that represents your Supermarkets. Make up your mind. Until then, stay out of my life. And, Chris, here's your fancy cellular phone back. I have no one outside of Syria I need to call.

"Oh, and by the way, be careful when you press the SEND button. You never know what might happen . . ."

Demolition Man

7. Pepsi's "Come alive with the Pepsi Generation" was translated into Chinese as "Pepsi brings your ancestors back from the grave."

8. Frank Perdue's chicken slogan "It takes a strong man to make a tender chicken" was translated into Spanish as "It takes an aroused man to make a chicken affectionate."

9. The Coca-Cola name in China was first read as "Ke-kou-ke-la," meaning "Bite the wax tadpole" or "female horse stuffed with wax," depending on the dialect. Coke then researched 40,000 characters to find a phonetic equivalent, "ko-kou-ko-le," translating into "happiness in the mouth."

10. When the Parker Pen people marketed a ballpoint pen in Mexico, the ads were supposed to have read, "It won't leak in your pocket and embarrass you." Instead, mistranslation resulted in the ad reading, "It won't leak in your pocket and make you pregnant."

> *—from a list of Ten Great Global Marketing Mistakes,*
> *published in the* Sarasota Herald-Tribune,
> *January 19, 1998*

In 1993, Sylvester Stallone and Wesley Snipes starred together in a little-known, little-remembered, but perversely brilliant movie called *Demolition Man.* The movie takes place in the year 2032, when globalization has come to completely dominate American life and it is illegal to swear, smoke, use salt, be poor, exchange fluids, use profanity, drink alcohol or have children without a license. Archcriminal Simon Phoenix (Snipes) emerges after being imprisoned for more than thirty years in a deep-freeze prison that uses cryogenic technology to flash-freeze all inmates. When he emerges, he finds a quiet, peaceful, crime-free Southern California that is just ripe for plucking by a hardened gangster like himself. The local officials, unused to having crime anymore, quickly discover that they need an old-fashioned cop to combat this old-fashioned criminal. So they unfreeze

John Spartan (Stallone), who is also serving time as an ice cube in the same freezer-prison for a previous bloody encounter with Phoenix, in which many innocent civilians were killed. But the plot is irrelevant. What is most memorable about the movie is that in this futuristic, globalized Southern California, there is only one restaurant: Taco Bell.

Stallone discovers this fact when, after being unfrozen, a local official offers to host a dinner party in his honor because Stallone saved his life. Stallone is shocked to discover that the dinner party is going to be held at a Taco Bell. He has the following exchange with his fellow cop, played by Sandra Bullock, as they are driving to dinner:

Stallone: "He says that I saved his life, and I'm not even sure that I did, and my reward is dinner and dancing at Taco Bell? I mean, hey, I like Mexican food, but come on."

Bullock: "Your tone is quasi-facetious, but you don't realize that Taco Bell was the only restaurant that survived the franchise wars."

Stallone: "So?"

Bullock: "So now all restaurants are Taco Bells."

Stallone: "No way."

The two of them then walk into this very fancy Taco Bell, where the piano player, who sounds like Barry Manilow, is singing the advertising jingle for Green Giant canned vegetables:

> Good things from the garden
> Garden in the valley
> Valley of the Jolly Green Giant

This is because by the year 2032 the only songs left are advertising jingles. As the group sits down for dinner, Stallone asks someone to pass him the salt.

Bullock: "Salt isn't good for you, hence it is illegal."

According to Hollywood, this is what America will look like when globalization reigns across the land, and all culture and environment is homogenized, standardized and sanitized. It is a chilling sci-fi portrayal of the future, but what worries me most is that there may be more than a grain of truth, and salt, to it.

When I traveled to Doha, Qatar, in the fall of 1997, I stayed at the Sheraton Hotel, which is located right at the tip of the Doha corniche, overlooking the bluish-green Persian Gulf. The Doha corniche is a ten-mile-long seafront walkway, paved with white stones and lined with gardens and palm trees. Women in native Qatari robes, some wearing black masks with only slits for their eyes, stroll up and down the corniche. Qatari men ogle and ululate at them, while mothers pushing baby carriages and families walking together amble by, all caressed by the cool breeze coming off the Gulf. My first morning in Doha, I went out for a stroll on the corniche, and as I soaked up the colors, the rainbow of people and the whole tableau, I said to myself: "This place is really tastefully done. If there is an authentic Persian Gulf culture and scene, this is it." And the more I walked, the more I enjoyed myself—until I rounded one corner and suddenly it appeared before me, like a huge blot on the horizon:

Taco Bell.

Yes, right there, in the middle of the Qatari corniche, Taco Bell—with a twenty-foot-high picture of the emir of Qatar protruding from its roof. I looked at that and thought to myself: "Oh no, oh jeez, what is that doing here? Why did they have to put a Taco Bell right in the middle of this beautiful corniche? Here I was having my authentic Qatari moment, here I was feeling far from home in a unique corner of the world, and I have to see Taco Bell." And the worst thing was: *It was crowded!*

The writer Thomas Wolfe said, "You can't go home again," but I fear he was wrong. In the world of globalization, you won't be able to *leave* home again. Because globalization is creating a single marketplace—with huge economies of scale that reward doing the same business or selling the same product all over the world all at once—it can homogenize consumption simultaneously all over the world. And because globalization as a culturally homogenizing and environment-devouring force is coming on so fast, there is a real danger that in just a few decades it could wipe out the ecological and cultural diversity that took millions of years of human and biological evolution to produce.

There is really only one hope for stopping it or at least slowing it down. Just as countries need to develop the right surge protectors and software if they want to plug into the Electronic Herd financially without being overwhelmed by it, the same is true in the environmental and cultural spheres. Countries need to develop sufficiently strong cultural and environmental filters so that they can interact with the herd without being so overwhelmed by it that it turns their culture into a global mush and their environment into a global mash. If countries cannot do that, particularly developing ones, we will all be poorer. Everywhere will start to look like everywhere else, with the same Taco Bells, KFC's, and Marriotts, with the same malls, MTV and Disney characters, with the same movies, music and Muzak, with the same naked forests and concrete valleys. Touring the world will become like going to the zoo and seeing the same animal in every cage—a stuffed animal.

When I visited Bangkok in March 1996, people there were still talking about it. They called it "the Mother of All Traffic Jams."

The occasion was a four-day national holiday marking the start of the rainy season in Thailand the previous April. Richard Frankel, an environmental engineer in Bangkok, recalled the scene for me: "On Wednesday night we figured we would try to beat the traffic and get out of town. We planned to drive to Chiang Mai, two hundred miles north, and spend the holiday there. So we packed up the car, fed everyone and took off from the house. Our plan was to drive on the expressway around Bangkok, continue out past the airport and then head north. We left the house at 10 p.m. The kids were asleep in the back seat, everything was perfect—until we hit the expressway. The traffic was backed up bumper to bumper for sixty miles. By ten the next morning, we had only reached the airport, just a few miles from our house. Some people abandoned their cars. We finally managed to turn around and spent the holiday at home."

Bangkok represents the extreme example of what can happen when a developing country opens itself to the rush of global investment without the necessary filters and surge protectors to regulate growth. Think of the problem this way: By the year 2000, there were about 5.8 billion people on the planet. Let's say 1.5 billion of them were living what could be called a globalization lifestyle. That is, they were in the lower middle, middle or upper class of their societies, with a television, maybe a phone, some sort of vehicle to get around with and a home with a refrigerator and washer/dryer. They were, to put it another way, living a lifestyle based on heavy consumption of petrochemicals (from plastics to fertilizers), hydrocarbons (coal, gas and oil) and bent metals (cars, refrigerators, airplanes). In the next decade, if globalization continues to bring more and more people into this lifestyle, and if we cannot learn to do more things using less stuff, we are going to burn up, heat up, pave up, junk up, franchise up and smoke up our pristine areas, forests, rivers and wetlands at a pace never seen before in human history.

Visit Bangkok and see the future: rich city, poor life. Because of traffic jams, some Bangkok drivers won't leave home without a mobile phone and a portable potty in their car. Bangkok is a city of 10 million people with so little central planning that up until the late 1990s it not only had no subway system, it didn't even have a carpool lane. Many Bangkokers stopped entertaining on weeknights because of the uncertainty of when guests would arrive. "All the spontaneity of life is gone," environmental journalist James Fahn complained to me one afternoon as we sat in Bangkok's scraggly center-city park. "You can't just call up your buddy and say, 'Let's meet at a restaurant in fifteen minutes.' "

The traditional argument from developing countries has been: "We'll make our mess now and clean it up later when we can afford it." But as Bangkok demonstrates, when a city grows as fast and in as unbridled a fashion as it has, there may be no later. Many sidewalks are already gone. There is no room left for new parks. Canals have been cemented over for new buildings. The fish in the river are dead. Half the traffic cops have respiratory problems. In Bangkok, the free market and the Electronic Herd simply overran the government, or grew so much richer than the government that investors could evade every environmental regulation through corruption. As one American diplomat in Thailand remarked to me when I visited in 1996: "We've just opened a dozen or so new embassies in the former Soviet Union, and our job there is to explain to people that there is something called 'a market.' Our job in Thailand is to explain to people that there is something other than the market."

I was meeting in Jakarta once with Agus Purnomo, who heads the World Wide Fund for Nature in Indonesia, and I asked him: "What is it like to be an environmentalist in an emerging market? Is it like being the Maytag repairman, the loneliest man in town?"

"We are in a constant race with development." He sighed. "Before we even have a chance to convince the wider audience here that environmentally sound development is a viable way to do things, the plans to build roads, factories or power plants are moving ahead. We have a problem here with unemployment, so any developer who can sell promises of employment will get support. When that happens, we get labeled as against employment and get treated as outsiders."

But the devastation that is wrought happens now so quickly and is often irreversible, he added. "You lose a mountain, you lose it—you can't regrow it. If you cut the forests, you can grow them back, but you lose the biodiversity—the plants, the animals. I'm worried that in a decade, we'll all be environmentally aware, but there'll be nothing left to defend."

What to do? Can we develop a method of environmentally sustainable globalization? One hope is clearly that technology will evolve in ways that will help us preserve green areas faster than the Electronic Herd can trample them. As Robert Shapiro of Monsanto likes to say: "Human population multiplied by human aspirations for a middle-class existence divided by the current technological tool kit is putting unsustainable strains on the biological systems that support life on our planet. When three guys living on a lake dumped garbage in it, it was not a big deal. When thirty thousand do it, you'd better find a way not to make so much garbage, or to treat that garbage, or to have fewer people who make garbage—otherwise the lake is not going to be there."

That is going to require some real breakthroughs in information technology, biotechnology and nanotechnology (miniaturization down to the molecular and atomic levels that enables tiny power sources to run huge systems) so that we can create value on a smaller and smaller scale, while using less and less stuff. For instance, it is an encouraging sign that, thanks to biotechnology, we can now go into a plant and change the base pairs in its DNA so that it naturally repels insects without having to use fertilizers or pesticides. It is an encouraging sign that, thanks to information technology, things such as recording tape and film are now being turned into digits—1's and 0's—which are not endangered, produce no garbage and are infinitely reusable.

But technological breakthroughs alone will not be enough to neutralize the environmental impact of the herd, because the innovations simply are not happening fast enough—compared to how fast the herd moves, grows and devours. You can see it just in the way environmental destruction statistics are now expressed. *Time* magazine reported in 1998 that 50 percent of the world's 233 known primate species are now threatened with extinction and that 52 acres of the world's forests are lost *every minute*.

Because of this, conservationists must also learn to move faster. They need to quickly develop the regulatory software and conservation-enforcing procedures to ensure sustainable development and to preserve the most pristine areas. They need to intensify work with local farmers and native peoples whose livelihoods depend on healthy forests and other natural systems. They need to quickly cultivate local elites ready to build and maintain parks and nature preserves that the new bourgeoisie and urban underclasses don't have the time, resources or inclination to bother with. And of course, they need to promote effective birth control, immediately, because unbridled population growth will explode any environmental protection filters. Howard Youth, writing in *World Watch* magazine about how the Caribbean nation of Honduras had developed a green consciousness over the years, noted that this whole painstaking effort was being undermined by a shortage of condoms. "Flying over the Honduran countryside," he wrote, "you can almost see the country grow: spreading brushfires, new towns, new roads, new swatches of forest cut from the slopes create a patchwork of human activity . . . The biggest population growth is occurring in the countryside—in villages scattered widely over rugged terrain—and in many of these places contraceptives are not readily available . . ."

But while it would be nice if conservationists were able to move faster in all these areas, it is unrealistic to believe they will. So where does that leave us? It leaves us with this fact: For now, the only way to run as fast as the herd is by riding the herd itself and trying to redirect it. We need to demonstrate to the herd that being green, being global and being greedy can go hand in hand. If you want to save the Amazon, go to business school and learn how to do a deal.

It's not easy finding people who can combine a flair for greenmail and Greenpeace, but the closest I've ever met is Keith Alger.

I met Alger, forty-four years old, while on a tour of Brazil's Atlantic rain forest, where he was one of the leaders of a coalition that helped save what's left of the rain forest in Brazil's northeastern Bahia state, while also creating alternative employment there for some of the loggers. An American political scientist married to a Brazilian monkey specialist, Alger came to Brazil with the view that he would save the rain forest by helping educate Brazilians about its ecological significance. But he quickly learned that as long as he couldn't provide jobs for the loggers who would be put out of business by saving the rain forest, he would get nowhere. As Alger described it to me: "It is hard for people to be poor and it's very embarrassing if you cannot take care of your own surroundings. The farmers here would tell me that they wanted to save the rain forest, but their jobs were also endangered species. If they needed to buy a new car or send a son to college they would just have a logger take out a few hectares of their old trees, which they saved like money in the bank. If I wanted to save the rain forest, I had to help deliver jobs for them."

So Alger, who runs the Institute for Social and Environmental Studies of Southern Bahia, teamed up with the Washington-based Conservation International and a group of local environmentalists, and together they all became environmental entrepreneurs to save the rain forest. With one hand Alger and his Brazilian colleagues fought the loggers in a seven-year public policy battle that concluded in 1998 with the Brazilian government finally banning all logging in the Atlantic rain forest in southern Bahia. With the other hand, Alger's team and Conservation International built an ecopark through a dense swath of that very same rain forest. They hired a group of professional rock climbers, who used bows and arrows to shoot ropes over the hundred-foot-high trees and then weave the ropes and netting together to create a treetop canopy walkway, with connecting tree houses. The walkway, which is about a foot wide and does sway a bit as you step along it from treetop to treetop, is located outside the town of Una, where the Atlantic rain forest once covered the entire coast. Today only 7 percent of it has survived loggers and slash-and-burn farmers.

The canopy walk is spectacular. It is not every forest where a single hectare of land contains as many as 450 different tree species, all wrestling for sunlight. Tiptoeing through the treetops on the canopy walkway, you can look one of the rarest monkeys on earth, the golden-headed lion tamarin, right in the eye as he jumps from tree to tree. And you can examine termite nests as big as pumpkins hanging from rubber trees dripping with natural latex. Walking along the dirt pathways on the floor of the rain forest, which are also part of the Una Ecopark, you can march side by side with caravans of leaf-cutter ants carting away chunks of leaves to their anthill the size of a pitcher's mound.

With the help of Conservation International, Alger's team lined up funding to build the Ecopark from Ford Motor Company and Anheuser-Busch (Budweiser), both of whom do a lot of business in Brazil, as well as USAID (the U.S. government's Agency for International Development) and Banco Real, the Brazilian bank, which owned the nearby Transamerica Hotel and whose president told the local Brazilian officials: "I want my tourists to see trees in the background when they look out the window, not some moonscape that has been logged." Anheuser-Busch actually sent one of their theme park designers, from Busch Gardens in Florida, to help design the Ecopark.

Along with the park, Alger worked with the mayor of Una, himself a logger, to create jobs in other ways. For instance, the Transamerica Hotel employs 600 people, and now offers rain forest tours. Alger's coalition worked to increase farming within the rain forest with crops, such as cocoa and coffee, that can be harvested in the shade of the trees. Alger's team also wrote a professional grant proposal for the Una city government to the Brazilian federal government and won funding from the Ministry of Education for advanced teacher training for Una's school-teachers. Says Alger: "I put the mayor, who is a logger, out of business. I knew I had to deliver for this guy or they will say that we ran out on them."

One other place Alger looked was to the high-tech community, which today has enormous credibility in developing countries, where every governor and mayor dreams of having a microchip plant in his backyard. Intel, at the urging of one of its founders, Gordon Moore, who serves on the board of Conservation International, provided funding and computer hardware for Alger's team to properly map the rain forest and focus on what needed to be saved most. Using something called the Geographic Information System, Alger's team was able to feed maps into a computer and then ask it certain key questions.

"The most important thing we asked the computer was where are the key choke points and corridors between the different sections of the Atlantic rain forest," said Alger. "The GIS pointed us right to them. That was critical because these corridors connect two larger bodies of the rain forest and without them it just becomes a bunch of isolated fragments, which cannot support as many species, and therefore many of them will go extinct if these corridors are not preserved. We built the Una Ecopark on one of these corridors that the mayor had already licensed for logging."

Alger also enlisted the help of George St. Laurent, an adventurous, eccentric American entrepreneur, who had opened a computer factory for the Brazilian market, using an abandoned cocoa factory near Una. St. Laurent got tax incentives from the state government to open his high-tech plant there, but he told the local governor that he needed more than tax breaks if he was going to persuade computer engineers from São Paulo and Silicon Valley to move to northeastern Brazil. He needed some green, not just greenbacks. Maintaining a nice environment can be a critically important magnet for attracting high-tech knowledge workers, who often have many choices of where to live. Silicon Valley isn't in California for nothing. "I told [the governor] we need a nice environment," said St. Laurent. "I told him computer engineers can live anywhere. They want a high quality of life and places they can go on weekends. If they happen to live next to one of the most exciting biodiversity systems, they would rather be part of it than watch it be destroyed." To help Alger win the support of the local government, St. Laurent promised to donate some computers to the local schools.

Eventually, the pressure from the Brazilian government, and Alger's coalition, brought around the mayor of Una, Dejair Birschner—grudgingly. The mayor told me:

"When I first heard about these environmentalists, I thought they were going to persecute us. About two years ago I started to realize that they were worried about helping to develop the region. Una has 32,000 inhabitants and 1,700 square kilometers. The three biggest employers are the Transamerica Hotel, Unacaw (a large cocoa farm) and the municipality. [Life here] is awfully hard. Some forty percent of our people live in wooden shacks, and since the cocoa industry collapsed, things have gotten really bad here . . . I don't blame Keith for telling us the truth—that logging was not sustainable. We will have to produce jobs ourselves. But Keith will have to play his part too."

The lesson that Alger learned from all this is that the only way to save the rain forest is the same way you save a country's financial system—by treating it not as just an emerging market but as an emerging society. Save the society and you can save the trees.

Said Alger: "We started by working with some of the brightest local Brazilian graduate students from around here to form the Institute for Social and Environmental Studies of Southern Bahia. Then we began training people and equipping them with the skills to be modern conservationists. That meant teaching biologists how to think about business deals and teaching economists about the most modern geographic mapping techniques. Until recently, no Brazilian university taught this sort of integrated approach with these overlapping skills, which you need in order to be a successful environmental entrepreneur these days. We are now training a new generation in how to get the most bang from the buck, and the bang I'm talking about is both species conservation and economic and social opportunities for the human beings who live around those species. Without learning how to do both, we couldn't have saved a single tree."

.   .   .

The other method for greening globalization is to demonstrate to corporations and their shareholders that their profits and share prices will increase if they adopt environmentally sound production methods.

Jim Levine, an environmental engineer who sits on the San Francisco Bay Conservation and Development Commission and teaches companies to be both green and greedy, explained to me how it works: "What you have to do is get companies, shareholders and Wall Street analysts to realize that poor environmental performance equals wasted profits. Up until ten years ago, environmental performance in manufacturing was not a design objective. But now, with the government hitting companies over the head with both new regulations and new tax incentives to be green, and with the SEC telling companies they have to start accurately portraying their environmental liabilities to shareholders—such as where they are being sued for dumping and what the cleanup could cost—there has been a paradigm shift. Companies are starting to realize that if they go into Bangkok and build a plant that pollutes the environment and then the Thai government finally gets around to passing the laws and regulatory software to clean it all up, it will be a lot more expensive to deal with later, rather than building in green procedures from the start."

One of the leading companies in this new paradigm is the Chicago-headquartered health products company Baxter International, Inc. In 1997 Baxter had sales of $6.1 billion, on output from its sixty manufacturing plants worldwide. As part of its annual reporting to shareholders, Baxter includes an Environmental Financial Statement for all its operations. Its 1997 Environmental Financial Statement reported that green production practices implemented that year had saved the company $14 million, which more than covered the costs of the programs. In addition, it said that cost avoidance from green production practices since 1990 had already saved another $86 million. "This means," the report said, "that Baxter would have spent $100 million more in 1997 for raw materials production processes, disposal costs and packaging if no environmentally beneficial actions had been implemented by the company since 1990."

Most countries right now don't have effective "polluter pays" laws, but one day many will. Which is why Baxter says in its 1997 annual report that "it is better to have all our international waste today go to reputable waste sites. Thus we can be in better shape to avoid big potential liabilities in the future." Executives who don't think this way are not taking care of their shareholders and are robbing themselves of higher bonuses.

Sometimes, though, even this profit motive can't get the job done. Sometimes it is just more profitable to overexploit the land and to sell out to rapacious global interests. That leaves one last strategy, and it's a powerful one—learning how to use globalization against itself.

I also discovered this in Brazil, not in the rain forest but in the Pantanal wetland, which I visited with a team from Conservation International. We flew in a tiny prop plane to the Fazenda Rio Negro, a ranch and nature lodge on the Rio Negro, with a grass airstrip in its front yard. Our plan was to start our tour by interviewing Nilson de Barros, Superintendent for the Environment for Brazil's Mato Grosso do Sul state. I knew this was going to be an interesting interview when de Barros insisted that we conduct it in the middle of the Rio Negro. We boarded motorized launches at the Fazenda and set sail for the meeting point at a shallow bend in the river. There, de Barros and his team were waiting for us, standing in waist-deep water. Next to them was a boat with a cooler full of beer.

"First a beer, then a bath, then we talk," he said, cracking open a can of Skol as the river flowed by.

And I thought I had the best job in the world!

De Barros explained that the Pantanal region, located along the borders of Brazil, Bolivia and Paraguay, is the largest freshwater wetland in the world (the size of Wisconsin) and is home to the jaguar and a host of other endangered species. The Pantanal nature reserve, where we were standing in the middle of the river, is a sort of Jurassic Park without the dinosaurs. Along the river we passed scores of caiman lounging onshore, giant river otters bobbing up and down, with egrets, hyacinth macaws, toucans, ibises, marsh deer, spoonbills, jabiru storks, ocelots and rheas (ostriches) all poking out from the forest at different points. Unlike the Amazon, de Barros explained, the Pantanal is not threatened by poor residents who want to destroy the habitat to relieve their poverty. Indeed, the culture in the Pantanal is a rare example of man and nature thriving in harmony through an economy of ranching, fishing and now ecotourism. The danger to this region comes from globalization: There are the soy farmers on the plateau above the Pantanal basin who are eager to feed a rapidly expanding world soybean market. Pesticides and silt runoff from their farms are fouling the rivers and wildlife. At the same time, Brazil, Argentina, Uruguay, Paraguay and Bolivia have formed a trading bloc to make them more globally competitive. And to get their soy products to global markets from this region faster, they want to dredge and straighten the rivers—so barges can navigate them more easily and swiftly—but in ways that could seriously harm the ecosystem. Finally, a consortium of international energy companies, led by Enron, is building a potentially environmentally dangerous gas pipeline across the Pantanal from gas-rich Bolivia to energy-starved São Paulo.

But while globalization is the main threat to the Pantanal, it is also its main hope for salvation. For one thing, the residents of the Pantanal now have a chance to safeguard their traditional way of life, which is based on keeping the land natural, by selling ecotours and naturally fed beef to world markets ready to pay a premium for ecofriendly products. Moreover, having cutting-edge global companies involved here can be an asset. The soybean business has attracted the big global barge companies, which unlike many local firms can afford to use highly sophisticated technologies that are less harsh on the environment—such as modern barges that can navigate sharp river bends with high-tech propellers so the rivers don't have to be straightened.

But where globalization is really an asset is in the fact that it is creating "Super-empowered environmentalists," who, acting on their own, can now fight back rather effectively against both the Electronic Herd and governments. Thanks to the Internet, environmentalists in one country are quickly relaying how a multinational behaves in their country to environmentalists in other countries. Therefore, more and more multinationals are realizing that to preserve their global reputation and global brands in the face of Internet activism, they need to be more environmentally responsible. What happened in the Pantanal, in fact, is that local environmentalists engaged environmentalists in North America to put pressure on the Inter-American Development Bank, which was planning to fund the dredging and straightening of the river system. The Development Bank, sensitive to its global reputation, responded by pressuring the local governments sponsoring the project to scale it back and to do a full-blown environmental assessment. In the end, the governments involved figured out ways to improve navigation of the rivers in the Pantanal without altering their shape.

"This is such a contrast from just fifteen years ago," says Glenn Prickett, vice president for corporate partnerships at Conservation International. "Think about a country like Brazil. Fifteen years ago the generals were in charge there, and when foreign environmentalists criticized economic development in the Amazon, the generals just told them: 'Butt out. This is our sovereign territory. It is none of your business.' But then globalization and the Internet come along and the Brazilian government begins letting in, in fact inviting in, all these big global companies to invest. This creates a new dynamic. The power driving development has shifted to global companies and institutions, who by definition do business globally, need access globally, and therefore need to be concerned about their global environmental reputations. If Brazilian environmentalists get on the Internet and tell their colleagues in the United States and Europe that this global company is spoiling the environment in Brazil, the environmentalists in these other countries will get activated. Pretty soon this company could be facing a global campaign that would affect its business, not just in Brazil but worldwide."

With so many democracies around the world now, sometimes it only takes one environmentalist waving an E-mail message on the floor of his or her parliament to hold up a major power plant project or some other environmentally sensitive deal. Global companies are learning that by supporting conservation programs they can improve the image of their global brand among customers, who increasingly value the environment.

"There is no hiding place anymore for bad corporate behavior in a world of globally interconnected activism," said Prickett. "Customers, regulators and shareholders everywhere can now reward or punish companies for what they do in faraway places. For those who behave well, they can open doors and for those who behave badly they can close them."

The best companies have learned this lesson. As Charles O. Holliday, Jr., the chairman of DuPont, once explained to me, "In the old days, if we were going to put a chemical plant in a neighborhood, we thought that if we can just get the permission of the neighbors who live around that plant, we'll be fine. Not anymore. With the Internet and all, now it's like you have six billion neighbors that you have to satisfy . . . You can get government approval for lots of things, but now it's a question of whether you can build wider [public] coalitions."

This helps explain why Ford Motor is now funding Conservation International's research on the Pantanal, its wildlife management program there and the conversion of Pantanal cattle ranches into private reserves—and even lobbying in Brazil to support the Pantanal preservation. To be sure, Ford is not saving the Pantanal because it's fallen in love with its endangered species, but rather because it believes that it can sell a lot more Jaguar cars if it is seen as saving the jaguars of the Pantanal. And if that's what it takes to save this incredibly beautiful ecosystem and way of life, then God bless Henry Ford and the Internet.

If saving the rain forest from the Electronic Herd is difficult, saving the culture that grew up around that rain forest is an even more complex task.

In the Cold War system, not to mention earlier periods in history, countries and cultures simply didn't meet each other quite as frequently, directly and openly as they do today. Travel to many areas was more difficult, and there were countless walls, fences, iron curtains, valleys and trenches for individual cultures to hide behind and preserve themselves in. But today cultures are offered up for global consumption and tested against one another over the Internet and through satellite television and open borders in a brutal Darwinian fashion. I go to villages in northeastern China to see what the world looks like beyond the frontiers of globalization and I find the teenage girls in go-go boots. I walk through Singapore airport and what do I see but two little old Indian ladies, in traditional robes, sitting, transfixed, in the television lounge watching American wrestling on Rupert Murdoch's Sky TV. I couldn't help wondering, as I watched them watching these hulking wrestlers in Tarzan outfits body-slamming each other, what they made of it all. Plug into globalization without the right software and operating system and it will melt down your economy with the blink of an eye. Plug into it without the right environmental surge protectors and it will pave over your forests in a flash. Open your borders to globalization's cultural onslaught, without protective filters, and you could go to sleep at night thinking you're an Indian, an Egyptian, an Israeli, a Chinese or a Brazilian and wake up the next morning to find that all your kids look like Ginger Spice and your boys all want to dress like Hulk Hogan.

A month after I was in Qatar, where I encountered Taco Bell, I went to Kuala Lumpur, Malaysia, where I stayed in the Shangri-La Hotel, one of the grand old hotels of Southeast Asia. I love that name "Shangri-La." It sounds so exotic. I arrived in Kuala Lumpur late at night and couldn't really see much when I drove into town, so the next morning, as soon as I got up, I threw open the curtains of my hotel room and the first thing I saw on the adjacent building was a two-story-high picture of Colonel Sanders from Kentucky Fried Chicken.

"Oh jeez," I said to myself, "what is *that* doing here? I came fifteen thousand miles to Kuala Lumpur to stay in the Shangri-La, and the first person I meet is Colonel Sanders!"

On another occasion I was visiting a businessman in downtown Jakarta and I asked him for directions to my next appointment. His exact instructions to me were: "Go to the building with the Armani Emporium upstairs—you know, just above the Hard Rock Cafe—and then turn right at McDonald's." I just looked at him, laughed and asked: "Where am I?"

India is a country that has actively tried to resist much of this global cultural homogenization. But even there, among India's elites, the Electronic Herd is fast at work. On a stiflingly hot afternoon in New Delhi, during the summer of 1998, I interviewed seventy-eight-year-old former Indian Prime Minister I. K. Gujral, one of India's most enlightened politicians. He began by recalling something that a Canadian representative to a Unesco conference had said to him after the Indian statesman introduced a resolution meant to ensure that the "new information order" that was taking hold around the globe would be a two-way exchange of culture and information—not just the developed countries pouring their culture down the gullets of the developing nations. The Canadian representative had stunned Gujral by supporting his resolution. "I asked him why Canada would support this," Gujral recalled. "He said, 'Because we are already experiencing what you are fearing. There is no more Canadian music, theater, film, culture or language.' It has all been Americanized."

When I asked him why this issue was so important to him, Gujral, who was dressed in traditional Indian garb, basically said that unless you preserve at least some of your own olive trees in your own backyard, you will never feel at home in your own house. "What are my roots?" he asked aloud. "My roots are not only the fact that I live here in India. My roots are the fact that I hear someone reciting a couplet in my native language. I hear someone singing a song in my native language when I walk down the street. My roots are when I sit in my home with you in my native dress. Our traditions are a thousand years old. You cannot just let them go like that. The world will be much richer if the colorations and diversities are sustained and encouraged with different cultures."

I identify thoroughly with Gujral, maybe because I was born and raised in a relatively small community in Minnesota. Globalization can be deeply disorienting. To have your own cultural olive trees uprooted or homogenized into some global pulp is to lose your bearings in the world.

I was musing about this in Jerusalem one afternoon with my friend Yaron Ezrahi, the political theorist, when he made a trenchant observation. He said: "You know, Tom, there are two ways to make a person feel homeless — one is to destroy his home and the other is to make his home look and feel like everybody else's home."

How do we prevent this sort of homelessness? The first thing to do is to understand that Americanization-globalization is not just about push, it is also about pull. People all over the world want in on globalization, for a lot of reasons. Those Qataris who were packing into Taco Bell on the Doha corniche were not coming from some charming pub or neighborhood bistro full of polished brass and oak. Before Taco Bell was there on the corniche, there was probably a fly-infested sidewalk stand, some guy grilling on charcoals in less than sanitary conditions, no lighting and no bathroom. In its place Qataris were being offered something they had never tasted before, Mexican food, with a clean bathroom, international sanitation standards, smiling service and quality controls — all at a cheap price they could afford. No wonder it was crowded.

And there is something more they were being offered, something less visible but even more valuable to many of them. I first discovered it in Malaysia. I went to see the finance minister, and while I was waiting in his anteroom, his press aide introduced me to a Malaysian businessman also there to see the minister. He introduced him by saying: "This is Mr. Ishak Ismail, he owns all the Kentucky Fried Chicken franchises in Malaysia." I immediately took out my IBM ThinkPad and insisted on interviewing him.

"Tell me something," I asked. "What is the great appeal of Kentucky Fried Chicken to Malaysians?" Not only did they like the taste, he said, but they liked even more what it symbolized: modernity, Americanization, being hip. "Anything Western, especially American, people here love," explained Mr. Ismail. "They want to eat it and be it. I've got people in small [rural] towns around Malaysia queueing up for Kentucky Fried Chicken — they come from all over to get it. They want to be associated with America. People here like anything that is modern. It makes them feel modern when they eat it." Indeed, walking into Kentucky Fried

Chicken in the rural areas of Malaysia is the cheapest trip to America many Malaysians will ever be able to take.

The Malaysians go to Kentucky Fried and the Qataris go to Taco Bell for the same reason Americans go to Universal Studios—to see the source of their fantasies. Today, for better or for worse, globalization is a means for spreading the fantasy of America around the world. In today's global village people know there is another way to live, they know about the American lifestyle, and many of them want as big a slice of it as they can get—with all the toppings. Some go to Disney World to get it, and some go to Kentucky Fried in northern Malaysia. Ivy Josiah, a young Malaysian human rights activist, once expressed to me the mixed feelings her generation has about this phenomenon. "I get emotional when I think of how our traditional restaurant stalls are going to be eaten up by Kentucky Chicken, McDonald's and Chili's," she said. "We are losing our own identity. We grew up with those stalls. But younger people did not. You go in those stalls now and they have rats and bad water. For a Malaysian kid today the big treat is going to Pizza Hut. Globalization is Americanization. Elites here say, 'You should not have McDonald's,' but for the little people, who don't get to travel to America, they have America come to them."

For all these reasons it would be naive to think that somehow we can stop the global juggernauts of McDonald's or Taco Bell from opening franchises everywhere around the world. They proliferate because they offer people something they want, and to tell people in developing countries they can't have it because it would spoil the view and experience of people visiting from developed countries would be both insufferably arrogant and futile.

Yet, culturally speaking, something will be lost—for them and for us—the more these global franchises greet us atop every hill, in the terminal of every airport and around every corner. The only hope—and it is only a hope—is that countries will also learn to develop multiple filters to prevent their cultures from being erased by the homogenizing pull and push of global capitalism. Because given the force and speed of globalization today, those cultures that are not robust enough to do so will be wiped out like any species that cannot adapt to changes in its environment.

I believe the most important filter is the ability to "glocalize." I define healthy glocalization as the ability of a culture, when it encounters other strong cultures, to absorb influences that naturally fit into and can enrich that culture, to resist those things that are truly alien and to compartmentalize those things that, while different, can nevertheless be enjoyed and celebrated as different. The whole purpose of glocalizing is to be able to assimilate aspects of globalization into your country and culture in a way that adds to your growth and diversity, without overwhelming it.

Glocalism is actually a very old process, going back to ancient times, when, for instance, local cultures encountered the spread of Hellenism and tried to absorb the best without being overwhelmed by it. Judaism is a classic example of a religious culture that has absorbed influences from many different countries over generations, without ever losing its core identity. My teacher, the rabbinic scholar Tzvi Marx, notes that when the Jews first encountered the Greeks in the fourth century B.C.E., the one thing that was absorbed most thoroughly into Jewish thought was Greek logic, which was melded into biblical and rabbinic learning in that day.

"This absorption of Greek logic was relatively easy, because it was or-ganically related to what the rabbis and biblical scholars of that day were doing, which was cultivating truth," says Marx. "The sign of a healthy ab-sorption is when a society can take something from the outside, adopt it as its own, refit it into its own frame of reference and forget that it ever came from the outside. This happens when the external force being ab-sorbed touches something latent in your own culture, but maybe is not fully developed, and the encounter with the outside stimulus really en-riches that latent thing and helps it flourish." That is how species and cul-tures advance.

At the same time that the Jews were exposed to Greek logic, though, they were also exposed to the Greek celebrations of the body, not to men-tion the Greek preoccupation with Eros and polytheism. The Jews did not absorb these influences. They were viewed as alien and remained alien. The Greeks enjoyed watching naked gymnasts. The Jews did not, and never absorbed this part of Greek culture. Those who did were con-sidered to have assimilated and to have lost their original sense of self. Fi-nally, there were things which the Greeks ate and styles of dress which Jews in those days selectively adopted and enjoyed precisely because they were different, but never made them their own. To put it in absurd terms: They did not give up matzo ball soup to eat souvlaki, but they ate souvlaki and enjoyed it as something different.

Healthy glocalism is always a trial-and-error process, but it is an in-creasingly necessary one. In a world where so many of the protective walls, fences and trenches have been removed, and will continue to be re-moved, cultures that are good at glocalizing have a real advantage, and those that aren't need to learn to do so. Some cultures are obviously not good glocalizers, and this makes globalization very threatening to them. When countries or cultures are not good at glocalizing you get the sort of reaction of the Taliban Islamic fundamentalists in Afghanistan: They fear a trial-and-error encounter with globalization because they fear that everything will end up as error and with their culture overwhelmed, so they just bring down the veil over a whole country, or try to build higher and higher walls. But these walls are inevitably breached by the Electronic Herd, and when that happens, and people start to lose their own cultural identity, they end up becoming assimilated in their own country. Their own country becomes just a place through which other countries and cultures pass.

There is another danger. Some cultures may think they are glocalizing in a healthy manner, but in fact they are assimilating and losing their identity in a subtle, slow-motion manner. A trite but obvious example is the way McDonald's Japan has been absorbed by Japanese culture and architecture. With two thousand restaurants in Japan, McDonald's Japan, a.k.a. "Makudonarudo," is the biggest McDonald's franchise outside of the United States. McDonald's Japan has been so successful at integrating itself into Japan that the story is told of a little Japanese girl who arrives in Los Angeles, looks around, sees a few McDonald's, tugs her mother's sleeve and says to her: "Look, Mom, they have McDonald's in this country too." You could excuse that little girl for being surprised that McDonald's was an American company, not actually a Japanese company. (The McDonald's folks in Japan renamed Ronald McDonald "Donald McDonald" to make it easier for the Japanese to pronounce.) "You don't have two thousand stores in Japan by being seen as an American company," James Cantalupo, president of McDonald's International, told me. "Look, McDonald's serves meat, bread and potatoes. They eat meat, bread and potatoes in most areas of the world. It's how you package it and the experience you offer that count."

The fact that the little girl in this story didn't know that McDonald's comes from Chicago and was founded by a guy named Ray Kroc, who was not very Japanese, is to me a sign of an unhealthy glocalism. Something that should be treated as different—the Big Mac—and even enjoyed because it is different, is not. An unhealthy glocalization is when you absorb something that isn't part of your culture, doesn't connect with anything latent in your culture, but you have so lost touch with your culture, you think it does. Says Tzvi Marx: "They say in medicine that one way the cancer virus enters a cell is by disguising itself so that the cell doesn't know it is there and thinks that the cancer is an organic part of it-self—until it is too late, and the cancer has taken over the cell nucleus and all of a sudden that whole cell is gone." This can happen—with glo-calism acting as the cancer virus that fools you into thinking something belongs, but doesn't. I am glad that they have McDonald's in Japan, and I am glad that I have a sushi bar near my home in Bethesda. I'm glad that a little Japanese girl likes McDonald's, just as I am glad my girls like sushi. But it is important that this Japanese girl likes it *because* it is differ-ent, not because she is fooled into thinking that it is actually Japanese. When that happens, homogenization is just around the corner. When that happens, there is every chance this Japanese girl will eventually lose touch with what is really Japanese, and one day she will wake up like that cell and discover that she has been invaded and there's nothing left of her original self and culture.

G localism alone, though, even in its most healthy form, is not suffi-cient to protect indigenous cultures from globalization. Some hard filters are also needed. To begin with, you need zoning laws, protected area laws and educational programs to preserve unique regions and a cultural heritage from insidious homogeneous development. It doesn't mean saying no to every McDonald's, but it can mean saying no to Mc-Donald's in certain neighborhoods. This requires strong planning by bu-reaucrats who can't be easily bought off and by politicians ready to assign a real value to cultural preservation.

Southern France is preserved as southern France, in part, because Germany, through the European Union, subsidizes French agriculture so that small French farmers, and therefore small shopkeepers and small vil-lages, can survive intact—despite global pressures for consolidation of farms and the malling of villages. In other words, what we like about southern France is based on a politics that assigns a real value to cultural preservation. It is based on a common Euro-agriculture policy and trans-fer payments to support small-plot farming to keep the villages there in-tact, in part because they are seen as a source of cultural richness. We need these kinds of social safety nets for our cultures. Politicians have to educate the public about the value of such cultural safety nets and have to be willing to sell them.

In developing countries, where you do not yet have a middle class big

enough to appreciate or lobby for cultural preservation, and where zoning laws and environmental legislation are weak, easily corrupted or
nonexistent, you need to rely more heavily on another filter—the marketplace. To come to a logger in Indonesia, who has a family of twelve to
feed, and tell him that he really should not slash and burn the rain forest
because it is part of his country's cultural heritage simply does not work.
He will tell you, "You want to preserve it—you buy it." People have to see
that cultural preservation is related to their well-being and does not mean
sacrificing themselves in the race for prosperity. Tourism can play an important role in creating incentives for locals to maintain the character
and tradition of a place. Tourists always want to know: Can you breathe
the air? Can you drink the water? Those issues are important for a hote-
lier who wants to sell $20 dinners to tourists, instead of $1 dinners to locals. Sometimes the best way to protect a pyramid, an archeological dig or
a unique neighborhood is to make its preservation profitable for those
who live around it.

   While visiting Bali, Indonesia, in 1997, my wife and I toured one of its
most beautiful religious sites, Pura Tanah Lot, a temple built on a coastal
outcropping of rock. When the tide comes in, the outcropping and the
temple are isolated by the surf. It is a spectacular attraction that draws
millions of Indonesian tourists who come to visit and make Hindu offerings. We arrived around sunset, and as I went to take a picture of my wife
with the temple in the background, I noticed a golf cart speeding by. A
golf course had been built along the coast, just a few hundred yards from
the temple, and the cart path on one hole went right along the shoreline.
Now, I love golf, but I also love stunning natural settings and respect holy
temples. It was obvious that either no planning had gone into the approval of this golf course location or the bureaucrats in charge of planning had been bought off.

   No wonder the *Jakarta Post* carried a story the week we were there
about some artists on Bali who were holding an art exhibition protesting
the paving of their paradise. The *Post* said the exhibition included a
drawing of a golf ball dribbling into a Hindu procession; another depicted Bali as a golf ball being batted around by the world, and one
picture was of a village farmer swinging his hoe like a golfer teeing off—
only he is swinging away at developers. The show was wryly entitled:
"glo-BALI-zation."

   If Bali continues down this self-destructive path it will mean the end of
its tourist business. Indeed, the tour book we used to guide us in Bali, one
of the Knopf guides, which was written two years before we visited, said

the following about Pura Tanah Lot: "The intense touristification of the place is distracting, and it's not finished yet: a luxury hotel and golf course are planned nearby. For the time being, it's still a place worth visiting." When the tourist guides start warning you that a country is overexploiting its own culture and telling tourists to come see a site before it is lost, you know that country has entered a danger zone. I fear that the next edition of the Knopf guide to Bali will simply say: "Too late. Go somewhere else."

And that's why the profit motive, while necessary at times, is also not sufficient, because it can too easily lead to the commercialization and exploitation of every cultural icon. You also need a middle class and an elite with enough of a commitment to social activism to pay to preserve cultural icons, even when they are not profitable—or precisely because they are not profitable. When it comes to preserving noncommercial aspects of life, you cannot ask the market to do too much, and you don't want to ask the market to do too much.

"In the long run it would be an illusion to think that the market and the profit motive alone can be enough to protect a country's cultural or environmental assets," argues Fareed Zakaria, managing editor of *Foreign Affairs*, who is of Indian origin. "It simply will not be. Because what globalization does is empower the common man. It empowers common men and women to have all these choices, and when that happens it is inevitable they will make the choices that seem the most attractive, the most modern, the most appealing, the most convenient and the most commercial. And they may want strip malls along every street and Taco Bells on every corner—even though in the short run that will steamroll their local and national cultures. That is why it is not enough to just harness the market; you also have to regulate it. But to regulate it, you need elites who are ready to protect things from the market—to create spaces where the market will not rule or invade, and in so doing protect those totally irrational, noneconomic aspects of a country's national character. It is usually only elites, secure in their own wealth, who are ready to worry about these things. The Rockefellers helped set up the national park system in America. The Metropolitan Museum was founded by great capitalists who said we need a museum that has nothing to do with the market."

While all these filters for protecting culture and environment make sense in theory, you need them all working at once to have any hope of making an impact. The rain forest park alone will never pay enough to eliminate all logging; bureaucrats alone will never have enough political will to apply all environmental laws; green corporations alone will never be enough to slow the pace of degradation; Internet activism alone will never be enough to restrain the Electronic Herd.

That is why I hope, and I actually believe, that as we enter this next decade of globalization, someone, or some party, is going to build their politics around the notion of making all of these filters work together. I'm not talking about Greenpeace, I'm talking about mainstream parties and politicians.

It will have to start in the developed countries and then fan out. The good news is that this politics already has a name—"the livability issue." In America, Al Gore has started to lay claim to this issue. Livability, he argues, requires "smart growth" and smart growth requires politicians to build a set of laws, incentives and initiatives that can get all the filters working together. A key element of Gore's strategy is the creation of "Better America Bonds." Through federal tax subsidies, this program would allow communities to raise up to $9.5 billion in bonds that would be used to buy up still-green open space, restore decayed parks and refurbish areas, particularly inner cities, where the environment has been destroyed but can be reclaimed. The more inner cities are reclaimed, the less pressure for more urban sprawl into green areas.

Only a relentless, coherent politics of livability that enables a society to get all the necessary environmental and cultural filters operating in concert will have a chance of moderating the relentless, coherent, well-funded and efficient business plans of Nike, MTV, McDonald's, Pizza Hut, Enron and Taco Bell. It may be only a hope and a prayer today, but it is a necessary hope and a prayer—because there will be no sustainable globalization without environmental preservation and cultural preservation.

They all go together. Cultures are nurtured and sustained within their native environment. The most interesting and diverse tribes in the Amazon live in the most pristine, unpolluted, undeveloped regions. And the most interesting and diverse towns, neighborhoods, regions and communities in America, Qatar or southern France are the ones where the environment has not been paved over and malled over so that it looks like Everywhere U.S.A.

Israel provides a very interesting case study in this regard, because it is a place with a strong culture dating back thousands of years and an environment that is more familiar than any in the world, with every other hill and rock mentioned in the Bible. Today, though, the Society for the Protection of Nature in Israel (SPNI) is fighting the massive urban sprawl that is overtaking the country. If you planted a tree in the hills between Jerusalem and Tel Aviv, visit it soon. It may not be there much longer, because by 2020 the area from Haifa to Tel Aviv to Jerusalem is likely to become one big, seamless urban megalopolis. Israelis are building as if they were living in Australia—more is better, bigger is better, wider is better. If current population trends continue, Israel, outside the Negev Desert, will soon be one of the most densely populated countries in the world. Sadly, the golden arches of McDonald's now dominate a prominent hill as you enter and exit Jerusalem from the west.

Precisely because Israel can never limit Jewish immigration, it has to get much more sensitive about sustainable development; otherwise Israeli-Zionist culture will lose the environment from which it emerged and to which it is so intimately linked. "Every project that is approved against the national plan, and destroys open space, destroys part of Jewish heritage—the biblical landscape of David and Solomon's day," explained Avram Shaked, the conservation coordinator for the SPNI, as the two of us spent a morning watching some bulldozers bite several mouthfuls out of the Judean hills. "The Bible refers to the vineyards of Ben Shemen. Today Ben Shemen is the biggest highway interchange in the country. We still speak about 'the Land of Israel' in metaphysical terms, but we forget about the actual land."

Yoav Sagi, chairman of the SPNI, then chimed in: "We have to change the culture here from conquering the land to preserving the land. Because if Israel should one day become a normal country, with no more wars, what will sustain us here is the quality of life and connection to the land. But if we keep to this trend, we will have no quality of life and no land to be connected to."

When you strip people's homes of their distinctiveness—either by homogenizing them or by destroying them environmentally—you undermine not only their culture but also social cohesion. Culture, at its best, can be one of the most powerful forms of voluntary restraint in human behavior. It gives life structure and meaning. It sanctions a whole set of habits, behavioral restraints, expectations and traditions that pattern life and hold societies together at their core. When unrestrained globalization uproots cultures and environments, it destroys the necessary underlying fabric of communal life.

And this brings us back to sustainable globalization. You cannot build an emerging society—which is so essential for dealing with the globalization system—if you are simultaneously destroying the cultural foundations that cement your society and give it the self-confidence and cohesion to interact properly with the world. That is why my concern for developing countries that get steamrolled by globalization goes beyond a narrow preoccupation with wanting them to remain colorful places that we can all enjoy as tourists. My concern is that without environment there is no sustainable culture and without a sustainable culture there is no sustainable community and without a sustainable community there is no sustainable globalization.

I see this process very clearly in my own neighborhood. My favorite cafe these days, a few miles from our house in Bethesda, Maryland, is called the Corner Bakery. To begin with, I like the name Corner Bakery. It evokes something warm and neighborly, and inside they sell thirty different types of bread. It also has the aroma of an old-time bakery and the look as well, with polished dark wood and brass and a friendly staff. Yes, that's my Corner Bakery. There's only one problem with my Corner Bakery. It's not on a corner. It's in Montgomery Mall, a shopping center. Although the name and the feel of the place evoke the Main Street of old, there is no soul behind it. When you come in the Corner Bakery, there is no "hi, neighbor—hi, Pop—hi, Doc." It's just a bunch of strangers off the freeway. In other words, we've finally arrived in the post-McDonald's era. And we've seemingly returned to something in our roots—but the community and environment that sustained the old corner bakery aren't there behind the franchised Corner Bakery. So it's just a Potemkin facade, anchored not in a community but in concrete.

What I fear is that Malaysia and Thailand, India and Israel, Qatar and Indonesia will eventually reach a point in their development where they too will want to revive their corner bakeries—the sights, the smells, the colors, the street stalls, the architecture and the landscapes of old. Those were the nests in which their own distinctive cultures, their olive trees, were planted and nurtured. But they could discover that they have been erased forever, not by some new, evolved form of their old culture, which has happened throughout history, but rather by a sterile global culture smashed onto their society.

We cannot hope to preserve every culture in the world just as it is. And we cannot want a culture to be preserved if it lacks the internal will and cohesion to do so itself. As with species, cultures spawning, evolving and dying is part of evolution. But what is going on today, thanks to globalization, is turbo-evolution. It is almost not fair. In a world without walls, even some very robust cultures are simply no match for the forces of the Electronic Herd. They need help to survive, or they will be destroyed at a rate far faster than they can be regenerated by evolution, and we will end up with only one animal in the zoo.

As *National Geographic* observed in a special August 1999 issue on global culture, "There is no better measure of this crisis than the loss of languages. Throughout all of history something on the order of 10,000 spoken languages have existed. Today, of the roughly 6,000 languages still spoken, many are not being taught to children—effectively they are already dead—and only 300 are spoken by more than a million people. In another century fully half of the languages spoken around the world today may be lost . . . The biological analogy is apropos. Extinction when balanced by the birth of new species is a normal phenomenon. But the current wave of species loss caused by human activities has no precedent. By the same token, languages, like cultures and species, have always evolved, but today languages are being lost at an alarming rate—within a generation or two. 'When we lose a language, it is like dropping a bomb on the Louvre,' laments Ken Hale of the Massachusetts Institute of Technology. As languages disappear, cultures die. The world becomes inherently a less interesting place, but we also sacrifice raw knowledge, the intellectual achievements of millennia."

No one understands this better than James Wolfensohn, president of the World Bank. Wolfensohn told me once of a trip he took to Guatemala, not long after taking over at the World Bank. "I was in the high country and met with the Mayan elders. It was in a terribly poor village, bereft of everything. These people had nothing. We had come to look at ways we could help them improve health care and education. When we raised the issue of education, it was the thing they wanted to talk about most. Even more than water. They wanted our help in protecting the Mayan education, which was an oral tradition passed down over three thousand years. Here these people were so poor, but they have this incredibly rich history and culture—they had been studying mathematics and astronomy long before the West—and they wanted our help so they could keep passing it down to their children. The world will be a poorer place if we can't help them."

So Wolfensohn has started a program of cultural lending at the World Bank—in addition to normal development lending—on the assumption that losing the knowledge and culture of those Mayan elders would be like losing the DNA of a rare plant or animal species. Among the cultural lending projects the World Bank is now supporting are the restoration of the National Museum of Brazil, the restoration of mosques in Samarkand, the preservation of cultural sites in Bethlehem, a language dictionary in Uganda, the development of living culture projects for indigenous peoples in Peru and Bolivia and support for traditional artisans and craftsmen in Morocco. The only sad thing is that Wolfensohn has to struggle every year with the World Bank board, which is made up of Finance Ministers, to keep this program funded. Says Wolfensohn, "I say to them, 'Can you imagine England without its history? Can you imagine what it would be like to go to France without its culture? Well, if you can't conceive of that, why deny it to developing countries who need it even more? You can't get people to move forward unless they have a recognition of the base and the past from which they've come.'" The best part of Wolfensohn's program is that countries that get cultural aid have to use at least 15 percent of it to fund modern artists, painters, artisans, and poets, so that the World Bank isn't just putting cultures in museums but is nurturing them as living realities.

Globalization will be sustainable depending, in part, on how well each of us manages the filters needed to protect our cultures and environments, while getting the best out of everyone else's. If globalization becomes just a more efficient way to exchange cultures—for me to sample that Japanese girl's sushi and Kabuki while she tastes my McDonald's and Disney—so that people can actually pick and choose more, if it turns out to be a confederation of distinct cultures and not a homogenization of them, and if it promotes a more culturally diverse universe, rather than a soulless, standardized globe, it will be sustainable. As Yaron Ezrahi puts it: "Either globalization homogenizes us only on the surface, and local cultural roots remain, or it homogenizes us to our very roots and it becomes environmentally, culturally and politically lethal."

It is O.K. for Disney World to have a Chinese pavilion and a French pavilion and a Mexican pavilion. But God save us from a world where the Chinese pavilion at Disney World is our only remembrance of what China once was, and where the Animal Kingdom at Disney World is our only remembrance of what the jungle once was, and where the Rain Forest Cafe is the only rain forest you or your kids will ever see.

$$\left(14\right)$$

Winners Take All

Give me the Nikkei close and the Detroit score.
> —*Michael Jordan, speaking in a commercial in which*
> *he poses as a Wall Street executive*

Dennis, I came for you from Poland.
> —*sign in the crowd addressed to Dennis Rodman*
> *at the United Center, the Chicago Bulls' arena,*
> *April 11, 1998*

I am a season ticket holder to the Washington Wizards NBA basketball team, and the summer of 1996 was a dark moment for all Wizards fans. The Wizards' star forward, Juwan Howard, was a free agent that summer and the cash-rich Miami Heat were trying to lure him away with an offer in the range of $120 million over seven years. The Wizards were initially offering "only" $75 million to $80 million. At the peak of Howard's contract negotiations, I happened to run into political commentator Norman Ornstein of the American Enterprise Institute, also a Wizards fan, and we were bemoaning the seemingly inevitable loss of Howard to Miami.

"You realize," Ornstein said at one point, "it's all NAFTA's fault."

We both laughed, knowing there was a lot of truth behind what Ornstein was saying. Put simply, globalization creates much more of an open, unified global market for many goods and services. As a result, when a country plugs into this system, those with the skills or talent to sell their goods and services into this unified global market can really cash in, because they can sell to a marketplace the size of the whole wide world. Juwan Howard's good fortune was that the improvement in his jump shot and rebounding skills coincided with the fall of the Berlin Wall, NAFTA, the European Monetary Union, GATT, the collapse of communism and other market-merging forces that enabled the NBA to become a global sport and enabled fans from Moscow to Mexico to Miami to help pay

Howard's salary. The NBA in 1998 sold more than $500 million worth of NBA-licensed basketballs, backboards, T-shirts, uniforms and caps outside the United States, not to mention millions of dollars more in satellite and cable viewing rights.

Indeed, NBA basketball today has begun to rival soccer as the most global sport. How global is it? You know those Matrushka dolls that they sell in Russia—the wooden dolls with one doll inside a larger doll inside a larger doll. Well, when I visited Moscow in 1989 the hottest-selling Matrushka dolls were those of the different Soviet leaders and the last Czars. You could get Lenin inside Stalin inside Khrushchev inside Brezhnev inside Gorbachev. But when I visited Moscow for the Russian presidential election in 1996, I found that the hottest-selling Matrushka doll outside the Kremlin was Dennis Rodman inside Scottie Pippen inside Toni Kukoc inside Luc Longley inside Steve Kerr inside Michael Jordan! You don't like the Chicago Bulls? Hey, no problem. Street vendors in Moscow were selling every NBA team as a set of Matrushka dolls that year.

But while globalization helps to explain Howard's good fortune, it also helps to explain one of the most serious by-products of plugging into the globalization system—the fact that during the 1980s and 1990s, as globalization replaced the Cold War system, income gaps between the haves and have-nots within industrialized countries widened noticeably, after several decades in which that gap had remained relatively stable.

Economists will tell you that there are many reasons for this widening income gap. These include massive demographic shifts from rural to urban areas, rapid technological changes that increasingly reward knowledge workers over the less skilled, the decline of unions, rising immigration into developed countries which drives down certain wages and the shift in manufacturing from high- to low-wage countries, which also holds down salaries.

All these factors have to be taken into account when trying to explain the widening gap between haves and have-nots, but for the purpose of this chapter, I want to examine the factor that may be the most important, and has certainly been the most visible in my own travels. This is the phenomenon of "winner take all"—which refers to the fact that the winners in any field today can really cash in because they can sell into this massive global marketplace, while those who are just a little less talented, or not skilled at all, are limited to selling in just their local market and therefore tend to make a lot, lot less. USA Today noted that the Miami Heat's first offer to Howard of $98 million over seven years would pay the average salary of an elementary school teacher ($30,000 a year) for 3,267 years.

Economists Robert H. Frank and Philip J. Cook pointed out in their classic book, *The Winner-Take-All Society*, that globalization "has played an important role in the expansion of inequality" by creating a winner-take-all market for the globe. They note that with trade barriers and tariffs being reduced or eliminated all over the earth, travel costs being slashed, internal markets being deregulated and information now being freely and cheaply disseminated across borders, a single unified global market is being created in many industries and professions. The traveling salesman who used to be confined to a five-state area can now use faxes, satellite phones and the Internet to create a national or global clientele for himself. The doctor who was limited to one hospital can now give his diagnosis and advise treatment of patients through data transmission networks that stretch the world over. The singer who used to be heard only in his or her country can now use CD technology and worldwide pay-per-view cable systems, not only to reach a global audience, as the Beatles did, but to profit from it in myriad ways. At the same time, Frank and Cook argue, the elimination of formal and informal rules that limited competitive bidding for the best in any particular industry—rules such as the reserve clause in professional sports, which restricted a player's ability to put himself out to the highest bidder, or informal rules in industry which led companies to promote executives from within rather than scour the world for the best and the brightest—have also contributed to an open, global auction market. (Consumers can also benefit from this. If you are sick with some rare disease, you will appreciate being able to consult with the best specialist anywhere in the world through the Internet; and if you are a shareholder of a slumping Fortune 500 company, you will be pleased that it can lure the best free-agent executive from as far away as Australia, and won't feel compelled to promote some dolt from within.)

You put all these factors together and you end up with a situation in which the potential market for any good or service, for any singer or songwriter, for any author or actor, for any doctor or lawyer, for any athlete or academic, now extends from one end of the world to the other. This unprecedented openness and opportunity for mobility enables, encourages and in many ways requires firms, industries and professionals to try to cover this worldwide market—otherwise somebody else will. And when one of these players emerges as the winner—as "*The* Accounting Firm,"

"*The* Doctor," "*The* Actor," "*The* Lawyer," "*The* Singer," "*The* Salesman," "*The* Basketball Player," "*The* Man" or "*The* Woman" in any particular field, that person can potentially win not only the United States or Europe, not only Japan or China. He or she can reap enormous profits and royalties from everywhere at once. Ford Motor's double-edged advertising slogan says it best. "Ford: Winning the World Over."

"In this global village," write Frank and Cook, "the top players—those who can deliver the best product—can earn enormous profits. Consider Acme Radials, a hypothetical tire company in Akron, Ohio. If Acme were the best in, say, northern Ohio, they were once guaranteed a decent business. But today's sophisticated consumers increasingly purchase their tires from only a handful of the best tire producers worldwide. If [Acme] is one of the best, it wins and its profits will skyrocket; otherwise, its future will likely be bleak."

As Frank and Cook point out, while the winners can do incredibly well in this global market, those with only marginally inferior skills will often do much less well, and those with few or no skills will do very poorly. Therefore, the gap between first place and second place grows larger, and the gap between first place and last place becomes staggering. Of course, in many fields there is rarely one winner, but those near the top get a disproportionate share. The more that different markets get globalized and become winner-take-all markets, the more inequality expands within countries and, for that matter, between countries.

These inequalities are becoming one of the most disturbing social byproducts of this system. According to a report in the *National Journal*, the incomes of the poorest fifth of working families in America dropped by 21 percent between 1979 and 1995, adjusted for inflation, while the incomes of the richest fifth jumped by 30 percent during the same period. On May 30, 1998, *The Economist* reported that America had 170 billionaires, compared with 13 in 1982. "Just now the economy is doing so well that everybody is getting ahead," *The Economist* added. "But inequality has increased sharply over the past 30 years, and this has not gone unnoticed. In newspaper cartoons, Bill Gates has evolved from geek-hero to bullying monopolist—very Rockefelleresque. *Titanic*, the blockbuster movie, offered a bracingly Marxist view of events, and the delight of American audiences when one or two rich passengers went under was, er, chilling." Sadruddin Aga Khan, president of the Bellerive Foundation, which tracks the effects of globalization, reported that Bill Gates's fortune at one point was equal to the combined net worth of the 106 million poorest Americans.

There are many other examples of the impact of globalization on income gaps and the social consequences that flow from this. But, as I indicated above, you can learn everything you need to know about this subject by studying just one group of people—the National Basketball Association and, in particular, the bench of the 1997–98 World Champion Chicago Bulls.

NBA players and owners are among the greatest beneficiaries of today's globalization system—a system that no one has understood better, and understood how to exploit better, than NBA Commissioner David Stern. As Stern explained to me in an interview, thanks to the democratization of technology throughout the formerly communist world, the NBA found that it suddenly had "multiple outlets to broadcast its games—cable, satellite dishes, the Internet, fiber optics and traditional television—in multiple countries." He said the NBA today has relationships with more than 90 broadcasters around the world, bringing NBA basketball to more than 190 countries in 41 different languages. Even China broadcasts a game of the week on Saturday mornings. Thanks to the democratization of finance, the collapse of communism and the end to many travel and trade barriers, a huge transnational marketplace was created for all sorts of consumer goods. Companies wishing to sell into this marketplace were eager to associate their products with a global symbol that could be marketed across a lot of different borders and time zones at once. The NBA logo and NBA players became the global symbol that could jazz up these global brands—toothpaste, shoes or deodorant—and give them instant credibility with consumers from Buenos Aires to Beijing. And thanks to the democratization of information—and the rise of Michael Jordan—a single spokesperson could emerge who was admired from one end of that global market to the other, despite national differences.

"So Sprite is running a commercial at the same time in Denmark and Poland and both of them use an NBA logo, which gives their products an international cachet that can be understood in any market," Stern explained. To reinforce this, he added, "the NBA now has marketing-television offices in Paris, Barcelona, London, Taiwan, Tokyo, Hong Kong, Melbourne, Toronto, New Jersey, Miami—for Latin America—and Mexico City. And we now play eight regular-season games in Tokyo and two in Mexico City."

In 1990, NBA games were broadcast to 200 million households in 77

countries. By 1998 it had grown to 600 million households in 190 countries. More than 35 percent of fans who connect to the NBA's official
Web site, www.nba.com, live outside the United States. Computer users
from 50 countries regularly log onto www.nba.com. Since 1994, the
number of international players drafted into the NBA has quadrupled.

To explore this further, I interviewed Steve Kerr, the three-point shoot-
ing specialist, who played with Michael Jordan for many years on the
Chicago Bulls. Kerr's NBA career began just before the fall of the Berlin
Wall, when professional basketball was a primarily American sport, and it
is culminating today, when it is a global game. Kerr told me: "I went to
Tokyo a couple of years ago to participate in a basketball camp there that
Sean Elliott [another NBA star] runs, and I could not believe how often
I was recognized by people around Tokyo. One morning I got up at five
o'clock to go down to the Tokyo fish market to watch them auction off the
fish. It was sort of a touristy thing to do. You go in there, and there are all
these huge tunas lying around that they are selling for 50,000 dollars
apiece. The fish are on these pallets all over the floor, and I'm walking
around looking at these tunas, and all these fishermen are speaking
Japanese and auctioning off the fish. But everywhere I walk these [Japan-
ese] fishermen—fishermen!—keep coming up to me and saying, 'Ahh,
Steve Kerr—Chicago Bulls.' This is five a.m. in the Tokyo fish market!"

When the Chicago Bulls played a preseason exhibition tournament in
Paris in October 1997 (the tournament is called the McDonald's Championship—what else?), some 1,000 reporters and photographers were accredited for the games—more than for the NBA finals. Kerr recalled: "It
felt sort of strange to be walking down the streets of Paris and everyone
knows who you are."

My friend Allen Alter, the foreign editor of CBS News, was trying to
get visas for CBS to send a crew into North Korea in the winter of 1997.
He did what any good editor would do—he persistently wooed the two senior North Korean diplomats at the UN who were in charge of dispensing
visas. The North Korean diplomats mentioned during a dinner one night
that they were very interested in NBA basketball, so Alter sent them a tape
of the 1997 NBA finals: the Chicago Bulls versus the Utah Jazz. The next
morning the North Koreans, who, Alter said, virtually never returned
phone messages or faxes, sent him an unsolicited fax profusely thanking
him for the tape and telling him that "it is already on its way by diplomatic pouch to Pyongyang." A few weeks later a North Korean delegation
was visiting New York and one of the North Korean diplomats informed

Alter: "We are very interested in cheerleaders—they are very fascinating to my country." Evidently the "Dear Leader" of North Korea, Kim Jong Il, who was already known to have a fascination with Godzilla and the magician David Copperfield, had developed a taste for cheerleaders by watching NBA highlight reels.

Israel's leading political columnist, Nahum Barnea of the *Yediot Aharonot* newspaper, is an avid NBA fan and can easily satisfy his passion, because many NBA games are now aired live on Israeli television despite the seven-hour time difference. Barnea told me he was visiting his mother at her nursing home on the day of the sixth game of the 1998 Chicago Bulls–Utah Jazz NBA finals. While he was chatting with his mom, he turned on the Bulls-Jazz game on her room television, so he could watch and visit at the same time. When the game came on and Barnea's aged mother saw that her son was engrossed in a basketball shoot-out, she asked Nahum: "Which team is Israel?" It never occurred to Nahum's mom that her son could be so intensely interested in watching a basketball game that did not feature at least one Israeli team.

But the globalization of the NBA has real social repercussions. Just take the bench of the Chicago Bulls. At one end of this bench sat Michael Jordan. *Forbes* magazine estimated Jordan's nonbasketball income from endorsements at $47 million in 1997 and his salary that year was $31.3 million, for an overall income of roughly $80 million. In 1998, shortly before Jordan retired, *Fortune* magazine estimated that Jordan's total impact on the American economy since he joined the NBA in 1984 was "$10 billion"—taking into account the NBA ticket sales he spurred, the foreign broadcast rights and higher television ratings he produced and the worldwide Nike footwear, apparel and other products that Jordan endorsed. *The Sporting News* reported that "Jordan's value was underscored upon his return to the NBA in March 1995, after an eighteen-month hiatus in baseball. The stock market value of [his] five endorsees—McDonald's, Sara Lee, Nike, General Mills and Quaker Oats—soared $3.8 billion within two weeks." It was rather fitting that the Upper Deck Company, which makes baseball and basketball cards, ran an ad in *The Sporting News* showing Michael Jordan holding the world in his hands, only the world is the size of a basketball. Next to the globe in Jordan's hands are the words "Actual Size?"

Michael Jordan is indeed the winner who took it all. But there are twelve players on an NBA team. Sitting on the same bench with Jordan in his final season—sitting in fact just eleven places away from him—was someone whose shooting skills were only marginally less effective than his, someone whose jump shot was only slightly less accurate, someone whose free-throw shooting was only slightly less consistent, someone whose defensive skills were only slightly less intense. But he was still a great basketball player. After all, he was in the NBA and he was on the championship Chicago Bulls. His name was Joe Kleine. He sat eleven seats away from Jordan and his salary in 1997 was the NBA minimum of $272,250 a year—or roughly $79,727,750 less than Jordan's total. Same game, same league, same team, same bench! One reason for that huge gap was the fact that while Michael Jordan has a global market for his services and autographs, the market for Joe Kleine's services and autographs did not extend far beyond the United Center in Chicago.

After the Chicago Bulls–Orlando Magic game on April 11, 1998, I visited the Bulls' locker room to talk to Joe Kleine & Co. The global market realities were starkly on display there. Before the Bulls opened the locker room door after the game, approximately thirty reporters, both print and television, stood in a line in the hall outside. When the locker room door was finally opened, this group of thirty reporters all squeezed together in a semicircle around Michael Jordan's locker. In the throng was a Japanese television crew, speaking Japanese to one another. They were led by a young Japanese female TV reporter who kept blushing as these huge, nearly seven-foot-tall Bulls kept walking out of the shower with the skimpiest towels wrapped around their waists. You don't see that in Japan every day!

But imagine this scene: There is a locker room. There are twelve lockers with stools in front of them. Yet all thirty reporters are gathered in a semicircle around the empty locker of one player—Michael Jordan. The reporters' microphones and cameras are all aimed at his empty chair, all waiting for the moment when he will arrive, all hoping for a quote to transmit around the world. Meanwhile, the other eleven players are dressing at their lockers, attracting virtually no attention. (Scottie Pippen finally draws a few reporters when he emerges.)

Out of curiosity I ambled over to Joe Kleine, introduced myself and asked him whether he was disturbed by the widening income gap between players like himself and Jordan. Kleine indicated that he understood very well the principle of winner take all. As he put it: "Salaries have been moving forward in this league for everyone, but the superstars have made a great leap. In my case, though, I chose to come here and play for the minimum. That was my choice, so I can't resent it."

In society, as in the NBA, there are real social consequences that flow from these income gaps. On teams where the lower-paid players don't have the psychic compensation of playing with Michael Jordan or winning championship rings, this can be a serious issue. Because as the superstars get more, there is less left to pay everyone else, which was a major issue in the 1998–99 NBA lockout. In 1998, more NBA players (roughly 25 percent) made the NBA minimum than ever before. As *Petersen's Pro Basketball* magazine observed: "The NBA is beginning to reflect American society at large: The rich are getting richer, there are a lot of (relatively) poor people around and the middle class appears in danger of disappearing. 'Last year (1996–97) about a third of the league—110 out of 348 players—were making the league minimum,' NBA player agent Don Cronson said. 'The way things look, this year that number should go up to about 150. Between the restrictions of the salary cap and the incredible money paid to superstars, there's practically no money left over for the $1 to $2 million guys, who are usually the fourth-to-seventh-best players on the roster. So you'll have your top three and your bottom five, [who are] happy to just be in the league making peanuts. But your four to seven guys are the major contributors you need to keep happy—and they're not going to be happy, if they'll be there at all, that is. There is going to be a lot of jealousy and dissension, far more than ever before. A huge salary gap means serious locker room problems every time. That's just human nature. And it's certainly the nature of today's pro basketball player.' The best example of class separation last season was with the Houston Rockets, with their trio of superstars totaling over $21 million in salaries, only two members of the shrinking middle class (Kevin Willis and Mario Elie) on the roster and no fewer than eight minimum-salary players toiling for bottom feeder rates. 'From what I heard, that was one unhappy team,' Cronson said."

It's "a real problem," said Steve Kerr, who played on two other NBA teams before the Bulls. "You have a lot of teams with guys making the NBA minimum and they are starting, while you have former starters making four million dollars and they are coming off the bench. And it is impossible for there not to be ill feeling among those guys making the minimum, who are starting, and guilt feelings by those starters making four million dollars who are coming off the bench." Asked if he ever resented the difference between himself and Jordan, Kerr too made clear that he understood globalization and his place in the cosmos. "No, honestly not," he said. "I think about all the thousands of guys out there who are also very good players and they didn't make it to the league. All I can think is how fortunate I am."

This gap on NBA benches is also reflected in the growing gap in the owners' boxes. NBA owners used to be local businessmen from the community. Today, NBA owners are increasingly corporations with the global income needed to pay global salaries in a global sport. Who owns the New York Knicks? Cablevision System Corporation. Who owns the Atlanta Hawks? Time Warner. Who owns the Portland Trail Blazers? Paul Allen, a founder of Microsoft. Who owns the Philadelphia 76ers? Comcast Cable. Who owns the Seattle SuperSonics? The Ackerley Group Inc. media conglomerate. Abe Pollin, the owner of the Washington Wizards, was one of the few local owners left before he took Michael Jordan and an AOL exec as partners. A pillar of the Washington community and a generous philanthropist there, Pollin made his money in local Washington real estate and had to promise Juwan Howard the equivalent of nearly his entire net worth just to sign him for seven years and keep him from bolting to the Miami Heat. But owners like Pollin, who are part of their communities, are now a dying breed, and that diminishes the community as a whole.

"Rarely, if ever, has Charles Dolan, chairman of Cablevision, which owns the Knicks, stepped inside the locker room at Madison Square Garden," reported *The New York Times* (Jan. 10, 1999). "In what was more of a family atmosphere in the 60s and 70s, owners would invite players on vacations with them. Now there are players who have never met the owners of their teams." Indeed, when catcher Mike Piazza was traded from the Los Angeles Dodgers to the Florida Marlins and then to the New York Mets in May 1998, he complained that the Dodgers ownership was so distant it was impossible to communicate with them. Who owned the Dodgers? Rupert Murdoch's Australian conglomerate, Newscorp., which Piazza described as "out of touch, distant, like the Wizard of Oz."

Finally, that gap on the bench, and that gap in the owner's box, is reflected in a gap in the stands. Michael Jordan's fans may never have begrudged him his salary, particularly as long as he kept winning championships. But the widening gulf between winners and losers in the global economy that these sports salaries reflect has social repercussions. Rich and poor increasingly live separate existences, sending their children to different schools, living in different neighborhoods, shopping in different stores and going to different sporting events—or, worse, not going at all. It used to be that going to the game pulled a community together. But sports lovers will be able to do this less and less because to pay these huge salaries, ticket prices are being put out of reach of all but the rich, and stadiums are being segmented by classes, with the poor slobs who can afford only $75 tickets sitting crammed into the bleachers eating peanuts, while the rich sit in skyboxes, with plenty of leg room, and dine on crab cakes brought by waitresses. Even the players, many of whom come from impoverished backgrounds, speak about the social gap between them and the mostly white affluent crowds who pay to see them. "You go diving into the stands after a ball," one unidentified black player told *Sports Illustrated*, "and you land on some investment banker's cell phone. Meanwhile, the fellas you grew up with can't afford a ticket to get in. Yeah, you think about those things." To pay for Shaquille O'Neal's $121 million seven-year salary, the Los Angeles Lakers had to raise their *cheapest* seats from $9.50 a game to $21, and their most expensive courtside seats from $500 to $600 per game. As a result, notes Harvard University political theorist Michael J. Sandel, the ballpark, which used to be so central in homogenizing a community, "is no longer the kind of shared public space that brings together people from different walks of life."

Indeed, the gap between the world's sports stars and their fans has almost become otherworldly. "I was reading a story the other day about the boxer Evander Holyfield, who had built a 56,000-square-foot house," Steve Kerr said to me. "And I am sure he meant this in the right way, but the article quoted him as saying that he wanted to invite underprivileged kids to tour his house so they could see what they could achieve with hard work. A 56,000-square-foot house! The only way you can achieve that is by becoming the heavyweight champion of the world and there's only one of those. Everything is focused on what you can buy. We have players going into schools and telling kids, 'Stay in school so you can buy all this stuff that I have.' I'm not sure that's the right message. The message should be, stay in school so you can do what you want to do in life."

When I can't use my tickets to the Washington Wizards' games, I often give them to a friend of mine who is a doorman. He is so grateful and I am so sad. I am so sad that he is so grateful to get to do something that my dad and I did when I was growing up—which was to go to the Minneapolis Lakers' games without a second thought, when my dad was making $13,000 a year.

There is something wrong when so many people are now frozen out of that simple experience. Community gets eroded just another notch, so you are not surprised when you pick up *The Washington Times* on

November 12, 1997, and read the following item: "Two bystanders were killed in Philadelphia after a disagreement about who was the better point guard, Allen Iverson of the Philadelphia 76ers or Gary Payton of the Seattle SuperSonics. Words turned to gunfire Sunday after the game between the 76ers and Sonics. Derrick Washington, 21, and his cousin, Jameka Wright, 22, were killed in the crossfire in the Southwark Plaza public housing development."

I know that in many ways such a two-tier economy was really the norm for much of American history and the rise of the large middle class was really a mid-twentieth-century phenomenon. My dad never would have understood not being able to afford to go to a basketball game, but I am sure my grandfather would have. Unfortunately, it looks like my grandchildren will, too.

I use the example of the NBA not because I sympathize with players who make only $272,250, but because it is an easy device to explain the widening income gaps that are helping to feed a backlash against globalization around the world (which I will discuss in detail in the next section of the book). These widening income gaps are particularly noticeable outside the United States where middle classes tend to be much smaller and where antimonopoly and other income-equalizing laws are less stringent. This is one of the central economic dilemmas of the globalization system: the Golden Straitjacket, the Electronic Herd, free markets and free trade produce far greater incomes for a society as a whole. That is a fact. But that income is highly unequally distributed and the whole let-her-rip capitalism that comes with it is enormously socially disruptive. But to stick with a closed, regulated, bureaucratically run economy in today's world will impoverish a society as a whole, and can be even more socially disruptive—without generating any of the resources to ameliorate conditions for those left behind. Look at Fidel Castro's socialist Cuba in the 1990s. There was little in the way of income gaps there, but the society as a whole became so poor that Cuba in the mid-1990s became the sex tourism capital of the western hemisphere, as thousands of Cuban families had to assign a wife or daughter to take up prostitution to earn hard currency to survive. I met a Canadian diplomat while in Cuba who told me her job was to "get Canadian sex tourists out of jail." Eventually, in the latter part of the 1990s, Castro opened the Cuban economy a bit and allowed a limited amount of free enterprise, and this immediately produced huge income gaps. As my Cuban tour guide told me while I was on a 1999 visit to Havana: "In the old days, I might have two pairs of shoes and you would have three. But today, because I am a guide and I have access to foreign currency, you might have three pairs of shoes and I might have thirty." In the long run, these income gaps, if they continue to widen, could turn out to be globalization's Achilles' heels. There is someting inherently unstable about a world that is being knitted together tighter and tighter by technology, markets and telecommunications, while splitting apart wider and wider socially and economically. (The last chapter will consider some ways to address this.)

Consider the following news story that I happened to come across one day on the wires: "PORT-AU-PRINCE, Haiti (Reuters)—Haiti, the poorest country in the Western Hemisphere, will have cellular telephone service for the first time at the end of May 1998, providers of the service said Friday. Only a minority of wealthy families, foreign investors and business people will be able to afford the service. Per capita annual income in Haiti is about $250. Telephones will cost $450 and there is a $100 start-up service fee, along with charges of $20 a month for the service." In other words, for the elite globalized segment of the Haitian population a cellular phone is just an everyday tool; for most other Haitians it's two years' salary.

That is not stable, but unfortunately it is also not unusual. According to the 1999 United Nations Human Development Report, the Internet is linking people in a new global network, but access is still largely concentrated in rich countries. OECD countries, with 19 percent of the world's population, account for 91 percent of users. Bulgaria has more Internet hosts than the whole of sub-Saharan Africa, excluding South Africa. The United States and Sweden have 600 telephone lines per 1,000 people, while Chad has 1 telephone line per 1,000. South Asia, with 23 percent of the world's people, has less than 1 percent of the world's Internet users. English is used in almost 80 percent of Web sites, although fewer than one in ten people worldwide speak the language. Industrialized countries hold 97 percent of all patents worldwide. I am certain the Internet and information appliances will spread, and a lot more quickly than people think, but at the millennium this digital divide is indisputable and it is widening the gap between rich and poor.

According to the 1999 UN report, the fifth of the world's people living in the highest-income countries has 86 percent of world gross domestic product, 82 percent of world export markets, 68 percent of foreign direct investments and 74 percent of world telephone lines. The bottom fifth, in the poorest countries, has about 1 percent in each of these sectors. Not surprisinly, the wealthiest fifth consume 45 percent of all meat and fish, while the poorest fifth consume less than 5 percent. And the gap has been widening. In 1960 the 20 percent of the world's people who live in the richest countries had 30 times the income of the poorest 20 percent. By 1995, the richest 20 percent had 82 times as much income. In Brazil, for instance, the poorest 50 percent of the population received 18 percent of the national income in 1960. By 1995, they received only 11.6 percent, while the richest 10 percent of Brazil's population were taking home 63 percent of the national income. In Russia, the richest 20 percent of the population now takes home 11 times more of the national income than the poorest 20 percent. The 1998 UN Human Development Report noted that, thanks to globalization, market researchers today try to sell their products to "global elites," "global middle classes" and "global teens," because no matter where they live they now follow some of the same basic consumption patterns, showing preferences for the same "global brands" of music, videos and T-shirts. "What are the consequences?" the report asks. "First, a host of consumption options have been opened for many consumers—but many are left out in the cold through lack of income. And pressures for competitive spending mount. 'Keeping up with the Joneses' has shifted from striving to match the consumption of a next-door neighbor to pursuing the lifestyles of the rich and famous depicted in movies and television shows."

Visit just about any developing country today and you will encounter these yawning gaps around every corner. While on a visit to Rio de Janeiro, I went to interview people in the *favela* of Rocinha, a warren of crowded shacks and makeshift homes that is the biggest slum in South America. I noticed as we were driving toward the *favela* that we came to a fork in the road. If you turned right, you went up the driveway, past manicured gardens, to the American School in Rio, which is the most expensive school in the country, charging roughly $2,000 a month. It is located in the heart of Gavea, the toniest neighborhood in Rio, and enrollment is very restricted. If you turned left at the same intersection you entered the *favela* of Rocinha, where many people don't make $2,000 a year and enrollment is, shall we say, "unrestricted." Well over 100,000 people are crammed into the *favela*. As long as Brazil keeps growing economically, that intersection may be politically sustainable. But if growth in Brazil really slows down, that fork in the road can become a wishbone that could split the country.

In order to put the Golden Straitjacket on tighter to satisfy the Electronic Herd, Brazilian President Fernando Henrique Cardoso had to cut social security spending immediately after his reelection in October 1998. The *New York Times* Brazil correspondent, Diana Jean Schemo, wrote an article about some of those who were being squeezed as a result. Cardoso was already in political hot water with his people for describing as "bums" people who wanted to retire and go on social security. Schemo told the story of one worker, Nilton Tambara, a fifty-four-year-old retired metalworker, who had begun working at age eleven and had paid into the Brazilian social security system for thirty-three of the forty-one years he worked before retiring.

"Is there any way to stay calm in this country?" asked Tambara, as he stood outside a Wal-Mart store in São Paulo, complaining that he could not afford to buy a $16 aluminum ladder. "The categories that the government talks about—the rich, the middle class and the poor—don't exist. It's just the rich and the miserable."

In Cairo, Egypt, you have an estimated 500,000 people living inside tombs in the "City of the Dead"—five square miles of cemeteries in the heart of the Egyptian capital. But the City of the Dead is located less than ten miles away from Egypt's newest gated golf course community, called Katamya Heights, one of several such complexes that house a few hundred families in an oasis of homes, gardens, artificial lakes, fountains and hotels. Its advertising literature, which can be found on the Internet, boasts the following: "Katamya Heights is a resort community that caters to those who love the challenges of golf or tennis and the pleasures of family activities in a clean desert setting. The resort features 27 holes of championship golf, practice facilities and golf academy, a luxurious 50,000-square-foot clubhouse, with restaurants and lounges, swimming pool, health and recreational facilities. Price per person for golf, including transfers to/from Katamya Heights golf course: $165." Per capita annual income in Egypt in 1998 was $1,410—good for about nine rounds of golf.

Thailand is a country which is sharply split between an urbanized, export-oriented working and entrepreneurial class, living in the financial and manufacturing centers of the country and enjoying many benefits from globalization, and an impoverished, inward-looking rural sector, which, though indirectly affected by globalization, has little understanding of it and sees little benefit from it. When the Thai baht crashed in 1997, that rural segment of Thailand, still living primarily off the land, had little sympathy for the globalized city slickers, who were getting wiped out as the government was forced to let the baht float downward.

At the time, Thai singer-entertainer Ploen Promdan came out with a sort of Thai country-rap song called "The Floating Baht." The song consists of a dialogue between a banker and a farmer. I reproduce some of it here because it captures brilliantly how the gap between the globalized and the nonglobalized in a society, if untended, can widen to a point where people who speak the same language can't understand each other anymore, let alone feel a common bond.

Here is a rough translation: The song begins with the refrain, "Our baht is floating now, our baht is floating now. How long it will float will depend on the situation. Please watch the situation properly."

Banker: "O.K. Look here, everybody, today our baht is already floating."

Farmer: "Yesterday a two-year-old kid fell into the river but did not die."

Banker: "How come? What prevented him from drowning?"

Farmer: "Yes, the kid fell into the water, and the people saw him bobbing up and down, and they ran down to the river and found that he was clutching a floating baht."

Banker: "Don't you understand? I'm talking about our currency floating."

Farmer: "Well, if not for the floating baht, the kid would have drowned."

Banker: "I am talking about the floating currency, stupid."

Farmer: "Well, why are you telling us? What's so important about that?"

Banker: "I'm telling you because you should care about it. I am telling you because I was afraid you didn't know."

Farmer: "Why do we have to burden our minds with all these things?"

Banker: "These are philosophical thoughts for you to ponder."

Farmer: "Why do I want to go and think about this? We are not philosophers."

Banker: "You're a jackass."

Farmer: "Actually, if I hadn't been a jackass, I would have been the head of a finance house." [Most of Thailand's finance houses went bankrupt when the baht collapsed.]

Refrain: "Our baht is floating now. When the baht floats the price of every commodity floats up too."

Banker (in a lecturing voice): "When the baht floats, commodity prices float to that level. And to whatever level the baht floats, the price of goods also moves to that place within a day or two. Everything floats up, nothing floats down. That's how things work."

Farmer: "So why are you complaining and moaning all the time?"

Banker: "We complain, we shout, we curse and ultimately we will demonstrate in the streets and block the roads and people will notice us and sympathize with us and help us solve the problem."

Farmer: "Why are you so anxious for the problem to be solved?"

Banker: "So that things become better, you moron."

Farmer (laughing in his face): "Ha, ha, ha. Look at you, screaming like a kid. You were so reasonable and now all of sudden you're screaming."

Banker: "You moron."

Refrain: "The baht is now very weak and not as healthy as before and causing all kinds of problems to us. The price has gone up for everything we used to buy."

Banker: "Thai money flows out of the country, but foreign money doesn't flow in. Thai people like to flow out to foreign countries for holidays. They go in and out, and buy things when they are abroad."

Farmer: "Well, they like to do that. They have money. It is their money. So what's the problem?"

Banker: "It is still Thai money that they are taking out, and it deteriorates the situation when they take money out of the country. The Thai baht loses its value, and then there is a loss of capital for investing in things too."

Farmer: "How do you know?"

Banker: "It is in the news every day and every week. Don't you follow the news?"

Farmer: "I never listen to the radio. I never read. I am not interested in any of this story. I only watch Thai kick boxing and the soccer championship."

Banker: "Please turn yourself around and give some thought and concern to the problems of the country."

Farmer: "I am afraid that the Thai kick boxer will lose his championship to the foreigner. Isn't that something to worry about?"

Banker: "Don't you know that our country has borrowed huge sums of money from abroad?"

Farmer: "How huge?"

Banker: "Huge loans, massive loans. You are a moron. You don't understand a word I am saying, do you? I am wasting my breath talking to you. When you borrow this money from abroad you have to pay it back."

Farmer: "Shouldn't the man who borrowed the money have the right to enjoy it?"

Banker: "It's people like you who are screwing up the country and wasting money. You are part of the Thai nation, the Thai family, which is responsible for this overspending. We're all in this together."

Farmer: "Oh, but I'm not married. And I have no family."

III

The Backlash
Against the System

The Backlash

Ray Boyd: "What's wrong, Mommy?"
Dorothy Boyd: "First class, that's what's wrong. It used to be a better meal. Now it's
a better life."

— from the movie Jerry Maguire

The annual Davos World Economic Forum is as good a barometer of global affairs as you can find. Every February the world's great globalizers gather together in the Swiss mountain retreat to celebrate and debate globalization. The meeting is attended by top industrialists, political figures, economists, technologists, scientists and social scientists from every corner of the world. Each year, one or two individuals stand out as the trendsetters. One year it was China's economic czar Zhu Rongi; one year it was Yasser Arafat, Yitzhak Rabin and Shimon Peres; another year it was the Russian reformers; another year the battered Asian economic leaders. In 1995 the star of the Davos World Economic Forum was George Soros, the billionaire financier. I know because I was invited to attend a press conference, at which representatives of all the world's major media organizations gathered around a conference table and interviewed Soros as if he were the president of a superpower. And he seemed to think he was. Reporters from Reuters, Bloomberg, AP–Dow Jones, *The New York Times*, *The Washington Post*, *The Times* of London and the *Financial Times* grilled Soros on his views about Mexico, Russia, Japan and global economic trends, and then ran out of the room to file his remarks by telephone. His opinions were carried on the front pages of the *International Herald Tribune* and many other newspapers the next day.

Watching this scene, I felt that I was witnessing an important transition. Soros personified the Electronic Herd. He was a lead bull. Maybe *the* lead bull. And this was just around the time when many people were beginning to realize that this Electronic Herd was replacing the Soviet

Union as the other superpower in our two-superpower world. Only a few years earlier Soros had administered a stunning economics lesson to British Prime Minister John Major. Major thought the British pound was properly valued. Soros did not, and in September 1992 Soros led the herd in a campaign to force the British pound down to its "right" level. Major scoffed at Soros, then sneered at him, then resisted him, then raised a white flag and devalued the pound by 12 percent. Soros walked away with a profit of $1 billion from a couple of months' work. Goodbye, Soviet Union. Hello, Electronic Herd.

Interestingly enough, a year after first seeing Soros hold court with his own news conference in Davos, I went back to Davos, eager to see who would be the star in 1996. I was standing at a computer terminal in the main hall retrieving my E-mail messages when I noticed George Soros walk by. But what struck me was that this year no one was paying any attention to him at all. In fact, he seemed to be all alone. What a difference a year makes. I don't think he could have hired a news conference that year. Why? Who was the star of Davos 1996? None other than Gennadi A. Zyuganov, the head of the Russian Communist Party!

The Davos Forum is the ultimate capitalist convention. How could this dinosaur from the Jurassic era of the Cold War—Gennadi Zyuganov—have been the man of the hour? Because the business and political elites gathered in Davos that year were understanding, many for the first time, that this powerful phenomenon called globalization was also producing an equally powerful backlash in some circles. At that time it looked like Zyuganov was actually going to defeat Boris Yeltsin for the Russian presidency, and therefore the backlash forces were actually going to take power in a major country. So all the executives at Davos wanted to talk to Zyuganov—the "beast of the backlash"—and find out what he was going to do with private property, the Russian budget and ruble-dollar convertibility. I interviewed Zyuganov at the time, and it was clear to me that *he didn't have a clue* what he was going to do. He seemed to be spending most of his time hiding from the Western business elites. Like other ideological backlashers against globalization, Zyuganov had more attitude than workable programs, more ideas about how to distribute income than about how to generate it.

Since then, though, the backlash against globalization has become more apparent and widespread. Let there be no doubt, globalization has fostered a flowering of both wealth and technological innovation the likes of which the world has never before seen. But this sort of rapid change, as the previous chapters indicate, has challenged traditional business practices, social structures, cultural mores and environments and, as a result, has generated a substantial backlash—with one of its loudest and most visible manifestations coming at the World Trade Organization summit in Seattle in late 1999. This is not surprising. Markets generate both capital and chaos; the more powerful markets become as a result of globalization, the more widespread and diverse their disruptions.

Beyond this general sense of disruption and dislocation, the opponents of globalization resent it because they feel that as their countries have plugged into the globalization system, they have been forced into a Golden Straitjacket that is one-size-fits-all. Some don't like the straitjacket because they feel economically pinched by it. Some worry that they don't have the knowledge, skills or resources to enlarge the straitjacket and ever really get the gold out of it. Some don't like it because they resent the widening income gaps that the straitjacket produces or the way it squeezes jobs from higher-wage countries to lower-wage ones. Some don't like it because it opens them to all sorts of global cultural forces and influences that leave their kids feeling alienated from their own traditional olive trees. Some don't like it because it seems to put a higher priority on laws to promote free trade than it does on laws to protect turtles and dolphins, water and trees. Some don't like it because they feel they have no say in its design. And some don't like it because they feel that getting their countries up to the standards of DOScapital 6.0 is just too hard.

In other words, the backlash against globalization is a broad phenomenon that is fed by many different specific emotions and anxieties. This backlash expresses itself in different forms, through different characters in different countries. This chapter is about those different emotions, forms and characters, and how they have come together to create a whirlwind that—for the moment—is only buffeting the globalization system but one day might become strong enough to destabilize it if we don't take the serious backlashers seriously.

As I mentioned earlier, in the summer of 1998 I took a tour of Brazil with Conservation International, which had built an ecopark in the Atlantic Rain Forest in cooperation with people from the nearby town of Una, in an effort to help them create a tourist industry that might be able to spawn enough jobs for them to quit logging. Conservation International invited Dejair Birschner, the forty-eight-year-old mayor of Una, to show me around and to explain how all this was affecting his town. The mayor was a Paul Bunyan type, whose father and grandfather had been loggers, but now the environmentalists had basically put him out of business. As we walked through the rain forest, Mayor Birschner patted every other tree. He knew each tree species in the rain forest by its Brazilian name. I took an immediate liking to this Brazilian lumberjack. There was something very solid about him. After our walk, we sat on a picnic table on the edge of the Atlantic Rain Forest and talked about the challenges facing the mayor. The mayor explained to me that intellectually he understood that logging was not sustainable anymore. But as much as he knew this, he also knew that his little town was not prepared for life without logging. We talked for about thirty minutes, and when I was done interviewing the mayor, I thanked him and started to pack up my IBM ThinkPad laptop, when he said to me, "Now I want to ask you something."

"Please," I answered, "ask anything you like."

The mayor then looked me in the eye and said, "Do we have any future?"

His question hit me like a fist in the stomach. It almost brought tears to my eyes, looking across the table at this proud, sturdy man, a mayor no less, asking me if he and his villagers had any future. I knew exactly what he was asking in his question: "My villagers can't live off the forest anymore and we're not equipped to live off computers. My father and grandfather made a living off logs and my grandchildren might make a living off the Internet. But what are all the rest of us in between supposed to do?"

I cobbled together an answer, trying to explain in simple terms that he and his people did have a future, but they needed to start making a transition from an agro-economy to a more knowledge-based economy, beginning by better educating the town's children. The mayor listened, nodded his head, thanked me very politely and then got up to go to his car. As he was leaving, I pulled the interpreter aside and asked him if he could ask the mayor, when they got to the mayor's car, what he thought of my answer.

A few minutes later, the interpreter returned. He reported back that the mayor just wanted to remind me of something he had alluded to in our interview: When he gets to the office every morning he has 200 people waiting for him, asking for jobs, housing and food—not to mention out-of-work loggers threatening his life. If he can't provide them with jobs, housing and food, they will eat the rain forest—whether that's sustainable or not.

"He just wanted you to understand that," the interpreter said.

Mayor Birschner represents a whole generation of people around the world today who feel threatened by globalization because they fear that they just don't have the skill sets or the energy to make it into the Fast World. I call them them "the turtles." Why? Because high-tech entrepreneurs in Silicon Valley always like to compare their supercompetitive business to the story about the lion and the gazelle in the jungle. Every night the lion goes to sleep in the jungle knowing that in the morning, when the sun comes up, if it can't outrun the slowest gazelle, it will go hungry. Every night the gazelle goes to sleep in the jungle knowing that in the morning, when the sun comes up, if it can't outrun the fastest lion, it's going to be somebody's breakfast. But the one thing that the lion and the gazelle both know when they go to sleep is that in the morning, when the sun comes up, they had better start running.

And so it is with globalization.

Unfortunately, not everyone is equipped to run fast. There are a lot of turtles out there, desperately trying to avoid becoming roadkill. The turtles are all those people who got sucked into the Fast World when the walls came down, and for one reason or another now feel economically threatened or spurned by it. It is not because they all don't have jobs. It is because the jobs they have are being rapidly transformed, downsized, streamlined or made obsolete by globalization. And because this global competition is also forcing their governments to downsize and streamline at the same time, it means many of these turtles have no safety net to fall into.

In the Broadway musical *Ragtime*, there is a scene in which Henry Ford explains the genius of his assembly line. I always remember the verses because they capture so well the world that was once safe for turtles—but is no more. The Broadway version of Henry Ford sings:

> See my people? Well, here's my theory
> Of what this country is moving toward:
> Every worker a cog in motion.
> Well, that's the notion of Henry Ford.
> One man tightens and one man ratchets
> And one man reaches to pull one cord.

Car keeps movin' in one direction.
A genuflection to Henry Ford!
(Speed up the belt, speed up the belt, Sam!)
Mass production will sweep the nation,
A simple notion the world's reward.
Even people who ain't too clever
Can learn to tighten a nut forever,
Attach one pedal or pull one lever . . .

Today, alas, people who ain't too clever can't learn to make micro-chips forever. Good jobs require many skills. I once did a story about how the U.S. Agency for International Development (AID), which usually works to provide job training and economic assistance to developing countries in Africa, was trying to use some of its techniques to help revitalize the inner-city slums of Baltimore. Or as the headline in the *Baltimore Sun* put it: "Baltimore To Try Third-World Remedies." One reason Baltimore had summoned AID was that its own turtles simply couldn't make it in the Fast World. One city official explained the problem succinctly: In the 1960s, she said, the biggest employer in Baltimore was Bethlehem Steel Corp. You could get a job at the steel plant with a high school education or less, make a decent living, buy a house, raise your kids and send them to college. It meant the American dream was open to turtles from even the most disadvantaged neighborhoods. Today the biggest employer in Baltimore is Johns Hopkins Medical Center. Unless you want to be a janitor, you can't even get a job interview at Johns Hopkins without a college degree. Turtles need not apply. And you certainly can't apply for a job there if you are one of the 150,000 Baltimore residents—out of 730,000—who are functionally illiterate. (Baltimore officials kept wondering why the urban poor were not taking fuller advantage of the well-funded social programs in the city, when they discovered that most of them couldn't read the signs. This was one reason they summoned AID: it had developed a whole series of cartoon characters and other visual devices to bypass illiteracy in Africa. "You want to know what the real irony is?" Dr. Peter Beilenson, Baltimore's Commissioner of Health, said to me when I came to interview him. "The company that develops these communications programs for AID is from Baltimore. Its office is about three blocks from here.")

As globalization progresses, replacing many manual repetitive jobs with machines and requiring more skills to do the jobs that are left, the number of good jobs available to turtles becomes fewer and fewer. A *Washington Post* story from June 1998, about the General Motors strike in Flint, Michigan, told the reader everything about the plight of turtles today. It read: "In the past 20 years, GM has cut employment in Flint to 35,000 workers from 76,000, and it says 11,000 more jobs could be eliminated over the next few years . . . Among its total U.S. workforce, GM has trimmed 297,000 hourly jobs over the past 20 years, cutting the overall number of jobs to 223,000 . . . Some of the jobs were moved to Canada and Mexico, where plants were either more efficient or less costly, *but the bulk of the people were simply replaced by machines* [italics mine]."

The same article quoted George Peterson, president of AutoPacific Inc., a California-based auto industry research and consulting firm, who said that in non-UAW plants in the United States—such as the Marysville, Ohio, factory of Honda Motor Co.'s U.S. subsidiary—workers have multiple skills and are capable of performing multiple tasks. This kind of versatility, he said, helps Honda cut production costs. "It's still possible to have a full-time job in this industry, *if you are willing to do more than one job* [my italics]," Peterson said, referring to the UAW's concerns over job security.

So not only do you need more skills than ever if you want to get a job in manufacturing today, but you need multiple skills to keep your job from going to a robot. This makes it very hard on the turtles.

A nalysts have been wondering for a while now whether the turtles who are left behind by globalization, or most brutalized or offended by it, will develop an alternative ideology to liberal, free-market capitalism. As noted earlier, in the first era of globalization, when the world first experienced the creative destruction of global capitalism, the backlash eventually produced a whole new set of ideologies—communism, socialism, fascism—that promised to take the sting out of capitalism, particularly for the average working person. Now that these ideologies have been discredited, I doubt we will see a new coherent, universal ideological reaction to globalization—because I don't believe there is an ideology or program that can remove all of the brutality and destructiveness of capitalism and still produce steadily rising standards of living.

Another reason the backlash against globalization is unlikely to develop a coherent alternative ideology is because the backlash itself involves so many disparate groups—as evidenced by the coalition of protectionist labor unions, environmentalists, antisweatshop protestors, save-the-turtles activists, save-the-dolphins activists, anti–genetically altered food activists and even a group called "Alien Hand Signals," who came together in December 1999 to protest globalization at the Seattle WTO summit. These disparate groups are bound by a common sense that a world so dominated by global corporations, and their concerns, can't help but be a profoundly unfair world, and one that is as hostile to the real interests of human beings as it is to turtles. But when it comes to actually identifying what the real interests of human beings are and how they should be protected, these groups are as different as their costumes. The auto workers, steel-workers and longshoremen, who were in Seattle to demand more protectionism, doubtless couldn't care much whether America allows imports of tuna caught in nets that also snare turtles. Indeed, I wouldn't want to be the turtle that gets in the way of one of those longshoremen offloading a boat in Seattle harbor. This makes the power of the backlash hard to predict, because while all the groups can agree that globalization is hurtful to them, they have no shared agenda, ideology or strategy for making it less so for all.

That's why I suspect that the human turtles, and many of those who simply hate the changes that globalization visits on cultures, environment or communities, are not going to bother with an alternative ideology. Their backlash will take a variety of different spasmodic forms. The steelworkers will lobby Washington to put up walls against foreign steel. Others, such as the radical environmentalists who want to save the rain forest, will simply lash out at globalization and all its manifestations, without offering a sustainable economic alternative. Their only message will be: STOP.

As for the poorest human turtles in the developing world, those really left behind by globalization, they will express their backlash by simply eating the rain forest—each in their own way—without trying to explain it or justify it or wrap it in an ideological bow. In Indonesia, they will eat the Chinese merchants by ransacking their stores. In Russia, they will sell weapons to Iran or turn to crime. In Brazil, they will log the rest of the rain forest or join the peasant movement in the Brazilian countryside called "Sem Teto" (Without Roofs), who simply steal what they need. There are an estimated 3.5 million of them in Brazil—agricultural people without land, living in some 250 encampments around the country. Sometimes they live by the roads and just close the roads until they are paid or evicted, sometimes they invade supermarkets, rob banks or steal trucks. They have no flag, no manifesto. They have only their own unmet needs and aspirations. That's why what we have been seeing in many countries, instead of popular mass opposition to globalization, is wave after wave of crime—people just grabbing what they need, weaving their own social safety nets and not worrying about the theory or ideology.

But while this backlash may be a bit incoherent and only loosely connected, it is very real. It comes from the depth of people's souls and pocketbooks and therefore, if it achieves a critical mass, can influence politics in any country. Societies ignore it at their own peril.

In almost every country that has put on the Golden Straitjacket you have at least one populist party or major candidate who is campaigning all the time now against globalization. They offer various protectionist, populist solutions that they claim will produce the same standards of living, without having to either run so fast, trade so far or open the borders so wide. They all claim that just putting up a few new walls here and there will make everything fine. They appeal to all the people who prefer their pasts to their future. In Russia, for instance, the communist members of the Duma continue to lead a backlash against globalization by telling the working classes and pensioners that in the days of the Soviet Union they may have had lousy jobs and been forced to wait in breadlines, but they always knew there would be a job and always knew there would be some bread they could afford at the head of the line. The strength of these populist, antiglobalization candidates depends to a large degree on the weakness of the economy in the country that they are in. Usually, the weaker the economy, the wider the following these simplistic solutions will attract.

But these antiglobalization populists don't only thrive in bad times. In 1998, a majority of the U.S. Congress refused to give the President authority to expand NAFTA to Chile—little Chile—on the argument that this would lead to a loss of American jobs. This wrongheaded view carried the day at a time when the American stock market was at a record high, American unemployment was at a record low and virtually every study showed that NAFTA had been a win-win-win arrangement for the United States, Canada and Mexico. Think of how stupid this was: The U.S. Congress appropriated $18 billion to replenish the International Monetary Fund, so that it could do more bailouts of countries struggling with globalization, but the Congress would not accept expansion of the NAFTA free trade zone to Chile. What is the logic of that? It could only be: "We support aid, not trade."

It makes no sense, but the reason these arguments can resonate in good times as well as bad is that moments of rapid change like this breed enormous insecurity as well as enormous prosperity. They can breed in people a powerful sense that their lives are now controlled by forces they cannot see or touch. The globalization system is still too new for too many people, and involves too much change for too many people, for them to have confidence that even the good job they have will always be there. And this creates a lot of room for backlash demagogues with simplistic solutions. It also creates a powerful feeling in some people that we need to slow this world down, put back some walls or some sand in the gears—not so I can get off, but so I can stay on.

A nd don't kid yourself—the backlash is not just an outburst from the most downtrodden. Like all revolutions, globalization involves a shift in power from one group to another. In most countries it involves a power shift from the state and its bureaucrats to the private sector and entrepreneurs. As this happens, all those who derived their status from positions in the bureaucracy, or from their ties to it, or from their place in a highly regulated and protected economic system, can become losers—if they can't make the transition to the Fast World. This includes industrialists and cronies who were anointed with import or export monopolies by their government, business owners who were protected by the government through high import tariffs on the products they made, big labor unions who got used to each year winning fewer work hours with more pay in constantly protected markets, workers in state-owned factories who got paid whether the factory made a profit or not, the unemployed in welfare states who enjoyed relatively generous benefits and health care no matter what, and all those who depended on the largesse of the state to protect them from the global market and free them from its most demanding aspects.

This explains why, in some countries, the strongest backlash against globalization comes not just from the poorest segments of the population and the turtles, but rather from the "used-to-bes" in the middle and lower-middle classes, who found a great deal of security in the protected communist, socialist and welfare systems. As they have seen the walls of protection around them coming down, as they have seen the rigged games in which they flourished folded up and the safety nets under them shrink, many have become mighty unhappy. And unlike the turtles, these downwardly mobile groups have the political clout to organize against globalization. The AFL-CIO labor union federation has become probably the most powerful political force against globalization in the United States. Labor unions covertly funded a lot of the advertising on behalf of the demonstrations in Seattle to encourage grassroots opposition to free trade.

One of my first tastes of this middle-class backlash against globalization came by accident when I was in Beijing talking to Wang Jisi, who heads the North America desk at the Chinese Academy of Social Sciences. We drifted from talking about America to talking about his own life in a China that was rapidly moving toward the free market, which many Chinese both welcome and fear. "The market mechanism is coming to China, but the question is how to impose it," said Wang. "I depend on my work unit for my housing. If all the housing goes to a free-market system, I might lose my housing. I am not a conservative, but when it comes to practical issues like this, people can become conservatives if they are just thrown onto the market after being accustomed to being taken care of. My driver complained to me the other day that when he was younger he contributed all his energy and everything he had to Maoism and to 'Socialist Construction.' But now he is forty-five or fifty and suddenly he is asked to go into the market. 'Is it fair,' he is asking of the government, 'that I devoted myself to whatever you asked of me for decades and now suddenly you forget me, you push me into the market when I get older? It is not fair. I have done nothing wrong. I have always followed your instructions, dear government, but now your instructions are to forget about the government.' [This driver] enjoys working here with us. He does not want to become a taxi driver and lose all his benefits. He does not want to go into the market."

You don't have to have been a communist worker bee to feel this way. Peter Schwartz, chairman of the Global Business Network, a consulting firm, once told me about a conversation he had before being interviewed in London for an economics program on the BBC: "The British reporter for the show, while escorting me to the interview, was asking me about some of my core ideas. I alluded to the idea that Britain was a good example of the takeoff of the entrepreneurial economy—particularly compared to the rest of Europe—and that the best indicator of the difference was the difference in unemployment in the U.K. and continental Europe. At that point he said to me: 'Isn't that terrible? Unemployment benefits are now so low in Britain it isn't worth staying on the dole anymore and people have to go to work.' "

Schwartz then added: "There are people who see this transformation [to globalization] as a big loss, not a gain. They are losing not just a benefit but something they perceived as a right—the notion that modern industrial societies are so wealthy that it is the right of people to receive generous unemployment insurance."

If you want to see this war between the protected and the globalizers at its sharpest today, go to the Arab world. In 1996, Egypt was scheduled to host the Middle East Economic Summit, which was to bring together Western, Asian, Arab and Israeli business executives. The Egyptian bureaucracy fought bitterly against holding the summit. In part, this was politically inspired by those in Egypt who did not feel Israel had done enough vis-à-vis the Palestinians to really merit normalization. But in part it was because the Egyptian bureaucrats, who had dominated the Egyptian economy ever since Nasser nationalized all the big commercial institutions in the 1960s, intuitively understood that this summit could be the first step in their losing power to the private sector, which was already being given the chance to purchase various state-owned enterprises and could eventually get its hands on the state-controlled media. The Islamic opposition newspaper *al-Shaab* denounced the economic summit as "the Conference of Shame." For the first time, though, the Egyptian private sector got itself organized into power lobbies—the American-Egypt Chamber of Commerce, the President's Council of Egyptian business leaders and the Egypt Businessmen's Association—and tugged President Mubarak the other way, saying that hosting a summit with hundreds of investors from around the world was essential to produce jobs for an Egyptian workforce growing by 400,000 new entrants each year. President Mubarak went back and forth, finally siding with the private sector and agreeing to host the summit, and bluntly declaring in his opening speech: "This year Egypt joined the global economy. It will live by its rules." But the Egyptian bureaucracy, which does not want to cede any power to the private sector, is still fighting that move, and every time there is a downturn in the global economy, such as the Asian collapse in 1998, the Egyptian bureaucrats go to Mubarak and say, "See, we told you so. We need to slow down, put up some new walls, otherwise what happened to Brazil will happen to us."

For a long time, I thought that this Egyptian reluctance to really plug into the globalization system was rooted simply in the ignorance of bureaucrats, and a total lack of vision from the top. But then I had an eye-opening experience. I did an author's tour of Egypt in early 2000, meeting with students at Cairo University, journalists at Egyptian newspapers and business leaders in Cairo and Alexandria to talk about the Arabic edition of this book.

Two images stood out from this trip. The first was riding the train from Cairo to Alexandria in a car full of middle- and upper-class Egyptians. So many of them had cell phones that kept ringing with different piercing melodies during the two-hour trip that at one point I felt like getting up, taking out a baton and conducting a cell-phone symphony. I was so rattled from ringing phones, I couldn't wait to get off the train. Yet, while all these phones were chirping inside the train, outside we were passing along the Nile, where barefoot Egyptian villagers were tilling their fields with the same tools and water buffalo that their ancestors used in Pharaoh's day. I couldn't imagine a wider technology gap within one country. Inside the train it was A.D. 2000, outside it was 2000 B.C.

The other image was visiting Yousef Boutrous-Ghali, Egypt's MIT-trained minister of economy. When I arrived at his building the elevator operator, an Egyptian peasant, was waiting for me at the elevator, which he operated with a key. Before he turned it on, though, to take me up to the minister's office, he whispered the Koranic verse "In the name of God, the Merciful, the Compassionate." To a Westerner, it is unnerving to hear your elevator operator utter a prayer before he closes the door, but for him this was a cultural habit, rooted deep in his tradition. Again, the contrast: Mr. Boutrous-Ghali is the most creative, high-tech driver of globalization in Egypt, but his elevator man says a prayer before taking you up to his office.

These scenes captured for me the real tension at the heart of Egypt: while its small, cell-phone-armed, globalizing elites were definitely pushing to get online and onto the global economic train, most others feared they would be left behind or lose their identity trying to catch it. Indeed I was struck, after a week of discussing both the costs and benefits of globalization, by how most Egyptians, including many intellectuals, could see only the costs. The more I explained globalization, the more they expressed unease about it. It eventually struck me that I was encountering what anthropologists call "systematic misunderstanding." Systematic misunderstanding arises when your framework and the other person's framework are so fundamentally different that it cannot be corrected by providing more information.

The Egyptians' unease about globalization is rooted partly in a justifiable fear that they still lack the technological base to compete. But it's also rooted in something cultural—and not just the professor at Cairo University asked me: "Does globalization mean we all have to become Americans?" The unease goes deeper, and you won't understand the backlash against globalization in traditional societies unless you understand it. Many Americans can easily identify with modernization, technology and the Internet because one of the most important things these do is increase individual choices. At their best, they empower and emancipate the individual. But for traditional societies, such as Egypt's, the collective, the group, is much more important than the individual, and empowering the individual is equated with dividing the society. So "globalizing" for them not only means being forced to eat more Big Macs, it means changing the relationship of the individual to his state and community in a way that they feel is socially disintegrating.

"Does globalization mean we just leave the poor to fend for themselves?" one educated Egyptian woman asked me. "How do we privatize when we have no safety nets?" asked a professor. When the government here says it is "privatizing" an industry, the instinctive reaction of Egyptians is that something is being "stolen" from the state, said a senior Egyptian official.

After enough such conversations I realized that most Egyptians—understandably—were approaching globalization out of a combination of despair and necessity, not out of any sense of opportunity. Globalization meant adapting to a threat coming from the outside, not increasing their own freedoms. I also realized that their previous ideologies—Arab nationalism, socialism, fascism or communism—while they may have made no economic sense, had a certain inspirational power. But globalism totally lacks this. When you tell a traditional society it has to streamline, downsize and get with the Internet, it is a challenge that is devoid of any redemptive or inspirational force. And that is why, for all of globalization's obvious power to elevate living standards, it is going to be a tough, tough sell to all those millions who still say a prayer before they ride the elevator.

This tug-of-war is now going on all over the Arab world today, from Morocco to Kuwait. As one senior Arab finance official described this globalization struggle in his country: "Sometimes I feel like I am part of the Freemasons or some secret society, because I am looking at the world so differently from many of the people around me. There is a huge chasm between the language and vocabulary I have and them. It is not that I have failed to convince them. I often can't even communicate with them, they are so far away from this global outlook. So for me, when I am pushing a policy issue related to globalization, the question always becomes how many people can I rally to this new concept and can I create a critical mass to effect a transition? If you can get enough of your people in the right places, you can push the system along. But it's hard. On so many days I feel like I have people coming to me and saying, 'We really need to repaint the room.' And I'm saying, 'No, we really need to rebuild the whole building on a new foundation.' So their whole dialogue with you is about what color paint to use, and all you can see in your head is the whole new architecture that needs to be done and the new foundations that need to be laid. We can worry about the color of paint later! Brazil, Mexico, Argentina, they now have that critical mass of people and officials who can see this world. But most developing countries are not there yet, which is why their transition is still so uncertain."

In Morocco, the government is privatizing simply by selling many state-owned enterprises to the same small economic clique tied to the royal palace that once dominated the state monopolies. This is why 3 percent of Morocco's population controls 85 percent of the country's wealth. Morocco's universities, which uniquely combine the worst of the socialist and French education systems, each year turn out so many graduates who cannot find jobs, and have no entrepreneurial or technical skills suited for today's information economy, that Morocco now has a "Union of Unemployed University Graduates."

As more countries have plugged into the globalization system and the Fast World, still another new backlash group has started to form—the wounded gazelles. This group comprises people who feel they have tried globalization, who have gotten hammered by the system, and who, instead of getting up, dusting themselves off and doing whatever it takes to get back into the Fast World, are now trying artificially to shut it out or get the rules of the whole system changed. The poster boy for this group is Malaysia's Prime Minister Mahathir. Hell hath no wrath like a globalizer burned. On October 25, 1997, in the midst of the Asian economic meltdown, Mahathir told the Edinburgh Commonwealth Summit that the global economy—which had poured billions of dollars of investments into Malaysia, without which its spectacular growth would never have been possible—had become "anarchic."

"This is an unfair world," Mahathir fumed. "Many of us have struggled hard and even shed blood in order to be independent. When borders are down and the world becomes a single entity, independence can become meaningless."

Not surprisingly, in 1998 Mahathir was the first Asian globalizer to impose capital controls in an effort to halt the wild speculative swings in his own currency and stock market. When Singapore's Minister for Information, George Yeo, described Mahathir's move at the time, he said, "Malaysia has retreated to a lagoon and is trying to anchor its boats, but the strategy is not without risk."

Indeed it is not. If you think you can retreat permanently into an artificially constructed third space, and enjoy all the rising living standards of the Fast World without any of the pressures, you are really fooling yourself and your people. Nevertheless, Mahathir's retreat, which proved to be only temporary, was received with a certain amount of sympathy in the developing world—although it was not copied by anyone. As we enter this second decade of globalization, there is an increasing awareness among those countries that have resisted the Golden Straitjacket and the Fast World that they cannot go on resisting. And they know that a strategy of retreat will not produce growth over the long run. For several years I would meet Emad El-Din Adeeb, editor of the Egyptian journal *Al Alam Al Youm*, at World Bank meetings and other settings, and for several years he would express to me strong reservations about Egypt's joining this globalization system. When I saw him in 1999, at the Davos Forum, he said to me, "O.K., I understand we need to get prepared for this globalization and that is partly our responsibility. There is a train that is leaving and we should have known this and done our homework. But now you should slow the train down a bit and give us a chance to jump on."

I didn't have the heart to tell him that I had just come from a press lunch with Bill Gates. All the reporters there kept asking him, "Mr. Gates, these Internet stocks, they're a bubble, right? Surely, they're a bubble. They must be a bubble?" Finally, an exasperated Gates said to the reporters: Look, of course they're a bubble, but you're all missing the point. This bubble is going to attract so much new capital to this Internet industry that it is going to drive innovation "faster and faster." So there I was: in the morning listening to Bill Gates telling me that the Fast World was about to get even faster and in the afternoon listening to Adeeb tell me he wanted to hop on but could someone just slow it down a bit.

I wish we could slow this globalization train down, I told Adeeb, but there's no one at the controls.

•   •   •

I was once having coffee at the Internet cafe in Amman, Jordan, which is called Books@Cafe and is just down the street from the incredibly well-preserved ruins of one of the great Roman amphitheaters in the Middle East. I visited there in September 1997, and the owner, Madian al-Jazerah, stopped by my table to introduce himself. He insisted that I have a piece of banana cream pie on the house. Why banana cream pie? I asked. Well, he explained, it was made by the wife of the Israeli deputy ambassador in Amman.

"Let me get this straight," I said, "the banana cream pie at the Internet cafe in Amman is made by the wife of the Israeli deputy ambassador! That's great. I love it."

Well, it wasn't so great for everyone, he explained. When the Islamic fundamentalists in Amman found out that the banana cream pie at the Internet cafe in Amman was made by the wife of an Israeli diplomat, they called for a boycott of the Internet cafe until it removed the pie from the menu. "And they called for the boycott on the local Internet," the owner said. (Obviously, the boycott failed and the pie is still on the menu!)

The anti-Israeli-made banana cream pie fundamentalists represent still another backlash against globalization. It is the backlash of all those millions of people who detest the way globalization homogenizes people, puts Israeli-made banana cream pie in the face of a Jordanian Muslim, brings strangers into your home with strange ways, erases the distinctiveness of cultures and mercilessly uproots the olive trees that locate and anchor you in the world. Many people obviously are ready either to abandon a lot of their local culture in favor of an Americanized-globalized consumer culture or to juggle the two together in their lives, clothes, eating habits and outlook. And people's capacity for juggling these sorts of things should never be underestimated. If people weren't such good jugglers, McDonald's and Disney would not enjoy such worldwide popularity. But some people are not into juggling. In fact, they are ready to go to war to protect their local culture from the global. Their war cry is: "I don't want to be global. I want to be local." For globalizers, hierarchy is about those who are most connected. For fundamentalists, hierarchy is about those who are most disconnected—from anything but their one source of truth.

Where this cultural backlash becomes the most politically destabilizing is when it gets married to one of the other backlashes—when groups that are economically aggrieved by globalization merge with those who are culturally aggrieved. This phenomenon is most apparent in the Middle East, where fundamentalists of many stripes have become highly adept at weaving the cultural, political and economic backlashes against globalization into one flag and one broad political movement that seeks to take power and pull down a veil against the world. The first flag of the Algerian opposition was an empty sack used to hold couscous, the popular North African grain, which symbolized the frustration of Algerian workers, and particularly young people, at not having any work. Slowly, though, those carrying that empty couscous sack made common cause with Islamic fundamentalists opposed to the Westernizing, secularizing ways of the Algerian regime, and together they produced a powerful backlash, under the green Islamic fundamentalist flag, against those in Algeria who wanted to link the country to the globalization system.

Benjamin Netanyahu's election to Prime Minister of Israel in 1996 was partly a political backlash against the problems of the Oslo peace accords, but it was also a cultural backlash against the globalization and integration implicit in Israel's peacemaking with the Arabs. Israeli religious scholar Moshe Halbertal once remarked to me that Shimon Peres's vision that his grandchildren and Yasser Arafat's grandchildren "would all make microchips together" was something fundamentally threatening to many religious Jews in Israel. They feared that if the ghetto walls fell around Israel and Israel assimilated into the Middle East—the same way American Jews assimilated into America—it would not be good for Judaism. They worried at some level that "Peace Now" and "Jewish Now" could not really coexist—particularly when peace seemed to mean more globalization, more integration, more Blockbuster Video, more smut-ridden cable stations and Pizza Huts. Hence the signs that appeared in ultra-Orthodox neighborhoods on the eve of Netanyahu's 1996 election: "Vote for Bibi. He's good for the Jews." In Israel too, though, the cultural backlash against globalization has merged with the economic and political one. In the wake of the peace agreement with Jordan, Israeli textile manufacturers began doing the logical thing, which was moving their low-skilled textile jobs from Israeli development towns, such as Kiryat Gat, across the river to Jordan, where wages are a fraction of what they are in Israel. Suddenly, Israeli textile workers, who are not ready for the Intel factory that is also being built in Israel, find their jobs going to Jordan—a place where their jobs could never have moved without peace and globalization. The workers in Kiryat Gat worry that "Peace Now" and "Jobs Now" won't go together, and, since many of them are Oriental Jews, they react by throwing their political support to Shas, the ultra-Orthodox Sephardi party, which is opposed to globalization on religious-cultural grounds and is mostly interested in "Messiah Now." So Messiah Now, Jewish Now and Jobs Now all get merged together into one protest movement that is hostile to globalization.

To be sure, there is nothing wrong with trying to anchor your society on a foundation of religious and traditional values. These are important olive trees that anchor a society. Not everyone advocating such values is somehow engaged in violent fundamentalism. But when this fundamentalism is driven not by real spirituality but by a backlash against globalization it often lapses into sectarianism, violence and exclusivity. And the more noninclusive you become, the less networked you are, the more you will fall behind, and the more you fall behind, the more you will want to retreat and reject the outside world with more exclusivity.

But you don't have to be a Muslim or Jewish fundamentalist to want to join the backlash against globalization because of how it can make you feel like a stranger in your own backyard. This is a universal phenomenon. I was touring Asia when the Australians held their 1996 national election and was struck by how much of their campaign revolved around biscuits and bathing suits. Yes, the issue in Australia was this: John Howard, who was then head of Australia's Conservative Party, claimed that Paul Keating's ruling Labour Party, in its zeal to have Australia integrate with the global economy and become more open to foreign investment, had created a situation in which Australia's most cherished companies were being bought up by global corporations based abroad and owned by foreigners. Howard charged that Australians were losing their national icons, indeed their very sovereignty and identity, to the global marketplace, even though they were improving their economy. In particular, he pointed to the fact that Arnott's Biscuits, which every Australian schoolchild grew up with, had been sold to a U.S. company (Campbell's Soup, no less!), which would probably start tampering with its recipe for Iced Vo-vos—Australia's most famous cookie, made of marshmallows and coconut. The same was true, Howard said, of Australia's famous Speedo bathing suits, which, he complained, had been sold to a U.S. firm. What happened to Iced Vo-vos and Speedo bathing suits actually became a hot topic of one of the election debates. And these olive-tree-hugging arguments helped Howard defeat the Lexus-loving Keating in a landslide.

A year later I was riding through the farmland of Indiana in the spring of 1997 on my way to Purdue University, being driven by a very thoughtful Purdue history professor, John Larson. As we got near Lafayette, I saw a huge factory looming on the horizon. "What is that?" I asked. "It's the Subaru factory," Professor Larson explained as we got closer. Then he added that this Subaru factory was Indiana's "first experience as a Third World country."

"How so?" I asked.

"For the generation, like mine, that grew up in the 1950s, it was America that was doing all the outreaching," said Larson. "We did all the globalizing. But when the Japanese car people were looking for a site for the Subaru factory, they came in here the way Americans go into India, asking all these questions: 'Can we have what we want? Do we trust you people? Do you have a stable workforce? What is the education level here? Will we get tax breaks?' The community leaders here were eager for the investment, but some people asked: 'Who are these Japanese to ask about our schools?' "

Once the Subaru people decided to put their factory in Lafayette, someone suggested that they rename the highway that ran in front of the factory something like "Subaru Highway," in honor of this company that was coming in and bringing all these jobs. "But then the local VFW heard about it and they raised a huge fuss," explained Larson. "They said you can't rename that highway. Don't you know what its name stands for?" The highway was already called Bataan Highway—named in honor of the peninsula in the Philippines where thousands of Americans died on a death march after being captured by the Japanese in April 1942.

"The Subaru people were very sensitive and said that by all means we shouldn't rename the Bataan Highway 'Subaru Highway,' " said Professor Larson. "Since then, people have gotten quite used to the Japanese and they have been well accepted. Japanese managers rotate in and out of here with their families. Their kids go to the local schools—except on Saturday when the Japanese kids also go to their own schools to keep up with their language and because they don't think our math training is rigorous enough."

The Groundswell
(Or the Backlash Against the Backlash)

In the winter of 1995 I visited Hanoi. Every morning to get my exercise I would walk around the pagodas on Hoan Kiem Lake, in the heart of Hanoi, and every morning I would stop to visit a tiny Vietnamese woman crouched on the sidewalk with her bathroom scale. She was offering to weigh people for a small fee. And every morning I would pay her a dollar and weigh myself. It wasn't that I needed to know how much I weighed. I knew how much I weighed. (And my recollection is that her scale was not particularly accurate.) No, doing business with that lady was my contribution to the globalization of Vietnam. To me, her unspoken motto was: "Whatever you've got, no matter how big or small—sell it, trade it, barter it, leverage it, rent it, but do something with it to turn a profit, improve your standard of living and get into the game."

That lady and her scale embody a fundamental truth about globalization which too often gets lost in talk of elite money managers, hedge funds and high-speed microprocessors. And it is this: globalization emerges from below, from street level, from people's very souls and from their very deepest aspirations. Yes, globalization is the product of the democratizations of finance, technology and information, but what is driving all three of these is the basic human desire for a better life—a life with more freedom to choose how to prosper, what to eat, what to wear, where to live, where to travel, how to work, what to read, what to write and what to learn. It starts with a lady in Hanoi, crouched on the sidewalk, offering up a bathroom scale as her ticket to the Fast World.

In central Hanoi today, every inch of sidewalk seems to be covered by someone selling something off a mat, out of a trunk or from the shelves of a storefront. Every inch of road is occupied by people who have traded their sandals for a bicycle, their bicycle for a motor scooter, their motor scooter for a Honda Civic, their Honda Civic for a Toyota Camry and, yes, even their Toyota Camry for the occasional Lexus. Because we tend to think of globalization as something that countries connect to outside themselves, or something imposed from above and beyond, we tend to forget how much, at its heart, it is also a grassroots movement that emerges from within each of us.

This explains why, along with the backlash against the brutalities, pressures and challenges of globalization, there is a groundswell of people demanding the benefits of globalization. This groundswell is propelled by millions of workers who have been knocked around by globalization, but who nonetheless get up, dust themselves off and knock again on globalization's door, demanding to get into the system. Because if they have half a chance, the turtles don't want to be turtles, the left-behinds don't want to remain behind and the know-nots want to know something more. They want to be lions or gazelles. They want to get a piece of the system, not to destroy it.

I happened to be in Rio de Janeiro when the Brazilian government privatized the state telephone company, Telebras. There was a big street protest in Rio against the privatization. What struck me most, though, was that the next day the Brazilian newspaper O Globo carried an interview with one of the demonstrators, asking him why he had come. He answered that he came to the demonstration because "I thought I might get a job." The poor guy wasn't against privatization. He just wanted a share.

People will accept a lot more stress associated with globalization than one might think—in part because Russian miners, Mexican peasants and Indonesian laborers understand at some level that they don't really have any choice but to get up to speed for the Fast World, and in part because many of them don't want it any other way. Obviously, if market forces get totally out of whack—if people feel that the system has become so crazy that the connection between hard work and a better standard of living gets severed and therefore no amount of painful reforms or belt-tightening will get them a share—then this system is in danger. But we have not reached that point—yet.

Think about the Russian workers who after the fall of communism were not paid for weeks or months. Why didn't they burn down the Kremlin? Because they've been to that play before and they know how it ends. They want a different ending this time—prosperity, freedom,

choices—and they are ready to make incredible sacrifices for it. My favorite story out of Russia in 1998 was told to a friend of mine by a Russian
economist about a Russian tank driver in a town behind the Urals who
drove his tank to city hall and demanded all his long-overdue paychecks.
When the frightened townsfolk surrounded the tank and asked the driver
if he intended to blow up city hall, he said, No, no, no—the only reason
he drove his tank was because he didn't have any other way to get there
and couldn't afford a taxi. He just wanted to get paid.

Indeed, for all the churning that global capitalism brings to a society,
the spread of capitalism has raised living standards higher, faster and for
more people than at any time in history. It has also brought more poor
people into the middle classes more quickly than at any time in human
history. So while the gap between rich and poor is getting wider—as the
winners in today's globalization system really take off and separate themselves from everyone else—the floor under the poor has been rising
steadily in many parts of the world. In other words, while relative poverty
may be growing in many countries, absolute poverty is actually falling in
many countries. According to the 1997 United Nations Human Development report, poverty has fallen more in the past 50 years than in the previous 500. Developing countries have progressed as fast in the past 30
years as the industrialized world did in the previous century. Since 1960,
infant mortality rates, malnutrition and illiteracy are all significantly
down, while access to safe water is way up. In relatively short periods of
time, countries that have been the most open to globalization, like Taiwan, Singapore, Israel, Chile and Sweden, have achieved standards of
living comparable to those in America and Japan, while the ranks of the
middle class in countries like Thailand, Brazil, India and Korea have
swelled, due partly to globalization.

Consider the following article from *The Economist* (Jan. 8, 2000):

BEWARE: multinational companies are on the rampage, destroying jobs, stamping on wages and generally wrecking local eco-
momies. Or so critics of globalisation make out. But a cool look at
the numbers tells a different story, as is clear from a new cross-
country study by the OECD [Organization for Economic Cooperation and Development]—the first to take a detailed look at the
contribution of foreign firms to national economies.

Fact one: foreign firms pay their workers more than the national
average—and the gap is widening. In America, for example, for-

eign firms paid 4 percent more than domestic ones in 1989; in 1996 they paid 6 percent more.

Fact two: in most countries, foreign firms are creating jobs faster than are their domestic counterparts. In America the workforce of foreign firms rose by 1.4 percent a year between 1989 and 1996, compared with an annual rise of 0.8 percent at domestic ones. In both Britain and France employment at foreign firms increased by 1.7 percent a year; at domestic ones it fell by 2.7 percent. Only in Germany and the Netherlands did foreign firms shed workers.

Fact three: foreign firms spend heavily on research and development (R&D) in the countries where they invest. In 1996 they accounted for 12 percent of America's R&D spending, 19 percent of France's and a remarkable 40 percent of Britain's. Indeed, in some countries foreign firms spend more of their turnover on R&D than domestic ones. In Britain, for example, foreign firms spent 2 percent of their turnover on R&D; domestic firms only 1.5 percent.

Fact four: foreign firms tend to export more than domestic ones. In 1996 foreign firms in Ireland exported 89 percent of their output, domestic ones only 34 percent. The gap was 64 percent to 37 percent in the Netherlands, 35.2 percent to 33.6 percent in France and 13.1 percent to 10.6 percent in Japan. The big exception is America, where domestic firms exported 15.3 percent of their output, foreign ones only 10.7 percent.

These benefits of foreign investment are even bigger in the OECD's poorer economies. Take Turkey. Foreign firms' wages are 124 percent above average; their workforce has risen by 11.5 percent a year compared with 0.6 percent in domestic ones; and their R&D spending is twice as high as in domestic firms.

No wonder, then, that while the backlash against globalization is alive and well, this backlash is constantly being tempered by the groundswell for more globalization—more people wanting into the system. You don't need to be a political scientist to figure that out. All you have to do is walk down the street in practically any developing country:

You'll meet Chanokphat Phitakwanokoon, a forty-year-old Thai-Chinese woman, who sells cigarettes and Bao Chinese dumplings from her little stand on Wireless Road in the heart of downtown Bangkok. I was staying at a hotel near there in December 1997, the week the government closed most of the country's finance houses, and I asked the *New*

York Times interpreter to accompany me on a walk to get some reactions from the street merchants. The first person I chatted with was Chanokphat. I began by asking her "How's business?"

"Off by forty or fifty percent," she said sullenly.

I asked her if she had ever heard of George Soros, the billionaire hedge-fund manager who was then being blamed for speculating on the Asian currencies and triggering their collapse.

"No," she said, shaking her head. She had never heard of Soros.

"Well, let me ask you this. Do you know what a stock market is?" I asked.

"Yes," she answered without hesitation. "I own shares in Bangkok Bank and Asia Bank."

"How in the world did you think of buying bank shares?" I asked.

"My relatives were all buying, so I bought too," she answered. "I put them away in the bank. They are not worth much now."

At that point, I looked down and noticed that she wasn't wearing any shoes. Maybe she had shoes somewhere, but they weren't on her feet. I couldn't help thinking to myself: "She has no shoes, she has a fifth-grade education, but she owns bank stocks on the Thai stock exchange." Some questions then occurred to me: What are her interests? Is she going to lead a march to burn down the IMF office that is imposing all these conditions on Thailand to reform its economy? Or, because she is now somehow part of the system, would she be prepared to work harder, save more and sacrifice more, even to the IMF, if it would help revive the Thai economy? Something tells me it's the latter. That's the groundswell at work.

You'll meet Teera Phutrakul, who heads one of the biggest mutual funds in Thailand. I went to interview him one afternoon in Bangkok about whether there would be a backlash in Thailand against Western and American bankers who might try to move in and buy up Thai banks and businesses, now that their currency was so cheap and many firms were flat on their backs. Teera thought for a moment and then answered by telling me a story: A few weeks ago, a friend of his had had his wallet stolen. In his wallet he had credit cards from four banks: American Express and three Thai banks. Right away he called American Express and the three Thai banks and reported his missing credit cards. American Express asked him if he wanted a new card sent over by motor scooter the same day. He still has not heard from the three Thai banks.

"So," said Teera, "ask yourself this: 'Will my friend really care if those three Thai banks are now bought up by Citibank and have their standards brought up to the same level as American Express?' " Will he feel a sense of nationalist outrage? Maybe, but it probably won't last long if those Thai banks start reemploying people and if they suddenly start to run as efficiently and profitably as Citibank and American Express. That's the groundswell at work.

You'll meet Liliane, a thirty-two-year-old Brazilian social worker who lived in the Rocinha *favela* in Rio and works for the municipal government. She gave me a tour of a day-care center in the *favela* and along the way explained that she had saved for years to finally be able to move her family out. Now that they were out of the *favela* and into the Fast World, the last thing she wanted was for that world to fold up, even if it was a struggle to get in. She said to me: "When I was young everyone in our neighborhood in the *favela* had to watch TV in one house. I am now moving to a place that is one hour and twenty minutes from my work, instead of twenty minutes, but it is not in the *favela* and it is away from the crime. I am moving there for my children because there are no drug dealers. I make nine hundred reals a month. [Now] I can buy a telephone. Now our house is made of bricks, not wood, and at the end of the month I still have some money left. When we had inflation, no one could buy on credit because you could not afford the inflation interest rates. Today even the poor people here have a phone, they have cable television and they have electricity. I have all the basic things that rich people have. Now we can complain about the service [from the electricity or the phone company]. Before, we didn't have them, so we couldn't complain about them." That's the groundswell at work.

You'll meet Fatima Al-Abdali, a Kuwaiti environmental health scientist, who owns the most popular Internet cafe in Kuwait City, Coffee Valley, where you can sip latte and surf the Net. Educated in America, Al-Abdali wears a veil, as a sign of Islamic piety, but is a total Web-head underneath. I gave a lecture on globalization in Kuwait, and she was one of the people in the audience. Afterward, she invited me to visit her cafe and meet some students there. The cafe was located in an urban shopping mall. As I sat down at a corner table, I said to her: "Look, I'm a little confused. Do the math for me. You are wearing an Islamic head covering, you are obviously a religious person, but you were educated in an American university and now you are bringing the Internet to Kuwait. I don't quite see how it all adds up."

Her answer, in essence, was that so many times in the past the Arab-

Islamic world had been invaded by outsiders, with their often alien influences and technologies. Well, she said, they were being invaded again. But this time she was going to own that invasion, not let the invasion own her. She was going to put a veil around that Internet and make sure the youths who frequented her cafe used it properly. I admired the effort. Don't lash out against it—own it yourself.

"I had this idea three years ago for an Internet cafe," she told me in 1997. "I knew it was coming and that if I didn't open one, someone else would. I realized we can have some control over it, so let's teach people the good parts and make it consistent with our own culture, rather than wait to be invaded by it. I adopted it, and adapted it, and on our Web page now we are slowly introducing some [Islamic] women's rights issues."

Al-Abdali invited some students from Kuwait University to join us. One of them mentioned in passing that they had just held student elections at the university and the Islamic fundamentalist candidates got wiped out by the independent, liberal and secular parties. Student elections are very important in the Arab world, because they tend to be the most free and therefore often the most indicative of public attitudes, at least among young people. I asked Abdul Aziz al-Sahli, a twenty-one-year-old communications student, why the Islamists were so roundly defeated. "The Islamists are not that impressive anymore," he said. "The secular parties are helping the students more with the small things that students care about now—Xeroxing, E-mail problems, library books, parking. The society is less ideological now. We need to look for a job." That's the groundswell at work.

You'll meet two Australian friends of mine, social scientists Anne and Gerard Henderson. The Hendersons stopped by to see me one day in Washington and told me about their daughter, who was attending university in Australia: "Our daughter, Johannah, is twenty-one years old," explained Gerard. "One day she and the girl she was sharing a flat with got a letter from the Australian phone company, Telstra, announcing that one-third of the company was being privatized and every householder who had a Telstra phone was entitled to buy a batch of shares. She called us and asked if she should do it and we said yes. So she took up the offer. She has very little money—it was three Australian dollars a share and she bought three hundred shares. She hasn't even started to earn a salary yet. She might be a librarian, or a teacher, or a good hardworking wage earner, but she is the only one in the family who took up the Telstra offer. The workers in Telstra bought up about ninety percent of the shares of-

fered, and they have become less militant since. People just understand
that this sort of thing is important. The Conservatives used the antiglobalization arguments to defeat [Paul Keating's Labour government] in
1996 and then they simply embraced the same arguments. There is no alternative, unless you want to go backward. Ten years ago my daughter
would have gone with the flow against globalization, but a few shares of
Telstra, which was all she could afford, has suddenly [made her] interested in what happens in Wall Street because that affects her now."

That's the groundswell at work.

I f the intellectual critics of globalization would spend more time thinking about how to use the system, and less time thinking about how to
tear it down, they might realize what a lot of these little folks have already
realized—that globalization can create as many solutions and opportunities as it can problems. But can it create the biggest solution of all? Is
there anything about globalization, and the rise of the Internet and other
modern technologies, that can make a difference for those at the bottom
of the bottom of the barrel—the 1.3 billion people still living on one dollar a day?

A lot of politically correct nonsense has been written about this question. Globalization critics will trot out all sorts of statistics that indicate
that 90 percent of the world, or some such figure, doesn't have a telephone or has never made a phone call. Therefore, they argue, globalization and the rise of the Internet can and will do nothing for them—only
widen the gap between them and the rest of the world. This is simply
wrong.

To begin with, it is wrong on the level of technology. While it may be
true that in the year 2000 most people on the planet have never made a
phone call, it will not be true by 2005 and it will be history by 2010. According to telecommunications industry estimates, by roughly 2005 one
billion low-cost portable Internet connections will be deployed around
the world—be they through cell phones, pagers or Palm Pilots. And by
2010 there'll be about three billion deployed. Since there are only a billion families on the planet, and these devices will become incredibly
cheap, there is no reason that the vast majority of the poor won't become
wired. (A techie friend of mine figures that by 2010 about 100 million
toasters should be online, as every piece of electronics gets fitted for software and becomes networked.)

Therefore, the real question is whether, once this technology is widely available, will it be able to make a difference in combating poverty, in ways that previous technological leaps have not? In raising this question, I do not mean to suggest that technology, or its absence, is the only variable in combating poverty. In fact, how societies are governed remains the most important variable. Creating a stable political, legal and economic environment friendly to entrepreneurship, in which people can start businesses and raise their productivity, is the precursor for effectively fighting poverty anywhere. As Nobel Prize–winning economist Amartya Kumar Sen makes clear in his outstanding book *Development As Freedom*—freedom, the ability of a person to make decisions about his or her life, is not only the most efficient means for building a healthy, developed society, but also its ultimate goal. When you put assets in the hands of the poor in a politically distorted environment, such as Liberia or Burma, not much happens. But when you put assets in the hands of the poor in reasonably stable and free environments a lot will happen. That's why, as Sen points out, there has never been a famine in a country that is democratic, has multiparty politics and a free media, including modern India. "Political freedom," Sen notes, "gives voice to the vulnerable sections of the population and provides them with the power to demand and receive protective support in times of emergency crisis."

Poor countries such as Kenya and Zambia have fallen behind in the globalization age not because globalization failed them, but because they failed to put in place even the minimum political, economic and legal infrastructure to take advantage of globalization. Prosperity did not run away from them; they failed to make the choices that would encourage it to stay. Countries such as Uganda, Poland and South Korea have made the right choices and reaped the benefits. Nations don't fail to develop, per se; they fail to develop good government.

As such, we can refine the key question even more. Is there something about globalization that can both enhance freedom and contribute to the alleviation of poverty in ways that previous systemic changes and technological leaps have not? The answer on both counts is yes. I have already tried to explain in chapters 9 and 10 how globalization can promote better, more accountable government and give individuals, activist groups and companies much greater power to become shapers of the new world without walls. What's noteworthy is how much the poor are beginning to understand this and exploit it. As harsh as the globalization system can be, it also gives those brutalized by it a greater ability to tell people about their pain or get organized to do something about it, and this helps explain and sustain the groundswell.

Thanks to the Internet, for instance, it is no longer just the few big media conglomerates who talk to the many. It is now the many who can talk to the many. I learned this from Chandra Muzaffar, president of a Malaysian human rights organization called International Movement for a Just World. I went to see this gentle Malaysian Muslim at his barren office in a suburb of Kuala Lumpur. I went for the express purpose of hearing him blast globalization in the name of the left-outs and left-behinds, for whom his organization is such a strong advocate. But I got a subtler, more interesting message from him.

"I think that globalization is not just a rerun of colonialism," said Muzaffar. "People who argue that have got it wrong. It is more complex than that. Look around. As a result of globalization, there are elements of culture from the dominated peoples that are now penetrating the north. The favorite food of Brits eating out is not fish and chips today, but curry. It is no longer even exotic for them. But I am not just talking about curry. Even at the level of ideas there is a certain degree of interest in different religions now. So while you have this dominant force [Americanization], you also have a subordinate flow the other way . . . There are opportunities now for others to state their case through the Internet. Iran is highly linked to the Internet. They see it as a tool they can use to get their point of view across. In Malaysia, Mahathir now gets some coverage [all over the world] through CNN. The campaign for banning land mines was launched through the Internet. This is what globalization does for marginalized groups. To argue that it is just a one-way street is not right and we should recognize its complexity. People operate at different levels. At one level they can be angry about injustices being done to their society from Americanization and then talk about it over McDonald's with their kids who are studying in the States." That's the groundswell meeting the backlash.

It is true even in the most developed societies. *Forbes* magazine — hardly an advocate of the know-nots — ran a very smart piece in July 1998 after Time Warner–CNN's disastrous June 7, 1998, report that U.S. Green Berets had deliberately nerve-gassed turncoats in Laos in 1970. No sooner did the program air than U.S. Army veterans alleged that this so-called exposé about Operation Tailwind was based on spurious reporting and dubious sources. Despite numerous complaints, the global news giant CNN would not retract the story. (Global news giants don't apologize to anyone, especially to some retired soldiers.)

"Time Warner may have expected the resulting anger to subside," noted *Forbes*. "[But,] fighting mad, Vietnam vets mobilized on the Internet—the only medium easily available to them. Without the Internet it would have taken months to dig up the facts—and by then few would have much cared. 'It allowed me to do in three days what [CNN producer] April Oliver did in eight months,' says Air Force Major General (retired) Perry Smith, CNN's military consultant, who quit the network in protest over the show, then helped rebut it. Smith says the night the show aired he dashed off a list of questions about what really happened in Laos. Simply by pressing a button, he dispatched the questions to over 300 of his best sources—'my E-mail brain trust,' explains Smith. 'The E-mails started flying from all over.' " Tailwind was classified top secret, so had the Vietnam vets had to wait for the Pentagon bureaucracy to decide whether or not to declassify information they needed to refute CNN, the furor over the story would have passed. But by using an E-mail network, which cost them almost nothing, they were able to assemble on their own all the testimony they needed from soldiers who were on the scene at the time, and then stick it in CNN's face in a matter of days.

In the end, the E-mail-armed veterans, living off their pensions, forced CNN's high-priced president, Rick Kaplan, to go on his own network, looking like a pathetic deer caught in the headlights, disown his own story and abjectly apologize over and over again in order to save his own job and restore some credibility to his network. The final score: Vietnam Veterans with E-mail, 1. Time Warner–CNN, the world's largest media conglomerate, 0.

But while the Internet and globalization can, and increasingly will, create more freedom of expression for individuals and more transparency in government, why do I believe it can also help the poor confront poverty in some unique ways? "Because the Internet scales like no other technology," said Alan Hammond, chief scientist of the World Resources Institute. "One Web site translated into Hindi, Mandarin, Swahili and Spanish would have a potential user base of two billion people. It can help people, even the poorest people, invent their way out of poverty, and create digital dividends, rather than a digital divide."

Consider just one example—the story of Bangladeshi-American banker Iqbal Z. Quadir. "In early 1993," he explained, "I was employed at an investment firm in New York, where my colleagues and I worked together on the same reports requiring cumbersome and frequent exchanges of floppy disks. When a simple link installed among our computers eliminated the need for physical exchanges of disks, we produced reports faster and worked more comfortably and creatively. This reminded me of my experiences in a village in rural Bangladesh during the country's war of independence in 1971. The war started in urban areas, forcing my family to take refuge in a relatively remote village. The region had no modern infrastructure, except for two motorized boats that carried passengers and cargo between two towns and touched near this village as one of their stops in between. For several months, the war forced these boats to suspend their services. When they started running again, there was an immediate positive effect on village life. Farmers and fishermen received a better price for their produce, and more things became available for purchase. The improvement was so dramatic that even at the age of thirteen I observed it clearly. In addition, during this period I spent a whole day walking between two villages. My parents had sent me to a village ten kilometers away to collect some medicine from a village pharmacist. After walking for most of the morning, I arrived at my destination only to learn that the pharmacist had left for the city to replenish his supplies. It took me all afternoon to walk back home. Thus, when the computer link in my office snapped in 1993, I saw the wasted day in 1971 in a new light. Connectivity is productivity, be it in a modern office or an underdeveloped village; connection enables, disconnection disables.

"If connectivity meant productivity," recalled Quadir, "then it must be a weapon against poverty. But how was my native Bangladesh doing in 1993 on this battlefront against poverty? Research made me rediscover that Bangladesh chugged along mostly without phones, causing me to wonder how much human energy was wasted in an unconnected nation of 120 million. There were two phones per thousand people and virtually none in rural areas where over 100 million of the population resided. This was particularly disturbing because it was a time when new forms of connectivity, such as the Internet and E-mail, were beginning to transform even mature economies, such as the United States. About this time in 1993, I learned that the government of Bangladesh would initiate a process to issue cellular licenses in 1994. This was very relevant. To achieve rural connectivity, one would need to think in a new way and establish and operate a new telephone company—in this case a cellular one—for which a license would be needed from the government. I had to organize quickly. Although attracting commercial investments for a telecommunications service in rural Bangladesh was perceived to be extremely difficult, I felt there had to be a way. If connectivity indeed meant productivity, there had to be a way to collect part of that productivity gain to pay for the necessary investment. The key point, I kept in mind, is not how much money a village has to purchase telephone services, but how much money the village can make if the services are made available. The villagers would pay for the phone service from what they make from the phone services."

But how to get started?

"One bright spot in this gloomy situation was a remarkable institution called Grameen Bank," said Quadir. "This microlending bank operated in 35,000 villages through 1,100 branches and 12,000 workers. Typically, a woman would borrow one hundred to two hundred dollars without collateral from Grameen Bank to purchase, say, a cow. The cow would then produce milk that she would sell to her neighbors, enabling her to make a living and pay off the loan. This process allowed the poorest of the poor to stand up on their feet. To me, connectivity could play a similar role. I proposed that a cellular phone could serve as 'cow'—at least from the perspective of the bank's borrowers. A woman could borrow, say, two hundred dollars from the Bank, purchase a handset and sell telephone services, by going door to door to villagers, thereby making a living and thus paying off her loan. My proposal caught the attention of Muhammad Yunus, the remarkable founder of Grameen Bank, without whom none of this would have been possible. With Yunus encouraging me to explore the possibilities, I left my venture-capital profession in early 1994 and convinced a socially conscious American investor named Joshua Mailman to form a company with me in New York.

"The result, two years later, was a partnership called GrameenPhone Limited—a commercial operation providing cellular services in both urban and rural Bangladesh. Grameen Bank's arm for administering the village phone operators typically selects women by past borrowing records with the bank. For instance, if a woman has demonstrated certain skills in learning new things, she is favored as a candidate for retailing phone services. Another factor is the location of her house; a central location in the village is preferred. Grameen also ensures that at least one member of the family of a village-phone operator knows English letters and numbers. The average daily earning of two dollars by phone operators is, of course, one indication of the phone's utility. However, there is also plenty of anecdotal evidence of how people living in villages with phones are thinking and doing things differently after the phones arrived. For instance, one lady is thinking about raising a large number of chickens, a business she had not pursued earlier for fear of not being able to call a veterinarian on time if the chickens developed a disease. Another man wants to cultivate bananas on a large scale because he is now able to obtain market prices on time to make the correct shipping decisions. One woman contacted the doctor in time to save her child, who was running a high fever. The migrant workers throughout the world with roots in Bangladeshi villages can now call home to know how their families are doing and if the money they are sending home is indeed reaching its destination. There is also a great deal of positive social impact. With some of the poorest women in the villages holding in their hands instruments of global communication, there are ripples in the highly stratified villages. Even a relatively rich person in the village is walking up to a poor woman's home for a service he needs."

Quadir says that he takes several lessons away from this experience. One is that digital technologies should unleash new thinking and create new business models that could be appropriate for poor countries. But institutions need to be created in these countries that can deliver the technology to the common people so that they themselves can harness its power. That is what GrameenPhone did. Another lesson is that there is no such thing as "economic development" without entrepreneurship. Entrepreneurship is the most potent force for uplifting countries, and what the Internet and globalization can do, with some imagination, is enable even the poorest Bangladeshi to be an entrepreneur.

"Since poor countries, by definition, have large poor populations, they must rank the energy of the poor as one of their most important strengths to move such poor countries forward," concluded Quadir. "In other words, the phone may be a 'cow' for the lady who operates it, but it acts as a 'horse' for the village, pulling the whole village out of poverty."

What such stories teach us is that while globalization can produce a profound sense of alienation, as power keeps moving up to more and more abstract levels that are difficult to touch, affect or even see, it can also do the opposite. It can push down to the local level and to the weakest individuals more power, opportunities and resources to become shapers than ever before.

These stories also help to explain why the backlash against globalization so far has not garnered enough critical mass anywhere to really disrupt this new system. Too many people still want into this system, and are finding ways to get there, even if it is painful at times. That is because too many people in developing countries understand that globalization is a tool to make them better off, faster, than anything they have ever had before. Is every job a good one? Absolutely not. Is everyone in Sri Lanka paid the same as everyone in Seattle? No. But are the jobs created by the Electronic Herd in developing countries better than the alternatives, of grinding poverty or child prostitution? Absolutely. Are they the first and necessary step out of poverty? Absolutely. As economist Paul Krugman has bluntly pointed out: "The raw fact is that every successful example of economic development this past century—every case of a poor nation that worked its way up to a more or less decent, or at least dramatically better, standard of living—has taken place via globalization; that is, by producing for the world market rather than trying for self-sufficiency. Many of the workers who do that production for the global market are badly paid by First World standards. But to claim that they have been impoverished by globalization . . . you have to forget that those workers were even poorer before the new exporting jobs became available and ignore the fact that those who do not have access to global markets are far worse off than those who do" (*Slate*, Nov. 23, 1999).

This is why so many representatives from developing countries were so upset at the 1999 Seattle World Trade Organization summit when the United States and other developed countries threatened to cut them off from global trade unless they got their worker and environmental standards up in short order—which was just a politically correct pretext used by American labor unions to limit trade with those countries which have lower wages. Without those lower wages these developing countries could never take the first step up the development ladder, which is the necessary precondition for them to improve their worker and environmental standards. No wonder then that the backlash against globalization is often stronger among Western intellectuals than emerging-market workers—who may not like a lot of things about globalization, but who know that the alternatives are a lot, lot worse.

Sometimes the news is in the noise—in what is being shouted on the streets of Seattle and painted on the walls in graffiti. But sometimes the news is actually in the silence—in what isn't being said. The greatest wisdom you can acquire as a reporter is understanding the difference between the two, and knowing when the silence is speaking volumes. I feel that the most important news story from Asia and Russia in 1998 and 1999 was the relative silence with which the lower and middle classes in

Thailand, Korea, Malaysia, Indonesia and the former Soviet Union accepted the verdict of the global markets—that their countries had fundamental software and operating system problems—and were ready to take the punishment and are now trying to make the necessary adjustments.

How long this will last is impossible to predict, but it keeps confounding all those who have been predicting globalization's imminent demise. After every global economic disturbance, or after every Indian nuclear test, or every noisy Seattle WTO summit, some pundit writes that it all goes to show that globalization is "finished," the system is breaking down and the poor will rise up against it. Globalization is forever being buried by people who don't understand the first thing about it, or about people's real aspirations, and who have never spoken to the likes of Liliane or Teera, Chandra or Iqbal, the Hendersons' daughter or the miners in Russia, let alone to a little old lady with a scale in Hanoi. When all of *them* give up trying to be in the Fast World, and when all of *them* declare that they would rather go back to their old, closed, regulated systems, and give up trying for a better lifestyle—for them or their kids—then I will acknowledge that globalization is "finished" and that the backlash has won.

Until then, let me share a little secret I've learned from talking to all these folks: With all due respect to revolutionary theorists, the "wretched of the earth" want to go to Disney World—not to the barricades. They want the Magic Kingdom, not *Les Misérables*. And if you construct an economic and political environment that gives them half a sense that with hard work and sacrifice they will get to Disney World and get to enjoy the Magic Kingdom, most of them will stick with the game—for far, far longer than you would ever expect.

America and the System

Rational Exuberance

When Federal Reserve Chairman Alan Greenspan made his famous comment in early 1997 warning investors in the U.S. stock markets against "irrational exuberance," because of the way they were pushing up share prices beyond any seemingly rational price-earnings calculations, I wrote a column in the form of a letter to Greenspan, as though he were an advice doctor at a newspaper. It began like this: "Dear Dr. Greenspan, I have a terrible problem. I'm feeling irrationally exuberant about the U.S. stock market and I just can't shake it. I know you've said 'irrational exuberance' is bad for my health, and I've tried everything: Hypnosis. Valium. Short selling. Even rereading your speeches from 1987. But nothing works. Every time I come to Europe, or visit Japan, I return home itching to invest more in the U.S. market. Please, please help me. Sincerely yours, Mr. Full E. Invested."

I went on to say that I didn't know what the right level of the U.S. stock market should be, and believed that if America didn't continue to do the basics of increasing productivity and keeping interest rates and inflation down, the stock market would go down just as it had gone up. But the point I wanted to make was that if there was some extra zip in the U.S. markets, it was not only because there was plenty of "irrational exuberance" about the American economy but also because there was some rational exuberance about America as well.

Since I spend a great deal of time overseas and away from Wall Street—looking at my country from the outside in—I am constantly exposed to the rational exuberance about America in the rest of the world. This rational exuberance is built on the following logic: If you look at globalization as the dominant international system today, and you look at the attributes that both companies and countries need to thrive in this system, you have to conclude that America has more assets, and fewer liabilities, in relation to this system than any other major country. This is what I call rational exuberance. It is the intuition among global investors that while many in Europe and Asia were still trying to adjust their societies to globalization, and some were barely up to the starting line, Uncle Sam was already around the first turn and in full sprint.

A useful way to analyze this rational exuberance is to ask the following question: If a hundred years ago you had come to a visionary geo-architect and told him that in the year 2000 the world would be defined by a system called "globalization," what sort of country would he have designed to compete and win in that world? The answer is that he would have designed something that looks an awful lot like the United States of America. Here's what I mean:

First of all, he would have designed a country that was in an ideally competitive geographic position. That is, he would have designed a country that was both an Atlantic and a Pacific power, looking comfortably in both directions, and at the same time connected by landmass to both Canada and Latin America, so that it could easily interact with all three key markets of the world—Asia, Europe and the Americas. That would come in handy.

He would have designed a country with a diverse, multicultural, multiethnic, multilingual population that had natural connections to all continents of the globe, but was, at the same time, bound together by a single language—English—which would also be the dominant language of the Internet. He would also have bestowed upon this country at least five different regional economies joined by a single currency, the dollar, which would also be the reserve currency for the rest of the world. Having a single country with different regional economies is a great asset because when one region might be slumping the other could be surging, helping to smooth out some of the peaks and valleys of the business cycle. All of that would be helpful.

He would have designed a country with extremely diverse, innovative and efficient capital markets, where venture capitalism was considered a noble and daring art, so that anyone with a reasonable (or even ridiculous) invention in his basement or garage could find a venture capitalist somewhere to back it. That would be nice. Because when you talk about speed, nothing is faster at throwing money at new ideas than American capital markets. If you compare a list of the twenty-five biggest companies in Europe twenty-five years ago with a list of the twenty-five biggest European companies today, the two lists are almost the same. But if you take a list of the twenty-five biggest companies in America twenty-five years ago and compare it with a list of the twenty-five biggest American companies today, most of the companies are different. Yes, America's financial markets, with their constant demands for short-term profits and quarterly earnings, often won't let corporations "waste money" by focusing on long-term growth. That's true. But these same markets will give someone with a half-baked idea $50,000 overnight to try to turn it into the next Apple computer. Massachusetts has a bigger venture capital industry than all of Europe combined. Venture capitalists are very important people in this day and age, and not just as a source of money. The best of them provide real expertise for start-up companies. They see a lot of them and they understand the stages through which companies have to go in order to develop, and they can help carry them through, which is often as important as seed money.

Our geo-architect would certainly have designed a country with the most honest legal and regulatory environment in the world. In this country, both domestic and foreign investors could always count on a reasonably level playing field, with relatively little corruption, plenty of legal safeguards for any foreigner who wants to make an investment and take out his profits at any time, and a rule of law that enables markets and contracts to work and safeguards and encourages innovation through patent protection. The U.S. capital markets today are not only more efficient than those of any other country, they are also the most transparent. The U.S. stock markets simply will not tolerate secrecy, so every listed company must file timely earnings reports, along with regularly audited financial statements, so that mismanagement and misallocation of resources is easily detected and punished.

He would have designed a country with a system of bankruptcy laws and courts that actually encourages people who fail in a business venture to declare bankruptcy and then try again, perhaps fail again, declare bankruptcy again, and then try again, before succeeding and starting the next Amazon.com—without having to carry the stigma of their initial bankruptcies for the rest of their lives. In Silicon Valley, says renowned venture capitalist John Doerr, "it is O.K. to fail and in fact it might even be important that you failed before on someone else's money." In Silicon Valley, bankruptcy is viewed as a necessary and inevitable cost of innovation, and this attitude encourages people to take chances. If you can't fail, you won't start. Harry Saal, who founded one of the most successful software diagnostic systems in Silicon Valley, after being involved in several start-up ventures that went belly-up, once told me over coffee in Palo Alto: "The view here is that you are always better and wiser for having failed. Which is why when people here fail after having tried something, they often have an easier time raising money the next time around. People say, 'Oh, he went bankrupt on that first venture? I bet he learned something from that, so I'll bankroll him again.'"

In Europe, bankruptcy carries a lifelong stigma. Whatever you do, do not declare bankruptcy in Germany: you, your children and your children's children will all carry a lasting mark of Cain in the eyes of German society. If you must declare bankruptcy in Germany, you are better off leaving the country. (And you'll be welcomed with open arms in Palo Alto.)

On that subject, our geo-architect would certainly have designed a country that was hard-wired for accepting new immigrants, so that in theory anyone could come to its shores and be treated as constitutionally equal to anyone else, thus enabling that country to be constantly siphoning off the best brains in the world and bringing them together in its companies, medical centers and universities. Roughly one-third of Silicon Valley's scientists and engineers today are foreign-born immigrants, who then turn around and project Silicon Valley values and products all over the world. According to University of California at Berkeley urban affairs expert AnnaLee Saxenian, research by the Public Policy Institute of California found that in 1996, 1,786 Silicon Valley technology companies, with $12.6 billion in sales and 46,000 employees, were run by Indian or Chinese immigrant executives alone. Donald Rice, the former boss at Teledyne, started a biotech company, UroGenesys, in 1997 to work on cures for prostate problems. He based his company in Santa Monica, California. One day, he described his staff for me: "We have nineteen employees. Three were born in Vietnam, two scientists and one administrator; two were born in Canada, both scientists; one was born in Germany, a scientist; one was born in Peru, a scientist; one was born in Malaysia, a scientist; one was born in China, a scientist; one is from Iran, a scientist; and one is from India, a scientist. The rest of us are native-born Americans. I cannot think of another country in the world where you could so easily put such a team together." That's for sure. Has anyone out there tried to become a Japanese citizen lately? How about a Swiss? To be a Japanese you pretty much have to be born a Japanese. To be a Swiss you pretty much have to be born a Swiss. To be an American you just have to want to be an American. That doesn't mean that we let everyone in who wants to be an American, but when citizenship is a legal question, not an ethnic, racial or national one, it makes it much easier for a country to absorb new talent. As a friend of mine in Silicon Valley likes to say: "I'm not afraid of Japan or the other Asians. Our Asians will beat their Asians any day."

The more knowledge workers you can attract to your shores, the more successful you will be. As far as America is concerned, I say bring 'em in, and not only the rich, educated entrepreneurs. I would never turn back a single Haitian boat person. Anyone who has the smarts and energy to build a raft out of milk cartons and then sail across the Atlantic to America's shores is someone I want as a new immigrant. As T. J. Rodgers, chief executive of Cypress Semiconductor, remarked, while complaining about limits set by Congress on the number of temporary work visas allotted for foreign engineers: "The winners and losers in the information age will be differentiated by brainpower. But we have senators who don't see that. They want to send back the first-round draft choices of the intellectual world so that they can compete against us in their homelands. Four out of my ten vice presidents are immigrants. Some 35 percent of my engineers are immigrants. My vice president of research—the guy who designs my most advanced chips—is from Cuba." Would you like the jobs in your country depending on only the engineers your country could produce, or would you like to have access to the top 10 percent of all engineers in the world? America is the only country that really has that access today. Japan, Switzerland, Germany—they have no real traditions of immigration, and that will be a huge disadvantage for them.

Our geo-architect certainly would have designed a country with a democratic, flexible federal political system that allows for a high degree of decentralized political decision-making and therefore enables different regions and localities to adjust themselves to world trends without waiting for the center to move. Indeed, a federal system—with fifty states all having an incentive to compete and experiment in finding solutions to the intertwined problems of education, welfare and health care—is an enormous asset in the era of globalization, when such problems can be highly complex and you rarely get the right answer without experimenting a few times.

Our geo-architect certainly would have designed a country with the most flexible labor market in the world—one that enables workers to move easily from one economic zone to another, and one that enables employers to hire and fire workers with relative ease. In a period of rapid change, ease of movement is critical. In America, lose your job in Maine one day and you can get a new one in San Diego the next day, if you're prepared to move. Lose your job in Tokyo one day and I wouldn't recommend looking for one in Seoul the next. Lose your job in Munich one day and, even with a common European currency and market, it is not so easy to get one the next day in Milan. That is a real liability.

Moreover, the easier it is to fire workers, the more incentive employers have to hire them. This little paradox is one of the explanations—maybe even the most important explanation—for why America has so outpaced both Japan and Western Europe in the 1990s in absorbing the information revolution into its economy.

Ask yourself a simple question: Why is it that when technologies, from the Internet to personal computers, are available to every developed country, some adopt them quickly into their businesses and others don't? Well, the short answer is that most of these new technologies improve productivity in a factory, and living standards in a society, because they displace labor. The robot does the job more efficiently than an assembly line worker. The voice-mail chip in your phone does the job better than an operator. In other words, the key to the information revolution is not that it increases labor output per unit, but rather that it reduces the labor input per unit—with all the efficiencies and cost savings that entails. The amount of physical labor required to do any task gets reduced. That means if you have a culture and society that allows you to easily and freely displace workers with new technologies, then you will reap the benefits they offer in terms of improved productivity, improved profits, greater general prosperity and ultimately more job creation.

It all adds up to a more competitive country. America today has a society and culture in which Schumpeterian creative destruction is allowed to work. Alan Greenspan once pointed out that in mid-1999 roughly 300,000 jobs were getting destroyed by new technologies in America every week. But 300,001 new jobs were also being created by these new technologies each week, which is why America's aggregate unemployment rate was holding steady at a low level. Because American companies can easily fire workers, and displace them with technologies, they are unafraid to purchase these new technologies and they can more easily pay for them by getting rid of a worker. But that also makes them much less afraid to hire people.

In Europe and Japan, by contrast, it is very hard to fire someone. So imagine if a new voice-mail system came along that could really revolutionize your company's phone system and allow you to eliminate ten phone operators. A typical Western European company would have to buy the new voice-mail system *and keep the ten phone operators*, or buy them out at a very high price. The result is that either that company is going to be very wary about hiring anyone, or it will forgo buying the new technology because it can't afford to pay the bill for the new equipment and the wages for the old worker at the same time. The rate of return on the new capital investment would be too low. In that vein, it may turn out that one of the key turning points in American history, going into the millennium, was Ronald Reagan's decision to fire all of the striking air traffic controllers in 1981. No single event did more to alter the balance of power between management and workers, and thereby open the way for American companies to fire workers, absorb the information revolution and be able to hire more workers. No wonder, then, that millions of jobs were eliminated in America and many millions more created in America in the 1990s, while the labor market in Western Europe was largely stagnant, with unemployment frozen in the 12 percent range.

Our geo-architect would have designed a country where government-protected cartels are abhorred, so every company and bank has to fight and stand on its own, and monopolies will not be tolerated. That would be important. Even when a U.S. firm becomes a much-envied, world-class gem, like Microsoft, it still has to answer to the Justice Department antitrust division. That is one of America's great hidden strengths. People who say that America, to preserve its strength, must preserve giant companies like Microsoft—no matter what they do—have it all wrong. It is the fact that a bunch of Justice Department lawyers making $75,000 a year could take on Microsoft, the biggest company in America, and *win!*—that is the real source of our strength. There will always be another Microsoft as long as there is a Justice Department antitrust division ready and able to keep the road clear of monopolists, as well as judges such as Thomas Penfield Jackson who are not afraid to throw the book at them. It was an ironic coincidence that Judge Jackson's November 1999 finding that Microsoft was a monopoly that had harmed consumers came down the same week as the tenth anniversary of the fall of the Berlin Wall. It is worth remembering what those people who tore down that wall wanted so badly on the other side. To be sure, they wanted what Bill Gates was selling—Windows, Disney World, Big Macs and the good life. But they also wanted what Judge Jackson was selling—the rule of law. And if postcommunist societies have learned anything in these past ten years, it is that the rule of law is the foundation on which all of America's prosperity is built. As Russia, most of all, has discovered, no prosperity is sustainable without it. It's America's rules-based system of governance, in which no person or company is above the law, which is at the core of the American way. I was as distressed as anyone about the reports of alleged Chinese stealing of U.S. nuclear secrets in 1999. That is intolerable. But at the same time, I couldn't help but feel there was something pathetic about what the Chinese were alleged to be doing. Because our biggest secret—the real source of our strength—is one that they can't steal. It's how we live. When the Chinese photocopy *that*, then I will start to worry about them as competitors. But as long as they are just trying to steal our latest military secret, they should know that as soon as they steal it, our system will produce a better one.

Our geo-architect would have designed a country that is tolerant of the oddball, the guy with the ponytail or the gal with the ring in her nose who is also a mathematical genius or software whiz. America is a country where the minute one person stands up and says, "That's impossible," someone else walks in the door and announces, "We just did it." Says Intel vice president Avram Miller: "The Japanese don't get it, because they are focused on homogeneity. When it was building a gazillion of all the same thing, they were the world experts and we mistook it for some special genius. But the world does not want a lot of the same thing today, and in a world where everyone wants something different—and the technology that will give them something perfectly tailored [to their own needs and specifications]—America has a real advantage."

Our geo-architect would have designed a country whose corporate sector, unlike Europe's or Japan's, had, by the mid-1990s, already gone through most of the downsizing, privatizing, networking, deregulation, reengineering, streamlining and restructuring required to fully adjust to, and exploit, the democratizations of finance, technology and information and to avoid Microchip Immune Deficiency. Just as America won the space race, it is now winning the cyberspace race. American companies spend more on information technology per capita than any others in the world.

He also would have designed a country with a deeply rooted entrepreneurial culture and a tax system that allows the successful investor or innovator to hold on to a large share of his or her capital gains, so there is a constant incentive to get enormously rich. In our ideal country, Horatio Alger is not a mythical character but sometimes your next-door neighbor, who just happened to get hired as an engineer at Intel or America Online when they were getting started and ended up being paid in stock options that are now worth $10 million.

Our geo-architect certainly would have designed a country that still had a lot of environmentally attractive, wide-open spaces and small towns, to attract knowledge workers. Because today, thanks to the Internet, fax machines and overnight package delivery, high-tech firms and knowledge workers can escape from urban centers and settle virtually anywhere they want. So having lots of lush green valleys not far from oceans or mountains can be a real asset. That's why states like Idaho, Washington, Oregon, Minnesota and North Carolina have booming high-tech sectors today.

He would have designed a country that values the free flow of information so much that it defends the rights of the worst pornographers and the most incendiary racists to do their things. That would be an asset. Because in a world in which information, knowledge, goods and services will flow with increasing speed across the Fast World or through cyberspace, those countries comfortable with such openness, and the cacophony and chaos that sometimes attend it, those countries comfortable competing on the basis of imagination, not behind walls of protection, will have a real advantage. America, with its Freedom of Information Act, which barely allows the government to keep secrets for long, has nurtured this culture of openness from its foundation.

And, most important, our geo-architect would have designed a country whose multinational companies and little entrepreneurs are increasingly comfortable thinking big and thinking globally, and excel now in virtually every fast, light, networked, knowledge-intensive field of endeavor. America today excels at software design, computing, Internet design, Internet marketing, commercial banking, E-mail, insurance, derivatives, genetic engineering, artificial intelligence, investment banking, high-end health care, higher education, overnight package delivery, consulting, fast food, advertising, biotechnology, media, entertainment, hotels, waste management, financial services, environmental industries and telecommunications. It's a postindustrial world, and America today is good at everything that is postindustrial.

In a winner-take-all world, America, for the moment at least, certainly has the winner-take-a-lot system. This makes America a unique superpower. It excels in the traditional sources of power. It has a large standing army, equipped with more aircraft carriers, advanced fighter jets, transport aircraft and nuclear weapons than ever, so that it can project more power farther than any country in the world. And deeper too. The fact that America has both a B-2 long-range stealth bomber and the short-range F-22 stealth fighter now being developed means that the U.S. Air Force can fly into any other country's air defense system virtually undetected. At the same time, as detailed above, America excels in all the new measures of power in the era of globalization.

But remember this: Only a decade ago the Asians and the Europeans seemed to be dominant, and America-in-declinism was all the rage. Now, as John Neuffer, an American analyst at the Mitsui Marine Research Institute in Tokyo, told *The New York Times*, everything is suddenly reversed: "The Japanese don't see the light at the end of the tunnel, and Americans don't see the cliff they may walk over."

That doesn't mean there are no cliffs out there. There always are. Whatever organic competitive advantages America may possess at this moment in history, it still has to get the basics right in order to compete. It still must ensure that productivity, the ability to produce goods and services at lower and lower costs so that wages can rise without inflation, steadily improves. The upsurge in productivity America witnessed in the late 1990s was a new technologically driven phenomenon and it is not at all clear if growth will continue at such a high rate, slow back down to the slower pace of the previous twenty-five years, or speed up. Japan, for the moment, may have more liabilities than assets in this era of globalization, but Japan in many key industries is still an enormously effective manufacturer, with an always useful high savings rate and a very hardworking populace. Japan is also still an engine of innovation in areas such as high-end manufacturing, inventory management and electronics. There are a lot of good Japanese entrepreneurs who have simply been stifled by their system. So Japan's macroeconomic stumblings in the 1990s do not make it a bust—they just require it to adjust. As long as the Japanese and Western Europeans stick with their rigid, protected welfare systems, which by making capitalism less destructive also make it less creative and enriching, they won't be a challenge to America. But the further ahead America gets in this era of globalization, the more I expect these countries will seek to mirror and mimic America. This inevitable adjustment will be enormously painful, but they will be forced to do it in order to maintain anything like their current standards of living.

It is not that these societies are not producing entrepreneurial minds suited for this era. French brains work just like American brains. The only question is, What is the economic and social context in which those brains are allowed to flourish and develop? The reason many of France's best software engineers have flocked to Silicon Valley is that they simply do not feel they can thrive in today's French system. On March 21, 1998, *The Washington Post* reported from Paris about the brain drain from France to Silicon Valley because of the flexibility offered by the American system: Reza Malekzadeh, a twenty-four-year-old graduate of one of France's most prestigious business schools, moved to the States, changed jobs three times in three years and had become director of U.S. operations for the network-systems firm Softway International, Inc., in San Francisco. "I couldn't do in France what I do here," he said. "In France, even when you are fifty years old, they talk about you as [a product of] the school you went to. Here, people only care about what you can do, not how old you are or where you went to school fifteen years ago." He is now one of the 40,000 French citizens living in Northern California. Change the context in France and, no doubt, many of them will return and fewer will stop coming to Silicon Valley.

America also must use this moment, when it has a few extra assets, to deal with its still very real liabilities: crime-ridden inner cities, an insane lack of gun control, widening income gaps, underfunded public schools, a culture of litigation that can be debilitating to everyone from small businessmen to large corporations, an underfunded social security system, a consumer credit card culture that encourages too many people to spend too far beyond their means and rack up a mountain of consumer debt that in the event of a recession could pose a real danger to the whole financial structure, and a political system increasingly perverted and corrupted by lax campaign finance laws. Addressing these problems would *really come in handy* in the era of globalization.

I remain hopeful that America will use its assets wisely, and I don't think I am alone in this rational exuberance. But if we get complacent, bust will follow boom as surely as the dusk follows the dawn. Which is why I always heed the words of Treasury Secretary Larry Summers, who liked to say about America in the 1990s: "The only thing we have to fear is the lack of fear itself."

18

Revolution Is U.S.

Sooner or later McDonald's is in every story: Where did O.J. eat just before the murder of Nicole? McDonald's. What did Commerce Secretary Ron Brown serve U.S. troops just before he died? McDonald's.

—saying in the press office at McDonald's headquarters in Oak Brook, Illinois

How can you shout "Death to America!" when you're wearing blue jeans?

—twenty-one-year-old female Iranian student wryly commenting to
New York Times *reporter John Burns about the other students in the*
protest rally in Teheran marking the twentieth anniversary of the
Iranian revolution,
November 4, 1999

O, wad some Pow'r the giftie gie us,
To see oursels as others see us!

—Robert Burns

I believe in the five gas stations theory of the world.

That's right: I believe you can reduce the world's economies today to basically five different gas stations. First there is the Japanese gas station. Gas is $5 a gallon. Four men in uniforms and white gloves, with lifetime employment contracts, wait on you. They pump your gas. They change your oil. They wash your windows, and they wave at you with a friendly smile as you drive away in peace. Second is the American gas station. Gas costs only $1 a gallon, but you pump it yourself. You wash your own windows. You fill your own tires. And when you drive around the corner four homeless people try to steal your hubcaps. Third is the Western European gas station. Gas there also costs $5 a gallon. There is only one man on duty. He grudgingly pumps your gas and unsmilingly changes your oil, reminding you all the time that his union contract says he only has to pump gas and change oil. He doesn't do windows. He works only thirty-five hours a week, with ninety minutes off each day for lunch, during which time the gas station is closed. He also has six weeks' vacation every summer in the south of France. Across the street, his two brothers and uncle, who have not worked in ten years because their state unemployment insurance pays more than their last job, are playing boccie ball. Fourth is the developing-country gas station. Fifteen people work there and they are all cousins. When you drive in, no one pays any attention to you because they are all too busy talking to each other. Gas is only 35 cents a gallon because it is subsidized by the government, but only one of the six gas pumps actually works. The others are broken and they are waiting for the replacement parts to be flown in from Europe. The gas station is rather run-down because the absentee owner lives in Zurich and takes all the profits out of the country. The owner doesn't know that half his employees actually sleep in the repair shop at night and use the car wash equipment to shower. Most of the customers at the developing-country gas station either drive the latest-model Mercedes or a motor scooter—nothing in between. The place is always busy, though, because so many people stop in to use the air pump to fill their bicycle tires. Lastly there is the communist gas station. Gas there is only 50 cents a gallon— but there is none, because the four guys working there have sold it all on the black market for $5 a gallon. Just one of the four guys who is employed at the communist gas station is actually there. The other three are working at second jobs in the underground economy and only come around once a week to collect their paychecks.

What is going on in the world today, in the very broadest sense, is that through the process of globalization everyone is being forced toward America's gas station. If you are not an American and don't know how to pump your own gas, I suggest you learn. With the end of the Cold War, globalization is globalizing Anglo-American-style capitalism and the Golden Straitjacket. It is globalizing American culture and cultural icons. It is globalizing the best of America and the worst of America. It is globalizing the American Revolution and it is globalizing the American gas station.

But not everyone likes the American gas station and what it stands for, and you can understand why. Embedded in the Japanese, Western European and communist gas stations are social contracts very different from the American one, as well as very different attitudes about how markets should operate and be controlled. The Europeans and the Japanese believe in the state exercising power over the people and over markets, while Americans tend to believe more in empowering the people and letting markets be as free as possible to sort out who wins and who loses.

Because the Japanese, Western Europeans and communists are un-comfortable with totally unfettered markets and the unequal benefits and punishments they distribute, their gas stations are designed to cushion such inequalities and to equalize rewards. Their gas stations also pay more attention to the distinctive traditions and value preferences of their communities. The Western Europeans do this by employing fewer people, but paying them higher wages and collecting higher taxes to generously support the unemployed and to underwrite a goody bag of other welfare-state handouts. The Japanese do it by paying people a little less but guaranteeing them lifetime employment, and then protecting those lifetime jobs and benefits by restricting foreign competitors from entering the Japanese market. The American gas station, by contrast, is a much more efficient place to drive through: the customer is king; the gas station has no social function; its only purpose is to provide the most gas at the cheapest price. If that can be done with no employees at all—well, all the better. A flexible labor market will find them work somewhere else. Too cruel, you say? Maybe so. But, ready or not, this is the model that the rest of the world is increasingly being pressured to emulate.

America is blamed for this because, in so many ways, globalization is us—or is at least perceived that way by a lot of the world. The three demo-cratizations were mostly nurtured in America. The Golden Straitjacket was made in America and Great Britain. The Electronic Herd is led by American Wall Street bulls. The most powerful agent pressuring other countries to open their markets for free trade and free investment is Uncle Sam, and America's global armed forces keep these markets and sea lanes open for this era of globalization, just as the British navy did for the era of globalization in the nineteenth century. Joseph Nye, Jr., dean of the Harvard University Kennedy School, summarized this reality well when he noted: "In its recent incarnation, globalization can be traced in part back to American strategy after World War II and the desire to create an open international economy to forestall another depression and to bal-ance Soviet power and contain communism. The institutional frame-work and political pressures for opening markets were a product of American power and policy. But they were reinforced by developments in the technology of transportation and communications which made it in-creasingly costly for states to turn away from global market forces." In other words, even within the Cold War system America was hard at work building out a global economy for its own economic and strategic rea-sons. As a result, when the information revolution, and the three democratizations, came together at the end of the 1980s, there was a power structure already in place that was very receptive to these trends and technologies and greatly enhanced their spread around the world. As noted earlier, it was this combination of American power and strategic interests, combined with the made-in-America information revolution, that really made this second era of globalization possible, and gave it its distinctly American face.

Today, globalization often wears Mickey Mouse ears, eats Big Macs, drinks Coke or Pepsi and does its computing on an IBM PC, using Windows 98, with an Intel Pentium II processor and a network link from Cisco Systems. Therefore, while the distinction between what is globalization and what is Americanization may be clear to most Americans, it is not—unfortunately—to many others around the world. In most societies people cannot distinguish anymore among American power, American exports, American cultural assaults, American cultural exports and plain vanilla globalization. They are now all wrapped into one. I am not advocating that globalization should be Americanization—but pointing out that that is how it is perceived in many quarters. No wonder the Japanese newspaper *Nihon Keizai Shimbun* carried a headline on June 4, 1999, about a conference in Tokyo on globalization that referred to the phenomenon as "The American-Instigated Globalization." When many people in the developing world look out into this globalization system what they see first is a recruiting poster that reads: Uncle Sam wants you (for the Electronic Herd).

Martin Indyk, the former U.S. ambassador to Israel, told me a story that illustrates this point perfectly. As ambassador, he was called upon to open the first McDonald's in Jerusalem. I asked him what he said on the occasion of McDonald's opening in that holy city, and he said, "Fast food for a fast nation." But the best part, he told me later, was that McDonald's gave him a colorful baseball hat with the McDonald's logo on it to wear as he was invited to eat the first ceremonial Big Mac in Jerusalem's first McDonald's—with Israeli television filming every bite for the evening news. The restaurant was packed with young Israelis eager to be on hand for this historic event. While Ambassador Indyk was preparing to eat Jerusalem's first official Big Mac, a young Israeli teenager worked his way through the crowd and walked up to him. The teenager was carrying his own McDonald's hat and he handed it to Ambassador Indyk with a pen and asked, "Are you the ambassador? Can I have your autograph?"

Somewhat sheepishly, Ambassador Indyk replied, "Sure. I've never been asked for my autograph before."

As Ambassador Indyk took the hat and prepared to sign his name on the bill, the teenager said to him, "Wow, what's it like to be the ambassador from McDonald's, going around the world opening McDonald's restaurants everywhere?"

Stunned, Ambassador Indyk looked at the Israeli youth and said, "No, no. I'm the *American* ambassador—not the ambassador from McDonald's!"

The Israeli youth looked totally crestfallen. Ambassador Indyk described what happened next: "I said to him, 'Does this mean you don't want my autograph?' And the kid said, no, I don't want your autograph, and he took his hat back and walked away."

No wonder that the love-hate relationship that has long existed between America and the rest of the world seems to be taking on an even sharper edge these days. For some people Americanization-globalization feels more than ever like a highly attractive, empowering, incredibly tempting pathway to rising living standards. For many others, though, this Americanization-globalization can breed a deep sense of envy and resentment toward the United States—envy because America seems so much better at riding this tiger and resentment because Americanization-globalization so often feels like the United States whipping everyone else to speed up, Web up, downsize, standardize and march to America's cultural tunes into the Fast World. While I am sure there are still more lovers of America than haters out there, this chapter is about the haters. It is about the *other* backlash against globalization—the rising resentment of the United States that has been triggered as we move into a globalization system that is so heavily influenced today by American icons, markets and military might.

As the historian Ronald Steel once pointed out: "It was never the Soviet Union but the United States itself that is the true revolutionary power. We believe that our institutions must confine all others to the ash heap of history. We lead an economic system that has effectively buried every other form of production and distribution—leaving great wealth and sometimes great ruin in its wake. The cultural messages we transmit through Hollywood and McDonald's go out across the world to capture and also undermine other societies. Unlike more traditional conquerors, we are not content merely to subdue others: We insist that they be like us. And of course for their own good. We are the world's most relentless proselytizers. The world must be democratic. It must be capitalistic. It must be tied into the subversive messages of the World Wide Web. No wonder many feel threatened by what we represent."

The classic American self-portrait is Grant Wood's *American Gothic*, the straitlaced couple, pitchfork in hand, expressions controlled, stoically standing watch outside the barn. But to the rest of the world, American Gothic is actually two twenty-something American software engineers who come into your country wearing long hair, beads and sandals, with rings in their noses and paint on their toes. They kick down your front door, overturn everything in the house, stick a Big Mac in your mouth, fill your kids' heads with ideas you've never had or can't understand, slam a cable box onto your television, lock the channel to MTV, plug an Internet connection into your computer and tell you: "Download or die."

That's us. We Americans are the apostles of the Fast World, the enemies of tradition, the prophets of the free market and the high priests of high tech. We want "enlargement" of both our values and our Pizza Huts. We want the world to follow our lead and become democratic, capitalistic, with a Web site in every pot, a Pepsi on every lip, Microsoft Windows in every computer and most of all—most of all—with everyone, everywhere, pumping their own gas.

I saw the sign above the front door as soon as I walked into the lobby of the Homa Hotel in downtown Teheran in September 1996. Written there were the words "Down with USA." It wasn't a banner. It wasn't graffiti. It was *tiled* into the wall.

"Jeez," I thought to myself. "That's tiled into the wall! These people really have a problem with America."

A short time later I noticed that the Iranian mullahs, who have always been more sensitive to the ups and downs of American cultural and military power than anyone else, had started calling the United States something other than just the "Great Satan" and the bastion of "imperialism and Zionism." The Iranians had started to call America "the capital of global arrogance." I found that a subtle but revealing shift. The Iranian leadership seemed to understand that "global arrogance" was different from imperialism. Imperialism is when you physically occupy another people and force your ways upon them. Global arrogance is when your culture and economic clout are so powerful and widely diffused that you know that you don't need to occupy other people to influence their lives.

As India's Finance Minister, Shri Yashwant Sinha, once said to me about America's relations with the rest of the world today: "There is no balance, no counterpoise. Whatever you say is law."

And that is what makes today's combination of Americanization and globalization so powerful. What bothers so many people about America today is not that we send our troops everywhere, but that we send our culture, values, economics, technologies and lifestyles everywhere—whether or not we want to or others want them. "America is different," German foreign policy expert Josef Joffe noted in a September 1997 essay in *Foreign Affairs.* "It irks and domineers, but it does not conquer. It tries to call the shots and bend the rules, but it does not go to war for land and glory . . . The United States has the most sophisticated, not the largest, military establishment in the world. But it is definitely in a class of its own in the soft-power game. On that table, China, Russia and Japan, and even Western Europe cannot hope to match the pile of chips the United States holds. People are risking death on the high seas to get into the United States, not China. There are not too many who want to go for an M.B.A. at Moscow University, or dress and dance like the Japanese. Sadly, fewer and fewer students want to learn French or German. English, the American-accented version, has become the world's language. This type of power—a culture that radiates outward and a market that draws inward—rests on pull not push; on acceptance not on conquest. Worse, this kind of power cannot be aggregated, nor can it be balanced. In this arena, all of them together—Europe, Japan, China, and Russia—cannot gang up on the United States as in an alliance of yesteryear. All their movie studios together could not break the hold of Hollywood. Nor could a consortium of their universities dethrone Harvard . . . This is why the 'strategic partnership' forged by Russia and China appears so anachronistic in 1997. What are they going to do about America? Boris Yeltsin will hardly want to shop for know-how and computers in Beijing. And China will not want to risk its most important export market."

In the near term it is only going to get worse, because the economic power gap between the United States and the rest of the world is going to widen more before it narrows. All you have to do is look at what is happening in cyberspace to understand that. There is a great land grab going on there—a grab for who will set up and own the key global commercial Web sites and cyber-exchanges. A cyber-exchange is a two-way auction site with multiple buyers bidding on offerings from multiple sellers. They usually start out as spot markets. Spot markets are vehicles for selling excess inventory, whether it is crude oil, steel, microchips or goods that didn't quite pass inspection standards. But because of the efficiency of these cyber-exchanges they are quickly evolving from spot markets to more sophisticated mega-market-makers.

The closest thing to these cyber-exchanges that the average consumer would see is eBay—the auction site, where individuals can buy or sell anything from their basements. But imagine eBays for a whole set of industries, where goods and services related to any aspect of that industry could be exchanged between buyers and sellers. For instance, you already have Metalsite.com, where construction firms from anywhere in the world can put out their steel or metal needs to the lowest bidder. There is already E-Chemicals.com and Chemdex.com for chemicals and life science products. And soon there will be E-rubber, E-plastics, E-cement, E-paper, and E-insurance.

In the old world, a company ensured a steady stream of supplies and raw materials by nurturing a carefully selected group of suppliers, with long-standing relationships built on a history of trust and building to certain specifications. But as more and more goods get commoditized, a company such as IBM will put out for bid on a cyber-exchange its specifications for microchips, toilet paper and even energy, and suppliers will come there and bid for the contracts. In a world without walls, these global exchanges will be the shapers of the rules and standards by which a whole host of goods and services will be bought, sold, auctioned and bartered around the world. And because of America's lead in the cyberspace land grab, these exchanges are being created largely in America by American firms.

"Most of this is still happening just below the horizon, and the numbers are still relatively small, so people don't see it yet," Joel Cawley, Director of Corporate Strategy for IBM, explained to me in early 2000. "But it's going to become increasingly important. Estimates are that these exchanges will mediate between thirty and forty percent of industrial E-commerce by 2004. Once these big exchanges do get up and running, and get on everyone's radar screen, it will be too late. The winners will be established, the network effects will have kicked in and the cost of switching from a key site, or starting up a new one, will be very high."

Consider Enron. It has set up an online marketplace through which companies all over the world are now able to buy and sell natural gas, electricity, coal, plastics, pulp, paper and oil—and, coming soon, bandwidth. Bandwidth is the basic electronic pipe down which companies send their Internet traffic. Through Enron's Pooling Point Operators— where connections between bandwidth buyers and sellers will be established and monitored—a school with excess bandwidth capacity during the summer will be able to sell its surplus to a company with rising bandwidth demand. Bandwidth deals that used to take months to close will take seconds.

"We were the first to do this sort of thing for trading natural gas and electricity," said Enron's CEO, Kenneth Lay, "but we think the bandwidth market will be the biggest of all. It is now a thirty-billion-dollar market and in three years or so it should be ninety to a hundred billion dollars. And it will be global." The Internet economy runs on bandwidth, so if Enron's exchange works, it could be the equivalent of discovering cyber-oil—for Enron and for the United States. "There are strong advantages to being the first mover in these sorts of global markets," said Lay. "When you are first, you get scale very quickly, and with that comes economies that lower your transaction costs, and that gives you more liquidity and the ability to do more complicated transactions than others. We will have competitors, I'm sure. But it's pretty much a winner-take-all environment. The early entrants into these markets will in large part determine how they are shaped. [And] once an entity establishes a strong market position in this kind of global market, it is awful tough to overtake them."

This will have geopolitical implications. If you think the Europeans already dislike certain American ways of doing business, wait until they wake up in a couple of years and realize that American firms have won the cyberspace land grab and shaped the rules and standards for a whole set of E-exchanges.

What will the French call the Americans then? By the end of the twentieth century they had already come up with a new term to describe the United States. It wasn't just a superpower anymore. The French decided that America needed a category all its own. America, a French diplomat at NATO headquarters remarked to me, is now a "hyperpower." Not surprisingly, as I traveled around, I found that not only the Iranians were calling America "the capital of global arrogance," but, behind our backs, so, too, were the French, the Malaysians, the Russians, the Canadians, the Chinese, the Indians, the Pakistanis, the Egyptians, the Japanese, the Mexicans, the South Koreans, the Germans—and just about everybody else. Iraqi President Saddam Hussein, who, like the Iranians, is ever sensitive to even subtle changes in America's international standing, shrewdly tried to tap into this newfound resentment by changing his propaganda line. In the first Gulf War crisis in the early 1990s, Saddam depicted himself as the Arab Robin Hood, come to steal from the Arab rich to give to the Arab poor. In the second Gulf War crisis, in the late 1990s, Saddam depicted himself as Luke Skywalker, standing up to the American Evil Empire. Every time he was interviewed on television, Saddam's foreign minister complained that America behaved like "the last days of the Roman Empire." This became Iraq's new propaganda line, from the top of the regime right down to the street. I was watching CNN one day and heard them do an interview with "a man in the street in Baghdad," who just happened to refer to America as an "international Dracula that sucks the blood of people around the world."

O.K., O.K., so the rest of the world thinks Americans are obnoxious bullies and are envious to boot. So what? What impact does this really have on relations between the United States and other governments? The short answer is that it makes America's relations with every country a little more complicated today. Some countries now go out of their way just to tweak America's beak; others sit back and enjoy the role of the "free rider"—they let America be the global sheriff, pay all the costs of confronting the Saddam Husseins and other rogues, and enjoy the benefits, while all the time complaining about America; others stew with resentment at American domination; others just quietly fall into line.

In fact, America's relationship to the rest of the world around the turn of the millennium was a lot like Michael Jordan's relationship was—in his heyday—with the rest of the NBA. Every other player and team wanted to beat Michael Jordan; every other player and team hated him for the way he could expose all their weaknesses; every other player and team measured themselves against Michael Jordan, and to some extent modeled their moves after him; every other player and team constantly complained that the referees let Michael Jordan get away with all sorts of fouls that no one else could. But despite all of that, none of the other teams really wanted to see Michael Jordan injured or retire, because anytime he came into town every seat was sold. He was the straw that stirred the drink for them all.

Consider just a few examples of this phenomenon: When Anatoly Chubais, one of the original architects of Russia's privatization program, was negotiating yet another Russian bailout by the IMF in the summer of 1998, the IMF was demanding more stringent terms than ever, and Chubais had little choice but to give in. At the height of the negotiations, the Russian television show *Kukli*, which features puppets dressed up as various Russian leaders, did a takeoff on "Little Red Riding Hood." Boris Yeltsin was Grandmother and then–Prime Minister Kiryenko was Little Red Riding Hood, trying to get to Yeltsin to influence the latest Russian bailout plan before anyone else. When Kiryenko arrived at Grandmother's house, though, he found Chubais already sitting next to Yeltsin. Chubais was dressed in a space suit and moon helmet. On the front of the suit were the Russian letters for "IMF" and an American flag. Chubais was literally depicted as an agent from planet America, there to tell the Russians what to do. When Kiryenko saw him sitting next to Yeltsin he said to the audience, "I guess I arrived too late."

At the 1999 Davos World Economic Forum, Minoru Murofushi, chairman of Japan's giant trading company the Itochu Corporation, was on a panel with then–Russian Prime Minister Yevgeny Primakov. Murofushi was commenting on Primakov's efforts to negotiate an end to Russia's economic crisis when, in something of a Freudian slip, the Japanese businessman said, "I know Mr. Primakov is meeting tomorrow with Mr. Fischer from IBM—I mean from the IMF." Oh well, IBM, IMF, what's the difference—they're both controlled by the Americans!

Yuan Ming, a professor of international relations at Beijing University, is one of China's leading experts on America. She once told me a story that indicated that China thought the only way to react to American global arrogance was with some arrogance of its own: "Our political leaders in their public speeches don't use the term 'globalization.' They use the term 'modernization.' There is a cultural reason for this. The historical lesson is still fresh in Chinese people's minds that China was forced into the international community in the last century by gunboats—so globalization represents something that China doesn't pursue but rather something that the West or America is imposing. Modernization, on the other hand, is something we can control. There is an annual New Year's television program that is shown on the main national television channel. It is one of the biggest TV events of the year in China. Almost a billion people watch it. Usually it is just singers and comedians. Three years ago, though, [in 1995] the show had a skit about two parents in a rural area calling their son who was studying in the United States. They ask him, 'How are you on this New Year's Day?' He says he's fine and that he plans to return home after finishing his Ph.D. in the United States. The parents are pleased to hear this. The line I remember most, though, is the parents telling the son that China is getting as good as America at many things. They say: 'You did some dishwashing for the Americans. Now we have to have some Americans come and do some dishwashing for us.' "

I was flying home from Japan on December 14, 1997, and was reading the letters to the editor in that day's *Japan Times.* I like to read them in whatever country I am in, because I always find interesting nuggets there. This letter was entitled "American Hubris," and it spoke for a lot of people. It said: "I am at (another) loss for words over the continuing bullying tactics of the United States. This time, I read that the U.S. refuses to sign any agreement [at the Kyoto Conference on climate change] unless three of its 'demands' are met . . . I would never belittle the U.S. history of 'helping' where it can—but the 'world's greatest country' (its claim, not mine) must learn humility. Its recent return to glory has been equally due to the failure of its competitors' political and economic systems. Pride comes before a fall. The U.S. government would do well to remember that." Signed: Andrew Ogge. Tokyo.

I visited India following its 1998 nuclear tests, and Indian Lieutenant General (retired) V. R. Raghavan, the former chief of operations of the Indian Army and now an analyst at the Delhi Policy Group, told me he had just taken part in an international seminar on the nuclear issue. The participants included British, American, Chinese and Indian experts, among others. "During one of the breaks we went out to tour a tiny Indian village and I showed them the shops and homes and the cow dung being used as an energy source," said General Raghavan. "But most fascinating was a visit we made to a middle school in the village. There were about thirty children in their early teens, and some teachers, and members of our group wanted to talk to them. So they set out some benches and had a chat. There was a lawyer from New York in the group and he asked the kids what they thought of China and the United States. Without any prompting these kids said that China is our biggest neighbor, we had a war with China, but China stands up for weaker nations and we have no problems with China. 'How about the United States?' he asked them. They said the United States is 'a bully, it elbows everybody and thinks only of itself.' People in the group couldn't believe it."

In 1997, I attended an academic conference in Morocco entitled "Globalization and the Arab World." Most of the Arab participants were French-educated Arabs from North Africa and France. (To be a French-

educated Arab intellectual is the worst combination possible for understanding globalization. It is like being twice handicapped, since both of
these cultures are intuitively hostile to the whole phenomenon.) I was
asked to give a brief introductory talk on globalization, which I did.
When I was done, a former Algerian prime minister, who was living in
exile and attending the conference, asked to respond to my remarks.
Speaking in French, he denounced everything I had to say. He argued
that "this globalization you speak about is just another American conspiracy to keep the Arab world down, just like Zionism and imperialism." I
listened politely to his remarks, which went on in this vein at great length,
and then I decided to respond in a deliberately provocative manner, in
hopes of bursting through his fixed mind-set. I said roughly the following
(with my profanities edited out): "Mr. Prime Minister, you spoke of globalization as just another American conspiracy to keep you down. Well, I
have to tell you something—it's much worse than you think. Much
worse. You see, you think we are back there in Washington thinking
about you and plotting how to keep you down, and turning all the dials
and pulling all the levers to do just that. I wish we were. God, I wish we
were. Because I like you, and I would turn the dials the other way to let
you up. But the truth is, *we aren't thinking about you at all!* Not for a second. We don't give a flying petunia about you. And it's not out of malice.
It's because we're trapped under the same pressures as you are, and we're
trying to keep one step ahead of the competition just like you are, and
we're worried about what the bond market is going to do next, just like
you are. So I wish I could confirm for you that there is a conspiracy to
keep you down, but I can't . . . Now if you want to build an Islamic bridge
to this globalization train, build an Islamic bridge. If you want to build a
Maoist bridge to this train, build a Maoist bridge. If you want to build a
Jeffersonian bridge to this train, build a Jeffersonian bridge. But promise
me one thing—that you will build a bridge. Because this train will leave
without you."

But for every North African who is reacting to Americanization-
globalization by shaking his fist at it, another is simply falling into line
and trying to get the best out of it. While I was visiting Casablanca in
1997, the guided-missile frigate USS *Carr* pulled into the port for a call.
The U.S. consulate in Casablanca held a reception for local officials and
guests on the deck of the *Carr* and invited me to attend. While some
young Moroccan girls elbowed one another to get pictures with the U.S.
sailors in their dress uniforms and guests dined on chicken fingers and

Budweiser on tap from a big steel keg, I fell into conversation with the governor of the Casablanca district. Sporting a tailored suit, the Moroccan official proudly explained to me in perfect French why he was sending his two children to the American school in Casablanca, and not to the French schools where he was educated.

"Two reasons," he offered. "First, in the world we are going into, if you don't speak English, you're illiterate. Second, the French system teaches you how to be an administrator. The American system teaches you how to survive on your own. That's what I want my kids to know."

Although French culture and education have been embedded in Morocco's major cities since 1912, there are now three American schools there, and they are in such demand they each have waiting lists for the waiting list. In fact, there is a real cultural competition now between America and France for the hearts and minds of the new generation in traditionally French-dominated North and West Africa, and it is a competition that America is increasingly winning—without even trying. It's all demand-driven. "The French higher education system has not adapted to this revolutionary period," remarked Dominique Moisi, who used to teach at France's renowned ENA, the National School of Administration, and is one of his country's leading experts on international affairs.

"The French system rewards people for their capacity to follow the path that is open to them. It does not encourage people to rebel or to develop their character. The mood out there is that if things are changing now in the 1990s, it is not because of France. America has become a mirror of our own doubts. We look at you and see what's missing."

Another popular reaction to Americanization-globalization today is the tendency of some countries to complain bitterly about America throwing its weight around, while they sit back and reap the fruits of American power. The Japanese will tell us privately that we are "dead right" in demanding that China live up to international copyright laws. And they will tell us that Japanese companies, such as Sony and Nintendo, suffer every bit as much from Chinese pirates as Disney and Microsoft. But Japan is not going to butt heads with Beijing on this issue. It will let Washington, the world's only superpower, do this while Japan holds America's coat and goes on doing as much business with China as it can—even taking advantage of whatever markets the United States loses in its confrontation with Beijing. At the end of the day, if the Americans are successful at winning new copyright concessions from China, Japan will enjoy this as well. How do you say "free rider" in Japanese?

Finally, there is a trend of countries looking for opportunities to complicate American diplomacy and check American power, both for traditional geopolitical reasons and for the sheer feel-good sport of it. Take Russia or France, for example: the more they are unable to achieve honor and dignity in the Fast World, the more they look to achieve it in all the wrong places instead—by challenging American diplomacy in Bosnia, by rushing a small unit of Russian troops into Kosovo before the U.S. and NATO troops can get there, or by tilting in favor of Saddam Hussein in Iraq. In fact, the weaker Russia gets, the more it is tempted to magnify even its small differences with the United States and the more some Russians try to stick a finger in America's eye to feel better about themselves—to feel that somehow they are still America's equal. As Russian commentator Aleksei Pushkov once said to me: "The prevailing attitude here now is that Russia should be a balancing force to correct situations where America gets infatuated with its own power." I would put it a little differently. The unspoken motto of Russia and many others today is: "If you can't have a good war anymore to change the subject from your domestic troubles, at least have a good argument with the Americans."

Being the world's sole superpower doesn't guarantee that America will get its way everywhere, but it does guarantee that America will be criticized everywhere. Again, think of the NBA. Gary Payton is the all-star guard for the Seattle SuperSonics. He's a great player, but he's not Michael Jordan and he makes up for some of his shortage in skills by talking trash to his opponents, particularly to Michael Jordan before he retired. To my mind, France and Russia today are the Gary Paytons of geopolitics—the biggest trash talkers in the world, always trying to make up for their weaknesses by giving everybody a lot of lip, particularly Uncle Sam.

In the Marx Brothers' classic movie *Duck Soup*, there is a scene in which Chico and Harpo are talking to the evil, calculating European statesman Trentino, Groucho's political rival, who has hired Chico and Harpo as spies. When Chico and Harpo come to Trentino's office to report on the progress of their spying, his secretary walks in with a telegram. Harpo grabs it out of her hands, examines it closely and then rips it into shreds, tosses it on the floor and shakes his head. Stunned and surprised, Trentino turns to Chico with a quizzical look, as if to ask: "Why did he do that?" And Chico answers: "He gets mad because he can't read."

That scene reminds me of yet another trend in reaction to Americanization-globalization—the one that is actually dangerous. It is the reaction of those who either are not up to Americanization-globalization or
don't want to be up for it for cultural, economic or political reasons, and
want to rip it up every time it is shoved in their face. These are the
Harpos—angry men and women who, unlike their leaders, don't want to
have it both ways. They don't just want to bow to America and then criti-
cize it behind its back. They want to have it one way, the old way, their
way.

To paraphrase something Ronald Steel once said to me, the angry
men see Americanization-globalization as an uninvited guest: You try to
shut the door and it comes in through the window. You try to shut the
window and it comes in on the cable. You cut the cable, and it comes in
on the Internet over the phone line. When you cut the phone line, it
comes in over the satellite. When you throw away the cell phone, it's out
there on the billboard. When you take down the billboard, it comes in
through the workplace and the factory floor. And it's not only in the room
with you, this Americanization-globalization. You eat it. It gets inside you.
And when it comes in it often blows open a huge gap between fathers and
sons, mothers and daughters, grandparents and grandchildren. It creates
a situation where one generation sees the world radically different from
their parents, and it's all America's fault. The constant theme, for instance, of the Saudi millionaire terrorist Osama bin Laden is that America has to get out of the Arabian Peninsula, and out of the Islamic world at
large, because its way of life is "defiling the Islamic home."

Former Indian Prime Minister I. K. Gujral is no Osama bin Laden,
not at all. But I had a conversation with him in New Delhi once in
which he articulated the distress that some people feel at the way
Americanization-globalization gets inside their family and home. "I see
the same thing happening now in India—the changes in our dress, eating habits," said Gujral. "My granddaughter is four. She is always talking
about bubble gum, not Indian food, or she says, 'I don't like Pepsi, I like
Coke.' She even speaks English more often than Hindi. I asked her one
day why she doesn't speak to me in Hindi, and then she went to her
mother and asked: 'Doesn't Grandfather speak English?' I keep on observing my grandchildren because it is an insight. The other day my
granddaughter said she wanted pizza. So her grandmother said that she
would make a pizza for her the next day. My granddaughter said, 'No,
no, I want Pizza Hut.' "

In Shanghai, I interviewed Wang Guoliang, a top official at the Bank of Communications, one of China's big four state banks. Just for fun I asked him where he got his news about the world. He said every morning his secretary prepared a summary for him from the Internet and Reuters, but he also got a lot from his son.

Then, out of the blue, he launched into a lecture about fathers and sons that lapsed into a tirade against the Internet.

"My son is an expert at the Internet. Whenever he comes across something interesting on the Internet he shows it to me," said the Chinese banker. "But fathers should not be guided by sons. My son also makes suggestions to me, but I don't like most of what he suggests. The father should not listen to the son. It undermines authority. I told my son to read the Internet less and to study more."

I. K. Gujral and Wang Guoliang are too cultured and sophisticated to get violent about this, but not so the other angry men. The angry men don't have a full-blown alternative ideology to Americanization-globalization. They are like Harpo. They just prefer to rip up the message and stomp on it. And unlike their wimpy governments, who complain about Uncle Sam but toe his line, the angry men are ready to cross that line and pull the trigger.

Now we get to what is really scary. Americanization-globalization not only gives these angry men a much greater incentive to hate America; it also gives them much greater power, as individuals, to pull that trigger. Globalization super-empowers them in two very important ways.

First, with the world wired the way it is—with all of us so much more connected in so many more places so much more of the time—terrorists can now unnerve so many more people at once. Consider my winter vacation in December 1998: I was skiing in the Rocky Mountains and for the first time I noticed that in almost every ski lift in which I was riding up the mountain, someone was speaking to someone else on a cellular phone. A friend of mine was skiing with a handheld pager that gave him a running account of both the Dow Jones Industrial Average and his own stock portfolio. He checked it between runs down the mountain. While I was sending several draft chapters of this book at a Federal Express satellite office, for delivery half a country away by 10:30 a.m. the next day, I ran into NBA Commissioner David Stern walking down the street with a cell phone to his ear, negotiating an end to the NBA lockout. At the end of my day of skiing I would go home and check out one of the forty channels on the local cable television, telephone friends in Cairo and Jerusalem using my AT&T

credit card or use my AOL 800 number to check on the news wires and any
E-mail I might have received. At dinner on New Year's Eve, I was getting
my coat at our restaurant and the following conversation was going on at
the front desk between an angry customer and the maître d': "What do you
mean you didn't get my reservation? I sent it to you by E-mail weeks ago!
The name is Ashraf, A-s-h-r-a-f." Before going to bed I picked up a copy of
USA Today and it carried the picture shown in chapter 3 of a Hasidic Jew
pressing his cell phone up against the stones of the Wailing Wall. Remember the caption: "Shimon Biton places his cellular phone up to the Western
Wall so a relative in France can say a prayer at the holy site."

All this, *while I was on vacation in the mountains!*

Imagine what it's like when we're home or at the office. We are all just
so much more connected now. Every day more and more people know,
or can know, everything that happens around the globe instantaneously.
And in such a world, it takes smaller and smaller amounts of dynamite or
germ weapons or highly enriched uranium to create anxiety and havoc
that can touch billions of people all at once. Globalization also gives terrorists more bang for their buck in another way. When microchips and
miniaturization make things smaller and lighter, *everything* becomes
smaller and lighter. Sam Cohen, the inventor of the neutron bomb, observed in *The Washington Times* (June 7, 1998) that within ten years after
the first plutonium fission test at Alamogordo, U.S. bomb designers were
able to reduce warhead weight, for the same yield—20 kilotons—by a factor of approximately 100. The United States has developed a warhead for
the NATO battlefield that is launched by two men carrying a bazooka,
with a yield below one-tenth of a kiloton. So have the Russians. We found
that out when Russia's former national security adviser, Alexander Lebed,
claimed that 100 mini–nuclear weapons, known as "suitcase bombs,"
were missing from the armory of Russian special forces. That is why Geoff
Baehr, chief of network designs for Sun Microsystems, remarked to me
once: "My biggest worry, and it cannot be overstated, is that this entire infrastructure is very vulnerable to attack, not just from a computer hacker,
but from someone getting into the telephone switches. In this world the
attacker can go to the telephone front, go home and have a sandwich,
and come back and attack again."

When you combine the angry men that Americanization-globalization creates with the way in which globalization can super-

empower people, you have what I believe is the real, immediate national security threat to the United States in the twenty-first century: the Super-Empowered Angry Man. That's right, it's not another superpower that threatens America at the end of the twentieth century. The greatest danger that the United States faces today is from Super-empowered individuals who hate America more than ever because of globalization and who can do something about it on their own, more than ever, thanks to globalization.

In the Cold War system, a Super-Empowered Angry Man—a Stalin, for example—needed to take control of a state in order to wreak havoc on the world. But today's Super-Empowered Angry Man, or Woman, can use the powers embedded in globalization to attack even a superpower. It was said of the far-flung Roman Empire that all roads led to Rome—north, south, east and west. And it was through that road system that Caesar extended his writ far and wide. And they were great roads. But there is a funny thing about roads. They go both ways, and when the Vandals and the Visigoths decided to attack Rome they came right up the roads. So it could be with globalization.

The Super-Empowered Angry Men come in many different forms. They range from the very angry but less violent to the very angry and somewhat violent to the very angry and very violent. A good example of the angry but less violent are the computer hackers who attacked my own newspaper, *The New York Times*, a pillar of the American establishment. On September 13, 1998, these hackers broke into the *Times's* Web site, the first time hackers have ever broken into the Web site of a major news organization. Martin Nisenholtz, president of the New York Times Electronic Media Company, told me the story: "We had just put out the Kenneth Starr report on Clinton on a Friday and it was a great day for our Web site. We had the only fully indexed version of the Starr report online, so you could just hit keywords and find what you wanted, and we were breaking all kinds of records for usage. I was so comfortable with where we were that I had accepted an invitation to go to Philadelphia to speak at the Wharton International Forum. So Saturday night I went down to Philadelphia. On Sunday morning at 7:45, I got a call from our Web site editor that we had been hacked. It had happened once before when some group had tried to flood our servers with requests. But this was different. They had actually taken over our Web site and were publishing their own message on our home page under the logo HFG, 'Hacking for Girlies.' They had superimposed a picture of a naked woman onto the body of this

HFG logo. So we retook the site and published on top of them, and then they came back and retook the site, and published again on top of us. So we came back again and retook the site, and then they came back and retook it back. For two hours we had dueling home pages on our own Web site! They had broken into our system and had taken over our servers—which is where the Web pages are stored—and they had managed to establish access to our Web site. Once they were in there, they had the same access that we did to managing the New York Times Web site. We kept asking ourselves, should we bring the site down, and I said no. But finally, it became apparent that we had to. So at 10:20 a.m., we brought down the site and closed off all the hatches [the remote off-site entry points]. The way they got in was by exploiting a bug in the Unix operating system. We took out the servers that were hacked and rebuilt the site on virgin servers, unconnected to any remotes."

What I found most interesting were the messages that the hackers posted on the Times's Web page. The opening message was: "WE OWN YER DUMB ASS." Parts of their messages were in code, a sort of high-tech olive-tree language of their own. Hacking for Girlies was spelled H4CK1NG F0R G1RL3Z. Certain vowels were numbers, as in their closing message: "R3ST ASSUR3D, W3 WILL B3 BACK SOON."

The hackers were clearly taking pleasure, almost like Jesse James, in demonstrating that they were smarter than the global power structure, as represented by The New York Times and its Web site. Their message was that you may be rich but you cannot compete with the brains of the Internet underground, even though it has much less power. They seemed to be saying that their brains were the equalizer. At one point the hackers wrote: "Just because we type in all caps and don't use 'elite' speak doesn't mean we are kids, or we don't own your dumb ass. For everyone who calls us immature kids, it shows one more person has underestimated us. And worse, what does it say about [your] security? That 'immature kids' were able to bypass [your] 25,000 dollar firewalls, bypass the security put there by admins with XX years of experience or a XXX degree from some college. Nyah nyah."

The hackers' only demand was for the release of Kevin D. Mitnick, the notorious computer hacker who has been in prison since his arrest by the FBI in February 1995. Mitnick, once the most wanted computer hacker in the world, was accused of a long crime spree that included the theft of thousands of data files and at least 20,000 credit card numbers from computer systems around the nation. Operating through a computer modem attached to his cellular phone, Mitnick was captured after he penetrated the home computer of a renowned computer security expert, Tsutomi Shimomura, a researcher at the San Diego Supercomputer Center. Shimomura helped a posse of telephone company technicians and federal investigators use cellular-frequency scanners to hunt down and arrest Mitnick.

These hackers are basically Internet fundamentalists. They have their own tribal customs, their own folk heroes, their own language, their own conspiracy theories and their own source of truth. But they have no coherent political ideology in the sense of a real alternative system. They are true Harpos. They have an attitude, not an ideology. They just want to bring low the power structure that now exists. They want to demonstrate that the system doesn't control them, but that they can control the system.

Moving up the scale, though, you find those who are a little more angry and a little more violent. Like the Super-empowered angry Tamil separatists who attacked the Sri Lankan embassy in Washington in September 1998. *The Washington Times* told the story: "When the Sri Lankan Embassy developed an E-mail address, the Tamil Tiger guerrillas found a new application for terrorism. They immediately began flooding the embassy with bomb threats and so much 'spam'—junk E-mail—that diplomats could not use the address for legitimate business. One diplomat called it 'E-mail terrorism.' " The story noted that the Sri Lankan embassy last year finally turned to a computer expert to develop a new program to filter out E-mail from the Liberation Tigers of Tamil Eelam (LTTE). The Tigers' tactic was mentioned as a new threat in the State Department's report on global terrorism. It stated that a group calling itself the Internet Black Tigers had previously struck in August 1997 with E-mail "weapons" that had decommissioned the embassies' electronic-mail systems. "The group claimed in Internet postings to be an elite department of the LTTE, specializing in 'suicide E-mail bombings,' " the State Department said. The group used what it called "E-mail-to-FTP anti-server missiles" that overload a targeted E-mail address and cause such disruption in terms of volume that the recipient is forced to scrap his entire E-mail site.

Finally, there are the really angry and really violent Super-Empowered Angry Men who don't use just E-mail. These are Harpos with real guns. They sense that there is a world-ruling system that they are not, and never will be, part of. In their view, the United States, IBM, *The New York Times*, Wall Street and the global economy are all part of one power edifice that needs to be brought down. These violent Super-Empowered Angry Men include the Aum Shinrikyo (Supreme Truth) sect in Japan, the Osama bin Laden gang in Afghanistan, the Unabomber and the Ramzi Yousef group in New York. Aum Shinrikyo preached a crazy cocktail of Hinduism, Buddhism and various worldwide conspiracy theories involving America, Jews, Freemasons and global capitalists. The Japanese sect killed twelve people and injured several thousand in March 1995 when it released sarin nerve gas in the Tokyo subway. According to *The Economist*, though, Aum Shinrikyo had amassed roughly a billion dollars in assets and had actually purchased an advanced Russian helicopter equipped to spray deadly chemicals. Osama bin Laden, the Saudi millionaire who in August 1998 bankrolled the bombings of the American embassies in Kenya and Tanzania, killing more than 200 people, communicated regularly around the world with satellite phones through his own Jihad Online (JOL). *The New York Times* reported that the FBI downloaded a captured personal computer from one of Bin Laden's operatives in Kenya, Haroun Fazil, and found an E-mail message inside in which he detailed how he kept tabs on global events through CNN, used the Internet to communicate with others in the Bin Laden underground network and referred to himself as "the media information officer of the East Africa cell."

Ramzi Yousef was the mastermind of the February 26, 1993, World Trade Center bombing in New York, which killed six people and injured more than a thousand. He came from a generation of angry young men from the Third World who have been longing for their chance to do what their parents could not do. That is, to turn their rage against the West, in revenge for all the turmoil it has visited on their societies, but to do it by using Western technology while rejecting the Western value structure behind it. They love the idea that you can just cream off the technological know-how, charge it on your Visa card and still live a fundamentalist lifestyle with the windows closed and a veil on. Where the Internet fundamentalists were only ready to use a mouse and a Unix bug to make their points, Ramzi Yousef & Co. were ready to use dynamite and a Ryder truck. But they basically had the same objective—to spit in the face of Americanization-globalization and stomp on it, by using the system against itself.

Ramzi Yousef is really the quintessential Super-Empowered Angry

Man. Think about him for a minute. What was his program? What was his ideology? After all, he tried to blow up two of the tallest buildings in America. Did he want a Palestinian state in Brooklyn? Did he want an Islamic Republic in New Jersey? No. He just wanted to blow up two of the tallest buildings in America. He told the Federal District Court in Manhattan that his goal was to set off an explosion that would cause one World Trade Center tower to fall onto the other and kill 250,000 civilians. Ramzi Yousef's message was that he had no message, other than to rip up the message coming from the all-powerful America to his society. *The Economist* once noted that "it used to be said of terrorists that 'they wanted a lot of people watching and not a lot of people dead.'" But not the Super-Empowered Angry Men. They want a lot of people dead. They are not trying to change the world. They know that they can't, so they just want to destroy as much as they can.

My favorite part of the Ramzi Yousef story, though, was the fact that one of his coconspirators, Mohammed Salameh, went back—after the World Trade Center explosion—to the Ryder truck rental agency where he rented the van that was used in the bombing. Salameh had put down a $400 deposit to rent the van and he wanted to get his deposit back—even though he had blown up the van. (He told the rental people the van had been stolen.) For Salameh the world was two different realms. In the morning you blow up the World Trade Center to kill as many Americans as you can for the sake of good over evil; in the afternoon you try to get your money back on the basis of American legal principles and contract law. Nothing better captures the ability of the Super-Empowered Angry Men to exploit the technology of the modern world without imbibing any of its values. When Ramzi Yousef was asked by investigators how in the world Salameh could have gone back to get the deposit—which helped police track down the bombers—he answered in one word: "Stupid." Indeed, Salameh helped lead the FBI to Ramzi Yousef. Police eventually tracked him to the Philippines, broke into an apartment he was using there and found all his latest plots on the C-drive of his off-white Toshiba laptop computer, which Philippine police said Yousef abandoned as he fled his Manila apartment in January 1995, shortly before his apprehension. A big part of the U.S. government's conspiracy case against Ramzi Yousef (besides trying to blow up the World Trade Center in 1993, he planned to blow up a dozen American airliners in Asia in January 1995) relied on the files found on his laptop, which contained flight schedules, projected detonation times and sample identification documents bearing photographs of some of his coconspirators. Ramzi Yousef was truly the Super-Empowered Angry Man—a detonator in one hand and a hard-drive in the other.

What is interesting about Ramzi Yousef and the other Super-Empowered Angry Men coming out of the Arab Islamic world today, notes Middle East expert Stephen P. Cohen, is that "they used to believe that they had to overthrow their own governments and get control of their own states before they could take on America. Now they just do it directly on their own as individuals." Globalization not only makes it possible for them to attack the United States as individuals, it not only gives them the motivation to do it, it also gives them the logic. The logic is that their own states don't represent the real power structure anymore. The relevant power structure is global. It is in the hands of the American superpower and the Supermarkets and they are the ones who tell all other governments what to do. Therefore if you want to bring down the real power structure you have to go after the superpower and the Supermarkets and not bother with the government of Pakistan or Egypt.

What bothers these Super-Empowered Angry Men is not only the notion that the United States is so technologically superior but that it makes a claim that its values are superior as well, when, in the view of the terrorists, these American values are nothing more than soulless consumerism and mindless technology worship. The following exchange took place at the close of Ramzi Yousef's trial, between him and the trial judge, Kevin Thomas Duffy. It is the Super-Empowered Angry Man versus the superpower.

Ramzi Yousef: "You keep talking about collective punishment and killing innocent people . . . You were the first one who killed innocent people, and you are the first one who introduced this type of terrorism to the history of mankind when you dropped an atomic bomb which killed tens of thousands of women and children in Japan and when you killed over 100,000 people, most of them civilians, in Tokyo with firebombings. You killed them by burning them to death. And you killed civilians in Vietnam with chemicals, as with the so-called Orange agent. You killed civilians and innocent people, not soldiers, in every single war you went to. You went to war more than any other country in this century, and then you have the nerve to talk about killing innocent people. And now you have invented new ways to kill innocent people. You have so-called economic embargo, which kills nobody other than children and elderly people, and which, other than Iraq, you have been placing the economic embargo on Cuba and other countries for over thirty-five years. The government in its summations and opening statement said that I was a 'terrorist.' Yes, I am a terrorist and I am proud of it. And I support terrorism so long as it was against the United States government and against Israel, because you are more than terrorists; you are the one who invented terrorism and [are] using it every day. You are butchers, liars and hypocrites."

Judge Kevin Thomas Duffy then replied—effectively telling Yousef to take his nihilistic rage and shove it: "Ramzi Yousef, you claim to be an Islamic militant. Of all the persons killed or harmed in some way by the World Trade Center bomb, you cannot name one who was against you or your cause. You did not care, just so long as you left dead bodies and people hurt. Ramzi Yousef, you are not fit to uphold Islam. Your God is death. Your God is not Allah . . . You weren't seeking conversions. The only thing you wanted to do was to cause death. Your God is not Allah. You worship death and destruction. What you do, you do not for Allah; you do it only to satisfy your own twisted sense of ego. You would have others believe that you are a soldier, but the attacks on civilization for which you stand convicted here were sneak attacks which sought to kill and maim totally innocent people . . . You, Ramzi Yousef, came to this country pretending to be an Islamic fundamentalist, but you cared little or nothing for Islam or the faith of the Muslims. Rather, you adored not Allah, but the evil that you yourself have become. And I must say that as an apostle of evil, you have been most effective."

Is there any defense against such people? It would be nice to believe that with the right sort of social and economic or cultural programs, societies could eliminate the motivation, the resentment and the rage of all those who feel steamrolled by Americanization-globalization. But we cannot. People like Ramzi Yousef have a very high degree of motivation or depravity. Feeling their pain will not turn them around, and neither will social work. There will always be a hard core of Ramzi Yousefs. The only defense is to isolate that hard core from the much larger society around them. The only way to do that is by making sure that as much of that society as possible has a stake in the globalization system. How one does that is one of the themes of the last chapter of this book.

One should have no illusions, though. The Super-Empowered Angry Men are out there, and they present the most immediate threat today to the United States and the stability of this new system. It's not because Ramzi Yousef can ever be a superpower. No, no, no. It's because in today's world so many people can be Ramzi Yousef.

19

If You Want to Speak to a Human Being, Press 1

I f there is a common denominator that runs through this book it is the notion that *globalization is everything and its opposite*. It can be incredibly empowering and incredibly coercive. It can democratize opportunity and democratize panic. It makes the whales bigger and the minnows stronger. It leaves you behind faster and faster, and it catches up to you faster and faster. While it is homogenizing cultures, it is also enabling people to share their unique individuality farther and wider. It makes us want to chase after the Lexus more intensely than ever and cling to our olive trees more tightly than ever. It enables us to reach into the world as never before and it enables the world to reach into each of us as never before.

As I have tried to demonstrate, since the onset of globalization as an international system, different countries and communities have seesawed between being attracted to its benefits and repelled by its negatives. Up to now, in the ebb and flow between globalization and the backlash against it, globalization has consistently come out on top in every major country that has plugged into the system. In no major country has the backlash against globalization managed to take power and in no major country has the backlash against globalization become so popular that this country would be willing to undermine the whole system—the way the Austro-Hungarian Empire did before World War I or Germany and Japan did before World War II.

Will it always be thus? Is globalization irreversible? My sense is that it is "almost" irreversible. Why do I say "almost" irreversible and not just plain old irreversible? Globalization is very difficult to reverse because it is driven both by enormously powerful human aspirations for higher standards of living and by enormously powerful technologies which are integrating us more and more every day, whether we like it or not. Theoretically, these aspirations and these technologies can be choked off, but only at a huge price to a society's development and only by building ever higher and ever thicker walls. I don't think that is likely to happen around the world, but it's possible. It is possible if the system gets so out of whack that not only disadvantaged minorities feel abused by it but also big majorities, in big countries.

And how could that happen? It could happen because the biggest threat to globalization today is globalization. That is, the system contains within it the potential for its own destruction. It contains within it traits and tendencies that, if allowed to run riot, could become so oppressive that large majorities in a large number of countries would start to feel like losers, and therefore rebel against the system or try to erect new walls. What follows are the most important reasons why that could occur.

Just Too Hard

When visiting Bangkok during the 1997 Thai economic turmoil, I was talking with an American diplomat there about what this setback meant for Thailand. Specifically we talked about all the things that Thailand was going to have to do in a very short period of time to get its software and operating systems up to speed to thrive in the globalization game. The diplomat ticked off a whole laundry list for me, and when he got done I said to him: "You know, we're asking Thailand to do in twenty years what it took the United States two hundred years to do."

"No, no," he said to me, shaking his head. I had it all wrong. "We're not asking them to do it in twenty years . . . We're asking them to do it in one year!"

It is now obvious that a country's power and status in the era of globalization is going to be a function, in part, of how much it is able and willing to develop the right software and operating systems needed to thrive. But what if the process of developing these institutions, liberalizing markets and putting on the Golden Straitjacket proves to be just too hard for too many big countries? While politicians and their followers will put up with a lot of pain and austerity in order to get to Disney World, there are limits. As Henry Kissinger once put it, political leaders "cannot survive as advocates of near-permanent austerity on the basis of directives imposed from abroad." Building software can take a long time, shaping your country into the right kind of plug to interact with the Electronic Herd can take a long time, and some countries may not be up to this task politically and economically—at least not in the time frame that the herd seems to demand. Others may not be up to it culturally. Cultures change slowly. It is a lot easier to develop a new-model Lexus than it is to evolve a new variety of olive trees, which can take generations.

If one dates today's globalization system from the fall of the Berlin Wall, then we could say the system is about to enter its second decade. What we have seen in the first decade of the globalization system is what happens when some small countries—Bosnia, Albania, Algeria, Serbia, Syria and many African states—are unable to make the transition. But these states are weak enough and small enough that the system just builds a firewall around them.

As we enter the second decade, though, we are encountering a much more serious question: What if some very large states, such as Russia, China and Japan—not to mention Indonesia, Brazil or even some members of the European Monetary Union—fail to make the transition? What if they find it too painful to put on the Golden Straitjacket, or their societies just can't make the cultural, political and economic shift to a more brutal, in-your-face, Schumpeterian capitalism, where you shoot the failed companies and don't keep them on respirators for years on end. The three democratizations may have made the collapse of the Soviet Union and China's communist-era economy inevitable. They may have made the collapse of Albania's or Indonesia's corrupt regimes inevitable. They may have made the collapse of Japan's rigged and overly protected economic system inevitable. But this doesn't mean their success at the new globalization system is inevitable.

Let's look at the three most important of these countries—Russia, China and Japan—today. What do you see when you examine them closely? What I see are three big, powerful nation-states, which on the outside look like 280-pound wrestlers, rippling with muscles, but on the inside each of them is suffering from congestive heart disease. Their hearts—that is, their operating systems and software, which are responsible for pumping blood to their industrial muscles—are clogged up and pump too much blood to their feet and not enough to their head and other areas. Russia needs a total transplant. China needs a quintuple bypass. And Japan needs some radical cholesterol-lowering drug treatment.

(France, Germany and some other countries of Western Europe don't need quite such radical treatments, but they will need to go on serious no-fat diets, if they are going to fit into their own version of the Golden Strait-jacket—the European Monetary Union. That diet is going to be painful at times, and will require some real lifestyle changes, which is why the European Monetary Union and single currency is going to be a lot harder to sustain politically than many people realize.)

I grew up in an age when the biggest external threats to America were the military strength of Russia and China and the economic strength of Japan. I suspect my girls, now ages twelve and fifteen, will grow up in a world where the biggest threats to America will come from the military *weakness* of Russia and China and the economic *weakness* of Japan. Adjusting to this new system is going to be extremely difficult for all three. To be sure, these countries are different, and the challenges they face are different, but not as different as you might think.

Japan

Here's a little secret: Japan's economy was always a lot more communist than capitalist. Walt Mossberg, the technology columnist of *The Wall Street Journal*, liked to say, "Japan was the world's most successful Communist country." In fact, it was the only country in which communism actually worked. Really. Throughout the Cold War, Japan was dominated by a single party, the Liberal Democratic Party. While Japan was ruled by the LDP, the state was run by a nomenklatura, an elite bureaucracy, just as Russia and China were. These elite bureaucrats often determined where resources should be allocated. The media in Japan were incredibly docile and, while not formally controlled by the government, were essentially guided by it. Japan had a deeply conforming population, with huge costs inflicted on those who did not conform. Nonconformists were not sent to Gulags but rather to their own internal Siberia. In Japan the nonconformists were labeled the "Madogiwazoku," which is translated as "the looking-out-the-window crowd," because they were often given desks that faced out the window and were basically shunned. This conforming population was ready to accept long working hours in return for a rising standard of living, lifetime employment contracts and a certain stability of life. Japan had a forced savings program in which the population, and corporations, were compelled to save and invest and not consume. If Soviet communism had worked half as well as Japan's version, Moscow never would have lost the Cold War.

Obviously this is a little tongue-in-cheek. Japan's economy also had a free-market element. A third of the Japanese economy today is made up of cutting-edge, globally competitive corporations, such as Sony, Mitsubishi, Canon and Lexus. These are among the best companies in the world and they have generated huge savings for Japan. Those savings have protected the other two-thirds of the Japanese economy—the communist segment, which is made up of bloated, sclerotic, dinosaur firms that have survived for years thanks to protectionist barriers erected by Japan's one-party state. Japan has built up so much savings from the Cold War that it has gotten through the first decade of globalization without sinking—even though its economic growth has been virtually stagnant since 1992. Korea, by contrast, modeled itself after Japan, but did not have the stockpiled savings that Japan had when all the walls came tumbling down. So Korea has had to adjust painfully, brutally and on short notice.

Eventually, if Japan is to avoid permanent stagnation, the communist segment of the Japanese economy is going to have to be "privatized" just like China's and Russia's. Inefficient firms and banks are going to have to be taken out and shot and their dead capital transferred to more efficient firms. This is already causing enormous social turmoil inside Japan.

America is a society where there is a close match between its cultural norms—flexibility and transparency—and the norms of business most valued by the globalization system, flexibility and transparency. Japan does not have that match. It has a culture of secrecy and opacity and a system renowned for rigidity. The greater the discrepancy between a country's cultural norms and the norms of the globalization system, the more painful is the process of adapting to it. In the Muslim world, pious women will bring down a personal veil over their face to keep the world at bay. Japan is a whole country wearing a veil. It's very sheer and sometimes hard to see, but it's there, and it keeps a lot more of the world out than the casual visitor realizes.

Nevertheless, Japanese history also teaches us that Japan is capable of change and adaptation to new systems, but only after it reaches a crisis point that really forces the country's hand. I have no doubt that Japan will be a formidable economic power again, but only after it goes through some wrenching social, political and cultural adjustments. Just take one little Japanese tradition: The corporate boards of virtually every public company in Japan today—except the most cutting-edge, Americanized firms, such as Sony—are made up of retired and current executives of that company, and shareholders have virtually no voice. Independent, outside board members are largely nonexistent in Japan. There is no way that such an inbred system can possibly drive change and do creative destruction at the speed that is going to be required in the coming decade. It will have to change, and already is—painfully.

When I visited Tokyo in early 1999, a friend of mine at the Japanese Foreign Ministry began our conversation as follows: "My son informed [my wife and I] the other day that he wants to be a fund manager, but he doesn't want to work for a Japanese bank. He wants to be with an international bank. The Japanese institutions that young people of my generation would automatically like to join, like the major banks, are crumbling. That is new. My wife couldn't understand my son. So he said to her, 'If you want to understand what I want to do, watch this film.' He gave her a video of the movie *Other People's Money*, about a New York financier who takes over a dying company in New England [and revitalizes it]. My wife is still worried."

Another Japanese friend who works in executive recruiting informed me that she always had a hard time recruiting Japanese to work for American companies because these American firms, unlike Japanese ones, were known in Japan as practicing "the three Ks—*kitsui*, the Japanese word for 'very demanding,' *kaiko*, Japanese for 'firing people' when they did not perform, and *kyoso*, Japanese for 'competition.'" But times are a-changing in Japan, and so are the Japanese. My friend told me she now tells her clients: "Even if you think you are signing up for life with a Japanese company today, you could wake up in the morning and find yourself working for a foreign-owned company very soon, so you might as well join one now and learn to adapt to it."

China

China, too, will have a difficult adjustment—not for cultural reasons but for political ones. China has the will, it just doesn't have the way. The biggest mistake some strategists make is thinking that China is going to grow economically and militarily on a straight line from where it is now to a point twenty years from now, when it will supposedly rival the United States and become an equal superpower. I think not.

Don't get me wrong. In twenty years China may be an economic and military powerhouse capable of rivaling the United States—but it is not going to get there in a straight line. There is a huge speed bump on the road that it will have to get over first. Some 40 percent of the Chinese economy in January 2000 was still made up of state-owned industries and banks, many of them bankrupt or unproductive. The only way that China can take care of the millions of Chinese who work for these firms is by privatizing them, closing and merging the weak ones, and directing capital to the efficient and profitable ones. And the only way China can do this without massive unemployment is with a massive influx of foreign investment.

Sure, China has attracted a high degree of direct foreign investment in fixed factories, but its currency is not fully convertible and it does not have a stock or bond market in which foreigners can freely play. And China has crony capitalism in spades, which is beginning to repel many foreign investors. Moreover, the Communist Party in China basically runs a series of businesses and corrupt rackets to keep itself well funded and well entrenched. Just one example of this massive official corruption in China was spotlighted in October 1998 by a report on Chinese state grain purchases, which revealed that of the $65 billion set aside to buy grain from farmers since 1992, $25 billion, or nearly 40 percent, had "disappeared." According to *Time* magazine (Nov. 2, 1998), investigators found that much of the missing money had gone into luxury condominiums, futures trading and purchases of cars and mobile phones by government officials. China's dilemma is that it cannot attract enough capital from the Electronic Herd to transform the bankrupt state-owned half of China's economy without upgrading its whole operating system from DOScapital 1.0 to 6.0 and without instituting real rule-of-law software. And that is going to clash, head-on, with the habits and interests of China's corrupt ruling party.

This is why you cannot draw a straight line from where China is today to where it wants to be in twenty years and assume that it's just going to become a richer and richer authoritarian system with the Chinese Communist Party ruling just as it does today. That is nonsense. Sooner or later China will bump up against its self-imposed limits—the limits that come from continued adherence to communist ideology in many sectors and from the state's obsession with political control. When that happens, either China won't get richer or it won't be as authoritarian as it is now, but something will give, because what the Chinese government can get away with now is very different from what it will be able to get away with once it is fully integrated into the herd. Those who think otherwise make the mistake of listening too much to China's leaders and not looking at them, or the enormous challenges China will face, within the context of the globalization system. China's transition is not going to be pretty. When 1.2 billion people going eighty miles an hour hit a speed bump the whole world will bounce. It's when China hits this speed bump that it will pose its most serious threat to world stability—again, not out of strength but out of weakness. Because once it fully abandons communist ideology, and simultaneously confronts the full, wrenching force of adjusting to the globalization system, which means opening up economically and politically, the only ideology that the regime will be able to fall back on to hold the country together, to legitimate its rule and to divert the nation's attentions, is China's old and gnarled olive tree—its nationalism. A nationalistic China that finds the new globalization system "just too damn hard" could pose a real threat to the stability of the system.

Russia

The same is true for Russia but even more so, since it is starting from so much lower a base than China or Japan.

To be sure, Russia remains a heavily armed country, with nuclear weapons. But now that it is integrated into the globalization system, it is Russia's weakness, not its strength, that poses the immediate threat to world stability, and will for some time. When Russia's economy melted down in August 1998, it set off a financial contagion that did more damage to Western financial institutions in one month than seventy years of Russian communism. Some politicians and foreign policy analysts, though, have fallen so in love with the Cold War that they simply cannot see Russia today as anything other than the Soviet Union and today's international system as anything other than the Cold War. It is amazing to think that Nazi Germany, which launched a war against the world and exterminated six million Jews, has been transformed in two generations into a thriving democracy that is now accepted as one of the most vibrant in the world. But Cold Warriors still treat Russia as a country incapable of change and congenitally fated to be America's geopolitical foe— forever.

No, we shouldn't treat Russia today like Canada, just because it had a few elections. It is a big country, with a big history, and major stockpiles of nuclear arms, and it will continue to compete with America for influence, like any other big power. But this is also true of France. Russia is not the Soviet Union anymore. It is a nation in the midst of an uncertain transition that is taking place in the context of a very different international system. Russia may not be able to make the transition to DOScapital 1.0, let alone 6.0, but it is not preordained that it won't be able to. As with China and Japan, we have an enormous stake in the Russian transition—which we cannot determine, but can affect. We do not have it in our power alone to make Russia a better place, but we do have it in our power to make it a less dangerous, angry and isolated place. This is why NATO expansion was such a mistake. In the globalization system the most threatening problems for the United States are black-market sales of nuclear warheads, strategic nuclear missile reduction, environmental degradation, containing rogues such as Iraq or North Korea, and financial viruses. None of these issues can be addressed effectively by America without the cooperation of a reasonably stable and democratizing Russia. Therefore, enlisting Russia's cooperation, and doing whatever we can to advance political reform there, should be our first priority—not expanding NATO, which can only undermine cooperation with Moscow.

In early 1998, I was sitting in the Prague office of Czech Deputy Foreign Minister Karel Kovonda. In between his very eloquent explanations about why NATO should expand to the Czech Republic, he mused to me about how globalization was affecting his own neighborhood, and the Czech Republic generally.

"I relish the international atmosphere we have here now that the Cold War is over and the Czech Republic is open to the world," said Kovonda. "My baby goes to a nursery school with a little girl from Korea and kids from Croatia and Bosnia. I buy groceries now from China from my corner greengrocer. But the flip side is that I have some Ukrainian Mafia in the next building. All this in my little satellite city outside of Prague. And there is growing suspicion and discomfort here with the dramatic increase in foreigners now living in this country illegally, working in this country illegally, trading in this country illegally and doing business in this country illegally—either from out in the boondocks or right in Prague. You get both sides of globalization in the Czech Republic today, and as we are at the crossroads of Europe, we are the first stop for a lot of the East-to-West illegal migration, yet, on the other hand, our border with Germany [is now less open]. On my desk is a top-secret report on international organized crime and criminal activities in this country. In the old days under the communists a lot of this would never have been possible. When the communists were in power here, half the time you could not get a visa to come to this country and now you don't even need a visa. Smuggling nuclear parts and fissile material, this is the danger. We have had people caught smuggling fissile material from places east of us to places south of us. These are the kinds of dangers the population at large is not appreciative of . . ."

I just nodded my head, reluctant to ask where he thought all that dangerous fissile material was leaking from and how he intended to solve this problem while alienating Russia with NATO expansion.

In Russia, China and Japan you have leaders from the Cold War generation trying to manage the transition into the globalization era, and in many cases they simply don't have the tools. Although the Russians have eliminated central planning, communist ideology and the Commissars, they have not been able to so easily eliminate the culture of communism and substitute the culture of capitalism.

Indeed, in Russia, China and Japan we will have to wait for what Robert Hormats calls the "millennium generation"—those who are coming of age in the globalization system—to take power in these countries before there can be a sustained turnaround. Says Hormats: "Whenever people ask me, 'How in the world do you produce political change in Russia?' I always tell them it is a process that takes nine months and then twenty-one years. And Russia's in the middle of that process right now."

It's what happens in the meantime, while we wait for this new generation, that is worrisome. Earlier, I compared companies and countries, and there is a lot to that comparison. But there is one way in which countries will never be like companies. Companies can rise, fail, fall and disappear. Countries can rise, fail and fall—but they rarely disappear. Instead, they stick around as failed states. Imagine if IBM went bankrupt, but was still out in the marketplace, with all its unpaid salespeople and managers, selling computer parts on the black market, trying to cheat old customers and trying to prove their continued relevance by throwing wrenches into whatever their old competitors were doing.

One reason that the pre-1914 era of globalization collapsed into World War I was the fact that the Austro-Hungarian Empire, one of the principal players of the European balance-of-power system in that day, experienced a long, slow erosion of power that gained momentum between 1909 and 1914. The Austro-Hungarian Empire understood that it was falling out of the great-power race, economically, militarily and politically. Instead of suffering this humiliation quietly, it behaved like the gunslinger who finds himself in a poker game he can't win. He kicks over the table and starts shooting. In the case of the Austro-Hungarian Empire, it aligned itself with Germany to eliminate Serbia in a local war, knowing this would likely trigger a world war with Russia.

When Serbia, Albania and Algeria act up, it can be messy, but it won't threaten the system as a whole. But what we don't know is what happens if and when large states, like a Russia, a Japan or a China, fail at globalization but still have military power from the old system. As political scientist Robert A. Pastor observed in his book *A Century's Journey: How the Great Powers Shape the World*, the challenge faced by the globalization system, after the Cold War, was really very similar to the challenge faced by the Versailles system, after World War I: How do we integrate the losers into the winners' system? The peace of Versailles did a very poor job of integrating the losers and was resented by them—so much so that it sowed the seeds for World War II. The peace following World War II did a good job of integrating the biggest losers—Germany and Japan—and that helped to stabilize both Europe and Asia.

In the case of the post–Cold War world, the question is: How do we integrate the losers from the Cold War into a market-oriented globalization system composed of mostly democratic states? This is particularly difficult, notes Pastor, because the post–Cold War peace is different from the Versailles peace in that the victory of the Western allies was not unconditional in the Cold War. The West did not occupy Russia or China or Vietnam, and therefore its ability to influence and shape the internal politics of the Cold War losers was limited and greatly varied from country to country. Yet the system has a huge stake in the successful integration of countries such as Russia and China. The key ingredient for any stable international system, says Pastor, is that "the principal challengers believe they have more at stake in preserving the system than in toppling it." For now, that could still be said of Russia and China when it comes to the globalization system. But what if it turns out to be just too damn hard for them, or others? Will countries that can't make microchips make trouble instead?

This isn't just an issue for developing countries or the unskilled. It also applies to those *who can make microchips.* There is a sister issue to "just too hard" that increasingly comes up with people today, and that is the problem of "just too fast." The pace of change in this globalization system is now so fast, and the requirements for success so constantly evolving, that no one ever feels they are on solid ground in the way their parents at least seemed to feel in the world of walls, when a union card or a lifetime career with the same company seemed to guarantee stability in one's life. After the first edition of this book came out, I received a touching letter from a woman from Roanoke, Illinois, that eloquently expressed a concern I often hear from people, but for which I have no easy answer: What happens if the speed of change demanded by this new system is more than individuals, companies, or countries can handle? The letter read as follows:

> Dear Mr. Friedman, I hope this letter finds you and I hope you can solve a mystery for me. I have seen you on several talk shows and was impressed enough to buy your book. I have read the book several times but have not found the answer to my question: where do I fit in to today's market? My husband and I have always been self-employed without success. In 1984 I found my way into college where I hungrily ate every course I could afford, including computers, economics, stocks, business and accounting. The local economy was in deep recession, since what is bad for Caterpillar is bad for everyone. The work I found went nowhere and I finally retired. In the meantime, my husband had started selling home-grown computers and was making money for the first time. With the advent of computers under $1,000 his winning streak is coming to an end. We know all the essential elements of business, including the Internet and computers, but do not see our place in the global market. We know "how" to sell but we do not know "what" to sell. For example, I have all the tools to write the great American novel, but lack the talent . . . When the millionaires planted their seeds in the stock market we were broke. Where does the little guy fit into this great world market? We are not alone in this quandary. We have many friends sitting on the same fence, wondering what happened to us and where we should go next. Perhaps you could address this issue in your next personal appearance.

I wish I had a simple answer. It seems that a day doesn't go by anymore without some article in the newspaper warning workers and their bosses to downsize, learn new skills, cut old ties, Web-up, become faster, become more flexible, become more prepared to throw out the old and the new and bring in the even newer and get with the program. The only problem is the program seems to change every six months, and that is just too fast and too hard for many educated people, let alone the uneducated. How will people start to react if they find this system just too damn hard and too damn fast for too damn long?

Just Too Connected

Another way in which globalization can threaten globalization is when the system itself gets so greased, and wires the world so tightly together, that small groups of people—whether it be investors or Super-Empowered Angry Men—can threaten the whole edifice by their excesses. If you talk to Wall Street investment banks today they will tell you that the thing that absolutely took them by surprise in the market meltdown of August–September 1998 was how much more interconnected the system was than they realized. None of their risk models— which were based on past correlations between investments and certain events—had anticipated the sort of chain reactions that in 1998 made a mockery of the whole concept of diversification. Companies that thought they were diversified by investing in different financial instruments, with different maturities, in different currencies, in different markets, in different countries found out quickly that all their investments were part of one big interlinked chain from which they could not escape when markets started to nose-dive. One link in the chain pulled down the other. Thanks to globalization, this chain is becoming longer and longer, tighter and tighter every day, and the scary truth is we still don't fully understand what it means to be so interlinked or how to protect ourselves when one of those links weakens. This interconnectedness not only applies to financial markets but was also graphically on display with the Y2K bug, which was created when computers were built with internal clocks that, in order to save memory space, rendered dates with just six digits—two for the day, two for the month and, you guessed it, two for the year. That meant they only went up to 12/31/99. So when the calendar hit January 1, 2000, many older computers would register that not as 01/01/2000 but as 01/01/00, as though it was 1900 all over again. Fortunately, good advance preparations and purchases of new computers by countries and companies rendered the Y2K threat pretty harmless by the time the millennium rolled around. New Year's 2000, rather than being a global nightmare that

united us all in fear, turned into a global party that united us all in cele-
bration.

Now that we have survived Y2K, though, it doesn't mean that all our
overconnectedness problems are behind us. Think about another fact:
When a nuclear blast takes place high in the atmosphere, it sets off an
enormous electromagnetic charge. If some terrorist or rogue state were
to set off even a small blast in the skies over America it could freeze up
and melt down every computer in the country in a way that would make
Y2K look like a day at the beach. Tim Weiner, in his book *Blank Check*,
about secret U.S. government programs, explained the phenomenon:
"A warhead exploding 300 miles above Omaha would instantly zap the
United States from coast to coast with a tidal wave of charged electrons.
Every electronic system, every radio transmission, every computer bank
in the country would experience something like a lightning strike magnified a millionfold. An intense surge of up to 50,000 volts per meter
would flow through the circuitry that wires the entire nation. The phenomenon was discovered in 1962, when the U.S. exploded three nuclear weapons high over the Pacific. Although the tests took place 800
miles from Hawaii, street lights went off across Oahu and burglar
alarms went haywire in Honolulu." Unlike the Y2K problems, the effects of this electromagnetic pulse, says Weiner, remain what engineers
call a "known unknown"—a problem that is known to exist but has no
known solution.

There is one more way that being too connected could become problematic for us. That is if being connected—or rather overconnected—becomes socially unbearable. Sitting in my office one day in the summer of
1999 I came across the following item on the Associated Press wired out
of Israel. It said that an Israeli man "was pulled over Monday after a policewoman nabbed him driving through the coastal town of Netanya with
a mobile phone in each hand. Engrossed in his conversation, he was operating the steering wheel with his elbows, the daily *Haaretz* reported.
The volunteer policewoman flagged him down when she saw his gray
Mitsubishi meandering from side to side."

I can't think of anything that better illustrates the disease of overconnectedness than this story of an Israeli motorist, with a cell phone
pressed to both ears, driving his car with his elbows. This is the real, lasting Y2K virus for developed countries. It is the anxiety that is going to be
produced when telecommunications combines with the "Evernet"—the
technology that will allow people to get online from their watch, their cell

phone, their car, their toaster or their Walkman—so that everyone will be able to be connected all the time, everywhere.

This virus of overconnectedness is spreading daily and has no known cure. I was in a restaurant with my daughter one day in the summer of 1999, when I found myself seated between two families, both of whose fathers were speaking loudly into cell phones as if they were in their offices. I wanted to scream, "Look, I'm on vacation. I'm trying to get away from my office. I don't want to be in your office. I don't want to hear about your problems. *Turn off that phone!*" In October 1999, I was in Chicago at the bris, the Jewish ritual of circumcision, of my new nephew. Just before the mohel, a white-bearded rabbi, was about to perform the circumcision, a cell phone rang. We all looked around for who was interrupting this solemn ceremony, when the mohel sheepishly put down his scalpel and pulled a cell phone out of his pocket. More and more I find myself reacting to people with cell phones the same way I react to someone smoking a cigar at the dinner table next to me—with rage.

I can't wait for the day when they have soundproof cell-phone sections in restaurants. "Cell phone or no cell phone?" the hostess will ask before she seats you. I also can't wait for the day that Motorola comes out with a device that enables you to jam all the cell phones around you, as easily as opening your garage door. Zap! No more dial tones within fifty feet. So sorry! It is not surprising that overconnectedness is becoming the disease of the Internet age. Because as the Internet and globalization shrink both time and distance, it can be great for business, but it is becoming socially claustrophobic. *The New Yorker* once illustrated this point with a cartoon. It showed a man escorting his date back to her apartment door after dinner. She squeezes his hands and says, "I'd love to ask you in, Howard, but they start trading in Hong Kong in ten minutes." Time and distance provide buffers and breathing space in our lives, and when you eliminate both, you eliminate some very important cushions. Several rabbis have written me that they believe, and indeed hope, that overconnectedness will lead to Jews learning to appreciate the Sabbath more. The idea of a day of rest when you turn off all your cell phones and just disconnect could take on a whole new appeal.

A friend who works on Madison Avenue said to me that before cell phones and beepers, when someone called the office for him and he was out his secretary would simply say, "Allen is out." Now when someone calls, and the secretary says he's out, the next thing the caller says is, "Well, connect me to his cell phone or beep him wherever he is." The presumption now is that he is always reachable—that he's never out. Out is over. Now, you're always in. And when you're always in, you're always on. And when you're always on, you're just like a computer server. You can never stop and relax. When was the last time you heard someone say, "Well, let me sleep on that"? There is no time or space to sleep on anything anymore. A Wall Street exec remarked to me that he used to love going to Japan, working all day and then hitting the great Tokyo restaurants at night. But now, with better communications, he works all day, and just when he's about to hit the Tokyo sushi bars, the faxes, beeper messages and cell-phone calls start coming in from New York. "I haven't been out to dinner in Tokyo in five years now," he said. "I end up working a nineteen-hour day now whenever I'm there."

I was interviewing a senior British defense official one day when he mentioned that he had recently put his cell phone down on the X-ray machine conveyor belt at an airport, and then forgot to claim it on the other side. When he realized five minutes later that he didn't have his phone he rushed back and got it. The security officer at the X-ray machine told him he got two calls in those five minutes, both of which, he discovered later, were from other senior defense officials. "The guy could have started a war if he had said the wrong things," the British official quipped of the baggage inspector who had found his phone.

I forgot to ask the British official if he was working or on his way from a holiday when he forgot his phone, but, then again, he probably wouldn't have known the difference himself. When we are all connected all the time the boundary between work and play disappears. Working moms and dads can now be home more. That's good, in theory. But what it often means is that the workday becomes nineteen hours long. I have a friend who works in a high-stress, senior government legal job. He told me he often comes home early and on weekends with his cell phone and tries to work at home, in order to be with his teenage daughter. Even though it means that twenty minutes out of every two hours he is on the cell phone, he figures it is better than nothing. His daughter disagrees. She eventually got so upset with the interruptions that she finally said to him, "Dad, just stay at the office."

I'm with his daughter, though I have to confess to having been as guilty as her dad at times. And it's only the beginning. The Y2K computer problem was over after a few months. But the Y2K social disease is going to be with us for a long time. To be sure, there are many virtues to being connected—from wiring your neighborhood and getting to know your neighbors better to having more flexible work hours. It's all a question of balance. If the balance tips toward overconnectedness, if people really start feeling choked by this system, they will get violent.

Just Too Disconnected

One of the paradoxes of a world in which we are all increasingly connected is that it makes it that much easier for us all to become increasingly disconnected. Because the more we are all wired and networked together, the easier it becomes for each of us to work alone, at home, from our beach house, tree house or from remotest Africa. The more we are all networked, the more we can all be freelancers. A friend of mine works for a large consulting firm, and recently, after a globalization-driven merger, he basically lost his office. The firm went to a system of motel desking in which people share desks, and you have office space only when you need it. All the files have been centralized and put online, and you are expected to just download everything you need. On paper it is all much more efficient, but, as my friend remarked to me one day, it has made his job a lot less satisfying.

"I have been doing legal work for a big firm for some twenty years now," he related. "Now, I am not that old, but in the old days (the 1980s) if you had a problem that you were trying to solve, you would walk down the hall to the water cooler, if there was one, and you would say, 'I have this problem with this corporation. They want to spin off these assets in this way. There are some capital gains we need to recapture. How do you think we should go about it?' And one of your colleagues would tell you that a couple of years ago we did it this way, and then someone else would walk by and say, well, it wasn't exactly like that, it was more like this. And maybe one guy there—Bill—would be the resident expert, and he would give you his sage advice. But you would work it out, face to face, with your colleagues in an informal way. Well, now half of us don't even have offices. I don't even have a desk of my own anymore. We rotate desks now to save office space. There is no water cooler and there is no Bill just down the hall, because he's working at home, thanks to telecommuting. I am sure Bill has a better lifestyle now, because he can work at home. And a lot of the answers he might have are now in the computer somewhere, but you have to know how to find them. What you miss, though, is Bill saying, 'Yeah, you could solve the problem this way, according to the book, but you have to watch out for this.' It's all the little intangibles you can't get from a search engine. Sure, you could E-mail Bill at 'Bill.com' and he would tell you the answer, but it's still just not the same."

A few months after talking to my friend, I came across an ad for a business software company called Office.com, whose motto is: "More informative than a trip to the water cooler." Yeah, I thought, but probably nowhere near as satisfying.

And it is not going to get any better. It is no longer just baseball and basketball players who are supposed to become free agents—now everyone is expected to move from job to job, team to team or company to company. In the new parlance, we are all "E-lancers" now.

Why is this happening? Nicholas G. Carr, an editor at the *Harvard Business Review,* summarized it well when he wrote in the June 1999 issue: "The old industrial model of organization—big groups of people doing specialized coordination—made economic sense for most of this century [in a world of walls]. But it is making less and less sense today. It's too costly and too unwieldy. Letting work shuttle freely between small, temporary teams that can organize and coordinate themselves in response to market stimuli is much more efficient . . . In the face of the new economics, it makes sense for companies to pursue ever greater levels of flexibility. But does it make sense for human beings?"

Carr raised this question as part of his review of a provocative book by the sociologist Richard Sennett, about the downsides of this sort of flexibility and disconnectedness. The book was entitled *The Corrosion of Character: The Personal Consequences of Work in the New Capitalism.* As Carr noted in his review, to be flexible is to lack attachments. The flexible company must always be ready to abandon strategies, products, people and even customers in order to move into a more lucrative market or adopt a more efficient and profitable way of doing business, as happened with my friend at his consulting firm. But forming connections and communities, holding on to one's olive trees—just being able to decorate your own desk and call it your home away from home—is one of the most defining characteristics of human beings. Globalization, by creating a world in which we are constantly being asked to break such connections, reinvent ourselves, think in the short term and stay flexible, sets us all adrift and leaves everyone feeling like a temporary worker. Paraphrasing Sennett's argument, Carr said this leaves us all "uncertain of who we are or how we should act. In the aggregate, it erodes the foundations of society. We don't bond with others; we 'team' with them. We don't have friends; we have contacts. We're not members of enduring, nurturing communities; we're nodes in ever-shifting, coldly utilitarian networks . . . But every time we reinvent ourselves, we erase the meaning that our past experiences granted us. In place of an ethical sense of ourselves as people with clear attachments, we are left with an ironic sense of ourselves as fabrications. We become unreal, virtual."

What is maybe most scary about all this, Sennett himself notes in his book, is that it is the result of something we call "progress." He writes: "What is peculiar about uncertainty today is that it exists without any looming historical disaster; instead it is woven into the everyday practices of a vigorous capitalism. Instability is meant to be normal." Schumpeter's creatively destructive entrepreneur is "served up as an ideal everyman. Perhaps the corroding of character is the inevitable consequence."

It must be noted, of course, that the very rootless flexibility that Sennett decries, though unnerving at times, can also be liberating. And while there are now fewer walls to protect you in your current job, there are also fewer walls to keep you out of a new one. Moreover, the flexibility of this system means the penalty for failure is much lower. As Carr himself observes, "You may have messed up your last assignment, but there is a good chance that your next one will be better suited to your talents."

Will we each find a floor, a desk, a shop, a Web site, a home we can grasp on to long enough to sink roots for our olive trees, or are we destined now to be constantly riding the elevators up and down? How people will feel about globalization, and whether they will rebel against it, will depend in part on how this question is ultimately answered.

Just Too Intrusive

In the summer of 1999, I visited Chicago and stayed at a large chain hotel. In the morning I went down to swim in the pool, and I put my room key in my bathing suit pocket. I then proceeded to lose the key in the pool. So I went back to the front desk, dressed in my bathing suit, and asked for a new room key.

"Can you show me a picture ID?" asked the desk clerk.

"No," I said. "I'm in my bathing suit! I have no ID."

"No problem," said the clerk. She typed a few things into her computer, and then looked up at me and said, "What are the ages of your two daughters?"

My daughters weren't with me. But I had stayed in this hotel a year earlier with them. I correctly answered the clerk's question about their ages and she handed me a new key. But I was upset. I couldn't help wondering: What else do they have on me and my family in that little computer, and who are they selling that information to? A few months later, I got a letter from an old friend, Richard Day, whom I met in Beirut in 1982, but had lost contact with. Richard, a consultant, was living in Dubai and his letter said basically the following: I found your address on a People Search site on the Internet. I was amazed that for a mere $99 I could order a complete credit check on you that included, among other things, a complete listing of your assets. I kept my $99 but it made me wonder what all of this is really coming to. Your daughters and my sons can check each other out in ways that you and I never dreamed were possible.

And it's just the beginning. Rule #1 of the Internet age is that we are all connected but nobody is quite in charge. That is, the Internet is Orwellian in its reach, but there's no Big Brother. What there is instead of Big Brother is a lot of Little Brothers. Beware of the Little Brothers. What the Internet does is super-empower individuals, Web sites, corporations and hotels—the Little Brothers—so they can amass huge amounts of information outside of any government supervision. Some will use it responsibly; others not. A 1999 study by the Center for Democracy and Technology found that less than 10 percent of all Web sites respected the OECD's basic privacy guidelines, which stipulate that people have the right to expect that any personal data they submit over the Internet will not be used without their consent, that they have a right to correct any errors and they have the right to assume that any confidential data will be protected from abuse.

One of the positive aspects of globalization is that it promotes transparency in financial dealings. Both countries and companies that want to plug into the herd have to disclose things to the market that in the past they could keep hidden. But just as there is nowhere to hide for countries and companies, so there is increasingly nowhere to hide for individuals. Every phone call you make, every bill you charge, every prescription drug you buy, every video you rent, every plane ride you take, every cash machine you use, gets logged somewhere in a computer of the Electronic Herd, and you have no idea when it might come back to haunt you. Have an affair with the President of the United States and a Special Prosecutor might one day trace every phone call you made to him and every tie you bought for him on a credit card. Are you into visiting the porno Web site "Hot Sex"? Well, just remember this: when you visit many Web sites today they are set up so that you automatically pick up what is known as a "cookie." A cookie is an electronic fingerprint that is placed in your Internet browser by the various sites you visit. Cookies can indicate where you go, where you shop and what you do online. When someone, say an online retailer, piles up all the cookies in your cookie jar they can form a pretty good picture of your habits, preferences, likes and dislikes, and then push back at you all sorts of direct marketing baked particularly for you.

Not worried, you say? Think about this: In 1998 I saw a television commercial for something called Guard Dog—a software product that provides Internet security and encryption for your home computer and for your own Web site. The commercial shows someone peeping through the closed shutters of a window and then a voice-over says: "The Internet is your window on the world," but it can also be "a window on you." To prevent that, buy Guard Dog software; "it keeps the Web from surfing you." A few months later I saw an item on ABC News that explained exactly why you might want Guard Dog. It reported the following: A national poll in the summer of 1998 found that "81 percent of people believe their personal information, including credit ratings, medical histories and financial records, is insecure." The report added that states such as Texas are already putting their state criminal histories online. The Texas criminal-record database is searchable for $3.15 per name searched. An offshore company called PublicData, based in Anguilla, British West Indies, buys public records in bulk and puts them online in a database searchable for as little as 3 cents per search. PublicData offers a list of records, including criminal records, indexes to some counties' court records and voter registration polls, driver's license records and so on. It gets worse. In December 1998, USA Today reported that a popular handheld computer that is designed to store dates, addresses and reminder notes "can be programmed to pick car locks by copying codes from remote-control keys, its manufacturer confirmed. With added software, the $369 Palm III can intercept an infrared car-lock signal up to about 10 feet away."

How we deal with all the Little Brothers is going to become an important political issue. There are lots of ideas. One of the most thoughtful comes from Harvard law professor Lawrence Lessig, in his book *Code, and Other Laws of Cyberspace*. Lessig argues that people suffer from the illusion that however cyberspace is right now is how it must always be. It can't be changed. It's a place to be discovered, not shaped. But cyberspace was not handed down by God. Its architecture is shaped by people with certain interests, who are, as we speak, "designing the hardware of cyberspace in ways that are determining the freedom and privacy that you and I will have there," says Lessig. The architecture of cyberspace is highly influenced by commerce and government, "both of which have an interest in knowing as much as they can about what people are doing and where," says Lessing. "So it's not an accident that the emerging Internet architecture makes it easier to track people and collect private data, because tracking people is what governments like and collecting private data is what commerce likes."

Government, argues Lessig, can't legislate privacy on the Internet because it has no way to really enforce it there. But it can create incentives for people to build privacy filters and other safeguards into the Internet. "Let's say the government says that data about you is your property and the only way that someone can take it away is by negotiating with you," he said. "That would create an incentive for Web designers to make it easier for each of us to negotiate about our personal data—what we want to give up for free, what we want to be paid for and what we don't want to give up at all."

The right to privacy is a core value from our Constitution and Founding Fathers. Are we moving into an age when such values will only be respected on land, but not in cyberspace? Justice Louis Brandeis spoke often about the need to preserve each citizen's "right to be left alone." But as the Internet moves into the center of how we communicate, educate and do business it raises a potentially deeper problem: the right not just to be left alone, but the right to remain opaque—to not have every move you make in life recorded in a computer somewhere and available for downloading to anyone, anywhere for $39. That is where we are heading, as the amount of personal data being piled up on all of us by Little Brothers in both the government and the private sector grows by leaps and bounds. "Advances in computing are having a twin effect," noted *The Economist* (May 1, 1999). "They are not only making it possible to collect information that once went largely unrecorded, but are also making it relatively easy to store, analyze and retrieve this information in ways which, until quite recently, were impossible." And the smaller, faster, cheaper and more interconnected computers become, the stronger become all the Little Brothers. If the Constitution ends where the Web begins, if

people experience globalization as something tha
lives and privacy, much more than it empowers the
the world, if they feel that the Web is surfing them,
surfing the Web, they will eventually erect new walls.

Just Too Unfair for Too Many People

Julia Preston, the *New York Times* correspondent in Mexico City in the late 1990s, tells a wonderful story that captures the tension between the winners and losers from globalization in Mexico.

"It was May Day 1996," Preston recalled, "and there was a very big demonstration in Mexico City. It was the first year after the austerity program and so it was an exceptionally large march, including a large number of unions which had been part of the government-labor alignment and had defied orders against demonstrating. I was walking in the middle of the 'Union of University Employees,' which has a long history of left-wing activism, and they were a particularly noisy bunch. They were chanting 'Muera Ortiz'—death to Ortiz, the finance minister. They were loud and hostile. In the middle of this demonstration my mobile phone rings in my purse and it is the secretary of Minister Ortiz on the phone, telling me the finance minister wants to speak with me. I said it was too noisy for me to speak from where I was standing in the middle of the demonstration, and I walked out of the crowd over to a building to get some quiet, and also to give myself some time to prepare for speaking to Ortiz. So he gets on the phone and I said, 'Mr. Minister, I have to tell you there are a large number of people here who don't agree with your economic policies.' He sort of chuckled and it quickly became clear that he wasn't interested. He was calling me to announce and celebrate the fact that Mexico had just placed its first thirty-year bond. It was the first time since the [1995] peso crash they had placed a long-term bond on Wall Street, without any American backing, and it had been received very well. So there he was—high as a kite—and there I was talking to him on the phone from the middle of this demonstration where people were calling for his death."

Ortiz could survive such a day—and globalization can survive such a day—as long as enough people in Mexico feel they are deriving enough benefits from this system to tolerate it. They may take to the streets occasionally to denounce a policy or to make a labor demand, but those Mexn workers are not joining ranks with Subcommander Marcos and the Zapatista guerrillas in wanting to disconnect Mexico from the system. Not yet.

In large part this is because the Electronic Herd and the Supermarkets, while they hammered a country such as Mexico, have also been quick to reward improved performance—buying more from Mexico and investing more in Mexico, as soon as it got its economic house in order. The growth that this has produced is what has enabled the Ortizes of the world to shrug off the calls for their death and to say to the workers, "Just stick with me for a little longer and I promise you this will all turn around."

But what happens if you have a recession in the United States and Western Europe at the same time, and Japan continues in stagnation and is unable to pick up the slack? The Electronic Herd could get emaciated, and instead of being able to reward Mexico, Brazil or Korea by buying their bonds when they do the right thing—when they reform their economies and when they put on the Golden Straitjacket—would be unable to do much at all. Instead of America and Western Europe being able to suck in all the imports from the developing countries, so they can export their way back to life, the big developed countries could be tempted to put up new protectionist walls against more imports to preserve their own shrinking job markets. Will the system continue to hold then? We don't know, because in the first decade of globalization we really have never faced this scenario. But this is the real stress test for the globalization system—how it survives a recession at the core—and until we go through it we really won't know whether the process of globalization is irreversible or not.

Just Too Dehumanizing

I was driving along the Beltway in Washington one day when I heard a news story on WTOP radio that caught my ear. It reported with great fanfare that when you call a particular New York cable television company, it offers the following new option: "If you want to speak to a human being, press 1."

I always press 1. I will always press 1. In fact, whenever I get that message, "If you don't have a Touch-Tone phone stay on the line and an operator will assist you . . ." I always stay on the line and wait to speak to the operator, even though I have a Touch-Tone phone. Always being able to press 1 is essential for globalization's success, always being able to stay on the line to speak to an operator is essential for globalization's success. Because at some level you need to feel that this system is built for human beings, not machines; otherwise it becomes deeply alienating.

But what happens if pressing 1 is no longer an option? What happens if globalization becomes just too standardizing, too dehumanizing?

My brother-in-law, Ted Century, is an inventor of medical devices, with his own basement machine shop. Ted is a salt-of-the-earth kind of guy who makes incredibly sophisticated precision devices with his hands. As I talked to him one afternoon about advances in online trading, the Internet, satellite technology and the like, he nodded his head for a while and then finally said, "Yeah, but where does quality of life fit into all this stuff?"

Ted and my sister Jane then launched into a story that had really been bothering them. "Every year in the summer we go from our home in Philadelphia down to South Jersey to buy local produce, particularly Jersey beefsteak tomatoes," said Ted. "They are these big, juicy tomatoes bursting with flavor. There is something in the sandy soil of South Jersey, about the way it retains water, that is really good for growing tomatoes and sweet corn, and that's why Campbell's always got tomatoes for their tomato soup from the small farmers there. But the great thing about these tomatoes was that they didn't travel well, so no one tried to sell them to a global market. They also came in all different shapes and sizes, with these ugly cracks at the top. But they tasted incredible. We used to make a special trip to the farmers' markets in South Jersey and buy them by the pound. We'd bring them home and cut them up for salads and cook them into tomato sauce. We had friends who ate so many of them at once their lips would get sore from the acid. You forget that tomatoes are a fruit, but the South Jersey beefsteak tomatoes were so sweet they tasted like a fruit. Well, in the summer of 1997, when we went to make our annual tomato-buying trip we noticed that they were harder to come by. Then, in the summer of 1998, we went out there to the farmers' markets to buy some and they were gone. Just gone. Instead, the farmers' markets had these tomatoes that were all the exact same size, with a sort of pink color and waxy taste. And at one farmers' market this guy opened his cooler for us and he had boxes and boxes of them neatly stacked inside. He said this new variety could be stockpiled longer and shipped farther. They all looked the same, and there were no more cracks. He said, 'Customers didn't like the cracks.' They were too ugly."

At this point, my sister Jane joined in: "What's worse," she said, "is that they still called these ersatz little laboratory tomatoes 'Jersey beefsteaks.' In other words, they got rid of the tomato, but they kept the brand name, so they can sell them all over the world as Jersey beefsteaks, even though they really don't have the same look or taste! I was profoundly depressed by this whole thing. It hit me that something that was a real piece of the quality of my life was gone forever, and I'm too young to be eating plastic food for the rest of my life. I saw it as a sign of the future, all the unique things in our lives being turned into plastic."

At the end of the conversation, my brother-in-law said to me, "The first thing that occurred to me after we got back from the trip, when we found out that they didn't sell our tomatoes anymore, was to get on the Internet and start checking for Jersey beefsteaks to see if anyone is still growing the real thing. Someone out there must be."

Ted's instinct was a good one. If there is still a market for them, and the seeds are still around, some farmer using the Internet, a Web site — www.tomatoes.Jerseybeefsteaks.com — a Federal Express account and a Visa account will surely set up a virtual farmers' market where it will be possible to order original Jersey beefsteak tomatoes from your home PC, charge them on Visa and have them delivered by FedEx the next day — at least I hope so.

The future of globalization may depend on it.

How we learn to strike the right balance between globalization's inherently empowering and humanizing aspects and its inherently disempowering and dehumanizing aspects will determine whether it is reversible or irreversible, a passing phase or a fundamental revolution in the evolution of human society.

In July 1998, The New Yorker ran a cartoon that showed two long-haired, scraggly bearded Hell's Angels types, one wearing a skull and crossbones T-shirt and the other sitting on his motorcycle. Each is obviously asking the other how his day went. One Hell's Angel finally says to the other: "How was my day? Advancing issues led declines."

And so it is with globalization. Globalization is always in the balance, always tipping this way or that. Our job as citizens of the world is to make certain that a majority of people always feel that advancing issues are leading the declines. Only then will globalization be sustainable. And no nation has a greater responsibility and opportunity to ensure this than the United States of America.

20

There Is a Way Forward

If a free society cannot help the many who are poor, it cannot save the few who are rich.

— *John F. Kennedy*

I n the winter of 1996, I accompanied then–U.S. ambassador to the United Nations Madeleine Albright on a trip to the war zones of Africa where UN peacekeepers were deployed. The tour took us to the civil wars of Liberia, Angola, Rwanda and Burundi. During the stop in Rwanda, the last on the trip, Albright asked her staff and the crew of her Air Force Boeing 737 to pose for a picture on the runway of Kigali International Airport. Her aircraft was painted white and blue, like a mini– Air Force One, and was emblazoned with the words "United States of America." Albright's staff and crew stood on the steps and beneath the wings. They included a Greek-American, a Czech-American, Jewish Americans, black Americans and white Americans. There were Air Force crewmen from small towns and State Department experts from Ivy League colleges, and they were all standing there shoulder to shoulder. As a reporter on the trip, I didn't think I belonged in the picture, so I stood over to the side and watched the Rwandan ground crew watching the American picture-taking session. The Rwandans had a slightly quizzical look. I couldn't help wondering to myself what they were making of this scene, which represented America at its best: the spirit of community, the melting pot, the willingness to help faraway strangers in need, the freedom and opportunity for each individual to work his way to the top and, most important, a concept of citizenship based on allegiance to an idea, not a tribe. As a picture, it represented everything that Rwanda was not. Rwanda had just emerged from an orgy of tribal warfare—Rwandan Hutus against Rwandan Tutsis—in which a million people were killed, some of them brutally hacked to death with machetes. Rwanda was all olive trees and no Lexuses, a country that was all gnarled roots choking one another, and no flowering branches.

As I watched that scene on the tarmac, I started to get mad—but not just about the tragedy in Africa—mad about the budget debate that was then going on in the U.S. Congress. It seemed to me then, and even more now, that we have something tremendously special in America. But if we want to preserve it, we have to pay for it, we have to nurture it. But when I listened at that time to the infamous 1994 class of freshmen Republicans, I heard mean-spirited voices, voices uninterested in any compromise, voices for whom the American government was some kind of evil enemy. I heard men and women who insisted that the market alone should rule, and who thought it was enough to be right about the economic imperatives of free trade and globalization, and the rest would take care of itself. I heard lawmakers who seemed to believe America had no special responsibility for maintaining global institutions, such as the UN, the World Bank and the IMF, which are critical for stabilizing an international system from which America benefits more than any other country.

And as I thought about all this on the tarmac of Kigali Airport, I said to myself, "Well, my freshmen Republican friends, come to Africa—it's a freshmen Republican's paradise." Yes sir, nobody in Liberia pays taxes. There's no gun control in Angola. There's no welfare as we know it in Burundi and no big government to interfere in the market in Rwanda. But a lot of their people sure wish there were. Take, for instance, the desk clerk in Luanda, Angola, who looked at me as if I were nuts when I asked her if it was safe for me to take a walk three blocks from the hotel, down the main street of the Angolan capital in the middle of the day.

"No, no, no"—she shook her head—"not safe." I'll bet she wouldn't mind paying some taxes to put more police on the street. And then there was the Liberian radio reporter who approached me in Monrovia and demanded to know why the U.S. Marines came to Liberia after the civil war broke out in 1989, evacuated only the U.S. citizens, and then left the Liberians to fight it out alone. "We all thought, the Marines are coming, we will be saved," the Liberian reporter remarked, "but then they left. How could they leave?" Poor guy, his country has no Marines to rescue him. I'll bet he wouldn't mind paying some taxes for a few good men. They don't worry about "big government" in Liberia. They don't worry about government at all—thanks to the gangs and warlords who have dominated that land for the past decade. No, Liberians may never again have to worry about government red tape. In fact, the only regulation I saw at the Executive Mansion in Liberia was a sign taped to a bullet-shattered window at the front door. It said: "Deposit Your Weapons Here."

Employers don't have to fret at all about pesky worker-safety rules in Angola, let alone services for the handicapped. The 70,000 Angolans who have had limbs blown off by land mines planted during the last twenty-five years of civil war seem to make do just fine on their own. You can see them limping around the streets of Luanda, in Felliniesque contortions, hustling for food and using tree limbs as a substitute for the human variety. And in Rwanda and Burundi no one was asked to pay for Head Start, unemployment insurance, Medicaid, national service or student loan programs. Instead, they just have brutal competition for scarce land, energy and water, with Tutsi and Hutu tribesmen taking turns downsizing each other to grab more resources for themselves.

They said at the time that the freshmen Republicans almost never went on congressional junkets. They thought it would look bad to their constituents back home. Most of them didn't even have passports. Too bad. They wanted all the respect and benefits that come with being the Michael Jordans of geopolitics, with being an American in today's globalization system, but without any of the sacrifices and obligations—at home or abroad—that go with it. They should come to war-torn Africa and get a real taste of what happens to countries where there is no sense of community, no sense that people owe their government anything, no sense that anyone is responsible for anyone else, and where the rich have to live behind high walls and tinted windows, while the poor are left to the tender mercies of the marketplace.

I don't want to live in such a country, or such a world. It is not only morally wrong, it will become increasingly dangerous. Designing ways to avoid that should be at the heart of American domestic and foreign policy today. Unfortunately, neither the Democratic Party nor the Republican Party has fully made the shift from the Cold War system to the globalization system in framing their own politics. They each behave at times as if the world is now safe for us to be both insular and mindlessly partisan on every issue. To the extent that there is any serious discussion about the shared national interest today, it's all about whether we can define a new common threat and not a new common mission. The "big enemy" is still the organizing principle for American internationalism, not the "big opportunity," let alone the "big responsibility."

America does have a shared national interest to pursue in today's globalization system—one that constitutes both a big opportunity and a big responsibility. Put simply: As the country that benefits most from today's global integration—as the country whose people, products, values, technologies and ideas are being most globalized—it is our job to make sure that globalization is sustainable. And the way we do that is by ensuring that the international system remains stable and that advances lead declines for as many people as possible, in as many countries as possible, on as many days as possible. In the Cold War system the fundamental political question was: Which hardware and operating system do you choose? In the globalization era, the fundamental political question is: How do you make the best of the only hardware and operating system that works—globally integrated free-market capitalism? America can be, and should be, the world's role model in answering this question.

America has had two hundred years to invent, regenerate and calibrate the balances that keep markets free without becoming monsters. We have the tools to make a difference. We have the responsibility to make a difference. And we have a huge interest in making a difference. Managing globalization is a role from which America dare not shrink. It is our overarching national interest today, and the political party that understands that first, the one that comes up with the most coherent, credible and imaginative platform for pursuing it, is the party that will own the real bridge to the future.

I n order to think about how to meet this challenge, you need to start by getting rid of the political language of the Cold War system, which doesn't really capture the issues at stake, and develop new terms appropriate to the globalization system. For this purpose, I have designed a matrix which I believe captures the four basic political identities people can choose from in the system of globalization (see diagram).

To find out who you are and who your rivals are in this new era, consider this matrix: The line across the middle from left to right is the globalization line. The first thing you have to do is locate yourself on this line in accordance with how you feel about globalization. At the far right end of this line are the "Integrationists." These are the people who really welcome globalization because they think it is either good or inevitable and want to see it promoted through more free trade, more Internet commerce, more networking of schools, communities and business, more electronic mail, so that we can ultimately have global

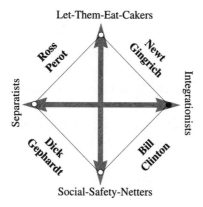

integration twenty-four hours a day, across twenty-four time zones and into cyberspace.

At the far left end of this globalization line are the "Separatists." These are people who believe that free trade and technological integration are neither good nor inevitable, because they widen income gaps, lead to jobs being sent abroad, homogenize culture into some global mush and lead to life being controlled by distant, faceless market forces. They want to see globalization stopped in its tracks. They want to cut it off and kill it now.

So the first thing you have to do is locate yourself somewhere on this line. Are you a Separatist? An Integrationist? Or something in between?

Now look at the line running from top to bottom of the matrix. This is the distribution axis. It represents what sort of policies you believe governments should adopt to go along with globalization and the Golden Straitjacket. At the lower end of this line are the "Social-Safety-Netters." I define Social-Safety-Netters as those people who believe that globalization will only be sustainable if it is democratized, in both the economic and the political sense. Economically this means designing trampolines and social safety nets that don't simply try to cushion the fall of the left-behinds, know-nots and turtles, but actually try to bring them into the system by helping them acquire the tools and resources to compete. And politically it means encouraging democratization in developing countries that are globalizing, because there is no sustainable economic growth without the growth of personal freedoms as well.

Obviously, not everyone agrees with this approach. That's why at the top of this distribution line—that is, at the other end from the Social-Safety-Netters—are the Let-Them-Eat-Cakers. These are people who believe that globalization is essentially winner take all, loser take care of yourself. They want to shrink government, taxes and safety nets, and let people truly reap the fruits of their own labor or pay the price of their own ineptitude. There is nothing that focuses the mind more on getting a job and keeping it, say the Let-Them-Eat-Cakers, than knowing that there is no net under you.

So next you have to locate yourself on this distribution axis. Are you a Social-Safety-Netter? Are you a Let-Them-Eat-Caker? Or are you somewhere in between?

All the key players in American politics today can be better understood and identified by this matrix than by the old labels of Democrat, Republican and Independent. Bill Clinton is an Integrationist Social-Safety-Netter. Former Speaker of the House Newt Gingrich was an Integrationist Let-Them-Eat-Caker. That's why Clinton and Gingrich were always allies on free trade but opponents on social security/welfare spending. House Minority Leader Dick Gephardt is a Separatist Social-Safety-Netter, and Ross Perot is a Separatist Let-Them-Eat-Caker. That's why Gephardt and Perot were allies against NAFTA and more free trade but opponents on social security/welfare spending, where Gephardt wants to spend money on social-safety-net programs and to defend workers' "rights," not just enhance their capabilities.

While I use this matrix to describe America today, you can easily adapt it to any country. Simply put yourself in this matrix and find out who you are and who your enemies will be in the next great political debate. I am an Integrationist Social-Safety-Netter. What does it mean to be an Integrationist Social-Safety-Netter? It means articulating a politics of sustainable globalization, a geopolitics of sustainable globalization (a foreign and defense policy), a geo-economics of sustainable globalization and, finally, an ethics of sustainable globalization (a way of thinking about where values, parenting and God fit into this system). In other words, it means articulating a new vision for a new international system.

Politics for the Age of Globalization

Let's start with a politics of sustainable globalization. It has to consist of two things: one is a picture of the world, so people understand where they are; and the other is a set of Integrationist Social-Safety-Net policies for dealing with it.

You need a picture of the world because no policy is sustainable without a public that broadly understands why it's necessary and sees the world the way you do. And politicians beware: For a lot of reasons it is very easy to distort and demonize globalization and end up where even if you are right on the economics, you lose control of the politics, so it works against you instead of for you. Why is this the case? Because people who are the biggest losers from globalization—workers who have lost their jobs to robots or foreign sweatshops—know exactly who they are. This makes them very easy to mobilize against more integration, technology or free trade. People who are beneficiaries of globalization, of more open trade and of foreign investment, often don't have a clue who they are. They often don't make the connections between globalization and their rising standards of living, and therefore they are difficult to mobilize. Have you ever heard a worker in a microchip factory say, "Boy, am I lucky. Thanks to globalization, soaring demand for American high-tech exports, the labor shortage for skilled workers in this country and rising expectations in the developing world my boss had to give me a raise. Ain't NAFTA wonderful."

Another reason globalization is easy to distort is that people don't understand that it is largely a technology-driven phenomenon, not a trade-driven one. We had a receptionist at the Washington bureau of *The New York Times*, but the company eliminated her job. She didn't lose her job to a Mexican, she lost it to a microchip—the microchip that operates the voice-mail device in all our office phones. The fact is, that microchip would have taken away her job if we had had no trade with Mexico. That microchip would have taken away her job had we had a thirty-foot-high wall stretching from one end of the Mexican-American border to the other. But politicians don't want to acknowledge this. None of them is going to stand up and say: "I want you to get up now, unplug your phone, go to your window, throw your phone out and shout: *'I'm not going to take it anymore! Save American jobs! Ban voice mail! Potato chips, yes! Microchips, no!'* " That's not a winning political message. It's much easier instead to rail against Mexicans and foreign factories. Because foreign workers and factories are easy to see, and microchips are not, they loom much larger in our consciousness as the problem. That's why trade, which is tangible, has come to symbolize for many people all the anxieties associated with rapid change and globalization—even though the main causes of those anxieties are new technologies and deregulation.

Bill Clinton defeated both George Bush and Bob Dole because a majority of American voters intuitively sensed that they were in a new era and that Clinton grasped this and had some credible ideas of how to deal with it—while Dole and Bush didn't get it at all. Unfortunately, once in office, Clinton never fully developed that intuitive sense and made it explicit, with a real picture of the world that could be repeated over and over again. It started from his first week on the job when he defined America's central problem as affordable health care—not sustainable globalization. What should Mr. Clinton have said at his first inaugural? Something like this:

"My fellow Americans, my tenure as your President is coinciding with the end of the Cold War system and the rise of globalization. Globalization is to the 1990s and the next millennium what the Cold War was to the 1950s through the 1980s: If the Cold War system was built around the threat and challenge of the Soviet Union, which was dividing the world, the globalization system is built around the threat and challenge of rapid technological change and economic integration that are uniting the world. But as it unites the world, globalization is also transforming everyone's workplace, job, market and community—rapidly destroying old jobs and harvesting new ones, rapidly eliminating old lifestyles and producing new ones, rapidly eliminating old markets and multiplying new ones, rapidly destroying old industries and inventing new ones. Foreign trade, which represented just 13 percent of gross domestic product in 1970, is now up to nearly 30 percent of American GDP—and rising. Technological change is now so fast that American computer companies manufacture three different models of each computer every year. Not only is this a new world; it is, for the most part, a better one. Even if they have to struggle at times with this system, China, Indonesia, Korea, Thailand, Malaysia, Brazil, Argentina have seen their standards of living rise faster, for more of their citizens, than at any time in their history—thanks to the increasing effectiveness of financial markets in facilitating trade and investment by people in one country into the factories of another. Globalization has been the engine of unprecedented economic growth and we must never lose sight of that. Indeed, as Treasury Secretary Larry Summers points out, thanks in large part to increasing globalization more than one quarter of humanity is now enjoying growth at rates in which their living standards will quadruple within a generation. Quadruple! And far from coming at the expense of the United States, this worldwide growth has led to the lowest unemployment rate in America in nearly fifty years. But globalization also presents an unprecedented challenge: While it is the engine of greater long-term prosperity for every country that plugs into the globalization system, it is also the engine of greater dislocations in the short run. And it is not enough to tell a factory worker who has suddenly lost his job to a lower-wage factory abroad that, while his situation is unfortunate, our society as a whole is better off because it can now purchase the steel or tennis shoes he once made at a cheaper price. It is not enough to tell the office worker whose job has been phased out in favor of a new computer system that, while the loss of him is unfortunate, our society as a whole is better off because it will be much more productive with that new network system installed. The benefits of globalization tend to be measured in the long run, and for society as a whole, but the dislocations come immediately and for specific individuals who know they have been hurt.

"Therefore, given this mismatch between the long-term opportunities and growth that globalization presents for greater well-being, and its disruptive political, environmental and social impacts, the United States needs a broad strategy to make globalization sustainable—to get the best out of it while softening the worst. Think of the world as a wheel with spokes. At the hub of this wheel is what I would label 'globalization and rapid economic and technological change.' That is, in plain language, the *one big thing* that is going on out there. Because it is at the center, we need a different approach to health care, welfare, education, job training, the environment, market regulation, social security, campaign finance and expansion of free trade. Each one of these areas has to be adjusted, adapted or reformed to enable us as a society to get the most out of this globalization system and to cushion its worst aspects. Globalization demands that our society move faster, work smarter and take more risks than at any time in our history. As your President I make you two promises. One is that I will make it my business to equip each of you, and our society at large, to meet this challenge, with the right combination of integrationist programs and social safety nets. The other is that I will be a tireless defender of our trade laws to ensure that globalization, while it challenges the American worker, does not allow others to take advantage of our openness by dumping their products here while limiting our access to their markets. I'm not here to tell you this is all going to be easy. In fact, I'm here to tell you that it is going to be really hard. But if we can strike the right balance—and I think we can—we can be the vanguard for the world on how to manage integration in the age of globalization, just as we were the vanguard for the world on how to manage containment in the age of the Cold War. God Bless America."

This is what Clinton believed, but it is not what he always said. And one reason his health-care proposals got chewed apart by his opponents— not the only reason, but one reason—was that they were not effectively located in a clear and constantly repeated picture of the world, with globalization at the center and the requisite policies flowing from it. As a result, notes Harvard University economist Dani Rodrik, "the connections and complementarities in all these areas got lost in the public debate," and it made it much easier for ideologues and extremists, as well as economic populists, nationalists, know-nothings, nativist xenophobes and opportunists, to often skew the debate on any one issue—like trade or health-care reform—and drive it into a dead end.

If we don't educate the public about the real nature of the world today and demystify globalization, the Separatists will always exploit this confusion for their own ends. In 1998, President Clinton could not get NAFTA expanded to Chile because a union-led minority, who believed that they were not benefiting from more free trade, were very active in opposing the expansion of NAFTA, while the majority that was benefiting from expanded free trade never understood who they were and therefore never got mobilized to defend their interests.

A politics of sustainable globalization, though, needs more than just the correct picture of what is happening in the world. It also needs the right balance of policies. Specifically, it demands a new social bargain between workers, financiers and governments that will make for sustainable globalization. Give them their due—the Thatcherites and Reaganites helped to prepare their countries for this era of globalization, and were instrumental in bringing it about by offering an unadulterated free-market vision for globalization. Their view was: "Let the market rule everywhere as much as possible and things will all be O.K." But a pure market vision alone is not enough. It is too brutal and therefore politically unsustainable. The Left, meanwhile, or what's left of the Left, has tried to hold on to the paternalism of the welfare state as much as possible. This is not economically sustainable.

What is needed instead of either of these extremes is a new social compact that both embraces free markets but also ensures that they benefit, and are tolerable for, as many people as possible. You stabilize globalization by democratizing globalization—by making it work for more and more people all the time. Finding the appropriate social bargain to

democratize globalization has been the task of the center-left—the Bill
Clintons in America and the Tony Blairs in England. Many people call
this approach "The Third Way." I don't buy that. The new social bargain
that Clinton and Blair have been groping for—which is what I call Integrationist Social-Safety-Nettism—is actually the *only* way for a country to
thrive and survive in this new system. There is no Third Way. There is
only one way—this balanced way.

We Integrationist Social-Safety-Netters believe that you dare not be a
globalizer in this world—an advocate of free and unfettered trade, open
borders, deregulation and Internet for all—without also being a social
democrat. Because if you are not willing to spend what it takes to equip
the have-nots, know-nots and turtles in your society to survive in this new
system, they will eventually produce a backlash that will choke off your
country from the world. You will not be able to maintain the political
consensus you need for openness. At the same time, we believe you dare
not be a social democrat, or safety-netter, today without being a globalizer, because without integration with the world you will never generate
the incomes you need to keep standards of living rising and to take care of
the left-behinds.

The question we all now face is: Where is the appropriate equilibrium
point between integrationism and social safety nets in today's globalization system? There are three elements we have to balance: The trapeze,
the trampoline, and the safety net.

The Trapeze

First, we want as open, and growing, a free-market-oriented economy as
possible, in which people are encouraged to swing free and take crazy
leaps. Without risk takers and venture capitalists, there is no entrepreneurship and without entrepreneurship there is no growth. Therefore, at
the heart of every healthy economy are the free-swinging trapezes of free
markets. Because there is no better safety net than a healthy economy
with low unemployment. In the growing, increasingly globalized U.S.
economy, the unemployment rate for those with less than a high school
education declined from 10.75 percent in 1994 to 6.75 by 1999, enabling
large numbers of young people, particularly minorities, to find employment, learn skills and gain the dignity that comes from holding a job. Yes,
not everybody has a great job—some people are flipping hamburgers and

others are designing Web pages. But a job, any job, is the beginning of self-respect and stability in a person's life.

Whenever I think about this issue, I always recall a story that Russian journalist Aleksei Pushkov told me back in April 1995 about one of his neighbors in Moscow. "He was this poor driver who lived in the apartment off the entryway. Every Friday night he would get drunk and sing along—over and over in a very loud voice—to two English-language songs: 'Happy Nation' and 'All She Wants Is Another Baby.' He had no idea what the words meant. When he got really drunk, he'd start beating his wife and she would start screaming. He was driving us crazy. I wanted to throw a grenade at him. Anyway, about eight months ago, I don't know how, he got a share in a small car-repair shop. Since then, no more 'Happy Nation,' no more singing all night, no more beating his wife. He leaves every morning at eight-thirty for work and he is satisfied. He knows he has some prospects in life now. My wife said to me the other day, 'Hey, look at Happy Nation'—that's what we call him—'he's an owner now.' "

This is why a trapeze strategy doesn't just mean government getting out of the way and letting the free markets rip, it also means thinking about how government can make more people owners and successful free-marketers. In America, that means initiatives that will improve access to investment capital in the most distressed, low-income communities, so we are not just training people for jobs that are not available. American inner cities are emerging markets every bit as much as Bangladesh, and they sometimes need some of the same sort of market-oriented assistance programs. As Treasury Secretary Larry Summers has pointed out: "The world over, private financial markets fail when it comes to the very poor. Mainstream banks do not seek out poor communities—because that's not where the money is. Other barriers tend artificially to restrict the flow of capital to certain neighborhoods or minority groups, creating clear market failures. Yet if you deprive the people of these districts of the chance to lend or save, they are a good deal more likely to stay that way."

One way to begin to democratize access to capital in America is to revitalize the Community Reinvestment Act, which uses government pressure to encourage commercial banks to make affordable credit to distressed neighborhoods. But there are some loans commercial banks will never make. That is why I would encourage the government-supported venture capital fund started in 1999 for low- and moderate-income neighborhoods. Known as the Community Development Financial Institutions

Fund, it gives start-up financing to entrepreneurs ready to make risky investments in underdeveloped districts, where they see the market possibilities—for anything from private day-care centers to low-income housing to a beauty salon to entertainment facilities—but where venture-capital financing wouldn't normally be made available.

The Trampolines

Second, even with a growing economy every society also needs trampolines—programs that can catch workers who fall behind in this rapidly changing environment and retrain them so they can bounce back into the economy. A trampoline is strong enough to catch you before you hit the ground, but not so cushy that you can live on it forever, and it can be very useful for constantly shrinking the pool of left-behinds. Without question, the most important trampoline is lifelong learning.

Every worker needs to understand that economic security in this world without walls cannot come any longer from the largesse of a welfare state or from holding fast to a union card. It can only come from holding a report card. In an age when technological change is so rapid, and the walls around companies and countries so small, only new skills and lifelong learning can ensure job security. "In your career, knowledge is like milk," says Louis Ross, chief technology officer for Ford Motor Co. "It has a shelf life stamped right on the carton. The shelf life of a degree in engineering is about three years. If you're not replacing everything you know by then, your career is going to turn sour fast." As Jim Botkin and Stan Davis note in their book *The Monster Under the Bed*, in the knowledge economy you don't earn a living, you "learn a living."

Government's job is not to shield workers from this reality, but to empower them to deal with it, and to let them know that it is not a battle they will have to fight on their own. To that end, I believe that each White House should offer in this era of globalization an annual piece of legislation that I would call "The Rapid Change Opportunity Act." It would go alongside whatever integrationist policy the Administration was pursuing that year—whether it be NAFTA expansion to Chile or any other free-trade arrangements. The Rapid Change Opportunity Act would vary each year. Its goal would be to create both the reality and the perception that the government understands that globalization is here, and that it spreads its blessings most unevenly. Therefore, the government is constantly going to be adjusting its trampolines to get as many people as possible up to speed for the Fast World, by expanding their capabilities and life choices. This is the only sustainable way to widen the winner's circle of those benefiting from globalization.

If I could have waved a magic wand, the Rapid Change Opportunity Act for 1999, for example, would have included the following: pilot projects for public employment for temporarily displaced workers; tax breaks for severance pay for displaced workers; free government-provided résumé consultation for anyone who loses a job, and a further extension of the Kassebaum-Kennedy Act, so that laid-off workers could keep their health-insurance policies longer; and a national advertising campaign for one of the best, but most underreported, bipartisan achievements of the Clinton era, the Workforce Investment Act. Signed in August 1998, it consolidated the government's 150 different job-training programs into three broad grants: Individual Training Accounts that workers can use for any training they believe will most advance their job opportunities; one-stop career centers for every job-training program; and an increase in youth-training programs by $1.2 billion over five years. In addition, I would have included in my Rapid Change Opportunity Act some increased U.S. lending to the Asian, African and Latin American development banks to promote training of women, microlending to women and small businesses, and environmental cleanup in every developing country with which America has significant trade. I would have included an increase in funding for the International Labor Organization's new initiative for building alternatives to child labor in countries where children are most abused. I would have included an increase in the already existing Trade Adjustment Assistance program, which provides some small income support and training for anyone who can show that his or her job was eliminated because of trade. I would have expanded the already existing Dislocated Worker Training program to assist anyone who lost a job because of new technology. And finally, I would have launched a national advertising campaign to better inform people about the already existing Lifelong-Learning Tax Credit, which allows citizens to write off from their income taxes up to $1,000 of the cost of any education or training program they sign up for to upgrade their education or technical skills.

I would also have included programs for reinforcing families and communities, which help provide workers with the psychological supports that are needed to thrive in today's high-pressure, high-speed labor markets. These could have included anything from increasing support for child day-care centers for working parents to insisting that every worker have a choice between flex time, which he can use for himself or family, and overtime pay. We need to have more self-reliant individuals in this system, but individuals cannot thrive in a vacuum. They need to be supported by more active, healthy and responsive communities that can help cushion people from either unchecked markets or overbearing governments. Trying to build more civic capacity, from the PTA to community policing, to fill that gap between markets and government is critical in this new system.

The point is that we Integrationist Social-Safety-Netters believe that there is much that government can still do in this era of globalization that is not all that expensive, does not involve radical income redistribution—or lavish compensatory welfare spending programs that would violate the economic rules of the Golden Straitjacket—but can meaningfully expand the winner's circle. These sorts of initiatives say to citizens: "While today's globalization system is asking you to leap from trapeze to trapeze, higher and higher, faster and faster, farther and farther, the government is not going to just let you fall to the jungle floor and be eaten by the lions of globalization. While it won't give you a handout anymore, it will give you a hand up." Even if we waste some money on these hand-up programs, the costs are so small compared to the benefits and efficiencies that come from keeping our markets as free and open to the world as possible. Something like a Rapid Change Opportunity Act is a tiny price to pay for maintaining the social cohesion and political consensus for integration and free trade. Hence my mottoes: "Protection, not protectionism. Cushions, not walls. Floors, not ceilings. Dealing with the reality of the Fast World, not denying it."

The Safety Nets

Third, and finally, we still need traditional safety nets—social security, Medicare, Medicaid, food stamps and welfare—to catch those who simply will never be fast enough or educated enough to deal with the Fast World, but whom you don't want just falling onto the pavement. In the globalization system, though, we are going to have to rethink what constitutes a safety net. For instance, in an era in which access to the Internet is going to be essential for learning, reserving an airline ticket, dealing with the government, communicating, not to mention shopping at the best price, we may decide that universal access to the Internet is a basic human right.

Obviously, there is a trade-off between the trapeze, the trampoline and the safety nets. What politics is about in America today, and in so many other countries, is trying to locate that new equilibrium point—trying to determine what is the right mix of an open-integrationist economy that is always producing more and more jobs, with the right trampolines and safety nets. Clearly, that equilibrium point has been and will continue moving to the right of center, from the center-left where it was during the Cold War, when governments felt it was both necessary and possible, in a world of walls, to prevent workers from being attracted to communism by maintaining elaborate welfare-state programs. Those days are over. But it doesn't mean simply surrendering everything to the private sector. Thanks to Integrationism, America's Golden Straitjacket is producing enough gold—with a substantial budget surplus projected into the new millennium—to afford both social safety nets and trampolines.

N o politics of sustainable globalization would be complete, though, if it relied exclusively on economic programs. While expanding access to globalization is critical, particularly for developing countries, simultaneously democratizing their political systems is just as important. This is one of the real lessons of globalization's first decade: Getting your society up to speed for globalization is an enormously wrenching process, and because of that it requires more democracy in the long run rather than less. In the Cold War, the leaders of developing countries had superpower patrons who would sustain them, no matter how they ran their countries. But those patrons are gone now and the masses are not going to sustain failed governments for long—not in an age when they can see how everyone else is living. (See dictionary entry for Indonesia.) If you fail now, you will fall—and unless your people catch you and support you, you will fall hard. (See dictionary entry for Suharto.)

As democracy scholar Larry Diamond has pointed out: "We have now seen a number of examples where countries in Latin America, Eastern Europe and East Asia have voted out of office governments they associated with the pain of globalization reforms. The new governments that came in made some adjustments but kept more or less the same globalizing, marketizing policies. How did they get away with that? Because the democratic process gave the public in these countries a sense of ownership over the painful process of economic policy reform. It was no longer something completely alien that was being done to them. They were being consulted on it and given a choice about at least the speed of the process, if not the direction. Moreover, as a result of the opportunity to participate in the process and throw out people who they felt had moved too harshly and abruptly, or too corruptly or insensitively, the whole process had much greater political legitimacy, and thus more sustainability."

Moreover, where parties and leaders have alternated in power—and political oppositions have come in and pursued pretty much the same policies of economic liberalization and globalization as their predecessors—the message sinks in to the public that there really is no alternative to the Golden Straitjacket. How many Latin American, Eastern European and now East Asian opposition leaders have come into office in the last decade and said, "Gee, it turns out we really are bankrupt. We really do have to open up. In fact, things are even worse than I thought, and we are going to have to accelerate these reforms because there's no way out. But we'll put a human face on them." Democratization helps make that coming to terms with reality possible. And that's why the countries that are adjusting best to globalization today are often not the naturally richest ones—Saudi Arabia, Nigeria or Iran—but rather the most democratic ones—Poland, Taiwan, Thailand, Korea.

Democratizing globalization—it's not only the most effective way to make it sustainable, it's the most self-interested and moral policy that any government can pursue.

Geo-economics for the Age of Globalization

I once wrote a fictional column about investing in the 1990s that went something like this: "So I decided to do a little international investing. I brushed up on my German and bought some German corporate bonds. I studied a little Japanese and picked up a few stocks on the Nikkei. I got a tip from a waiter at my local Chinese House of Hunan and bought a few shares on the Shanghai stock exchange. My broker tried to sell me some Lebanese government bonds, but I told him that I already had wallpaper in my office. I even did my thing for Russian reform, by brushing up on the Cyrillic alphabet and buying a few Russian T-bills. But after all my language training and foreign research, I discovered that I forgot to learn just two little English words: 'Alan Greenspan.' Because when Greenspan suddenly raised interest rates in the mid-1990s, making the extra interest I was getting on my foreign bonds less attractive, everyone started dumping these foreign markets and bringing their money home, and I got creamed." I was a bad lender. I had not done my homework. I was just chasing higher rates of return. I didn't know what I owned when I went into these countries. And I didn't know what I owned when I left.

Well, over the years I got a little smarter and became a better lender with my money. I started doing my international investing through a mutual fund that specialized in global markets and could scrutinize each investment. A short time after Russia's economy went into a tailspin in August 1998, I got a letter from that fund—Tweedy, Browne Global—reporting that its profits were down a bit because of the general turmoil in international markets that was triggered by Russia's default, but the fund was not down as much as many others because it had actually done its homework and stayed away from Russia. The Tweedy letter said of Russia: "We cannot understand investing in countries with little political stability, no laws protecting investors, and a currency that may be put to better use as Kleenex." Yes, the letter added, in early 1998 the Russian market increased fivefold, and then overnight lost 80 percent of its value—"a complete round trip." Russia, it turns out, was a bad borrower. It had no operating system and no software, and in the end all it could offer its investors was a round trip from zero to 80 percent and back again to zero.

I tell these two stories because they capture in microcosm the two biggest threats to today's global financial system—crises triggered by "bad lenders" and crises triggered by "bad borrowers." Just as you always have both drug users and drug pushers, in global economics you always have both bad borrowers, such as Russia, and bad lenders, such as myself. The big geo-economic question we need to address is: How do we stabilize this global economy to make it less susceptible to bad borrowing and bad lending, which today can get so big and spread so fast that it can rattle the whole system?

Let's start with the problem of the bad borrowers. I believe globalization did us all a favor by melting down the economies of Thailand, Korea, Malaysia, Indonesia, Mexico, Russia and Brazil in the 1990s, because it laid bare a lot of rotten practices and institutions in countries that had prematurely globalized. Exposing the venal and corrupt Suharto family in Indonesia was no crisis in my book. Exposing the crony capitalism in Korea was no crisis in my book. Exposing the totally corrupt insider dealings in Thailand was no crisis in my book. Exposing the absurd lengths to which the Mexican government had gone to attract short-term dollar loans, without an ability to repay, was no crisis in my book. All these systems would have crashed sooner or later.

But now that globalization has helped that happen sooner, the question is: What do we do with this opportunity? Some want to restrain the Electronic Herd from ever stampeding such countries again. Others want to encourage these countries to impose capital controls that will fence the herd out. Both these approaches are wrongheaded. The Electronic Herd is the energy source of the twenty-first century. Countries have to learn to manage it; restraining it is futile, and shutting it out for long will only deprive a country of resources, technology and professional advice, and prolong crony capitalism. Many experts point to Chile's capital controls as a positive example of what developing countries can do to prevent stampedes. Since 1991, Chile required foreign investors who put money into the Chilean market to keep it there for a minimum of one year. It also imposed an implicit tax on Chilean companies engaged in foreign borrowing. The results have been mixed at best. *Forbes* (May 18, 1998) quoted a study done by Sebastian Edwards, the former World Bank chief economist for Latin America, that showed the Chilean controls to have been only partially effective and significantly increased the cost of capital in Chile. For example, Chile's borrowing costs were roughly double those in Argentina, where a currency board prohibited capital controls. Capital controls are an invitation to let bureaucrats and cronies allocate capital rather than the marketplace. As a temporary measure to stabilize an economy, they can be useful and effective—provided the government fixes the currency at a very low, competitive rate. But in the long run, they are no solution. In relatively noncorrupt countries, such as Chile, capital controls will eventually lead to distortions; in already corrupt countries, they will make the corruption that much worse.

The right geo-economic approach, therefore, is to focus on strengthening these bad-borrowing countries so that they can plug into the herd again. Stampedes will still happen, and some countries no doubt will be unfairly hurt. But the herd is never irrational indefinitely. With rare exceptions, it doesn't run away from, or attack, countries with sound financial systems, pursuing sound economic policies. Some people talk about Thailand, Korea, Indonesia and Russia and bemoan what the herd did to them in stampeding away—as if they were practicing textbook economics and the herd just decided to bolt one day for no reason at all. That's nonsense. They were engaged in bad borrowing—and bad borrowing always involves governments and businesses running up massive short-term debts, usually denominated in a foreign currency, that cannot be spent rationally and are highly vulnerable to currency swings. Once the herd realizes the excess, it bolts. As U.S. Treasury Secretary Larry Summers once put it: "While it has become fashionable to blame capital account crises on a voracious global capital market, a large part of the problem in these crises came from governments' own efforts to attract short-term inflows that could not reasonably be sustained. We saw this, for example, in Mexico, with the increasing resort to issuing dollar-indexed 'Tesobonos' in the lead-up to crisis; we saw it in Thailand in tax breaks for offshore foreign borrowing; and we saw it in Russia, in the government's effort to attract foreign capital to the domestic bond market."

Economists and bankers today will debate the details for rehabilitating a bad-borrowing country and making it more stampede-proof. And each country is somewhat different. But, generally speaking, the approach has to include the following four steps:

Step one is to make clear to bad-borrowing countries that their goal should be to restore the necessary conditions for growth and attracting back the Electronic Herd. That means a credible commitment to improve its economic operating system over time from DOScapital 1.0 toward 6.0. This clearly requires some mix—it will differ from country to country—of budget cutting, closing down of inefficient, bankrupt firms and finance houses, currency adjustments, interest-rate adjustments, debt write-downs and the breakup of crony capitalist practices. The aim of such reforms is to stabilize their currencies, eventually lower their interest rates to stimulate demand at home and improve the prospect that contracts will be respected. In many cases this step needs to include a process for actually making it easier for the Electronic Herd to buy companies in these weakened economies. I realize the last point is controversial. It sounds as if I'm trying to make the world cheap and safe for American capitalism. I am not. I am trying to make the world safe for globalution and the creative destruction that is essential to capitalism— eliminating inefficient firms and replacing them with better-managed and capitalized ones operating according to the best international standards. I don't care whether the foreign buyers are American, German, Japanese or Indian. I only care about their standards and capitalization.

The state of Arizona used to have a notorious crony banking system. The best thing that ever happened to Arizona was when interstate banking allowed banks that had better technology, were better run and better capitalized—from New York, Chicago and San Francisco—to come in and buy up Arizona banks. An important reason Argentina recovered faster from the Latin American financial crises of the early 1990s was because a good portion of its banking system was taken over by the best international banks.

Having the Electronic Herd come back to your country—with the confidence to invest long-term capital, to transfer technology and to provide cutting-edge management for factories—is one of the most effective and quickest ways to build a better local operating system. And, frankly, the fear of the herd bolting away again is one of the best long-term sources of discipline to keep a country constantly improving its software and operating systems. Korea, unlike the other Asian tigers, always tried to block foreign investment during its development drive from the 1960s to the 1990s. Instead, it financed its own growth through its own savings and borrowings, in order to remain financially independent. But the Asian economic crisis forced Korea to permit foreigners to buy into its ailing industries, and these foreigners are slowly bringing a new business culture to Korea, with more transparency and shareholder control.

Step two is to persuade these bad-borrowing countries to reform not just their operating systems but also their political ones—to curb corruption and tax cheating and improve their rule-of-law and democracy software, so that, when the belt-tightening comes, people have a sense that there is some basic fairness to the reform process. It was simply no accident that the two countries least affected by the Asian economic downturn in 1998 were the two countries with the most vibrant democracies and the freest press—Taiwan and Australia. (Some would say that China was not affected, but China's economy was not fully plugged into the system and still had a lot of walls around it in the financial arena.) Countries basically get the economic outcomes they deserve, and those outcomes are directly related to the quality of their operating systems and software and their degree of democracy.

Which is why step three is to ensure that any balance of payments assistance, recovery loans or debt restructuring provided by the IMF or any other international financial institutions is provided on the condition that steps one and two are taken. The explicit goal of any IMF assistance should be restoring stability, growth and confidence so that the Electronic Herd, both within the affected country and from abroad, will want to resume investment. Treasury Secretary Summers had it exactly right when he argued that the future role of the IMF should be to catalyze market-based solutions and to promote the disclosure of accurate, timely and wide-ranging financial data that can be used by the herd to make better-informed investment decisions. In a world in which the private sector is now the overwhelming source of capital and innovation for growth, there can be no sustained recovery without it.

Step four has to be a commitment to use some of the IMF, or other assistance, to maintain minimum social safety nets in these countries and provide public works jobs to soak up some of the unemployed. These minimum safety nets are often the first things to get shredded in any rescue program. International bankers, who tend to focus only on preventing bank defaults in other countries and not worry about their depressions, pooh-pooh the issue of safety nets when it comes to helping the bad borrowers. This is insane. Because at the end of the day the real crisis in these bad-borrowing countries — and the real threat they can pose to the global system — is not economic, it's political.

Here's why: In exposing rotten practices in bad-borrowing countries, globalization not only flattened their crony capitalists but also steamrolled a lot of little folks who were just working hard, playing by the rules of their systems and assuming everything was O.K. They didn't know their countries had false bottoms. But when the floor caved in, in Russia, Mexico, Thailand, Indonesia and Brazil, it produced massive layoffs, unemployment, disinflation, fiscal contraction and collapsing real incomes. That's why it is critical to maintain some basic safety nets and jobs programs during the recovery process. No jobs and no safety nets is no way for a government to buy the patience needed for reform policies to take hold and put a bad-borrowing country onto a sustainable growth track.

If large numbers of people start to go hungry in big countries, their leaders will be sorely tempted to just opt out of the system, build walls of protection and engage in beggar-thy-neighbor policies of competitive devaluations — even if it makes no long-term sense. These are the sorts of policies that helped make the Great Depression "Great" and brought us World War II.

The other type of global economic crisis that can threaten the whole system is the crisis of bad lenders — from banks to mutual funds to hedge funds—which are now able to lend so much money to so many people in so many places that when they engage in reckless lending on a massive scale, and then suddenly try to get their money back, they have the potential to inflict serious damage on both good economies and bad ones. Unlike bad borrowing, which poses a primarily political threat to the system, bad lending on a global scale poses a real financial threat to the system.

Bad lending comes in many forms. I was a bad lender when I invested in emerging markets without having a clue about how these countries really operated. Some of the worst lenders in recent years have been big banks. A friend of mine who works in the Hong Kong market once remarked that during the height of the Asian economic boom in the early 1990s Germany's Dresdner Bank was telling its manager in Asia quite bluntly: "Lend, lend, lend, otherwise we will lose our market share." Banks make money by lending, and each bank assumed that Asia was a no-brainer, and each did not want to lose that market to the other. So they shoved money out the door, just like drug dealers. Their motto to the developing world was: "C'mon, kid. Just try a little of this cash. The first loan's free." That's why at the beginning of 1999, even after the Southeast Asia–Russia crises, the top 500 banks from the thirty largest industrialized democracies still had outstanding loans to developing countries totaling $2.4 trillion. That's a lot of leverage hanging out there.

Another form of bad lending is when banks lend millions of dollars to hedge funds so that they can "leverage" their bets. The hedge funds raise $1 from investors, borrow $9 more from banks, and then use that leverage to magnify each of their bets in different stocks, bonds, derivatives and currencies around the world. Generally speaking, there is nothing wrong with leverage. The typical home mortgage is leveraging. You want people to take advantage of leverage. You want people to take risks—even crazy risks. This is how fledgling enterprises get funded and either go bankrupt or turn into Microsoft. The danger with leverage derives from the fact that the amounts of money that can be lent to hedge funds or emerging markets today are so enormous, and the system is now so greased and integrated, that when big risk takers—such as Long-Term Capital Management—make big mistakes they can destabilize everyone.

And that is why since the 1994–95 Mexico peso crisis the impact on the system of each of the global lending crises of the 1990s—and the amount of money that has had to be mobilized by governments and international lending institutions to prevent massive domino defaults—has been getting larger and larger each time. That is a very dangerous trend line.

So now we can frame the problem of bad lending: We want there to be leverage in the system. We want investors to take risks. But we want to reduce the ability of any one individual, bank, hedge fund, country or group of copycat investors to get so overleveraged that it sets all the dominoes toppling. The question is: How?

There are a lot of would-be geo-architects out there, all making proposals about how they would reinvent the world to deal with this problem. Henry Kissinger says states need to get together to find a way to tame these markets. Some economists say we need to throw some sand in the gears of the system — by taxing certain currency transactions or encouraging governments to impose limited capital controls. Some market types say we need a global central bank that would regulate the global economy the way the U.S. Federal Reserve regulates the American economy. Still others say we need to put limits on the amount of money banks can lend.

My own view is that none of these ideas is going to be implemented anytime soon, and many of them are nothing more than hot air, often proposed by people who wouldn't know the difference between a hedge fund and a hedgehog.

Let me offer a more realistic approach. To begin with, we need to proceed slowly and humbly. By this I mean that we have to understand that today's global economic system is still so new and so fast that even our best minds don't fully understand how it works and what happens when you pull a lever here or turn a dial there. Alan Greenspan is a lifelong scholar of international finance, as well as one of its most important practitioners today, but when I asked him in December 1998 about today's globalized financial system he gave me a rare on-the-record quote that should humble us all. He said: "I have learned more about how this new international financial system works in the last twelve months than in the previous twenty years."

As for those who have proposed that we put a little "sand in the gears" of this global economy to slow it down a bit, my response would be that I don't think it is ever very wise to put sand in the gears of a machine when you barely know where the gears are. If you put sand in the gears of such a fast, lubricated, stainless-steel machine, it might not just slow down. It could come to a screeching, metal-bending halt. Also, where do you put the sand when you are dealing with a fund manager sitting in Connecticut using a cellular phone, a high-speed modem and the Internet to invest in Brazil via a bank domiciled offshore in Panama? It's hard to put sand in a microchip, let alone in cyberspace. Moreover, the minute you start putting taxes on currency transactions, even more banks and hedge funds are going to flee the United States for the regulation-light Cayman Islands, already the fifth largest banking center in the world. (Long-Term Capital Management, incidentally, was run from Connecticut, but it was chartered in the Cayman Islands.) As for those who want to reduce the amounts that banks can lend to hedge funds or emerging markets, I would just point out that the American banking industry has one of the most powerful lobbies in Washington, and these banks will strongly resist any new lending limits which curb their ability not just to lose money but to make it. O.K., O.K., you say, well then, countries should impose capital controls, so this hot money won't be able to come in and go out so fast. China today has strict capital controls and in 1998 Chinese banks, individuals and corporations managed to elude those controls and funnel billions of dollars out of China—using various ruses—so they could play with that money offshore and out of the control of the Chinese state. If an authoritarian regime such as China's cannot effectively impose capital controls, how do you think Brazil is going to? Finally, still others have called for the creation of a global central bank—a U.S. Federal Reserve for the world. This is a wonderful idea, but not something that is going to happen anytime soon—not as long as we all live in 200 different countries with 200 different governments.

So, does that mean that there is nothing we can do? No. The good news is that in the wake of the 1998–99 crises, the market, without any new regulation or sand in the gears, disciplined itself to some extent. You saw signs of this everywhere: The chief executives of some of the biggest banks in the world—Barclays PLC, BankAmerica, United Bank of Switzerland—were all ousted in 1998, after their banks registered huge losses from trading and lending in high-risk emerging markets. And Bankers Trust, which lost $500 million in one quarter of 1998, largely on dealings with Russia, lost its independence as a result. It was taken over by Deutsche Bank.

Following these beheadings, all major banks have been restricting leverage, cutting off those fund managers who have gone to excess, demanding more transparency from those to whom they are still lending and scrutinizing more seriously not just the balance-of-payments figures of emerging markets but also their operating systems, legal systems and overall software. In other words, without any new laws or regulations being passed, everyone in the system started taking the issue of risk management more seriously. Banks started asking fund managers more often: "What is your total exposure, and how vulnerable am I as your lender to a worst-case scenario?" Investors started asking fund managers more often: "What are the greatest risks out there that you see for both of us, and how are we protected?" And the IMF, the U.S. Treasury and fund managers all started asking emerging-market countries more often: "What are you doing to improve your financial system and regulatory oversight?" and "What are the flows of private and public money coming in and out of your country? I want to know that constantly and in real time."

Fund managers learned that if they were going to continue to raise capital, they were going to have to be more open with both their investors and their bankers. I know a hedge-fund manager in London who in the middle of the 1998 crisis informed his clients that he had just set up a Web site. It could only be accessed with a password by clients, but once you were in you could see, on a daily, real-time basis, everywhere that this hedge fund was invested, how much it had leveraged and what the state of each investment was. This hedge fund manager told me: "I know now that if I am going to attract more investments, I have to provide more transparency. A lot of the leverage came from the banks pushing money out and not knowing what other banks were pushing out at the same time. The banks have behaved like idiots. I could tell the same thing to twenty different bankers each day and they wouldn't know. I am borrowing funds every day, so the banks are going to have to demand at the end of every day's trading to know what my total borrowings are. I already see that starting to happen. The banks are now saying, 'I don't care where you have borrowed, but I want to know where my lending to you fits into your total borrowings.'"

The only realistic solution is to find a way to take this ad hoc approach and extend it into the future, until the day when some new global financial regulatory system can be erected. If everyone from the IMF to Merrill Lynch to my aunt Bev would just ask all these questions more often, and keep asking them, we would have a chance of preventing two out of the next five crises and limiting the impact of one out of the next five. One of the most important things the IMF could do today would be to work with countries to ensure that they publish in a timely and credible fashion much more detailed versions of their overall balance sheets—including the government's outstanding foreign currency obligations and the size and maturity of the private sector's foreign borrowings. There is no greater restraint on human behavior than having other people watching and knowing exactly what you're up to.

"What you are trying to do is avoid excesses which can create a sufficiently large amount of risk that it harms not only the people who made the mistake but a lot of innocent bystanders as well," said William J. McDonough, president of the Federal Reserve Bank of New York, which orchestrated the rescue of Long-Term Capital Management by private bankers and investors. "The key is having, and sharing, information. If we have the information flow—and sometimes it is just a case of asking a few more questions—we can say to the banks that we regulate that this or that fund is getting too big and you are helping it get too big."

This may not seem very sexy—calling on everyone in the system to become a better regulator, a more open borrower, a smarter investor and a slightly more prudent banker and lender. But it's time we stopped kidding ourselves. There isn't going to be a global central bank for a long time. And in a world of networks, Supermarkets and Super-empowered individuals—including Super-empowered investors—there are some things that governments cannot stop and some forces that governments cannot totally control. Therefore, we have to work with the institutions we've got to produce better financial governance without a global central bank telling everyone what to do. It is clear that when the market players impose some discipline on themselves and the regulators take their duties seriously, and the IMF takes surveillance seriously, they can have a restraining effect, and they can at least dial down some of the excessive leverage that can threaten the system as a whole.

You simply cannot hope for more than that. Today's markets are so big, so diverse and, with the advent of the Internet, becoming so fast, that they can never be made immune from crises. Global financial crises will be the norm in this coming era. With the speed of change going on today, and with so many countries in different stages of adjustment to this new globalization system, crises will be endemic. So, dear reader, let me leave you with one piece of advice: Fasten your seat belts and put your seat backs and tray tables into a fixed and upright position. Because both the booms and the busts will be coming faster. Get used to it, and just try to make sure that the leverage in the system doesn't become so great in any one area that it can make the whole system go boom or bust. Anyone who tells you that they have a plan for eliminating all these crises is just pulling your leg. In fact, as you are reading these words, the next global financial crisis is already germinating somewhere.

Think of participating in the global economy today like driving a Formula One race car, which gets faster and faster every year. Someone is always going to be running into the wall and crashing, especially when you have drivers who only a few years ago were riding a donkey. You have two choices. You can ban Formula One racing. Then there will never be any crashes. But there also won't be any progress. Or you can do everything possible to reduce the impact of each crash by improving every aspect of the race. That is, you can make sure that there is an ambulance always on hand, with a well-trained rescue crew and plenty of blood of different blood types. (The market equivalent of that is for the IMF, the G-7 and the major world central banks to be able, in an emergency, to inject capital into markets to prevent system-threatening meltdowns.) At the same time, you can build each Formula One car stronger. (The market equivalent of that is getting every investor who puts a dime into an emerging market to ascertain whether it is developing the operating system and software to properly allocate capital and generate the incomes needed to pay back its lenders.) You can focus on training drivers better. (The market equivalent of that is making sure that the IMF, investors and banks are constantly pressing for more and more accurate and timely data on how an economy is developing and where capital, particularly short-term funds, is flowing.) And last, you should put as many bales of hay around the track as possible in case a car spins out of control—and to warn drivers that if they are hitting the hay they are close to hitting the wall. But you don't want so many bales of hay that you impede the race. (The market equivalent of that is vigilant banking and financial regulation, circuit breakers and alarm bells to detect and defuse problems as early as possible.)

If you don't want to do all these things, then you should forget about Formula One racing and become a jogger. But be careful, because as a jogger in this world you very likely will be run over by a Formula One car.

A Geopolitics for the Age of Globalization

It is not easy for this generation of Americans to grasp how important America is to the world in the era of globalization. Historically, the United States either has been isolated and aloof from world affairs or has been compelled to enter deeply into the world as part of a moral crusade to fend off another aggressive threatening power. Isolation is easy to explain and understand. Engagement in a bipolar world—with a big, menacing, nuclear-armed Soviet bear always growling on the other side—was easy to explain and understand. But what is not easy to explain or understand is engagement in a world in which the United States is the biggest beneficiary and the sole superpower, with multiple secondary powers, and with no immediately visible threat, but with many little threats and an abstract, complex globalization system to maintain. But this is the world we have, and in this world we can't afford either isolation or waiting around for some smaller adversary to become a life-threatening foe.

America, as noted earlier, is the Michael Jordan of geopolitics. It's great to be Michael Jordan, and like the commercial said, a lot of people wanted to be like Mike. But as good as Michael Jordan was, he was nothing without the NBA, with its twenty-nine teams and its global television contracts to showcase his skills. So it is with America. We're nothing without the rest of the world, and the world cannot thrive without us. Other nations may want to beat America's brains out in many endeavors. But, save for the Super-Empowered Angry Men, most of the world also understands that, without a strong America, the world would be a much less stable place.

Sustainable globalization requires a stable power structure, and no country is more essential for this than the United States. All the Internet and other technologies that Silicon Valley is designing to carry digital voices, videos and data around the world, all the trade and financial integration it is promoting through its innovations, and all the wealth this is generating, are happening in a world stabilized by a benign superpower, with its capital in Washington, D.C. The fact that no two major countries have gone to war since they both got McDonald's is partly due to economic integration, but it is also due to the presence of American power and America's willingness to use that power against those who would threaten the system of globalization—from Iraq to North Korea. The hidden hand of the market will never work without a hidden fist.

Markets function and flourish only when property rights are secure and can be enforced, which, in turn, requires a political framework protected and backed by military power. "To ignore the role of military security in an era of economic and information growth is like forgetting the importance of oxygen to our breathing," noted Harvard University government specialist Joseph Nye, Jr. Indeed, McDonald's cannot flourish without McDonnell Douglas, the designer of the U.S. Air Force F-15. And the hidden fist that keeps the world safe for Silicon Valley's technologies to flourish is called the U.S. Army, Air Force, Navy and Marine Corps. And these fighting forces and institutions are paid for by American taxpayer dollars.

With all due respect to Silicon Valley, ideas and technology don't just win and spread on their own. "Good ideas and technologies also need a strong power that promotes those ideas by example and protects those ideas by winning on the battlefield," says foreign-policy historian Robert Kagan. "If a lesser power were promoting our ideas and technologies, they would not have the global currency that they have. And when a strong power, the Soviet Union, promoted its bad ideas, they had a lot of currency for more than half a century."

This fact is simply too easily forgotten today. For too many executives in Silicon Valley there is no geography or geopolitics anymore. There are only stock options and electrons. When I asked an all too typical tech exec on a 1998 visit to Silicon Valley when was the last time he had talked about Iraq or Russia or any foreign war, he proudly answered: "Not more than once a year. We don't even care about Washington. Money is extracted by Silicon Valley and then wasted by Washington. I want to talk about people who create wealth and jobs. I don't want to talk about unhealthy and unproductive people. If I don't care about the wealth destroyers in my own country, why would I care about the wealth destroyers in another country?"

This view that Washington is the enemy, and that any tax dollar paid there is a tax dollar wasted, is grotesque. There is a saying in Silicon Valley that "loyalty is just one mouse click away." But you can take that too far. Execs there make boasts like: "We are not an American company. We are IBM U.S., IBM Canada, IBM Australia, IBM China." Oh yeah? Well, then, the next time IBM China gets in trouble in China, call Jiang Zemin for help. And the next time Congress closes another military base in Asia—and you don't care because you don't care about Washington—call Microsoft's navy to secure the sea lanes of the Pacific. And the next time the freshman Republicans want to close more U.S. embassies, call Amazon.com to order a new passport.

Sure, it may seem unfair that America assumes a disproportionate burden for sustaining globalization. It means there are a lot of free riders, many of whom, like the French, will piggyback on us while criticizing us all along the way. It comes with the role of being a geopolitical shaper. Neither the hidden fist nor the hidden hand will work, though, without also the open hand. The open hand means an America ready to use its wealth to pay a little more than others to stabilize the system and lend a more generous helping hand to others to stabilize the system. Why not? Who benefits most from this system? Did you ever hear Michael Jordan complain about having to carry his team or even the whole NBA on his back?

This doesn't mean America needs to be involved everywhere all the time, or pay for everything everywhere. There are big, important places and there are small, unimportant places, and diplomacy is about knowing the difference between the two, and knowing how to mobilize others to act where we cannot or should not go alone. But the very reason we need to support the United Nations and the IMF, NATO, the World Bank and the various world development banks is that they leverage and magnify our power and our aid. When we deposit a dollar in the Asian Development Bank it gets loaned out many times over to promote poverty alleviation and free markets. When we pay our UN dues we fund peacekeeping operations around the world that advance our interests without putting American lives on the line. These multilateral institutions also give those nations adapting to American geopolitical leadership some sense that they have a voice in the decision-making. Maintaining that sense is critical if America is to remain a successful shaper.

In order to sustain such a policy, it's pretty clear that those who care about American internationalism are going to have to build a new coalition to support it. The constituency that sustained American internationalism for fifty years and appreciated the importance of America to the rest of the world was the so-called Eastern Intellectual Establishment. That Eastern Establishment, to the extent it even exists today, doesn't carry much weight with the I'm-an-idiot-and-proud-of-it congressmen and senators who don't even own passports and boast that they never leave the country. The Administration, from whichever party is in power, is going to have to bring together the new globalizers—from the software writers to the human rights activists, from the Iowa farmers to the environmental activists, from the industrial exporters to the high-tech assembly-line workers—to form a new twenty-first-century coalition that can defend free trade and American internationalism.

I know this is not going to be easy. Americans were ready to pay any price and bear any burden in the Cold War because there was a compelling and immediate sense that their own homes and way of life were at stake. But a large majority don't feel that way about North Korea, Iraq or Kosovo, and while Russia may still have the capability to pose a lethal threat to America today, it is not doing so at this time. That's why Americans are in the odd position now of being held responsible for everything, while being reluctant to die for anything.

That's also why in the globalization era, counterinsurgency is out; baby-sitting is in. House-to-house fighting is out; cruise missiles are in. Green Berets are out; UN blue helmets are in. In today's world, it seems, there is no war America can lose for long abroad and no war that it can sustain for long at home. So when the American President today is faced with a military threat, his first question is not "What strategy will work to fundamentally put an end to this threat?" Rather, his first question is "How much do I have to pay to get this show off CNN so I can forget about it?" Everything gets contained, but nothing gets solved.

America truly is the ultimate benign hegemon and reluctant enforcer. But history also teaches us that if you take this reluctance too far, you can threaten the stability of the whole system. Paul Schroeder, professor emeritus of international history at the University of Illinois, is one of the great international historians of the twentieth century. He once remarked to me, "If you look at history, the periods of relative peace are those in which there is a durable, stable and tolerable hegemon who does the adjusting and preserves the minimal necessary norms and rules of the game. And that hegemon always pays a disproportionate share of the collective costs, even forgoes opportunities for conquest or restrains itself in other ways, so as not to not build up resentments and to make sure the system stays tolerable for others."

This was true, for instance, of the so-called Vienna system, from 1815 to 1848, which was dominated by Britain and Russia, two aloof but relatively benign hegemons who enforced the basic rules but also allowed a lot of local autonomy and prosperity. It was also true in the so-called Bismarckian period, under Germany, from 1871 to 1890.

"The difficulty," says Schroeder, "comes when the benign hegemonic power which is responsible for keeping the system stable is unable, or unwilling, to pay the disproportionate costs to do so, or its hegemony becomes intolerable and predatory rather than benign, or when enough actors rebel against its rules and insist upon a different kind of system that may not benefit that hegemon."

That is what we must avoid. The globalization system cannot hold together without an activist and generous American foreign policy. Attention Kmart shoppers: Without America on duty, there will be no America Online.

Olive Trees for the Age of Globalization

After this book was first published, I was shipping a boxload of books to a friend in San Francisco and a deliveryman came to my house to pick them up. The deliveryman was a heavyset, middle-aged African American and I invited him into the kitchen to wait while I was signing and packing up the books. Sitting at my kitchen table, he picked up a book and started leafing through it. After a few minutes, he put the book down and said to me, "So the Lexus—that represents technology and computers and stuff?"

That's right, I said.

"And the olive tree—that represents community and family and things like that."

That's right, I said. "You've got it!"

"So tell me something," he said. "Where does God fit into all this? I have been in the presence of our Lord Jesus Christ. Where does He fit in?"

I had to chuckle, only because I have been asked that question so many times while speaking to groups about this book. Indeed, some of the most oft-asked questions I have gotten are: Is God in cyberspace? How do I raise my kids in this Fast World? And what's it going to do to me and my community? I believe all three of these questions come from the same source. It is people asking: Even if we can get the right politics, geopolitics, geo-economics and geo-management for sustainable globalization, there is another, less tangible, set of policies that needs to be kept in mind—the olive-tree needs in us all: the need for community, for spiritual meaning and for values with which to raise our children. Those have to be protected and nurtured as well for globalization to be sustainable. One could write a book about these themes alone. Let me sketch out here in broad strokes how one might begin to think about them.

Let's start with the issue of religion. Is God in cyberspace? That depends what your view of God is. If your view of God is that He makes His presence felt through divine intervention, through the hand of God at work in the world, then you would have to say that either God is not present in cyberspace or cyberspace has made you an atheist. Because it is hard to look at cyberspace and say that it is being shaped by the hand of God, given the fact that the most popular sites in cyberspace are pornography, gambling and pop music. Indeed, it is said that the most oft-used three-letter words on the World Wide Web are "sex" and "MP3"—the protocol for downloading rock music—not "God."

My own view of God, growing out of my own Jewish tradition, is different. I share the postbiblical view of God. In the biblical view of God, He is always intervening. He is responsible for our actions. He punishes the bad and rewards the good. The postbiblical view of God is that we make God present by our own choices and our own decisions. In the postbiblical view of God, in the Jewish tradition, God is always hidden, whether in cyberspace or the neighborhood shopping center, and to have God in the room with you, whether it's a real room or a chat room, you have to bring Him there yourself by your own behavior, by the moral or immoral choices and mouse clicks you make.

My teacher Rabbi Tzvi Marx pointed out to me that there is a verse in Isaiah that says, "You are my witness. I am the Lord." According to Rabbi Marx, second-century rabbinic commentators interpreted that verse to be saying, "If you are my witness, I am the Lord. And if you are not my witness, I am not the Lord." In other words, explained Rabbi Marx, unless we bear witness to God's presence by our own good deeds, He is not present. Unless we behave as though He were running things, He isn't running things. In the postbiblical world we understand that from the first day of the world God trusted man to make choices, when He entrusted Adam to make the right decision about which fruit to eat in the Garden of Eden. We are responsible for making God's presence manifest by what *we* do. And the reason that this issue is most acute in cyberspace is because no one else is in charge there. There is no place in today's world where you encounter the freedom to choose that God gave man more than in cyberspace.

So what I should have told that deliveryman was that although God is not in cyberspace, He wants to be there—but only we can bring Him there by how we act there. God celebrates a universe of such human freedom, because He knows that the only way He is truly manifest in the world is not if He intervenes, but if we all choose sanctity and morality in an environment where we are free to choose anything. As Rabbi Marx puts it: "In the postbiblical Jewish view of the world, you cannot be moral unless you are totally free, because if you are not free you are really not empowered, and if you are not empowered the choices that you make are not entirely your own. What God says about cyberspace is that you are really free there, and I hope you make the right choices, because if you do I will be present."

There is nothing about globalization or the Internet that eliminates the need for ideals or codes of restraint on human behavior. The more we are dependent on this technology, the more we need to come to it armed with our own ideals and codes of restraint. Indeed, the reason God so much wants to be in cyberspace, and the reason we should want Him there, argues Israeli religious philosopher David Hartman, is because in some ways cyberspace is the world that the prophets spoke about, "a place where all mankind can be unified and be totally free. The danger is that we are unifying mankind in cyberspace—all speaking one language, all using one medium—but without God." And we certainly don't want to be unifying mankind through the Internet without any value system, without any filters, without any alternative conception of meaning other than business and without any alternative view of human beings other than as consumers looking for the lowest price.

But these much-needed values are best learned off-line, outside the Internet. The only way people are going to find God on the Internet is if they bring Him there in their own heads and hearts and behaviors—drawing on values they learn in the terrestrial world—in the olive groves of their parents' home or their community, church, synagogue, temple or mosque.

W hich leads to another frequently asked olive-tree question: How do I prepare my kids for the Fast World? A lot more parents in America started to think about that after they realized that the news stories about the 1999 shootings at Columbine High School contained two sets of initials they never saw thrown together in the news before: NRA and AOL. That the NRA, the National Rifle Association, should feel guilty about the Columbine massacres went without saying. The idea that two high school kids were able to use their allowances to amass an arsenal that included the Intratec AB-10—a fingerprint resistant, high-volume, paramilitary assault weapon—a Hi-Point 9-millimeter carbine, a sawed-off pump-action shotgun and a sawed-off double-barreled shotgun should make anyone who opposes gun control ashamed of themselves.

But what about AOL, America Online, the Internet provider that housed the warped Web site of Eric Harris, one of the student gunmen? The AOL Web postings attributed to Mr. Harris included instructions on how to build pipe bombs ("shrapnel is very important"), an illustration of a creature toting a shotgun and a knife while standing on a pile of skulls and the song lyrics, "What I don't do I don't like. What I don't like I waste."

Should we as parents be as worried about the Internet as the Intratec? The short answer is no. AOL is not the equivalent of the NRA—but that doesn't quite end the matter. As the Internet moves into the center of our lives—how we communicate, educate and do business in the new millennium—we have to remember something essential: What makes the Internet so exciting and troubling is that, unlike *The New York Times* for example, it has no editor, no publisher and no censor. You and your kids interact with the network totally naked. But precisely because the Internet is such a neutral, free, open and unregulated vehicle for commerce, education and communication, personal judgment and responsibility are critical when using this technology. The only real filter is the one your kids bring in their own heads or hearts when they go online, and since kids often lack the judgment microchip, it is even more critical that parents and educators provide it. If we don't all take responsibility for building the internal software into our kids so that they can interact with this naked technology properly, we are going to have a problem.

I grew up in a small suburb of Minneapolis. You had to go at least an hour from my house to find trouble. On the Internet, trouble is just a few mouse clicks away. You can wander into a virtual neo-Nazi beer hall or pornographer's library, hack the NASA computers or roam the Sorbonne library, and no one is there to stop or direct you. To put it another way, the more the Internet makes us all broadcasters, all researchers, all consumers and all retailers and, alas, all potential bomb makers, the more critical it is that our teachers, parents and communities are still making us all citizens. That's work that can only be done off-line. The Internet and computers are just tools—wonderful tools that can extend and expand one's reach enormously. But you still need to know what to grasp and how to get the best out of them. These tools can help you think, but they can't make you smart. They can browse and search but they can't judge. They can enable you to interact far and wide, but they teach you nothing about how to be a good neighbor. They can empower you to touch the lives of many people, but they can't tell you what to say at a PTA meeting, or why to say it. That's the parenting paradox of the Internet. The best thing parents can do to prepare their kids for the Internet age is not to teach them more whiz-bang, high-tech skills, or buy their kids faster modems and computers, but rather to stress more old-fashioned fundamentals. The faster your kids' modems, the faster they can get online, the stronger must be their own personal software, if you want to see them thrive. And personal software can only be built the old-fashioned way: by stressing reading, writing and arithmetic, church, synagogue, temple, mosque and family. Those things can't be downloaded from the Internet; they can only be uploaded by parents and teachers, priests and rabbis. And that's why if I had one wish it would be that every modem that is sold would come with a Surgeon General's warning on it. It would say: "Judgment Not Included." You have to provide that yourself—the old-fashioned way from under the olive tree.

I began this book with a discussion of Cain and Abel and I will end it with a discussion of the Tower of Babel. What was the problem with the Tower of Babel? Isn't it what globalizers dream about today—a world in which we all speak the same language, have the same currency, follow the same accounting practices? It was precisely their sameness that allowed the people of the world in biblical times to cooperate and build that Tower of Babel—to build a tower that might actually reach to the heavens. I was talking about this one afternoon with my friend Rabbi Marx when he suddenly looked up from his coffee and asked: "Was the Tower of Babel the original version of the Internet?" After all, the Internet, too, is a sort of universal language outside the bounds of any particular culture. It is a universal mode of communication that, at least on the surface, seems to make us all intelligible to one another, even if we don't all speak the same language. And it allows us to connect with all sorts of people with whom we never shared an olive grove.

But what did God do with the Tower of Babel? He put a stop to it. And how did He put a stop to it? By making the people all speak different languages so they could no longer cooperate. Why did God do that? Rabbi Marx explains it like this: "God did it in part because He felt that the people were trying to transcend their own human limitations in building a tower to the heavens, in a way that might challenge Him. But He also destroyed the tower because He felt that their common language and approach was ultimately dehumanizing. It denied all particularity in men and women in favor of a universal language and a universal project. And therefore God's solution and his punishment was to stop the tower by making all the people speak different languages."

It was God's way of getting people back in touch with, and in balance with, their olive trees, which reflect their own individuality and their particular links to a place, a community, a culture, a tribe and a family.

Yes, globalization and the Internet can bring together people who have never been connected before—like my mom and her French Internet bridge partners. But rather than creating new kinds of communities, this technology often just creates a false sense of connection and intimacy. It's like two beepers communicating with each other. Can we really connect with others through E-mail or Internet bridge or chat rooms? Or is all this standardizing technology just empowering us to reach farther into the world while exempting us from the real work required to build relationships and community with the folks next door? I used to chat with and meet people from all over the world while riding the ski lifts up the mountains in Colorado. I still ride the lifts, but now everyone has a cellular phone. So, instead of meeting people from all over the world on the lifts, now I just overhear their conversations on their cellular phones with their offices all over the world. I really hate that. E-mail is not building a community—attending a PTA meeting is. A chat room is not building a community—working with your neighbors to petition city hall for a new road is. Can we really build cybercommunities that will replace real communities? I'm very dubious. That's why I, for one, won't be surprised if I wake up one day and discover that the Almighty has made the Internet crash just the way He did the Tower of Babel.

I keep thinking about this young Kuwaiti I met at the Internet Cafe in Kuwait City who told me: "When I was a student we didn't have the Internet. What we had were a few liberal professors and we would get together with them quietly in their homes and talk about politics. Now as a student you can sit at home and converse with the whole world." But, he confessed, he and his professors don't get together anymore like they used to. There is a danger that as a result of the Internetting of society, the triumph of all this technology in our lives, and globalization über Alles, people will wake up one morning and realize that they don't interact with anyone except through a computer. When this happens, people will really become vulnerable to those preachers and New Age religious fantasies that come along and promise to reconnect us to our bodies, our souls and the olive tree in us all. This is when you will start to see *truly* crazy revolts against monotony and standardization—people being different for the sake of being different, but not on the basis of any real historical memory, roots or traditions.

Balancing a Lexus with an olive tree is something every society has to work on every day. It is also what America, at its best, is all about. America at its best takes the needs of markets, individuals and communities all utterly seriously. And that's why America, at its best, is not just a country. It's a spiritual value and role model. It's a nation that is not afraid to go to the moon, but also still loves to come home for Little League. It is the nation that invented both cyberspace and the backyard barbecue, the Internet and the social safety net, the SEC and the ACLU. These dialectics are at the heart of America, and they should never be resolved in favor of one over the other. But they also should never be taken for granted. They have to be constantly nurtured, tended to and preserved—and we can do this by supporting our public schools, paying our taxes, understanding that the government is not the enemy and always making sure we're still getting to know our neighbors over the fence and not over the Web.

America is not at its best every day, but when it's good, it's very, very good. In the winter of 1994, my oldest daughter, Orly, was in the fourth-grade chorus at Burning Tree Elementary School in Bethesda, Maryland. At Christmastime all the choruses from the local public elementary schools got together for a huge performance in the Bethesda town square. I came to hear my daughter sing. The chorus conductor was an African American man, and for the holiday songfest he wore a Santa Claus outfit. The first song the chorus sang that evening was the Hanukkah classic, "Maoztzur," to the tune of "Rock of Ages." Watching this scene, and hearing that song, brought tears to my eyes. When I got home, my wife, Ann, asked me how it was. And I said to her: "Honey, I just saw a black man dressed up as Santa Claus directing four hundred elementary-school kids singing 'Maoztzur' in the town square of Bethesda, Maryland. God Bless America."

A healthy global society is one that can balance the Lexus and the olive tree all the time, and there is no better model for this on earth today than America. And that's why I believe so strongly that for globalization to be sustainable America must be at its best—today, tomorrow, all the time. It not only can be, it must be, a beacon for the whole world. Let us not squander this precious legacy.

Acknowledgments

This book has been four years in the making, and many people have helped me along the way. My publisher, Arthur Sulzberger Jr., not only provided me the time off to write this book, but, more important, he made me the *New York Times* foreign affairs columnist, which enabled me to see and understand globalization firsthand. For that I am deeply grateful. Howell Raines, the editor of the *New York Times* Editorial Page, has been a great supporter of my work and also helped to make this book possible, for which I am also deeply grateful. I would be remiss, though, if I did not also thank the current Executive Editor of *The New York Times*, Joe Lelyveld, and his predecessor, Max Frankel, for several years ago creating a beat for me at the intersection of finance and foreign policy, which first got me interested in many of the themes of this book.

I have been blessed by having many good friends with whom I could chew over different ideas that have gone into this work. No one has taught me more about the history of American foreign policy than my friend Michael Mandelbauin, who teaches international relations at the Johns Hopkins School of Advanced International Studies. Our weekly discussions of foreign policy have been a source of great intellectual stimulation for me. My friend Yaron Ezrahi, professor of political theory at the Hebrew University of Jerusalem, has encouraged this project from the beginning, and shared with me often and generously his wonderful insights into democratic theory, art and journalism. I constantly benefit from his intelligence and friendship. My soul brother from my Middle East days, Stephen P. Cohen, from the Center for Middle East Peace in New York, is not an expert on globalization, but his original mind and wonderful feel for international politics have enriched this book in so many ways. As a friend and teacher, he is a blessing. My friend Larry Diamond, senior research fellow at the Hoover Institution at Stanford University and co-editor of the *Journal of Democracy*, has been my tutor on the subject of democratization and commented on this book at every stage. One of the luckiest things that ever happened to me was meeting him while monitoring village elections in northeastern China. Jim Haskel, from Goldman Sachs, telephoned me out of the blue one day to comment on a column I had written for the *Times* and we have not stopped talking since. He is a pro at information arbitrage and I have greatly benefited from his comments on this book while it was in draft. Robert Hormats, vice chairman of Goldman Sachs International, has been another of my regular interlocutors on this subject. No one has a better feel for the intersection of finance and foreign policy than Bob, and every time we get together we come up with a new idea. Stephen Kobrin, director of the Lauder Institute at the Wharton School, arranged for me to conduct a very stimulating seminar on this book with some of his colleagues at Wharton, and then took the time and trouble to read the text in draft form. Steve's own writings on globalization, and his comments, have been a great help to me. World Bank economist Ahmed Galal, surely one of the finest of Egypt's new generation of economists, also took the time to listen to different arguments in this book, read it all in draft and share his thoughts in many ways that were enormously helpful.

Glenn Prickett, vice president of Conservation International, accompanied me on a trip to the endangered environmental zones of Brazil and tutored me on all the issues involving environment and globalization. I owe him a great debt. Jeffrey Garten, Dean of the Yale School of Management, invited me to present some of this book to one of his graduate classes and has been a constant source of insight on the subject of globalization.

Treasury Secretary Larry Summers, his assistant Michelle Smith and I have had a running dialogue about international economics for six years, and more than a few ideas in this book were sparked by some insight Larry tossed off in one of our off-the-record brainstorming sessions. Economist Clyde Prestowitz has always been a source of insight on global trade for me, and I am grateful for his help. Former Treasury Secretary Robert Rubin, Federal Reserve Chairman Alan Greenspan, Bank of Israel Governor Jacob Frenkel, economists Henry Kaufman and Ken Courtis, New York Fed president William J. McDonough, hedge-fund manager Leon

Cooperman, bond trader Lesley Goldwasser, World Bank chief economist John Page, National Economic Council chief Gene Sperling and World Bank president Jim Wolfensohn all took the time to discuss their views of globalization with me. From the private sector, Monsanto chairman Robert Shapiro, Cisco Systems president John Chambers, Baltimore businessman Jerry Portnoy, Minnesota farmer Gary Wagner and the senior executives of Compaq Computer all sat for multiple interviews for this book that were indispensable.

My teacher Rabbi Tzvi Marx, with his very special intellect, was extremely helpful in sorting out some of the cultural and religious aspects of globalization. And as usual my old friend Harvard government professor Michael Sandel was a source of intellectual inspiration. *Foreign Policy* editor Moisés Naím, foreign-policy historian Robert Kagan, China scholar Michael Oksenberg, *Wall Street Journal* technology columnist Walt Mossberg, Emory University professor Robert Pastor, *Foreign Affairs* managing editor Fareed Zakaria, Klaus Schwab, Claude Smadja and Barbara Erskine of the Davos World Economic Forum, and my brother-in-law Ted Century all encouraged this project in different but important ways. My mother, Margaret Friedman, and my in-laws Matt and Kay Bucksbaum were, as always, an endless source of support.

And now I herewith absolve all of the above of any responsibility for the final product.

The reader will notice that I quote a great deal from two outside sources. One is *The Economist*, which has been far, far ahead of every other news organization in understanding and reporting on globalization. The other is ads from Madison Avenue. For some reason, advertising copywriters have a tremendous insight into globalization, and I have not hesitated to draw on their work.

Finally, my regular golf partners at Caves Valley, Joel Finkelstein and Jack Murphy, and Dan Honig out in Colorado, kept me sane by not taking the least interest in this book but focusing entirely on taking my money on the golf course.

My assistant and researcher Maya Gorman was phenomenal. It is scary to think of some of the facts and news stories from different corners of the world that she was able to track down. I am in her debt for all her good work and good cheer.

My old publishing team of *From Beirut to Jerusalem* days—my editor Jonathan Galassi of Farrar, Straus and Giroux, his deputy Paul Elie and my literary agent Esther Newberg of International Creative Management—are the best in the business, bar none, end of story. It was a privilege to work with them on another book. LuAnn Walther's team at Anchor Books, the publishers of the paperback edition, were outstanding.

My daughters, Orly and Natalie, sat through repeated versions of this book in lecture form, and can recite whole passages themselves. They were always good sports and a boundless source of inspiration. But, as always, my first and last editor was my wife, Ann Friedman. No one has ever had a better partner in life, and it is to her that this book is dedicated.

INDEX

* Democratic ruled corporations vs owner controlled plutocracy
  to drive the free market